Guidance
for
Governance

The Japan Center for International Exchange wishes to thank

The Nippon Foundation

Guidance
for
Governance

Comparing
Alternative Sources of
Public Policy Advice

edited by
R. Kent Weaver and Paul B. Stares

Tokyo • Japan Center for International Exchange • *New York*

The surnames of the authors and other persons mentioned in this book are
positioned according to country practice.

Copyediting by Pamela J. Noda.
Cover design by Anne Bergasse, abinitio Y.K.
Design and production by abinitio Y.K.
Cover photographs © Corbis Digital Stock © Photo Disc.

Printed in Japan
ISBN 4-88907-050-8

Distributed outside Japan by Brookings Institution Press
(1775 Massachusetts Avenue, N.W., Washington, D.C. 20036-2188 U.S.A.)
and Kinokuniya Company Ltd. (5-38-1 Sakuragaoka, Setagaya-ku, Tokyo 156-8691 Japan).

Japan Center for International Exchange
9-17 Minami Azabu 4-chome, Minato-ku, Tokyo 106-0047 Japan

URL: http://www.jcie.or.jp

Japan Center for International Exchange, Inc. (JCIE/USA)
1251 Avenue of the Americas, New York, N.Y. 10020 U.S.A.

Contents

Foreword   *vii*

List of Abbreviations   *ix*

1 Guidance for Governance: An Overview,
   R. Kent Weaver and Paul B. Stares   *1*

2 United States, *Andrew Rich*   *31*

3 Japan, *Yamamoto Tadashi*   *71*

4 United Kingdom, *Diane Stone*   *89*

5 Brazil, *Amaury de Souza*   *124*

6 Germany, *Martin W. Thunert*   *157*

7 India, *Kuldeep Mathur*   *207*

8 Poland, *Robert Sobiech*   *231*

9 Republic of Korea, *Mo Jongryn*   *252*

About the Contributors   *277*

Index   *281*

Foreword

M uch has been said and written in recent years about the importance of "good governance." However, amidst all the attention and discussion that this goal has received, the obvious has often been overlooked or understated—namely, that good governance depends to a large extent on good advice. Traditionally, politicians and senior political appointees have relied heavily if not exclusively on policy guidance provided by civil servants within the government departments and ministries that they control. Increasingly, however, alternative or nongovernmental sources of policy advice are playing a greater role in government decision making. This reflects, on the one hand, a growing *demand* for such advice either because it is seen to be less partial and more imaginative or because the growing complexity of government requires specialized forms of expertise not typically resident in government bureaucracies. On the other hand, the *supply* of such advice is growing as groups within civil society establish their own sources of expertise to assess government initiatives and influence them with their own recommendations.

While the role of alternative sources of public policy advice is accepted and well established in some countries, their contribution in others is quite limited in part because of their general paucity. With the goal of making a substantive contribution to the burgeoning debate on how to improve the quality of governance around the world, the Japan Center for International Exchange (JCIE) launched a study to understand better the role played by alternative policy advisory organizations in a range of democratic countries at different stages of economic and political development. Under the directorship of R. Kent Weaver, senior fellow in the Governmental Studies Program of the Brookings Institution and Paul B. Stares, associate director of the Center for International Security and Cooperation at Stanford University and former director of studies at JCIE, eight countries—Brazil, Germany, India, Japan, the Republic of Korea, Poland, the United Kingdom, and the United States—were surveyed by recognized experts according to a common framework of analysis to facilitate international comparisons. In addition to shedding light on how such organizations have evolved and function in different national contexts, the individual authors also offer recommendations on how the situation could be improved in their own country based in part on what they have learned from the other cases.

The initial findings of the study were presented at a workshop convened in Frankfurt on November 22–23, 1999. These were subsequently refined for presentation at the Global ThinkNet conference held in Tokyo on May 28–30, 2000. A report on the discussions that took place at this conference can be found in *Guidance for Governance in the 21st Century*, published by JCIE in 2000.

The editors of this book wish to thank not only the individual authors of the case studies for their contributions to the study but also the staff of JCIE for their support throughout the project. In particular, the work of Pamela J. Noda, director of publications of JCIE, is gratefully acknowledged.

Finally, the study was made possible by the generous financial support of the Nippon Foundation.

Yamamoto Tadashi
President
Japan Center for International Exchange

Abbreviations

AARP	American Association of Retired Persons
ABHI	Association of British Health-care Industries
ABONG	Brazilian Association of Non-Governmental Organizations (Associação Brasileira de Organizações Não Governamentais)
AfJ	Alliance for Jobs, Training and Competitiveness (Bündnis für Arbeit, Ausbildung und Wettbewerbsfähigkeit)
AL	Legislative Support Service (Assessoria Legislativa)
AOFF	Budget and Financial Review Service (Assessoria de Orçamento e Fiscalização Financeira)
APAO	alternative policy advisory organization
ASI	Adam Smith Institute (United Kingdom)
BDA	Confederation of German Employers' Associations (Bundesvereinigung der Deutschen Arbeitgeberverbände)
BERA	British Educational Research Association
BIOSt	Federal Institute for Russian, East European and International Studies (Bundesinstitut für Ostwissenschaftliche und internationale Studien)
BNDE	National Bank of Economic Development (Banco Nacional de Desenvolvimento Econômico)
BNDES	National Bank of Economic and Social Development (Banco Nacional de Desenvolvimento Econômico e Social)
BOB	Bureau of the Budget (United States)
BoE	Bank of England
CAP	Center for Applied Policy Research (Germany)
CBI	Confederation of British Industry
CBO	Congressional Budget Office (United States)
CEA	Council of Economic Advisors (United States)
CEBRAP	Brazilian Center for Analysis and Planning (Centro Brasileiro de Análise e Planejamento)
CEDEC	Center for the Study of Contemporary Culture (Centro de Estudos de

	Cultura Contemporânea)
CEE	Central and Eastern European
CEM	Center for the Study of the World Economy (Centro de Estudos da Economia Mundial)
CEPR	Centre for Economic Policy Research (United Kingdom)
CES	Center for Economic Studies (Germany)
CFCE	Federal Foreign Trade Council (Conselho Federal de Comércio Exterior)
CHE	Center for Higher Education Development (Germany)
CMN	National Monetary Council (Conselho Monetário Nacional)
CMO	chief medical officer
CMPS	Centre for Management and Policy Studies (United Kingdom)
CNCT	National Science and Technology Council (Conselho Nacional de Ciência e Tecnologia)
CNI	National Confederation of Industry (Confederação Nacional da Indústria)
CNPq	National Council for Scientific and Technological Development (Conselho Nacional de Desenvolvimento Científico e Tecnológico)
CNPS	National Social Security Council (Conselho Nacional de Previdência Social)
CPIs	Congressional Commissions of Inquiry (Comissão Parlamentar de Inquérito)
CPRS	Central Policy Review Staff (United Kingdom)
CPS	Centre for Policy Studies (United Kingdom)
CRS	Congressional Research Service (United States)
CWDS	Centre for Women's Development Studies (India)
DAS	Comissão de Direção e Assessoramento Superior
DGAP	German Council on Foreign Relations (Deutsche Gesellschaft für Auswärtige Politik)
DGB	German Federation of Trade Unions (Deutscher Gewerkschaftsbund)
DIAP	Inter-Union Department of Congressional Assistance Services (Departamento Intersindical de Assessoria Parlamentar)
DIEESE	Inter-Union Department of Statistics and Economic and Social Studies (Departamento Intersindical de Estatística e Estudos Sócio-Econômicos)
DIW Berlin	German Institute of Economic Research (Deutsche Institut für Wirtschaftsforschung)
DÜI	German Overseas Institute (Deutsches Übersee-Institut)
ESG	Superior War College (Escola Superior de Guerra)
ESRC	Economic and Social Research Council (United Kingdom)
EU	European Union
FAPESP	Research Foundation of the State of São Paulo (Fundação de Amparo à Pesquisa do Estado de São Paulo)
FAT	Workers' Relief Fund (Fundo de Amparo ao Trabalhador)
FBDS	Brazilian Foundation for Sustainable Development (Fundação Brasileira para o Desenvolvimento Sustentável)
FCO	Foreign and Commonwealth Office (United Kingdom)

FEWER	Forum on Early Warning and Early Response (United Kingdom)
FFRDCs	federally funded research-and-development centers
FIESP	São Paulo State Federation of Industrialists (Federação das Indústrias do Estado de São Paulo)
FINEP	Research and Project Financing Agency (Financiadora de Estudos e Projetos)
FIPE	Institute for Economic Research Foundation (Fundação Instituto de Pesquisas Econômicas)
FJN	Joaquim Nabuco Foundation (Fundação Joaquim Nabuco)
FJP	João Pinheiro Foundation (Fundação João Pinheiro)
FOE	Friends of the Earth
FORD	Foreign Office Research Department (United Kingdom)
FUNCEX	Center of Foreign Trade Studies Foundation (Fundação Centro de Estudos do Comércio Exterior)
FUNDAP	Foundation for Administrative Development (Fundação do Desenvolvimento Administrativo)
GNP	Grand National Party (Republic of Korea)
GAO	General Accounting Office (United States)
HBS	Heinrich Böll Foundation (Germany)
HSFK PRIF	Peace Research Institute Frankfurt
HWWA	Institute for Economic Research (Germany)
IA	Atlantic Institute (Instituto Atlântico)
IBASE	Brazilian Institute for Social and Economic Analysis (Instituto Brasileiro de Análises Sociais e Econômicas)
IBRD	International Bank for Reconstruction and Development
IBRE	Brazilian Institute of Economics (Instituto Brasileiro de Economia)
ICS	Indian Civil Service
ICSSR	Indian Council of Social Science Research
IDESP	Institute for Economic, Social and Political Studies (Instituto de Estudos Econômicos, Sociais e Políticos de São Paulo)
IEDI	Institute for Industrial Development Studies (Instituto de Estudos do Desenvolvimento Industrial)
IE-UFRJ	Institute of Economics of the Federal University of Rio de Janeiro (Instituto de Economia da Universidade Federal do Rio de Janeiro)
IE-UNICAMP	Institute of Economics of the State University of Campinas (Instituto de Economia da Universidade Estadual de Campinas)
IEA	Institute of Advanced Studies (Instituto de Estudos Avançados)
IEA	Institute of Economic Affairs (United Kingdom)
IEPES	Institute for Political and Social Studies (Instituto de Estudos Políticos e Sociais)
IfW	Kiel Institute of World Economics (Institut für Weltwirtschaft)
IFS	Institute of Fiscal Studies (United Kingdom)
IISS	International Institute of Strategic Studies (United Kingdom)
IL	Liberal Institute (Instituto Liberal)
IMAZON	Institute of Amazon Man and Environment (Instituto do Homem e Meio

	Ambiente da Amazônia)
IMF	International Monetary Fund
IMPA	Institute for Pure and Applied Mathematics (Instituto de Matemática Pura e Aplicada)
INAE	National Institute of Higher Studies (Instituto Nacional de Altos Estudos)
INEP	National Institute of Educational Research (Instituto Nacional de Estudos Pedagógicos)
INESC	Institute of Socio-Economic Studies (Instituto de Estudos Sócio-Econômicos)
IPEA	Institute of Applied Economic Research (Instituto de Pesquisa Econômica Aplicada)
IPES	Institute for Economic and Social Research (Instituto de Pesquisas Sociais)
IPPR	Institute for Public Policy Research (United Kingdom)
IPRI	Institute for Research on International Relations (Instituto de Pesquisas em Relações Internacionais)
IPSU	International Public Service Unit (United Kingdom)
IRS	Roberto Simonsen Institute (Instituto Roberto Simonsen)
ISEB	Superior Institute of Brazilian Studies (Instituto Superior de Estudos Brasileiros)
ISER	Institute for the Study of Religion (Instituto de Estudos da Religião)
ISI	Fraunhofer Institute for Systems and Innovation Research (Institut Systemtechnik und Innovationsforschung)
ISPN	Institute for Society, Population and Nature (Instituto Sociedade, População e Natureza)
ITAS	Institute for Technology Assessment and Systems Analysis (Germany)
ITN	Tancredo Neves Institute for Political and Social Studies (Instituto Tancredo Neves de Estudos Políticos e Sociais)
IUPERJ	University Research Institute of Rio de Janeiro (Instituto Universitário de Pesquisas do Rio de Janeiro)
JCIE	Japan Center for International Exchange
KBN	State Committee for Scientific Research (Komitet Badań Naukowych)
KDI	Korea Development Institute
KERI	Korea Economic Research Institute
LDP	Liberal Democratic Party (Japan)
LNLS	National Laboratory of Synchrotron Light (Laboratório Nacional de Luz Sincroton)
LRS	Legislative Research Service (United States)
LSOs	legislative support organizations
MPC	Monetary Policy Committee (United Kingdom)
MPs	members of Parliament
NCSC&ST	National Commission for Scheduled Castes and Scheduled Tribes (India)
NDPBs	nondepartmental public bodies
NEAD	Agrarian and Rural Development Study Group (Núcleo de Estudos Agrários e Desenvolvimento Rural)
NEC	National Economic Council (United States)

NERC	Natural Environment Research Council (United Kingdom)
NGOs	nongovernmental organizations
NHRC	National Human Rights Commission (India)
NIESR	National Institute of Economic and Social Research (United Kingdom)
NIK	Supreme Chamber of Control (Najwyższa Izba Kontroli)
NIRA	National Institute of Research Advancement (Japan)
NPM	new public management
NPOs	nonprofit organizations
NSC	National Security Council (United States)
ODI	Overseas Development Institute (United Kingdom)
OECD	Organization for Economic Cooperation and Development
OMB	Office of Management and Budget (United States)
OPD	Office of Policy Development (United States)
OSCs	public interest civil society organizations (Organizações da Sociedade Civil de Interesse Público)
OTA	Office of Technology Assessment (United States)
PAN	Polish Academy of Sciences (Polska Akademia Nauk)
PARC	Policy Affairs Research Council (Japan)
PMPA	Public Management and Policy Association (United Kingdom)
POLIS	Institute for Social Policy Studies, Training and Consulting (Instituto de Estudos, Treinamento e Assessoria em Políticas Sociais)
PPI	Progressive Policy Institute (United States)
PRIO	Peace Research Institute Oslo
PRODASEN	Senate Data Processing Center (Serviço de Processamento de Dados do Senado)
PSI	Policy Studies Institute (United Kingdom)
PSPD	People's Solidarity for Participatory Democracy (Republic of Korea)
PUC-RIO	Department of Economics of the Pontifical Catholic University of Rio de Janeiro (Pontifícia Universidade Católica do Rio de Janeiro)
quango	quasi-autonomous NGO
R&D	research and development
RAE	Research Assessment Exercise (United Kingdom)
Rede IPEA	Public Policy Research Network (Rede IPEA [Instituto de Pesquisa Econômica Aplicada] de Pesquisas)
RES	Royal Economic Society (United Kingdom)
RIIA	Royal Institute of International Affairs (United Kingdom)
RITS	Third Sector Information Network (Rede de Informações para o Terceiro Setor)
RPC	Research Planning Committee (India)
RUSI	Royal United Services Institute for Defence Studies (United Kingdom)
RWI	Rhine-Westphalia Institute for Economic Research (Germany)
SEWA	Self-Employed Women's Association (India)
SIPRI	Stockholm International Peace Research Institute
SPD	Social Democratic Party (Germany)
SRS	Specialized Research Services (Germany)

SRU	German Council of Environmental Advisors (Der Rat von Sachverständigen für Umweltfragen)
SRW	Council of Economic Experts (Sachverständigenrat-Wirtschaft)
SWRC	Social Work and Research Centre (India)
SWP	Foundation for Science and Politics (Stiftung Wissenschaft und Politik)
TCU	Federal Audit Tribunal (Tribunal de Contas da União)
TAB	Office of Technology Assessment (Büro für Technikfolgen-Abschätzung)
THT	Terrence Higgins Trust (United Kingdom)
TUC	Trades Union Congress (United Kingdom)
UNI	Institute of Independent Entrepreneurs (Unternehmerinstitut)
VHAI	Voluntary Health Association of India
WNC	Women's National Commission
WWF	World Wide Fund for Nature
WZB	Social Science Research Center Berlin (Wissenschaftszentrum Berlin für Sozialforschung)
ZEF	Center for Development Research (Zentrum für Entwicklungsforschung)
ZEI	Center for European Integration Studies (Zentrum für Europäische Integrationsforschung)

Guidance
for
Governance

1 Guidance for Governance: An Overview

R. Kent Weaver and Paul B. Stares

The need for "good governance" has become a common exhortation in a wide variety of contexts from corporate boardrooms to international organizations. What makes for "good" as distinct from "bad" governance—used here in the context of the nation-state to mean "the traditions and institutions by which authority in a country is exercised for the common good" (World Bank Institute 2001)—has understandably received considerable attention. Indeed, it is fair to say that there is now general consensus on the desired qualities of good governance. Those most frequently cited are "accountability," "inclusiveness," "transparency," and "legitimacy."

All of these are attractive and necessary attributes to be encouraged in any system of governance. But good governance should also be judged in terms of the quality of the decisions taken and policies adopted, specifically whether they produce outcomes that are broadly efficient, equitable, sustainable, and cost effective. What makes such outcomes more likely, however, clearly depends to a large extent on the quality of the policy advice that is injected into the governance process to help guide key decision makers. Yet the role of policy expertise is largely missing from most discussions of effective governance even though it can be helpful—even critical—at every stage of the policymaking process.

Thus, at the earliest stages of defining the nature of a problem and getting politicians' attention to put it on the agenda for governmental action, policy experts can help to outline just how serious a problem is and elucidate the causes of that problem in a way that sets the parameters for governmental action. As policy responses to a problem are being formulated, policy expertise can be critical in identifying the most important alternatives, evaluating their advantages and disadvantages, and suggesting a reformulation of proposals if leading candidates have important flaws. When governments must finally accept or reject

1

a proposal for policy change, expertise can help policymakers decide whether to move forward, fine tune the proposal, or go back to the drawing board. Finally and perhaps most important, once a policy is in place, policy expertise can be critical in evaluating that policy and deciding whether to leave it alone, revise it, or make major changes. This is not to say that policy expertise is always supplied or used in a disinterested manner; on the contrary, policymakers' use of expertise "takes place in a busy public setting, in a swelling-information-rich environment fed continually by many interested parties, all intending to have some bearing on the activities of government" (Lacey and Furner 1993, 4).

In seeking to balance societal interests, governments have traditionally sought policy advice from primarily "line" government departments or ministries that have direct responsibility for supervising specific programs. Transport ministry bureaucrats provide the dominant repository for expertise on railways and airline policy, for example, and health ministry bureaucrats for expertise on issues like immunization policy, health care user-fees, and the closing of redundant hospitals.

Politicians and scholars of the policymaking process have long been uneasy about these relationships, however. Relying on line agencies for policy advice poses several potential problems (Weller 1987, 156). First, these agencies are unlikely to take a holistic view of society's—or even a particular government's—policy needs. Highway bureaucrats in a transport ministry, for example, might not pay sufficient attention to the impact of their advice and their actions on urban sprawl. Agricultural bureaucracies may be insufficiently attentive to broader trade policy considerations in government policy. Navy bureaucracies may be concerned primarily with their own objectives rather than those of other military services or the most efficient allocation of scarce defense expenditures.

Second, line government agencies may develop close relationships with, and even be "captured" by, the societal interests that they oversee. Agriculture bureaucracies may take as their central mission the welfare of farmers, banking agencies the welfare of banks, transport regulatory agencies the welfare of airlines and railways, and so on. Such relationships are understandable, but they may not be desirable for good governance. Even where bureaucracies are not guided by their own interests or "captured" by the interests of those they are supposed to supervise, they may be blinded by "conventional wisdom" in their sector and fail to think creatively about the nature of policy problems and potential solutions.

The impact of various social, political, and economic trends on the task of governance, moreover, has increased the need for policymakers to draw on alternative sources of policy advice to those traditionally relied upon. One critical trend is the growing complexity of issues. This has led both to a greater segmentation of bureaucracies in order to manage a widening set of issues and to a proliferation of nongovernmental actors and interests that must be taken into account and engaged in the policy process. The net result is to make the tasks of consensus building, policy coordination, and implementation increasingly difficult. Those responsible for managing the policy process have to comprehend both highly specialized forms of knowledge—whether it be scientific, technical, or legal in nature—as well as the complex linkages that exist among different issues, which often transcend disciplinary, bureaucratic, and administrative boundaries.

The nature of representative government is changing as well. The democratic process in many countries has become quite fractured, with the number of political parties growing and minority or coalition governments becoming commonplace. As a consequence, there is a now much greater demand for independent advice from the legislative branch of many governments to assess the policies advanced by the executive branch and, if deemed necessary, to help in formulating alternatives.

Demands from civil society have also grown. These take several forms. One is that governments are under increasing pressure, as indicated earlier, to make the policy process open, inclusive, and above all accountable to the general public. This has increased the demand for impartial and imaginative new sources of public policy advice. At the same time, public expectations for immediate results have risen. Short-term considerations thus predominate to an even greater extent than before, with the result that medium- and long-term concerns may be neglected.

Finally, global economic competition and recurrent fiscal imbalances in many countries, heightened by regional economic crises in Asia and elsewhere, have intensified concerns over governmental performance. Cozy relationships between bureaucracies and industries as well as inefficiencies in government programs, which once were tolerable and tolerated, are increasingly seen as unacceptable—if not by governments and citizens, then by international lending agencies.

Expert advice can, and often is, sought from individual experts on an ad hoc basis. Government leaders may assemble informal "kitchen cabinets," some members of which may be legitimate policy experts, while others are valued more for their political know-how. And legislatures may solicit expert advice by holding hearings, although without adequate staff they may have difficulty in aggregating conflicting testimony into a coherent portrait of the status quo, let alone a cogent proposal for change. Because of the limits of ad hoc advice, however, the executive and legislative branches frequently seek out, and in some cases even create, specialized organizations that have as a major objective the provision of policy advice. The focus of this study is on the role played by such entities, which we call alternative policy advisory organizations (APAOs): organizations outside of line government departments which serve as institutionalized sources of policy expertise for government policymakers (see Seymour-Ure 1987).

Of course, there are factors that work against the institutionalization of alternative policy advice especially within government. Line bureaucracies may resist the growth of bureaucratic rivals that challenge their programs or embarrass them politically. And central executives may feel overwhelmed by the mountains of information that they have to absorb from line agencies without creating new sources of expertise to provide information that may prove to be redundant or contradictory.

Although there is a growing acceptance of the role and value of alternative sources of public policy advice to improve the quality of governance, the availability and use made of such organizations varies considerably between countries. These variations reflect not only differences in governmental receptivity to alternative policy advice, but also such factors as political culture, legal provisions, the availability of funding, and human resources. As a consequence, there exists in some countries a plethora of alternative sources of public policy advice while in others there is a dearth. More is not necessarily better, however. Policymakers can become overwhelmed or confused by alternative sources of policy advice to the point that they ignore much of what they receive, including some that might be useful.

The broad purpose of this study is to assess the current state and role of alternative sources of policy advice in eight democratic countries in different regions of the world and in different stages of political and economic development. Each national case study follows a broadly similar analytical framework to facilitate comparison. Besides shedding light on how particular constellations of APAOs have evolved and function under different conditions, the individual case studies also permit us to reach some general conclusions about the relative influence of public policy advice in specific national contexts and, moreover, to make recommendations for how it can be improved drawing on the experience, where relevant, of other countries.

This introductory chapter provides an overview to the subject of APAOs and previews some of the findings of the case studies about the advantages and limitations of specific APAO types and the constraints that various environmental conditions impose on them. We begin by delineating our subject: What do we mean by alternative policy advisory organizations?

APAOS: A DEFINITION

While the boundaries of what constitutes an APAO are not entirely clear, they share these general characteristics:

(1) APAOs are institutionalized. Informal advisory networks, or even individuals, may be an important source of policy expertise for government

leaders, and many political leaders surround themselves with kitchen cabinets, which provide political or policy advice (Bakvis 1997). So long as they remain as informal bodies, they are outside our definition of APAOs.

(2) APAOs have a significant organizational life span, but not necessarily presumed perpetuity. Most APAOs have no sunset provisions that limit their life span. For our purposes, even a body with a predetermined endpoint—for example, a commission established to investigate a particular problem or tragic event—falls within our definition of an APAO. However, organizations with a very short life span—for example, a task force that is set up to investigate a particular problem, reports to political executives within a week, and then dissolves—are not considered here.

(3) APAOs are outside of or autonomous within line government departments. An independent advisory organization is sometimes placed within a government department for administrative convenience; yet this organization, by virtue of its independently appointed membership with fixed terms, has almost complete autonomy in offering policy advice. While APAOs must be fully independent of line agencies, formal independence is of course no guarantee of real independence. If a formally independent APAO is staffed by bureaucrats of a particular government agency, its independence may be nominal.

(4) APAOs may be based in either civil society or government. Governments clearly do not have a monopoly on policy expertise. Moreover, distance from government is a continuum rather than dichotomous: Expertise-bearing organizations that receive most of their funding from government—contract research think tanks, for example—are neither entirely of civil society or of government.

(5) APAOs offer policy advice as their central mission, although this may not necessarily be their exclusive mission. Most university-based research centers and service- and action-oriented nongovernmental organizations (NGOs), for example, do not fit our definition of APAOs because offering policy advice to government is usually a peripheral mission for them. Similarly, government statistical agencies, which provide data for analysis of social and economic trends, usually do not have policy advice as part of their mandate and thus would not be included in our definition. Central banks, likewise, play a key policy advisory role in many countries, but once again, this is not their central function.

(6) APAOs base their claim to legitimacy largely on their policy expertise and technical skills rather than on their representation of a specific societal interest. Although an organization may have substantive expertise in policy areas and may in fact provide information to government, to be

considered an APAO, its main credential must be its policy expertise, not its ideological point of view. Thus, organizations like employer and labor confederations, industry associations, trade unions, or environmental groups may be able to make a compelling case to the government, but their main credential is their representation of a social interest that the government should not ignore.

(7) Finally, APAOs provide substantive policy expertise, rather than expertise on politics, management, or the policymaking process. Politicians and governments, especially in wealthier countries, draw on an array of individuals who claim expertise on gauging public opinion, explaining policies to the public, and winning elections. These pollsters, consultants, and political professionals will offer advice on policy issues, but that advice is generally based on their estimation of the political salability of policy, not on its substantive merits. Within government, a parliamentary system may have an office of the prime minister whose primary function is to offer political advice or to manage the process of governance (see, for example, Bakvis 1997). Management consultants may be engaged similarly to reorganize government agencies or to make them run more efficiently. However, unless these organizations have a substantial internal capacity for policy expertise, they do not fit within our definition of APAOs.

APAOS: A TYPOLOGY

Alternative sources of policy advice come in a variety of organizational forms. As seen in table 1, they can be grouped along two dimensions: the organization's degree of autonomy from government and the centrality of policy advice to the organization's mission. But APAOs vary greatly in their organizational proximity to government: Some clearly are a part of government, others clearly are not, and still others—for example, contract research think tanks, which are heavily financed by government but organizationally independent, and temporary blue-ribbon commissions, which are generally appointed by government but operate at an arm's length—are somewhere in between.

It is apparent from table 1 that the distinctions between the organizations that have been categorized as APAOs and those that have not are hazy. NGOs, for example, may have both substantial research agendas and action-oriented agendas, and they may not distinguish or see conflict between these agendas. If their research does not meet the standard of value-neutral social science research, neither does the research of many organizations that fit more clearly within our definition of an APAO.

Table 1. Alternative Sources of Institutionalized Policy Advice and Expertise for Government

		Degree of Autonomy from Government		
		Government	Intermediate	Civil Society
Centrality of policy advice to organizational mission	Central	**Central policy review and advisory organizations within the executive** **Legislative support agencies** **Legislative committee staffs** **Independent government audit agencies** Central banks Treasury and Finance ministries	**Temporary blue-ribbon government commissions** **Permanent independent advisory bodies** **Contract research and ministerial think tanks** **Political party think tanks and research bureaus**	**Academic think tanks** **Advocacy think tanks** **Research-oriented NGOs**
	Peripheral	Government statistical agencies	Consulting firms to government International lending agencies (e.g., International Monetary Fund, World Bank) Supra-national organizations	Corporate think tanks Interest groups University research centers Action- and service-oriented NGOs Professional associations Personal staffs of legislators

Note: Organizations defined as alternative policy advisory organizations are shown in boldface.
NGOs: nongovernmental organizations.

It is nevertheless helpful to think in terms of types of APAOs even as we recognize that some organizations will not fit neatly into a single category. We outline the major types here, and we attempt to identify the advantages and limitations associated with each. Table 2 lists seven modal attributes that may be useful in providing policy advice and translating it into policy change: access to key decision makers, capacity for providing independent advice, responsiveness to the agenda of the government, credibility with policymakers, credibility with the public, capacity to offer a career path for policy experts, and institutional capacity to follow through on policy advice. Types of APAOs are rated—albeit very roughly—according to these attributes.

Obviously, significant variation can be found within each type of APAO, as extremely weak organizations with very few resources would not exhibit the potential advantages associated with their APAO type. Idiosyncratic relationships can be critical as well: For example, civil society–based APAOs may have relationships with particular politicians that can give them an unusually high degree of access to policymakers. The ratings in table 2 are intended, therefore, not to suggest a rigid set of APAO attributes, but to illustrate that there is no single preferred form of APAO. Actual advantages are rather the result of a series of trade-offs. Most government APAOs, for example, are likely to rank high in terms of responsiveness to the government's agenda and institutional capacity to follow through on advice, while civil society–based organizations are likely to produce advice that is truly independent. Given the distinctive advantages and limitations of specific APAO types, it is little wonder that wealthy, more democratic societies have many more APAOs of multiple types.

Central Policy Review and Advisory Organizations

Organizations that exist within the executive branch to provide a central policy review and advisory function are one of the most important, and most common, type of APAO. Central executives recognize the need for a broader—and sometimes longer-term—perspective than they are likely to get from the advice of line government agencies. The form that a central policy review and advisory organization may take varies widely in terms of whom it serves (the head of government personally or the cabinet collectively), its staffing (semipermanent, seconded from line agencies, or political appointment), the breadth of its policy mandate (all policy, domestic or foreign policy, or sector policy), the degree to which it offers political as well as policy advice, and—most critical for our purposes—the extent to which it relies upon its own independent policy expertise, rather than simply coordinating, managing, and acting as a gatekeeper for information from line government agencies.

Table 2. Attributes Associated with Specific APAO Types

APAO Type	APAO Attributes						
	Access to key decision makers	Capacity for providing independent policy advice	Responsiveness to agenda of government	Credibility with policy-makers	Credibility with public	Capacity to offer stable career path	Institutional capacity to follow through on policy advice
Governmental							
Legislative support agencies	?	?	+++	+++	+	++	+
Legislative committee staffs	?	?	++	?	0		
Independent audit agencies	++	+++	+	+++	+++	+++	++
Central policy review organizations	+++	?	+++	+++	+	?	+++
Intermediate							
Temporary blue-ribbon commissions	?	++	++	++	+++	0	0
Permanent advisory bodies	++	+	++	+++	++	+	+
Contract research and ministerial think tanks	++	+	+++	++	+	++	+
Political party think tanks and research bureaus	?	?	?	?	0	0	?
Civil Society APAOs							
Academic think tanks	?	+++	?	++	+	?	?
Advocacy think tanks	?	++	?	?	?	?	?
Research-oriented NGOs	0	++	?	0	+	0	?

+++ Potential to embody this attribute is extremely high.

++ Potential to embody this attribute is fairly high.

+ Potential to embody this attribute is modest.

0 Potential to embody this attribute is almost always limited.

? Potential to embody this attribute is highly variable; generalization is difficult.

APAO: alternative policy advisory organization; NGOs: nongovernmental organizations.

Many of the advantages and disadvantages of central policy review and advisory organizations are a consequence of their position. For example, because of their proximity to central decision makers, they are often called upon to address crises of the moment. Thus, their advice is more likely to be characterized by option evaluation of current and pressing issues, superficial analysis, discrete issues, and limited innovativeness, rather than by a fundamental rethinking of issues (Dror 1987, 200).

Other characteristics are dependent on the ways that particular central agencies are comprised. Organizations heavily made up of political appointees, like the Domestic Policy Council in the United States, may have the ear of their political masters, but when the central administration and organizational staff turn over, institutional memory is poor and the learning curve steep. Organizations relying on secondment from line bureaucracies may find their staff reluctant to stray from the views of their primary past and likely future employers. While having a permanent staff provides continuity for an organization, it may become so committed to its institutional point of view that it is no longer innovative (Seymour-Ure 1987, 183; Dror 1987, 197). The point is that there is no single best staffing arrangement for these organizations; rather there are a series of trade-offs to be resolved in the broader logic of governmental structure. Deviations from that logic are difficult to sustain—but also most useful in providing distinctive alternative policy advice.

Legislative Support Organizations and Independent Audit Agencies

Legislative support organizations (LSOs) can take many forms, but their overarching objective is to offer members of the legislature alternative sources of information to that provided by the executive. The most common type of these organizations is a parliamentary library or reference bureau that answers questions and provides information requested by legislators (Robinson 1998). In this capacity, legislative support organizations are simply repositories for published expertise. This role has been expanded in many countries, however. Legislative support organizations frequently go beyond providing materials produced elsewhere to summarizing and critiquing those materials, perhaps also performing independent policy analysis, preparing independent budget estimates, and holding seminars to bring legislators up to speed on issues.

Closely related to and partially overlapping with LSOs are organizations that can be called independent audit agencies, accountable to the legislature rather than the executive, which provide an independent oversight and watchdog function to ensure that government money is not being misallocated, wasted, or stolen. Auditing organizations may also expand their roles by looking beyond the question of proper expenditure of funds to consider whether a program is cost-effective or meets its goals. The U.S. General Accounting Office, which now performs policy analysis at the behest of Congress, is a classic example of an audit organization whose role has expanded (Mosher 1979).

As alternative sources of policy advice, LSOs and audit agencies have the advantage of their proximity to decision makers (see Robinson 1992). Their research agenda, as opposed to that of APAOs outside of government, is likely to be determined by the legislative agenda, and thus their potential for having timely impact is increased. Moreover, because LSOs and independent audit agencies provide a direct service to legislators, they may be viewed more sympathetically when it comes to funding. And as long as they are nonpartisan, for policy experts they may represent a reasonably secure career path in public service.

In many parliamentary systems, however, the legislature is not at all important to the policymaking process, existing merely as a vehicle for expressing a mandate to the governing party. In this situation, supporting an independent policy advisory organization for the legislature may be seen by the governing party as unnecessary at best and a potential nuisance at worst. LSOs and audit agencies may gain financial support only if the governing party is willing to take the long view toward a time when it will be in opposition and need expertise independent of the executive.

Legislative
Committee Staffs

Policy expertise may also be diffused among individual legislative committees or, in the case of a bicameral legislature, individual chambers. Clearly, the biggest advantage of legislative committee staffs is that their expertise is imbedded directly into the lawmaking process and, at least theoretically, outside of executive control.

Legislative committee staffs face limitations, however, primarily involving accountability and hiring. Should they be accountable to the committee chair (who usually is a member of the majority party), to senior members of each political party on the committee, or to all members? Each option has its drawbacks. If members of a legislative committee staff are hired by and accountable to the committee chair, their expertise is not likely to be truly autonomous. Where a single party holds a legislative majority in a parliamentary system, there will be pressure not to take too independent a line from that of the government. Indeed, in this volume, it is only with the two countries with presidential systems, Brazil and the United States, that the case study authors have rated legislative committee staffs as highly institutionalized and highly influential.

Even within the U.S. Congress, where committee staffs are larger and perhaps more consequential to policymaking than anywhere else, there is substantial variation in their composition. A few committee staffs have been organized in a relatively bipartisan fashion, but the dominant pattern, especially in recent years, has been toward majority and minority party staffs. Because the majority party generally gets more committee staff members than does the minority party, turnover can be significant when the partisan makeup of the legislature changes.

Obviously, these issues grow more complex in multiparty systems, whether parliamentary or presidential. Should committee staffs be divided on a partisan basis, or should they be divided between the governing party or coalition and those in opposition? Having separate staffs for each party is likely to be problematic when committee staffs are small and the number of parties is large, as staff may be spread across too many issues to provide in-depth expertise. And dividing committee staffs between the governing and opposition coalitions may lead to staff instability when the makeup of coalitions reshuffles.

Another alternative is to have committee staffs composed of nonpartisan civil servants, with stable career paths similar to those in the executive branch. This is the pattern adopted in Brazil, where, as Amaury de Souza indicates in his chapter, legislative committee staff members are nonpartisan, are hired by Assessoria Legislativa, the legislative support service, and hold permanent job tenure. There is no single answer to this question. What is clear, however, is that partisan legislative committee staffing patterns found in the U.S. Congress are probably not appropriate elsewhere, especially in countries with multiparty systems.

Permanent Advisory Bodies

Governments sometimes appoint permanent advisory bodies for independent advice on policy issues. These advisory bodies vary in mandate, agenda, and appointment. Germany's Council of Economic Experts is charged with a broad mandate, while many advisory bodies are limited to single issues, such as the arts or science policy. Sometimes advisory bodies are afforded substantial leeway over their own agenda; sometimes studies are undertaken only on request of government. In some cases, members of these bodies are appointed solely by the government, while in others interest groups have input as well.

Temporary Blue-Ribbon Commissions

Rather than create a permanent advisory body, governments sometimes opt for temporary blue-ribbon commissions to investigate a particular problem (see Pross et al. 1990; Weller 1994). Membership of these commissions frequently includes, at least in part, prominent citizens with some claim to expertise, alongside representatives of groups affected by the policy area. Generally, commissions are assisted by a special staff, which may be seconded from government departments or brought in from consulting firms or universities. It is these staff members who usually do the bulk of the actual work, gathering material and drafting the final report.

Again, the breadth of mandate of these commissions can vary. At one extreme is the Royal Commission on the Economic Union and Development Prospects for Canada, which was appointed in the early 1980s. Its resulting three-volume report of almost 2,000 pages, with more than seventy volumes of supporting research, was thought to exceed even the vastness of its name. At the other end are commissions with a much narrower scope, created to study, for example, a prison riot, an accident at a nuclear power plant, or the government's response to a flood.

How blue-ribbon commissions are used by governments also has wide variety. In Sweden, for example, such commissions have become an integral, regularized part of the policymaking process: They help to develop an expert consensus before the governing party begins to formulate legislation. In many countries, however, special commissions are sometimes used as a cynical ploy to deflect public pressure on the government to act on a salient issue. Indeed, the ploy is often successful, mollifying the public until such time that the issue becomes less salient.

By their very nature, these temporary special commissions usually have a clear mission and almost always have a limited time frame within which to achieve it. Self-perpetuation of the body thus does not become an end in itself.

Despite these advantages as a source of alternative policy advice, the effectiveness of temporary commissions of inquiry is compromised by the fact that their existence is at the will of the government, which determines the organization's membership, mandate, budget, and timetable. In many countries, the government will even decide whether or not the final report is to be released to the public. A variation on this theme has been known to occur when the governing party, which appointed the commission, loses power and a new government ushers in a very different set of priorities. The holdover commission may find itself facing a quick and quiet burial.

An equally serious, and more common, shortcoming of special commissions is lack of follow-through. Once their report is completed, special commissions are usually disbanded. Commission members may be called to testify before the legislature and to consult with bureaucrats and politicians, but there is no institutional capacity, or obligation, to keep the commission's findings and recommendations before the public. Unless the report finds an institutional champion in the bureaucracy or a powerful and committed backer among elected politicians, the half-life of the commission's work will be brief.

More fundamentally, the logic by which a temporary commission is appointed can wreak its own havoc. Sometimes members of a commission are appointed so as to represent all relevant interests on an issue. But by virtue of this, the commission may simply be a re-creation of the divided state of affairs that led the government to appoint a neutral, expert body in the first place. If commission members try to reach a unanimous agreement, which gives a report greater credibility, they may do so at the cost of all but the lowest common denominator that offends no one and is unlikely to deviate much from the status quo.

Another difficulty these commissions face is recruitment of expert staff. Because a temporary commission by definition does not offer stable, long-term employment, attracting qualified staff is not easy. The best personnel may be unwilling to relocate if there is no guarantee that they will be able to return to their prior jobs with salary and seniority intact. Many governments try to get around this by staffing temporary commissions with bureaucrats seconded from government ministries. But, as has been stated above, this approach has its drawbacks: Bureaucrats whose future livelihood depends on the goodwill of certain entities may be less than fully enthusiastic about policy recommendations that will be an anathema to their former department or clientele.

Contract Research and Ministerial Think Tanks

Like special temporary commissions, contract research and ministerial think tanks exist outside the formal structure of government, even as their research agenda is determined largely by government. Perhaps the earliest, and best-known, example of a contract research think tank is the RAND Corporation, which was created in the aftermath of World War II to provide expertise for the U.S. Department of Defense. Of course, government contracts with other organizations as well—for example, university research centers and academic think tanks. In Korea, think tanks have taken similar form to contract think tanks. Mo Jongryn in his chapter calls these organizations ministerial think tanks, enjoying the sponsorship and support of a specific government ministry but operating outside that ministry.

For government, the major advantage of contract research and ministerial think tanks is that because they rely on government funding, they are very responsive to requests for studies relevant to government's agenda. Thus their agenda is likely to focus on policy options that government is actually considering rather than on options that have little chance of enactment. At the same time, the fact that these think tanks are outside of government gives them added independence and credibility.

Yet, to the extent that think tanks are dependent on a single government agency for contracts, they may find themselves reluctant to criticize that agency, which would effectively be to bite the hand that feeds them. Even if think tanks do not engage in self-censorship, they may be perceived as biased, which hurts the credibility of their work (Weaver and McGann 2000). Moreover, they are likely to shy away from important issues that their sponsoring agency is anxious to keep off the policy agenda.

Academic Think Tanks

Academic think tanks, sometimes referred to as universities without students, are research organizations based outside of government that have as their major, if not sole, mission the work of policy-relevant research. They are similar to contract research think tanks in their emphasis on the social science norms of objectivity and completeness. They are supported primarily by nongovernmental sources such as philanthropies and corporations. Because of this, however, their research agenda is likely to be determined by the organization itself and by its donors rather than by government.

Academic think tanks that nurture and conform to the norms of social science are less likely than contract research or ministerial think tanks to avoid sensitive political issues, and at the same time they are less likely to be excluded from access to policymakers after a change in government. On the other hand, while academic think tanks produce studies within the scope of their experts' training, policymakers may find the research to be irrelevant, dense, long, theoretical, or poorly timed. And because of their nongovernmental nature, academic think tanks tend to lack a natural partisan constituency among policymakers.

Political Party Think Tanks
and Research Bureaus

Research bureaus and think tanks affiliated with a political party represent another source of expert policy advice, especially in the agenda-setting and policy-formulation stages. These organizations, which may take several forms, vary in the degree to which they are financed by government. In a few countries, like Germany and the Netherlands, political party foundations are financed largely by government, in rough proportion to the party's share of the vote in the preceding election. These organizations perform a variety of functions—civic education more prominently than policy research (see, for example, Weilemann 2000). In other cases, government financing is indirect or nonexistent, and the links between a party and its affiliated think tank are less formal.

By tapping their own expertise, political parties are able to develop more realistic and coherent electoral platforms and to act as a policy counterweight to government bureaucracies. This can be useful for political parties that have been out of power and have not had access to the expertise available to governmental bureaucracies. But in countries where political parties are themselves unstable, or undergoing regular realignment between elections (for example, Japan in the late 1990s), donors may have a hard time deciding which organizations to fund. Moreover, in such an environment, party-based research organizations do not provide the kind of secure career path attractive to highly qualified experts. And in political parties of all types, efforts to increase policy-research capacity must contend with politicians eager to devote resources to party building and electoral purposes instead.

Advocacy Think Tanks

Advocacy think tanks begin from a well-defined ideological point of view rather than from the social science norms of objectivity and completeness. Thus, they are frequently similar to party think tanks in their missions, although without close organizational links to a specific party or party and/or government financing. Again, the progenitors are largely American. The perceived success of the Washington, D.C.–based Heritage Foundation in influencing policy during the Reagan administration spawned a number of other advocacy tanks in the United States and abroad. Noteworthy has been the growth of conservative, free-market institutions, such as the Adam Smith Institute in the United Kingdom and the Frankfurt Institute in Germany.

The boundaries of this category of organization, as with other types of APAOs, are not entirely clear. In a number of countries, for example, there are business-oriented organizations (such as the Committee for Economic Development in the United States and the Studieforbundet Naringsliv och Samhalle in Sweden) that do not directly represent the interests of business but have close links to business. Some advocacy tanks also have linkages to organized labor. And some advocacy tanks have close informal links to a specific political party, even though they lack formal ties. The advantages and limitations of these organizations are fairly clear: When political parties sympathetic to the ideology espoused by an advocacy tank are in power, that organization may be looked to as a source of ideas and perhaps even personnel. When political parties hostile to that organization are in power, however, it may be consigned to the political wilderness.

Research-Oriented NGOs

Distinguishing NGOs that devote most of their resources to advocacy and social action from advocacy tanks that have expert policy research and advice as their central function is not easily accomplished. This category of research-oriented NGOs, then, describes where the two intersect, that is, organizations for which advocacy and policy advice are closely linked. Frequently, the policy advice offered by these organizations flows directly from the experience of their staff or clients in grass-roots social groups. Such groups are especially important in India where, as Kuldeep Mathur notes in his chapter, they have been active on issues such as women's rights and disabilities. In other cases, as with groups associated with the U.S. consumer advocate Ralph Nader (on health and auto safety issues, for example), social activism and research may be more distinct but also complementary.

The linkages of research-oriented NGOs to civil society may provide additional sources of information and financing, as well as political clout. On the other hand, their research may be perceived as less objective than that of academic think tanks, and they may have limited access to policymakers when parties hostile to their interests are in power.

CROSS-NATIONAL VARIATIONS IN APAO ACTIVITY

While APAOs come in many different forms, there are different levels of APAO activity and influence on the policymaking process across countries. Table 3 represents a rough assessment of the level of APAO activity in each of the countries studied in this volume, as determined by their respective authors. Activity ranges from nonexistent to stable, highly institutionalized, and influential. Indices for these determinations include organizational longevity, organizational turnover, and evidence suggesting impact on policymaking.

While these assessments are necessarily very rough, they suggest several interesting patterns, looking either across columns (countries) or across rows (APAO types). In a comparison of the surveyed countries, the United States stands out for its rich array of APAOs of almost every type, with Germany second. In their range of intermediate and civil society–based APAOs, the United Kingdom and Germany are fairly similar to the United States, but their APAOs within government are less institutionalized and less influential. Brazil, on the other hand, has a strong complement of government APAOs, but a relatively weak assortment based in civil society. Poland, Japan, Korea, and India share a pattern of much weaker APAO presence, although each has areas of some strength.

An equally interesting set of patterns emerges looking across APAO types. Some APAO types are widely diffused, showing up in nearly all countries, while others appear in only a few. Among government APAOs, none of the organizational subtypes is a substantial actor across all countries, but independent audit agencies are the most common. Among the intermediate APAOs, permanent advisory bodies appear frequently, while temporary blue-ribbon commissions and contract research and ministerial think tanks show a more mixed pattern. Political party think tanks and research bureaus, on the other hand, are weak or nonexistent in all of the countries studied with the exception of Germany and, to a lesser extent, the United Kingdom. Activity by civil society–based APAOs is also quite uneven across countries; they tend to be stronger in the United States, the United Kingdom, and Germany—the three countries that combine high gross domestic product (GDP) per capita, uninterrupted democracy for at least forty years, and a fairly strong tradition of civil society.

Table 3. Scorecard of APAO Activity

APAO Type	Country Ratings							
	U.S.	U.K.	Germany	Brazil	Poland	Japan	Korea	India
Governmental								
Legislative support agencies	+++	0	++	+++	+++	+	+	0
Legislative committee staffs	+++	+	++	+++	0	+	+	+
Independent audit agencies	+++	++	+++	+++	+++	+	0	0
Central policy review organizations	++	++	+	+++	+++	+	0	0
Intermediate								
Temporary blue-ribbon commissions	++	++	+++	0	+	++	++	++
Permanent advisory bodies	+++	+++	+++	+++	++	++	+	++
Contract research and ministerial think tanks	+++	+	++	++	+	++	+++	+
Political party think tanks and research bureaus	0	++	+++	+	0	0	+	+
Civil Society APAOs								
Academic think tanks	+++	+++	+++	+	0	+	+	++
Advocacy think tanks	+++	+++	++	++	+	+	+	+
Research-oriented NGOs	++	++	++	+	+	0	++	++

0 APAOs of this type are absent or almost nonexistent.
+ APAOs of this type are weak in numbers and resources. They are characterized by high organizational and/or staff turnover. Few if any of these organizations are more than a decade old and have survived at least one transition in top organizational leadership. Organizational survival is a real concern for most APAOs of this type. For civil society–based APAOs, only one or a very few APAOs of this type exist. Organizational visibility, access to policymakers, and evidence of impact on policymaking are all limited.
++ At least some APAOs of this type appear to be well-established, with stable financial support and acceptance of their role in the political process. However, for civil society–based APAOs, there are still significant questions about the long-term viability of a substantial share of APAOs of this type. Evidence of policy impact is sporadic or mixed.
+++ APAOs of this type are mostly well-established, with stable financing. Some have been around for a long time, and have experienced at least one successful transition in their organizational leadership. They have also experienced several changes in government without a marked decline in the role played by the APAO type as a whole, although specific organizations may have lost visibility, access, or influence. They are accepted participants in the policymaking process. Although their influence is frequently hard to evaluate, it is possible to point to numerous instances where they have had an influence. For civil society–based APAOs, these characteristics hold for a number of organizations and not just one or two atypical ones.
APAO: alternative policy advisory organization; NGOs: nongovernmental organizations.

EXPLAINING THE
VARIATIONS IN APAO ACTIVITY

A country's political, legal, and economic environment helps to explain the cross-national differences in levels of APAO activity. Some of these environmental factors can be viewed as structural conditions that affect APAO development—that is to say, they are fairly stable over time in their effect. But APAO development may also be influenced by windows of opportunity—temporary conjunctions of events that stimulate the founding or growth of APAOs and that may leave organizational legacies even after those conditions have disappeared or been weakened.

Among structural conditions, the *legal environment* is particularly important for civil society–based APAOs. Long-standing freedom of political association in countries like the United States and United Kingdom has provided the time for these organizations to develop and diversify. In countries like Korea and Poland, the weakening of restrictions on freedom of association are of relatively recent origin, but it is clear that it has stimulated the growth of civil society–based APAOs. Even where these restrictions do not exist, there may be limitations on incorporation of nonprofit organizations without the sponsorship of a government ministry, or limitations on donations to nonprofit organizations, and the effect has been to discourage the development of civil society–based APAOs. In Japan, as Yamamoto Tadashi points out in his chapter, the requirements for ministry sponsorship of NGOs have only recently been loosened (see also Ueno 1998).

The *financial environment* in a country is clearly relevant for APAO development as well. All other things being equal, we should expect that the more economically developed countries will have a higher level of activity by both governmental and nongovernmental APAOs. Greater social wealth both creates slack resources for investment in such activities and induces greater demand for higher quality policy advice, as it does for other things that may be considered unaffordable luxuries in poor countries, such as a clean environment. But this overall effect of wealth is mediated by other features of the financial environment. The cultural norms regarding corporate and individual philanthropy, for example, are likely to have a major impact on the activity of civil society–based APAOs. If corporations, foundations, and other sources of philanthropy donate to organizations that provide social services (for example, museums, hospitals, and universities) rather than to civil society–based APAOs, then the APAO environment is likely to be less rich. Studies of the United States have highlighted the role of philanthropy as a guiding force in the evolution of its dense network of think tanks (Smith 1991).

Laws that provide tax incentives for gifts to civil society–based APAOs as well as other nonprofit organizations are also likely to stimulate their development. In an increasingly globalized world, however, funding from governments, foundations, and multinational agencies can be a further source of assistance (Stone 2000b). In fact, the rapid growth and recent financial woes of East European think tanks can be attributed largely to the giving and subsequent withdrawal of financial support by Western foundations and aid agencies—a classic opening and closing of a window of opportunity that has nonetheless left a substantial organizational legacy (Struyk 1999, chapter 5).

A country's *political institutions* may also influence the development of APAOs. Institutional arrangements are especially important for APAOs within the governmental orbit. In general, we might expect that political systems where the legislature plays a policymaking role independent of the executive are more likely to develop a policy-advisory capacity responsive to the legislature (notably, legislative support organizations and committee staffs) than those where it does not. In such countries, legislatures not only have the need for independent policy advice, they are also likely to have sufficient leverage over the budget and other aspects of policymaking to ensure that they can obtain it. Indeed, both the United States and Brazil, with separation-of-powers institutions, have the strongest roles for legislature-based APAOs.

Windows of opportunity for the creation of new APAOs may open when the legislature feels a need to protect its institutional prerogatives vis-à-vis the executive, as with the creation of the Congressional Budget Office in the wake of struggles between President Richard Nixon and the Democratic-controlled Congress in 1974. Periods of minority government in parliamentary systems may also open windows of opportunity for expansion of activity by governmental APAOs, as legislators outside the governing party gain institutional leverage to win approval for new APAOs or funding for existing APAOs responsive to their needs. However, the Korean experience, as Mo relates in his chapter, suggests a chicken-or-the-egg problem in fostering APAOs responsive to the legislature: Even when there is a formal separation of powers between the executive and the legislature, a legislature with a history of subordination to the executive is unlikely to have either the leverage to obtain additional APAO resources or the political incentive to develop an autonomous policymaking capacity.

Several authors here note that legislators in parliamentary systems have few incentives to demand more resources for LSOs or legislative committee staffs because (1) reelection and prospects for career advancement are more important than policy activism, and (2) reelection and prospects for career advancement objectives are determined more by party loyalty and constituency than by policy activism. Indeed, the latter may be seen as detrimental to their careers. Moreover, opposition parties in parliamentary systems tend to concentrate on criticizing the government rather than on proposing constructive alternatives based on policy expertise, because they know the low probability of enacting them. Martin Thunert writes in his chapter that the expansion of legislative service organizations for the Bundestag in Germany can be attributed in part to a political window of opportunity in the early 1970s, when both major parties had recently experienced opposition status and thus saw the value of the expertise available to parties outside the governing coalition.

Federalism may also engender a richer array of APAOs, because it increases the number of governments seeking information and the number of sponsors of APAO activity. Thunert observes that *Länder* governments have been important sponsors and co-donors of academic think tanks, as well as of permanent advisory councils and (less frequently) temporary blue-ribbon commissions. In recent years in the United States, a huge number of advisory tanks focused on the state level have been founded (Rich and Weaver 1998). Yet, state legislatures vary widely in the degree to which they have developed legislative support organizations, legislative committee staffs, and other sources of institutionalized alternative policy expertise.

The relative weakness of political party think tanks in almost all the countries studied here is, on the surface, a somewhat surprising finding. But there appear to be several reasons that reflect common institutional and financial constraints. First, as indicated above, there are strong electoral incentives for political parties to devote their resources to electoral and party-building purposes rather than policy development; Germany, where government earmarks funds for policy research, proves the exception. Indeed, policy research that conflicts with positions already taken by a party could pose problems for party leaders.

Second, the advocacy think tanks that abound in many countries, especially the United States and United Kingdom, and that have an ideological affinity to a particular party serve as de facto party think tanks. The organizational independence and close informal links of these advocacy tanks may allow them to enjoy the advantages of proximity when their affiliated party is in power without entirely losing access or credibility when it is out of power.

Third, there may be financing advantages to being an independent advocacy tank rather than a party organ. Individuals, corporations, and foundations within the country may receive more favorable tax treatment for donations to independent organizations than donations to party bodies. Advocacy tanks in the developing and transitional economies may also be more likely to receive donations from foreign foundations than party-linked bodies.

The *labor market environment* for experts can affect APAO activity as well. If personnel with substantive and analytical skills in analyzing public policy are in short supply, as is the case in developing countries, finding staff for APAOs in addition to line government departments is not easy. But more subtle factors may also be at work. Particularly important is the capacity of APAOs to offer attractive career paths to potential staff. This is largely a matter of financial resources: NGOs, political party think tanks, and small advocacy tanks may not be able to offer policy experts the salary, prestige, or job security that comes with working for the government bureaucracy. Cultural and institutional factors are also relevant: In countries where lifetime employment with a single employer is the norm—and the desideratum for most workers—accepting short- or medium-term employment with an APAO may not be attractive.

The development of APAOs can also be affected by a broad set of factors that comprise the *information/expertise environment*. Obviously, the work of APAOs, especially nongovernmental groups, is likely to be inhibited if government is restrictive in disseminating the basic data necessary to perform independent policy analysis. APAO growth may also be inhibited if non-APAO organizations are already providing policy advice. A vibrant sector of policy-focused university research sectors, for example, may function as a substitute for independent academic think tanks. But if such organizations are nonexistent or lack adequate resources or have a weak focus on public policy, demand for APAOs may actually increase. Finally, there is the so-called emulation effect: If policymakers perceive APAOs to have been successful in the past, either at home or abroad, they may aspire to that success by creating new APAOs. Indeed, the chapters in this volume demonstrate that the rich array of APAOs in the United States has served as a model in other countries where policy elites and policy entrepreneurs are eager to have their own Council of Economic Advisors, Congressional Research Service, Heritage Foundation, Brookings Institution, or RAND Corporation.

The *cultural environment* is no less important. In particular, countries that have a high regard for neutral expertise tend to be hospitable to academic think tanks and permanent advisory bodies with heavy representation of academic experts. Germany stands out in this regard. On the other hand, in countries that are highly partisan and ideologically divided, civil society–based APAOs may have trouble gaining acceptance as neutral experts.

ARE APAOS IMMORTAL?

Among the countries in this study, prospects for creation of new APAOs vary greatly. But that is only part of the story. Equally important is whether APAOs, once created, can be sustained politically and economically.

APAOs are not immortal. Temporary blue-ribbon commissions, by their very nature, have limited duration. Even APAOs with presumed perpetuity may turn out to have limited tenure. Different types of APAOs face different hazards, but all seem to reflect structural conditions and windows of vulnerability, moments when an APAO may be particularly exposed. Government-based APAOs have natural ene- mies: bureaucrats who see a threat to their own policy priorities and their control over policy. In the United Kingdom, organizations such as the Central Policy Review Staff appear to have succumbed to this kind of bureaucratic opposition. Further, under pressure to reduce the size of government during periods of fiscal stress, government APAOs are uniquely vulnerable. It is much easier to abolish a small advisory commission or a legislative support organization with no service- delivery function than it is a large government ministry like Defense or Health. Nor are APAOs likely to have strong constituencies that will fight to protect them. The demise of the U.S. Office of Technology Assessment as part of the budget-cutting fever of the new Republican congressional majority in 1995 is a good case in point (Bimber 1996).

In a similar way, Mo points out, the incoming Kim Dae Jung government in Korea abolished 117 advisory commissions and merged twenty-seven others. Government APAOs that are strongly associated with a political party also encounter a window of vulnerability when their party loses power. Overall, however, such instances appear to be the exception rather than the rule. A more common pattern is that government APAOs which fail to secure powerful patrons are ignored and become irrelevant, at least for a while, or are downgraded in sta- tus and function. Thunert's discusssion of the fate of the planning bureau in the German chancellor's office in the 1960s and 1970s is an example of this.

Intermediate and civil society–based APAOs face somewhat different threats. Funding problems are usually central to their demise. Research-oriented NGOs seldom enjoy a strong financial base and are vulnerable to a decline in member- ship, foundation support, or government subsidies. In developing and transi- tional economies, changes in the funding priorities of foundations and national and multinational aid agencies may also lead to serious retrenchment or organi- zational demise. In practice, however, organizational shrinkage—cutbacks in staff, expenditures, and product lines—appears to be a more common fate for APAOs than outright death.

ASSESSING THE
INFLUENCE OF APAOS

Whether alternative sources of policy advice have an impact on policymaking depends on three broad factors. First, there must be an adequate supply of such advice. This in turn is likely to reflect matters such as the availability of financing and the adequate supply of policy experts. Second, there must be effective demand from policymakers for such advice; they must listen to, understand, and act upon that advice. Third, governments must have institutional capacity to change policy. If government elites perceive the wisdom of new policy ideas but are paralyzed by conflicting interest group pressures or veto points in governmental structure, governments may be no better off than if the advice had not been offered in the first place.

Assessing the influence and impact of APAOs on policymaking is difficult, as most of the authors here acknowledge (see also Stone 1996, chapter 7). Many APAOs can point to instances when their policy advice was taken and transformed into policy, but assessing and measuring the overall influence of APAOs is almost impossible. First, the process through which issues get—and lose—the attention of politicians is fluid. The leading analysis of agenda setting, by John Kingdon, suggests that issues and ideas get on the agenda when there is a conjunction of what he calls problem, policy, and political streams (Kingdon 1995; see also Baumgartner and Jones 1993). In the problem stream, increased attention may be drawn to a problem by a highly visible focusing event (for example, the Asian financial crisis) or by a newly developed indicator or an indicator that pushes through a highly visible threshold (see Stone 1989). APAOs may play a critical role in this process by producing indicators (for example, estimates of government expenditures wasted in a particular program, or the economic cost of failed policies) that help to redefine the nature of the problem.

In the policy stream, alternatives are frequently developed within communities of experts in a particular sector. Over time, proposals are refined, revised, and recombined. Proposals survive what is usually a long process of winnowing only if they appear to be technically feasible (having some prospect of being implemented and addressing the problem without making it worse), affordable, and congruent with the values of policymakers and the public (Kingdon 1995, 131–139).The political stream is equally complex. The attention of politicians is focused when they sense a national mood of concern on an issue or when an issue offers an opportunity for claiming credit. An election that brings new personnel into government with different values, perspectives, and priorities may also bring new issues to the agenda. Kingdon argues that brief opportunities to introduce change occur when the three policy streams come together and are joined, often through the efforts of a skilled political entrepreneur. Indeed, "advocates lie in wait, in and around government with their solutions in hand, waiting for problems to float by to which they can attach their solutions, waiting for a development in the political stream they can use to their advantage" (Kingdon 1995, 165).

Even if a problem is seen as pressing, it may not remain on the agenda long if no plausible policy alternative is available. Issues may fade from agendas for other reasons as well: The public and policymakers may become inured to the situation, especially if it is perceived to be insoluble, or they may lose interest as the memories of a visible event fade. Politicians may also feel that a problem has been "solved" after new legislation is passed; only if problems persist, or appear in a new form, will an issue reappear on the agenda. All of this would suggest that the influence of APAOs is likely to be intermittent rather than consistent, and as dependent on the interests of policymakers as on the characteristics of specific APAOs.

Policy choices, moreover, have complex parentage—only rarely is it said that advice from an APAO was the necessary, sufficient, and exclusive cause of that policy choice. In addition, APAO influence may take the role of policy brokerage rather than actual policy innovation (see Stone 1996). APAOs, especially those within government, may help to advance policy paradigms or proposals devised elsewhere by bringing them to the attention of policymakers or by adding their own support, thus giving ideas greater legitimacy.

A second reason why assessing the influence of APAOs is difficult, as noted at the outset of this overview and by several of the authors here, is that policy advice takes different forms at different stages of the policymaking process. This can range from broad paradigmatic rethinking of policy problems, causes, and solutions, to the development of specific policy alternatives, judgment on whether to accept proffered alternatives, and evaluation of current policies, which may or may not include the posing of alternatives if the status quo is found wanting. Aggregating measures of influence across these policymaking stages and types of advice is impossible to do in a meaningful way, even if the problem of attribution could be solved.

Third, policy influence may take place through multiple means. Whispering into the ear of politicians, when an APAO enjoys direct access to executive branch politicians, is one means. Another is working with opposition politicians and backbench legislators. This is not likely to lead to immediate policy change, but over the longer term a new party in power or new cabinet ministers moved up from back benches may look elsewhere for specific proposals. A window of opportunity might also occur whereby the legislature can make policy with substantial autonomy. Yamamoto's discussion of financial services reform in Japan is one such example.

Influence might also be realized through working with civil society groups, interest groups, or the media to push changes in policy. Even if political executives are resistant to change, they may be convinced when confronted with external pressure, especially during times of electoral vulnerablity.

Obviously, APAOs with ties to politicians and officials within the executive are most likely to whisper in the ears of politicians. Advocacy tanks, party think tanks, and research-oriented NGOs are most likely to use indirect approaches, especially if their political ideology or party identification is distant from that of the governing party.

The difficulties in measuring APAO influence leads us to reformulate the question of APAO influence by asking under what conditions APAOs are likely to make contributions to policymaking? In which countries? Which types of APAOs? Which types of advice? And through which channels? Here the case studies of countries offer a rich set of data. Although the patterns they suggest are far from simple, they are consistent with the arguments made earlier about the advantages and disadvantages of specific types of APAOs and the conditions that facilitate or hinder their development. They indicate, for example, that even where they exist, legislative support organizations and legislative committee staffs have relatively little influence in political systems where legislators themselves have little independent leverage to bring about policy change. In terms of types of policy advice, broad paradigmatic rethinking of policy problems and policy solutions is rare in almost all the countries examined here. Short-term policy concerns and putting out the fires of political crises are more the norm in both consolidated democracies and where free and open political contests are recent phenomena.

The case studies also suggest that APAO influence depends heavily on the opening of windows of opportunity that are largely beyond APAOs' control. Even the personal taste of political leaders can be a factor. Diane Stone notes in her chapter, for example, that the three most recent British prime ministers—Margaret Thatcher, John Major, and Tony Blair—have differed markedly in their overall openness toward alternative sources of policy advice and in the types of sources that they listened to. While marketing is becoming an increasing focus of many APAOs, especially those based in civil society (see the chapter by Andrew Rich), APAO influence is still frequently a matter of being in the right place at the right time.

PROSPECTS

While there appear to be general trends in the structural conditions that are likely to increase the supply of and demand for APAOs in the future, their overall prospects will still vary widely internationally. In the legal sphere, protections on freedom of association and speech are being loosened in many new democracies. Legal restrictions on the establishment of civil society–based organizations are being eased as well in Japan and Eastern Europe. Economically, increased per capita wealth will provide greater resources for APAO activity—but only in countries where growth is strong. Great differences will remain across countries in the capacity of philanthropies to support APAO activity and in their cultural inclination to do so. Support from the developed countries and multilateral sources for APAO activity in the developing world remains a large question mark.

The political environment can also be expected to encourage further APAO development, although unevenly. As indicated above, building demand for the services provided by alternative sources of policy advice remains a critical challenge in many countries. Politicians outside the executive (for example, backbench parliamentarians) have neither the incentive to seek out alternative policy advice in order to propose different policy options nor the opportunity to press those alternatives forward. Nevertheless, the growing assertiveness of legislatures in countries like Japan and Korea is likely to stimulate further APAO development, especially among APAO types directly responsive to the needs of legislators.

In addition, there are critical windows of opportunity—for example, periods of minority government in parliamentary systems—when APAO activity can be expanded and institutionalized. Even if those initiatives are partially reversed, they are likely to lead to an institutional legacy and to increased demand once conditions become favorable again. The supply of technically trained experts can also be expected to increase in most countries over time, as can the availability of data needed for policy analysis. But major differences are likely to remain across institutions and countries in the kinds of career paths that facilitate APAO recruitment.

In short, while we can expect a continued general growth in APAO activity, we should not expect a convergence toward high levels of APAO activity, or APAO influence on policymaking, across all countries. Major differentials are likely to remain—between rich countries and poor, between those with consolidated democracies and a strong civil society and those where democratic institutions and civil society are weaker, and between those where political institutions consolidate power in a single branch of government and those where power is diffused. Government financing is likely to be the major funding source for alternative policy in most emerging democracies, both because funding for civil society–based organizations is weak and because government employment can potentially offer greater career stability for the few experts than can most civil society–based APAOs.

Finally, as several authors in this volume state, much of the growth of alternative policy advice in the future is likely to be from sources that are transnational in nature rather than from sources that have an identifiable base in a single country (Stone 2000b). Indeed, the major multilateral lending agencies, the World Bank and the International Monetary Fund (IMF), are likely to have a far greater influence on economic policy in most of the developing and transitional economies than domestic APAOs because their advice carries with it both a carrot and a stick: Follow it and financial assistance will be forthcoming, fail to do so and risk being categorized as an economic rogue state.

OPPORTUNITY
FOR DRAWING LESSONS

The very different national experiences outlined in the following chapters suggest some important lessons for governments and civil society organizations seeking to improve the quality of alternative policy advice. The first is really a caveat: There is no single model of APAO appropriate for all societies. APAOs grow out of distinctive national environments, including differences in funding sources, the market among politicians for policy expertise, and the labor market for experts. Because these factors vary across countries, the types of APAOs that might be effective in some countries might, in others, find difficulty sustaining funding, an audience, or staff. Efforts to improve a country's capacity for alternative policy advice should be tailored to each nation's distinctive environment.

A second, and related, lesson is that the United States has unique conditions for nurturing and sustaining APAOs. These include a strong philanthropic tradition, an extensive university system for training experts, separation of powers, weak legislative parties, and federalism, all of which increase the demand for alternative sources of expertise. In no other country are all of these conditions present. Thus, simply copying U.S. institutions is not likely to work; lessons drawn from the U.S. experience will be of limited applicability elsewhere.

Third, having more APAOs in a country does not necessarily mean that these organizations as a whole have greater influence in that country. Indeed, a serious problem with civil society–based APAOs is that they are large in number but weak in resources, visibility, and credibility. Consolidating APAOs, securing a stable funding base, and achieving critical mass within organizations constitute the most important challenges for many APAOs in the years ahead.

In conclusion, it is appropriate to end with some general advice about policy advice. Despite the importance of specific national contexts in promoting APAO development, countries that currently discourage the creation of civil society–based APAOs by placing roadblocks in their path should consider changing those laws. In addition, multilateral lending agencies like the World Bank and IMF should encourage the development of alternative policy advisory capacity within governments and sponsor country-specific evaluations of that capacity (see Stone 2000a). In doing so, they will not only increase the salience of policy advice for governments, but will also signal the importance of a freer flow of information, which is essential for an effective democracy and, with it, good governance.

BIBLIOGRAPHY

Bakvis, Herman. 1997. "Advising the Executive: Think Tanks, Consultants, Political Staff and Kitchen Cabinets." In Patrick Moray Weller, Herman Bakvis, and R. A. W. Rhodes, eds. *The Hollow Crown: Countervailing Trends in Core Executives*. Basingstoke, U.K.: Macmillan.

Baumgartner, Frank, and Bryan D. Jones. 1993. *Agendas and Instability in American Politics*. Chicago: University of Chicago Press.

Bimber, Bruce. 1991. "Information as a Factor in Congressional Politics." *Legislative Studies Quarterly* 16(4): 585–605.

———. 1996. *The Politics of Expertise in Congress: The Rise and Fall of the Office of Technology Assessment*. Albany, N.Y.: State University of New York Press.

Dror, Yehezkel. 1987. "Conclusions." In William Plowden, ed. *Advising the Rulers*. Oxford and New York: Basil Blackwell.

Hammond, Thomas A., and Gary Miller. 1985. "A Social Choice Perspective on Expertise and Authority in Bureaucracy." *American Journal of Political Science* 34: 531–564.

Heclo, Hugh. 1974. *Modern Social Politics in Britain and Sweden*. New Haven, Conn.: Yale University Press.

Kingdon, John. 1995. *Agendas, Alternatives, and Public Policies*. 2nd ed. New York: HarperCollins.

Lacey, Michael J., and Mary O. Furner. 1993. "Social Investigation, Social Knowledge, and the State: An Introduction." In Michael J. Lacey and Mary O. Furner, eds. *The State and Social Investigation in Britain and the United States*. Washington, D.C., and Cambridge: Woodrow Wilson Center Press and Cambridge University Press.

Mosher, Frederick C. 1979. *The GAO: The Quest for Accountability in American Government*. Boulder, Colo.: Westview Press.

Pross, A. Paul, Innis Christie, and John A. Yogis. 1990. *Commissions of Inquiry*. Toronto: Carswell.

Rich, Andrew, and R. Kent Weaver. 1998. "Advocates and Analysts: Think Tanks and the Politicization of Expertise in Washington." In Allan Cigler and Burdett Loomis, eds. *Interest Group Politics*. 5th ed. Washington, D.C.: Congressional Quarterly Press.

Robinson, William H. 1992. "The Congressional Research Service: Policy Consultant, Think Tank and Information Factory." In Carol H. Weiss, ed. *Organizations for Policy Analysis: Helping Government Think*. Newbury Park, Calif.: Sage Publications.

———. 1998. "Parliamentary Libraries: Information in the Legislative Process." In George Thomas Kurian, ed. *World Encyclopedia of Parliaments and Legislatures*. Washington, D.C.: Congressional Quarterly Inc.

Seymour-Ure, Colin. 1987. "Institutionalization and Informality in Advisory Systems." In William Plowden, ed. *Advising the Rulers*. Oxford and New York: Basil Blackwell.

Smith, James Allen. 1991. *The Idea Brokers: Think Tanks and the Rise of the New Policy Elite*. New York: The Free Press.

Stone, Diane. 1989. "Causal Stories and the Formation of Policy Agendas." *Political Science Quarterly* (Summer): 281–300.

———. 1996. *Capturing the Political Imagination: Think Tanks and the Policy Process*. London and Portland, Ore.: Frank Cass.

———. 2000a. *Banking on Knowledge: The Genesis of the Global Development Network*.

London and New York: Routledge.

———. 2000b. "Think Tank Transnationalisation and Non-profit Analysis, Advice and Advocacy." *Global Society* 14(2): 154–172.

Struyk, Raymond J. 1999. *Reconstructive Critics: Think Tanks in Post-Soviet Bloc Democracies*. Washington, D.C.: The Urban Institute.

Ueno Makiko. 1998. "Think Tanks in Japan: Towards a More Democratic Society." In Diane Stone, Andrew Denham, and Mark Garnett, eds. *Think Tanks Across Nations: A Comparative Approach*. Manchester and New York: Manchester University Press.

Weaver, R. Kent, and James G. McGann. 2000. "Think Tanks and Civil Societies in a Time of Change." In James G. McGann and R. Kent Weaver, eds. *Think Tanks and Civil Societies*. New Brunswick, N.J.: Transaction.

Weilemann, Peter R. 2000. "Experiences of a Multidimensional Think Tank: The Konrad-Adenauer Stiftung." In James G. McGann and R. Kent Weaver, eds. *Think Tanks and Civil Societies*. New Brunswick, N.J.: Transaction.

Weller, Patrick. 1987. "Types of Advice." In William Plowden, ed. *Advising the Rulers*. Oxford and New York: Basil Blackwell.

———. 1994. *Commissions of Inquiry*. South Melbourne, Australia: Macmillan.

World Bank Institute. 2001. "Governance, Finance and Regulation." <http://www.world bank.org/wbi/wbigf/governance.html> (June 2001).

2 United States

Andrew Rich

E xperts have become ubiquitous in American politics. The number and variety of alternative policy advisory organizations (APAOs) have grown substantially in the United States since the mid-1960s, numbering in the thousands by the end of the twentieth century. From the Congressional Budget Office to the Heritage Foundation, from the Policy Institute of the AARP (formerly known as the American Association of Retired Persons) to the Harvard Center for Business and Government, experts and expertise abound within and outside of government with relevance to virtually every policymaking debate.

Their explosion in recent decades reflects an expanded demand for expertise in policymaking circles and a growth in the supply of entrepreneurial experts and their patrons in the United States. Members of Congress and the president have sought to create more sources of advice within government as their personal staffs have grown and become more professionalized. Their demands have extended to nongovernmental sources of policy expertise, helping to foster hundreds of new interest groups, think tanks, consulting firms, and university research centers. The growth of new sources of financial support, including private foundations, corporations, and individuals, has also facilitated an expanded presence of APAOs based outside of government.

As a new century begins, a sizable and diverse set of APAOs exists in the United States. Yet it is not clear that the influence of APAOs has expanded in proportion to their growing numbers. In a policy environment typically characterized as one where interests trump ideas and information in the competition to influence outcomes, expertise and policy advice in the United States are often portrayed as little more than the instruments of interests (Hall 1989; Schuck 1995). Studies suggest that in relation to Congress, "by all accounts, the most common form of legislative use [of expertise] is as support for preexisting positions"

(Weiss 1989, 425). Charles Lindblom observes: "Not usually an alternative to politics, analysis commonly operates as an indispensable element in politics. . . . Rather than making frontal attacks on policy problems, it more often meets certain needs of people, especially officials, to control others in political interaction" (1980, 28). Policy expertise is understood as valuable as ammunition in policy battles and as support for policymakers' preexisting positions.

It is in the context of these understandings of expertise that Nancy Shulock raises "the paradox of policy analysis." She asks the question: Why, if expertise is not used in a substantive way, does the United States produce so many—and increasing numbers of—policy advisory organizations (Shulock 1999, 226)? I examine this paradox in this chapter. I consider the environment for advisers in the United States and the range of APAOs active in contemporary policymaking—their characteristics and behaviors. I evaluate the different opportunities for experts to influence the policymaking process and the varying success different types of APAOs achieve. I conclude with reflections on the overall state of policy advice available in the United States and the likelihood—and desirability—of change or reform.

In the end, the analysis illustrates that experts and expertise serve multiple roles in U.S. policymaking and that their influence often extends well beyond providing support—either personal or research-based—for the preconceptions of decision makers. In a densely populated contemporary environment of APAOs, many experts succeed in making their analysis substantively influential in policy debates. APAOs based in or supported by government have a particular advantage insofar as they have close or direct access to decision makers. Other nongovernmental experts can also be substantively influential, and their success is often associated with the active marketing of their research.

It is nevertheless true that the purveyors of policy expertise that have proliferated in greatest number in recent decades are not those that most often make important substantive contributions to policy debates. The biggest growth of experts in U.S. policymaking, especially outside of government, has been among civil society–based advisory organizations that rely on preconceived ideologies and interests and those that observe—or are perceived to observe—lower standards of research than their forebearers. These organizations tend to appeal to relatively narrow audiences that are already predisposed toward their ideas, and their products are often used in the "supporting" role frequently attributed to expertise.

INSTITUTIONAL AND
POLITICAL ENVIRONMENT FOR APAOS

At the beginning of the twenty-first century, thousands of variously trained economists, political scientists, and policy analysts seek to advise government from more than a dozen government research agencies, 1,000 government advisory committees, more than 300 independent public policy think tanks, more than 500 university-affiliated research institutes, and dozens of interest groups and consulting firms. The United States provides an accommodating institutional and political landscape for a dense and diverse population of APAOs.

Institutionally, the United States has a separation of powers between the executive, legislative, and judicial branches. Formally, the Congress makes laws, the president implements laws, and the judicial branch decides challenges to their constitutionality. In reality, the three branches are not nearly so separate and distinct in their roles and behavior. Although the Congress has the responsibility for passing laws, the president, for example, can veto laws. A two-thirds majority vote of both houses of Congress is required to override a presidential veto. Moreover, the president has substantial informal leverage in setting the legislative agenda; the president can use the bully pulpit as the only nationally elected leader to foster public support for initiatives he or she may send to Congress.

A consequence of the separation of powers is that the three branches—and especially the legislative and executive branches—often compete. They compete over policy priorities and for public attention. This competition contributes to a higher demand for policy experts, both within and outside of government in the United States, than might be the case in countries with parliamentary systems of government.

The United States also has a system of federalism; political authority is split between the national government, fifty states, and thousands of cities, towns, and other local governments. The presence of such a range of governments, each with meaningful powers, expands the possible audiences for policy experts. Moreover, the frequent competition between different levels of government increases demands for policy advisory organizations.

In addition to these constitutionally prescribed attributes, the United States has relatively weak political parties, which contribute further to an environment in which APAOs are in high demand. Neither major political party in the United States (the Democrats or the Republicans) has a formal policy apparatus or a formal affiliation with a policy research organization. During elections, candidates tend to run independent, self-focused (as opposed to party-focused) campaigns. Candidates raise most money for their campaigns on their own, and they develop their own policy positions, tailored to accommodate the distinct concerns of constituents in geographically defined districts.

Political parties are relatively weak as well within governing institutions, especially the Congress. Rates of party-line voting are relatively high in the U.S. Congress, but more as a result of logrolling and existing shared interests among members than because of strong or highly centralized party leadership control or manipulation. All 535 members of Congress can—and often do—introduce substantively important legislation, regardless of their seniority. Members have electoral incentives to establish reputations as independent initiators of policy reform. A consequence of this incentive and their general independence is that all 535 members of Congress make demands on policy advisory organizations. They look to no single or central source for expertise.

The strength of the effects of these three attributes of the political system—separation of powers, federalism, and weak parties—has not been constant over time on the demand for policy advice. A further weakening of parties in recent decades, in particular, has actually intensified demands for policy expertise. Partly in reaction to weaker parties and the competition between branches and levels of government, the president and Congress substantially increased the size of their staffs in the 1960s and 1970s. In the decade following the Legislative Reorganization Act of 1970, the number of personal, committee, and professional congressional staff exploded from several thousand to more than 20,000. By 1980, with 23,528 staff, the U.S. Congress was by far the most heavily staffed legislature in the world (Malbin 1980, 10). The number of congressional staff decreased dramatically following the 1995 Republican takeover of Congress, but the U.S. Congress remained more heavily staffed than any other legislature. Similar staff growth occurred over the same period in the executive branch, without decreases in the 1990s. The large staffs enable the production of more analysis by personnel close to the president and Congress. Even more, these larger staffs produce more demands on APAOs, which produce information and expertise that these staffs can synthesize and provide to their bosses.

The separation of powers, the system of federalism, weak political parties, and the resulting independence and high levels of staff support to U.S. policymakers in recent decades combine to produce high demands for expertise and to provide experts with a variety of possible audiences and possible institutional points of access to political decision making. Within government, the competition between branches creates incentives for the president and Congress—and analogous branches at the state and local levels—to institutionalize a production capacity for (often competing) expertise in each branch. Expertise produced inside of government can also be useful in disputes between levels of government. Outside of government, the multitude of worthwhile access points to many hundreds of independent policymakers and their staffs allow policy experts to be optimistic about their chances of finding a patron for ideas.

Civil society–based APAOs have an additional advantage in the United States' century-long history of accommodating tax laws for nonprofit or third-sector organizations, which is the form these organizations usually take. The entry and incorporation requirements for third-sector organizations in the United States are minimal, requiring the formation of a board of trustees and a verifiable not-for-profit mission. Once incorporated, nonprofits enjoy a favorable tax status in the United States whereby their patrons can deduct financial contributions to the organizations from their taxable income, reducing their final tax liabilities.

Along with an accommodating institutional environment, features of the U.S. political culture have encouraged the proliferation of policy experts. Particularly in recent decades, the political climate has increased and diversified demands for experts and policy advice. APAOs first emerged in the United States at the beginning of the twentieth century. In this period, known as the Progressive Era, there was a growing confidence that expertise from the burgeoning social sciences could produce solutions to public problems and inform government decision making. Progressive reformers looked eagerly to experts to generate scientific knowledge that could move policymaking beyond the rancorous partisanship and logrolling of the previous century and endow government with more efficient and professional standards (Hammack and Wheeler 1994; Smith 1991, 24–72). The first APAOs, both inside and outside of government, formed during this period and were based on this ideal.

Beginning in the 1930s, a second wave of APAOs emerged, the ranks of which grew slowly into the mid-1960s. These new APAOs differed from the first generation insofar as faith in the power of pure scientific analysis and detached administrative solutions to social problems diminished when the country entered the Great Depression. Confidence in the ability of experts to solve problems declined, but direct government support for research increased substantially. In the wake of the Depression, the federal government took a more active role in providing public services. Public officials hired social scientists to work with them directly in designing new social and economic initiatives. Adjusting to a postwar economy, the federal government continued to grow in the 1950s, as a widespread consensus took hold among Americans that government could be an appropriate manager of social and political problems—even if it could not often serve to solve them. Experts with ideas for managing the economy, in particular, became crucial.

The consensus behind government management of the economy began to break down in the 1960s, and the opportunities for experts and policy advisers began to change. What emerged was a vibrant political debate in which participants took sides either for or against an activist government. Within this political context, experts were in greater demand than ever before, and they were rewarded not for maintaining a staid distance from decision making but for becoming aggressive advocates of ideas.

Concurrent with these changes, and in the decades since, the U.S. policymaking process has become generally more transparent, with a proliferation of interest groups and a greater variety of news media and, more recently, Internet sources reporting events to the public. Norms for policy issues to be debated using evidence have been reinforced, evidence that APAOs are well suited to supply. As one long-time Washington policy analyst puts it, in this day and age, "you can't really play in the policy game unless you have a study" (Rich 1999, 170).

It is in the context of this environment, which places high demands on suppliers of policy expertise, that I turn now to consider the backgrounds, characteristics, and behaviors of different types of APAOs active in the United States. My focus is on APAOs in national-level policymaking, but in many cases organizations similar to those described as active at the national level are present in state and local contexts as well. I begin with APAOs based inside of government and move to those that are intermediate and civil society–based. Examples of each type of APAO are listed in appendix A, along with background information about them.

APAOS INSIDE THE
EXECUTIVE BRANCH OF GOVERNMENT
Office of Management and Budget

The Bureau of the Budget (BOB), formed in 1921, was the first formal advisory agency to be formed in the federal executive branch. BOB was organized as part of the movement early in the twentieth century to bring efficiency and accountability to government. Its original mission was to systematize and coordinate the federal budgeting process. In its first forty years, the agency was staffed almost exclusively by professional budget analysts who produced objective technical studies for the president. BOB staff were mostly economists and academically trained analysts in career merit-based positions, invulnerable to changes in presidential administrations. Only BOB's director and deputy director were presidential appointees. As Walter Williams observes, "The office relied heavily on its career, professional staff who unquestionably were the elite career staff in the federal government. Career staff held most of the top spots, were at the center of power, and were viewed as the ultimate nonpartisan analysts" (1992, 104).

The agency's character changed during the late 1960s and early 1970s in response to presidential and congressional efforts at reorganization. President Richard Nixon wanted to establish greater political control over BOB. Congress likewise wanted a greater voice over BOB's operation. In 1970, the agency was renamed the Office of Management and Budget (OMB), and an additional layer of political appointees was added between the director and budget analysts. The new name reflected Nixon's desire to have the agency more involved in management and oversight than in new policy formation on his behalf. Congress gained some leverage over the agency in the reforms by requiring Senate confirmation of the OMB's director and deputy director. The reorganization created a new group of program associate directors who were appointed by the president and intended to organize and coordinate the work of the OMB and other government agencies to more effectively support the president's agenda (Heclo 1975). Once the reforms were in place, the OMB was larger and more politicized than BOB had been.

Since the 1970s, the OMB has balanced its political and analytic roles. Its size has been reduced as its formal responsibilities have remained relatively stable. The OMB consistently produces widely circulated budget estimates for presidential initiatives, and the agency remains responsible for drafting the president's annual budget proposal. In 1999, the OMB had approximately 500 staff, down from 610 in 1980. Most staff had bachelor's or master's degrees in the social sciences; most senior analysts had doctorates and had come to the agency from universities. The agency operated with a fiscal 1999 budget of US$57 million.

Council of Economic Advisors, National Economic Council, and National Security Council

BOB lost its near monopoly on providing analytic expertise to the president following World War II when the Council of Economic Advisors (CEA) and the National Security Council (NSC) were formed in 1946 and 1947, respectively. The formation of the councils reflected the expanded role and responsibilities of the federal government in the United States following the war. The federal government became more active, both abroad and domestically, with the emerging embrace of Keynesian economics.

Since its creation, the CEA has been chaired and staffed by academic economists, often on one- or two-year leaves from university appointments. The council, with a staff of thirty-five and a 1999 budget of US$3.8 million, provides ongoing analysis and advice to the president on the state of the economy and on policies that might promote economic growth. The CEA's influence with the president has fluctuated with each administration since its inception. Its role depends to a great extent on the predisposition of the president toward economic analysis. As Williams points out, generally, "the prudent use of policy analysts and analysis depends less on White House or agency institutional structure and process than on the personality, style, experience, and competence of leaders" (1990, 13).

In 1993, the new Clinton administration created an alternative economic unit in the Executive Office of the President. The National Economic Council (NEC), chartered by an executive order of the president in January 1993, became responsible for coordinating economic policymaking for the president and ensuring that economic policy decisions were "consistent with the President's stated goals."

With a staff roughly equal to that of the CEA, the NEC played a key role in the 1990s of brokering economic decision making for the president, coordinating research from the CEA as well as the Treasury, Labor, and other cabinet departments. Although equal in size to the CEA, the staff of the NEC has more often been lawyers and policy analysts than academic economists. Reflecting Clinton administration preferences, the NEC politicized the process of digesting and using economic analysis during the 1990s beyond what had been typical for the CEA.

In the foreign policy arena, the NSC tends to fulfill the combined roles that the CEA and NEC play in economic policy. The NSC coordinates foreign policy information for the president—with the secretaries of Defense, State, and Treasury among the formal members of the council—and produces independent analyses of foreign policy questions for the president. The NSC is staffed by a combination of academic foreign policy specialists and politically experienced foreign policy analysts. It had a staff of sixty in 1999 and a budget of US$6.9 million. Like the CEA, the extent to which the NSC has been relied on as a source of information and analysis by presidents has varied. Some presidents have relied more directly on the cabinet departments—State and Defense—for foreign policy information. Since President Nixon in the 1970s, however, the NSC has been a consistently important source of information and coordination on foreign policy questions for the president.

Office of Policy Development

In the 1970s, an additional advisory unit was created by President Nixon to help him devise domestic policy, a job Nixon did not trust to cabinet departments or the OMB (Williams 1992). The Domestic Council was first led by John Ehrlichman, a close political adviser to the president, and it was staffed by young aides with generally more political than policy experience. By one account, the agency in its early years, "achieved a remarkable place in domestic affairs. It succeeded to a degree never before attempted in gaining centralized political control over the Executive Branch for the President" (Waldmann 1976, 266). The agency's early success, which continued through the Ford and Carter administrations in the 1970s, stemmed as much from the close political ties it enjoyed with presidents as from the particular attributes of its products.

When Ronald Reagan became president in 1981, the Domestic Council was renamed the Office of Policy Development (OPD), and its role was downgraded. The size of the staff, which had reached sixty analysts during the Carter administration, was cut in half. Remaining positions were filled by low-level appointees, many of whom had worked in low-level positions in Reagan's campaign. The agency was reduced to reporting to a counselor to the president rather than to the president himself.

Under President Bill Clinton, the OPD remained small with a limited role in coordinating policy initiatives and political priorities. The agency, with a budget of US$4 million and a staff of thirty-one analysts by 1999, was a relatively low-profile unit in the Executive Office of the President. It was composed of a staff loyal to the president, many of whom had policy training, with master's degrees or doctorates in economics or political science. Staff of the agency remained political appointees, serving at the pleasure of the president.

Advisory Committees

Outside of the Executive Office of the President, the federal government has a long tradition of using advisory committees of experts to counsel the president and, more often, the leaders of executive branch agencies. In 1990, there were 1,071 advisory committees in the federal government (Smith 1992, 209). Many were science advisory committees—groups of prominent scientists advising the departments of Energy or Defense, for example, about current research and desirable practices. Many were intergovernmental advisory agencies, providing opportunities for officials from different levels of government to interact and form judgments about policy directions. Anywhere from a quarter to one-half of the advisory committees included representatives from the social sciences, of the type that are the focus of this volume.

Advisory committees are regulated under the Federal Advisory Committee Act, which passed Congress in 1972 and requires that proceedings of executive branch advisory committees be open to the public and that membership on advisory committees be politically balanced. In practice, advisory committees often counsel executive branch officials about desirable policy goals. They also serve a valuable political role for presidents. Advisory committees are venues where those with stakes in policy decisions can participate with and be heard by their regulators. As Bruce Smith points out, to the extent that advisory groups "become important forums for debating and potentially influencing the direction of agency policies, the constituencies served or regulated naturally seek a role in who is appointed to advisory positions, how they relate to the agency, and what advice is given" (1992, 45). In many cases, government decision makers are not ultimately looking for expert analysis from advisory committees. Rather, as Harold Seidman observes, "What the government basically wants from advisory committees is . . . support. Advisory boards may be used to lend respectability to new or controversial programs. . . . It is hoped that board members will act as program missionaries and assist in mobilizing support for the program both in their home communities and in the Congress" (1998, 199).

The success of advisory committees varies, as does their complexion and mission across policy areas. Advisory committees range from the Committee on

Construction, Safety, and Health in the Department of Labor to the Committee for Cable Signal Leakage, which advises the Federal Communications Commission. Most advisory committees produce annual, if not more frequent, reports and recommendations for the agencies where they are based. Some have budgets and professional staffs; others operate with minimal support. In 1993, US$144 million was spent on the staffing and support of all executive branch advisory committees (Seidman 1998, 201). The number of advisory committees and the amount spent on them shrank during the 1990s after President Clinton signed an executive order directing executive branch agencies to eliminate those that were obsolete.

APAOS INSIDE THE
LEGISLATIVE BRANCH OF GOVERNMENT
Congressional Research Service

For the legislative branch, the formation of the Legislative Research Service (LRS) in 1914 was the first foray into formal efforts to provide Congress with policy analysis and advice. The LRS was formed as a branch of the Library of Congress and, in its first forty years, the relatively small LRS staff served as reference librarians to members of Congress, answering basic informational inquires. In 1946, Congress gave the LRS more autonomy within the Library of Congress and authorized it to hire better-trained policy specialists. This mandate was reinforced and extended in 1970 when Congress changed the agency's name to the Congressional Research Service (CRS) and provided for an expansion of its staff to permit "'massive policy analysis' for Congress" (Robinson 1992, 184).

In its current form, the CRS fields roughly half a million inquiries annually from members of Congress and their staffs. More than two-thirds of these inquiries require only basic information and little research to answer, and members of Congress receive replies within twenty-four hours (Robinson 1992). The rest are often more detailed inquiries requiring original research and analysis by CRS staff. The CRS views members of Congress, their personal staffs, and their congressional committee staffs as its clients, and it usually treats their requests and consultations with them as confidential. CRS staff view their mission as providing objective or balanced information to members of Congress, and the agency enforces a careful review process for its products to ensure that they appear nonpartisan and do not endorse particular recommendations. The CRS has become especially well known for its *Issue Briefs*, which describe and analyze legislative debates and explain bills and the actions Congress has taken on them. The CRS develops more than 350 *Issue Briefs* every year. Each tends to be 10–15 pages in length and is made available to all congressional offices.

The agency's concerted efforts to produce nonpartisan research and to refrain from taking positions on policy matters has contributed to its sustained size and importance. In 1999, the CRS had a staff of almost 750 and a budget of US$71.4 million. Roughly one-third of its staff had backgrounds—and usually professional degrees—in library sciences; this group responded to roughly two-thirds of requests to the CRS that required basic information and reference material. Two-thirds of CRS staff were in policy analysis divisions, and they tended to hold doctorates or professional degrees in public policy, law, or economics. The director of the CRS is appointed by the director of the Library of Congress, in consultation with the Joint Congressional Committee on the Library.

General Accounting Office

In 1921, Congress created the General Accounting Office (GAO) to be the agency responsible for auditing government expenditures. The agency was designated in the same legislation in which the BOB was formed. Founded in an era endowed with the spirit to create efficient and responsible government, the GAO was intended to assist policymakers and bureaucrats to spend public dollars wisely. The agency was to be insulated from Congress and the president; it was organized so that its director, the comptroller general, would be appointed by the president and confirmed by the Senate to serve a fixed fifteen-year term. The comptroller general can only be removed by a majority vote of members of both houses of Congress. Upon retiring, comptrollers general retain their full salaries.

Although begun as an accounting agency, the GAO evolved into a unit that also conducts independent policy analysis and program evaluation. Following World War II, many of the GAO's auditing responsibilities were shifted to executive branch agencies, to be coordinated by GAO accountants. In the 1960s and 1970s, the GAO began to focus more on analysis and evaluation, and it became more responsive—and accountable—to Congress. Although the agency's relationship to Congress and the president was initially ambiguous, a 1986 Supreme Court decision clearly classified the GAO as a legislative support agency. While as late as 1969 only 10 percent of GAO reports were written to satisfy congressional inquiries, by 1988, more than 80 percent of GAO resources were devoted to responding to specific congressional requests (Havens 1992, 208–209). Like the CRS, the GAO seeks to be strictly nonpartisan and objective in its research and uses a careful peer review process to ensure accuracy in its products. Its reports are often the subject of congressional hearings, and its findings can fuel reform efforts in Congress by members of both parties.

In its contemporary analytic and evaluative role, the GAO is staffed mostly by graduates of public affairs and public policy programs, doctorate-level economists and computer scientists, and certified public accountants. In 1999, the GAO had a staff of 3,400, substantially off its high of nearly 15,000 at the end of World War

II when it was still auditing every government expenditure. The agency's 1999 budget was about US$350 million.

Office of Technology Assessment

In the early 1970s, the same period when Congress extended the size and roles of the CRS and the GAO, Congress created two new legislative advisory agencies: the Office of Technology Assessment (OTA) and the Congressional Budget Office (CBO). The OTA was formed in 1972 to provide congressional committees with unbiased analyses of issues involving technology. As one former OTA analyst observes, "Technology assessment as propounded by the academic community was understood as a mechanism for seeing into the future and thus avoiding the 'bad' effects of technology" (Carson 1992, 237). OTA was tasked with producing advice on how to avoid such bad effects. The agency was staffed by a combination of scientists and social scientists. It was administered—and its director appointed—by a bipartisan group of members of Congress.

Founded in 1972, OTA is unique among government-based APAOs insofar as it was shut down and eliminated by Congress in 1995. With a staff of roughly 140 and an annual budget of approximately US$20 million before being closed, the OTA produced between twenty and fifty reports a year for congressional committees during its twenty-three years of operation. Its studies were strictly nonpartisan and reviewed by nongovernmental specialists before their release to congressional committees and the public.

The OTA was eliminated in the fervor to cut government spending when the Republican Party won control of both houses of Congress in 1995. The cost-cutting Republican congressional leadership thought it important that Congress set an example in cutting its own appropriation, as other government agencies and services prepared to undergo downsizing. As one observer notes, "There was a widespread sense among legislators in 1995 that deficit reduction should 'start at home,' that Congress should demonstrate its willingness to make sacrifices along with the rest of the nation" (Bimber 1996, 69). The OTA was an easy target for budget-cutters because by its small size it could be completely eliminated at relatively little cost and its studies and forecasts, which tended to focus on the long term, would be less missed by members of Congress than the more immediately relevant products of other legislative support agencies.

Congressional Budget Office

The CBO, created by Congress in 1974, produced the most immediately relevant products of any congressional support agency, and, in fact, as the OTA was eliminated in 1995, the CBO absorbed more responsibilities. The CBO was formed to provide Congress with the projected budgetary and economic implications of pending legislation. It was founded in the same legislation that established new congressional budget committees. The CBO and the new committees were supposed to reestablish Congress' strength vis-à-vis the president in the budget-making process. In particular, the CBO was supposed to compete with and offset the influence of the executive branch's OMB. The CBO's major responsibilities were designated as—and remain—producing cost estimates of legislation before Congress, scorecards of the overall budgetary and economic effects of proposed legislation, and program analyses in areas with consequence for the federal budget. In 1995, Congress added to the CBO's mission the projection of private-sector and state and local government costs associated with proposed legislation.

The CBO is the only legislative support agency that makes projections, and its estimates are widely relied on by both proponents and opponents of legislation. In fact, under reforms to the budget-making process in the early and mid-1990s, Congress required that changes in the yearly budget be deficit neutral within certain spending categories. The CBO was designated to produce the binding estimates of whether proposed budget changes were truly neutral. Like the other legislative support agencies, the CBO strives to be nonpartisan and objective in its analysis. The director of the CBO is appointed for a fixed four-year term by the speaker of the House and the president pro tem of the Senate on the recommendation of the budget committees of both houses of Congress. The CBO director can only be removed by passage of a resolution in one of the houses of Congress. In 1999, the CBO had a budget of US$25.7 million. The staff of the CBO, which in 1999 numbered 232, are split between those with master's degrees in public policy and economics who have positions focused on producing basic cost estimates and those who are doctorate-level economists and statisticians and concerned with more sophisticated program analysis and new program estimates.

Congressional Committee Staff

In addition to legislative support agencies, Congress has the assistance of professional committee staffs. Congress is organized around nineteen committees in the House of Representatives and sixteen in the Senate. Since the Legislative Reorganization Act of 1946, each committee has had a staff of professional analysts. The Legislative Reorganization Act designated four professional staff plus six administrative clerks to each committee. Through reforms and extensions, by the early 1990s, every House committee except one had a staff of more than forty assistants. Six House committees had more than 100 staff—most of whom were professional analysts rather than clerks (Deering and Smith 1997, 164). Similar growth occurred in Senate committee staffs.

Although often hired for their expertise, congressional committee staff usually work for either the majority or the minority (Republican or Democratic) leader of the committee. Committee staff overall, which numbered around 2,000 by the end of the 1990s, typically work to develop partisan proposals for members of the committees and to organize hearings and committee meetings to consider legislation. Senior committee staff are often lawyers or policy analysts. Midlevel staff often have no advanced degrees. Most committee staff have political experience, often having worked previously as personal aides to members of Congress.

Committees vary substantially in the extent to which developing policy expertise is a priority in staff efforts and member deliberations. Some committees (e.g., tax, budget, commerce, energy, judiciary, and labor) deal with highly partisan subjects where members make decisions as much based on ideological predilections as on research (Deering and Smith 1997, 88). On some issues and in some committees, expertise and policy analysis play a more dominant role.

ASSESSING GOVERNMENTAL APAOS

The overall volume of policy advice and APAOs available within government increased tremendously after the mid-1960s. In the executive branch, beyond the advisory organizations located close to the president, agency-based efforts to improve advisory capacities emerged as well. These efforts began with the creation in 1961 of the Office of Systems Analysis in the Department of Defense. Defense Secretary William McNamara staffed the agency with a generation of whiz kids, young analysts who advised the agency on strategic and programmatic matters. In the late 1960s and early 1970s, additional executive branch agencies created policy analysis units modeled on the Office of Systems Analysis (Radin 1992). From the Department of Health, Education, and Welfare to the Department of the Interior, units were formed within executive branch agencies that reported directly to department heads on program evaluation and new policy ideas.

The growth in executive agency advisory staffs in the 1960s and 1970s is remarkable not only because it further reflects a growing interest in and commitment to experts, analysis, and information within government, but also because these new staff and agencies contributed further to demands for expertise and policy analysis from other sources. To be sure, when the size of personal congressional staffs grew and the executive branch bureaucracy ballooned, more of the new staffs' time could be devoted to analyzing and understanding policy issues independently. But even more, these expanded staffs reinforced and increased demands for the services of APAOs.

If the 1960s and 1970s marked the beginning of a period of significant growth in the commitment of the executive and legislative branches to policy expertise, these decades were also a time when substantial differences in how the branches produced and placed value on these goods were established. The characteristics and efforts of legislative support agencies such as the CBO, the GAO, and the CRS reflected incentives generally to produce consistently objective, nonpartisan research because they served—and were funded by—an ideologically divided Congress (Bimber 1996). Each support agency pursued a strategy of avoiding partisan conflict by producing nonpartisan research. In the executive branch, by contrast, the OMB, the CEA, the NEC, the NSC, and the OPD served a single political actor—the president—and consequently had incentives to produce work consistent with his priorities if they hoped to be influential, relied on, and endorsed for future funding. The motives and objectives of APAOs have varied based on differences in the clients served in each branch.

INTERMEDIATE APAOS

Temporary Task Forces

In addition to the permanent APAOs within government, there are a range of intermediate APAOs with looser or less permanent connections with government that are active in the United States. Among intermediate APAOs, temporary presidentially appointed task forces are most centrally located in the policymaking process. Presidents create temporary task forces to investigate important policy issues and to promote policy prescriptions with Congress and the public. They also use them to defer consideration of controversial issues taking on a high degree of public interest—often with the hope that interest will die down by the time task forces finish their work.

In the 1990s, President Clinton used task forces to organize his efforts on two issues at the top of his agenda: health-care reform and government reorganization. When he took office in 1993, Clinton formed a task force on health-care reform headed by his wife to design a proposal for universal health insurance in the United States. Likewise, Clinton designated a task force headed by Vice President Al Gore to investigate ways to make the federal government more efficient and effective. Both task forces were headed by well-known public figures (the first lady and the vice president) and staffed by a combination of government and nongovernment analysts. In addition to analysts detailed from government agencies, many academics and think-tank experts volunteered as consultants to the task forces. Business, labor, and interest group officials also contributed to the proceedings of the task forces.

In both health-care reform and government reorganization, President Clinton had outlines for what he viewed as desirable reform before the work of the task forces was under way. The task forces served to develop the details of the president's plans, promote the president's agenda, and provide opportunities for input from interested parties. The chairs of the task forces bore responsibility for shepherding proposals to Congress and promoting them with the public. Although in both cases the task forces served to highlight and organize the president's plans on the issues, neither effectively set the course for reform. In the case of health-care reform, in particular, the task force process was unsuccessful at creating anything approaching a consensus among interested parties about appropriate directions for reform. The exclusion of some industry representatives from the task force process—and their opposition to what the task force produced—resulted in a strong and successful campaign against the president's health-care initiative.

The experience of the health-care task force is one among many that suggest lessons for how and when task forces succeed in the United States—succeed, that is, when they are intended to promote policy change rather than simply contribute to delay or stalemate. Presidential task forces are most successful when they are appointed to address a widely perceived problem or crisis and when they propose reforms that minimize immediate pain to powerful constituencies. Task forces improve their chance of success when they delay decisions until agreement is achieved by competing sides in policy debates. Along with presidentially appointed task forces, the president and Congress can jointly appoint temporary blue-ribbon commissions that, while serving similar purposes as temporary task forces, have a more official membership and tend to play a more official, albeit not always a more important, role in policy development. In 1982, President Reagan appointed Alan Greenspan to chair a bipartisan commission to devise a solution to the pending crisis in the Social Security program. After nearly failing and dissolving several times, the Greenspan Commission eventually succeeded insofar as it provided cover for and surface credibility to the eventual compromise by President Reagan and the speaker of the House from the opposing party. As Paul Light observes, "The commission had succeeded mainly as a front for secret bargains. . . . By giving the leaders a chance to lead, by putting politics back into politics, the commission had provided the political cover needed for compromise" (1995, 184). While drawing extensively on experts and expertise in its proceedings, the Greenspan Commission illustrates that the influence and success of presidential task forces in the United States are typically far more dependent on the possibilities for political compromise than on the content or quality of expertise provided.

Federally Funded Research-and-Development Centers

Unlike presidential task forces, federally funded research-and-development centers (FFRDCs) are nongovernmental and permanent organizations. Most of the thirty-nine FFRDCs in existence in 2000 were chartered in the decade following

World War II and tasked with producing technical and analytic research for the defense, aviation, space, and energy agencies. These organizations are incorporated either as nonprofits or as units of universities. They receive full support from the federal government. FFRDCs tend to be large, with annual budgets in the hundreds of millions of dollars and staff of 500–2,500 people. Their analysts tend to be a combination of scientists, social scientists, and engineers, many with advanced degrees. Their products are often lengthy, technical, proprietary reports for their government clients.

MITRE Corp. provides an example of this type of organization. It operates three FFRDCs: one for the Defense Department, one for the Federal Aviation Administration, and one for the Internal Revenue Service. What distinguishes MITRE and the other FFRDC nonprofits from other types of APAOs is the exclusive research agreement each has with the government, which prohibits it from sharing findings and information with nonclients. Unlike presidential task forces, which tend to address high-profile, contentious subjects, the FFRDCs tend to work on projects unknown to the general public. They seek influence more with the administrative bureaucracy within government than with the Congress. MITRE, for example, works exclusively for the three aforementioned government agencies and seeks to produce objective, rigorous results consistent with the demands of its government contracts. In 1998, MITRE had a staff of more than 4,000 and an annual operating budget of US$521 million.

Contract Research Think Tanks

In many ways similar to the FFRDCs, contract research think tanks depend almost exclusively on government contracts for support. However, contract research think tanks, such as the RAND Corporation and the Urban Institute, operate with greater organizational independence than the FFRDCs. They produce prescriptive as well as evaluative research, and they sometimes seek financial support from nongovernmental sources to finance work of interest to their directors or researchers. Contract research think tanks tend to be staffed by policy analysts with master's degrees in public affairs and by Ph.D. economists. Their great reliance on government for financial support in turn provides opportunities for them to be influential, like the FFRDCs, with the government bureaucrats who support their work.

CIVIL SOCIETY–BASED APAOS

The growth in intermediate and especially government sources of policy advice that began in the 1960s and 1970s reinforced demands for expertise based in civil society. The number and diversity of civil society–based APAOs exploded over the same period. Independent public policy think tanks have more than quadrupled in number. Schools of public affairs and policy research institutes at universities have proliferated across the country. And an assortment of research-oriented consulting firms and interest groups has emerged.

In conjunction with this explosion of organizations, sources of support for civil society–based expert organizations have come to range from government to private foundations, from corporations to individuals. The missions of APAOs have come to range from those that are full service, conducting research on a diversity of social, economic, and foreign policy questions, to an increasing number of boutique or specialized organizations focused on one or a few narrow issues. The products of these APAOs have come to range from technical monographs to press releases, from full-length scholarly books to pithy policy briefs, from internal workshops to elaborate press conferences.

Think Tanks

More than three hundred independent public policy think tanks were operating in the United States by the end of the century, up from fewer than seventy in 1970. Contract research think tanks, already discussed, were ten to fifteen of the organizations in this group. The rest—the overwhelming majority—conformed to two general models: those that operated like "universities without students" and those that were aggressively advocacy-oriented (Weaver 1989).

University-without-student think tanks, including the American Enterprise Institute, the Brookings Institution, and the Hoover Institution, tend to place a premium on producing rigorous, balanced research. Many were founded during the first decades of the century on the ideal of neutral competence. Whatever their age, university-without-student think tanks tend to be staffed by doctorate-level economists, political scientists, and sociologists, and they are funded principally by long-established private foundations such as the Rockefeller and Ford foundations. They often produce book- and monograph-length studies with more long-term than immediate implications. Roughly one-third of think tanks active in American policymaking are of this style. Their ranks include many of the largest think tanks, so university-without-student think tanks consume roughly half of the resources invested in think tanks.

The largest number of contemporary think tanks conform to the second style of organization, that of advocacy think tanks. Advocacy think tanks also represent the fastest growing segment of the think-tank population. The founding of the Heritage Foundation in 1973 signified the birth of this new type of politically aggressive and often openly ideological think tank. These organizations tend to produce analysis and information relevant to immediate rather than long-term policy debates. They tend to be staffed by analysts with more political than academic credentials, usually holding bachelor's or master's degrees rather than doctorates. Their products tend to be in shorter, more quickly digestible formats—policy briefs and press releases—rather than books and monographs. And advocacy think tanks tend to be supported by corporations and small, ideological foundations (e.g., the Bradley Foundation, the John M. Olin Foundation, the Sarah Scaife Foundation), which emerged in the United States in the 1960s and 1970s with an interest in shaping the content of policy debates.

Their marketing style and ideological allegiances often make advocacy think-tank products useful to members of Congress as they seek to build support or opposition for legislative proposals among colleagues. They serve in the roles fulfilled by party-aligned think tanks in other countries, since the parties are relatively weak in the United States, as already discussed, and play little role in policy development. Ideologically aligned advocacy think tanks, rather than party think tanks, are helpful as elected officials work independently or in intra- or cross-party coalitions to develop policy proposals. The only think tank in the United States that resembles a party think tank is the Progressive Policy Institute (PPI), the research arm of the Democratic Leadership Council, a coalition of centrist and conservative Democrats. The PPI has no formal tie to the Democratic Party, however.

University-Based Institutes and Schools of Public Affairs

Beginning in the 1960s and extending into the 1970s and 1980s, new schools of public affairs and public policy emerged at universities across the country, often splintering off of departments of economics and political science. The Goldman School of Public Policy was founded at the University of California at Berkeley in 1969, for example; the LBJ School of Public Affairs was formed at the University of Texas in 1970. This growth largely reflected increased demands for practically trained policy analysts within government and in nongovernmental venues. Agencies needed analysts trained to evaluate public programs and develop innovative policy prescriptions. Many new schools of public affairs formed to satisfy this need, with roughly three hundred schools operating across the country by the end of the twentieth century.

Along with a demand for their graduates, these new schools of public affairs, along with more than six hundred policy research institutes that existed within universities by the end of the 1990s, were spawned by the availability of new forms of government and private foundation support. The federal government made major new grants to universities and other nongovernmental APAOs to foster graduate training in public affairs. Likewise, private sources of support, most notably the Ford Foundation, made the training of policy analysts a major priority.

New support was available to universities for policy-oriented research as well. Among the commitments made in President Lyndon Johnson's "War on Poverty" in the 1960s were provisions in the legislation for each new program that the government created to set aside "one percent of all money appropriated for the purpose of evaluation" (Rich 1999, 103). Universities became one of the major recipients of government funds for program evaluation beginning in the 1960s.

Consulting Firms

Over the same period, increased government and foundation support for policy research fostered as well the emergence of an industry of consulting firms, which provided commissioned studies to the government and other clients. Proliferating in substantial numbers in recent decades, consulting firms range in size and focus. Most tend to be specialized, with focuses on particular substantive areas or methodological techniques. Many are for-profit, as opposed to nonprofit, organizations. Analysts at consulting firms typically have graduate training, either master's or doctorates in their areas of focus. The nature and quality of consulting firm products vary considerably, based on the firm and clients. Whether the products of consulting firms are publicly available is usually decided by the client.

In addition to support from government and private foundations, consulting firms have profited from the desire of corporations to fund policy analysis. Beginning in the mid-1960s, corporations became more active in national policymaking as the federal government grew and imposed greater regulation on the private sector. Corporations have supported studies by consulting firms in efforts to defend themselves with Congress and presidents. In the debate over telecommunications deregulation in 1995, for example, the local telephone companies paid the WEFA Group, a for-profit econometrics consulting firm founded in 1963, to produce studies demonstrating the likely positive economic effects of telecommunications deregulation. WEFA was staffed by statisticians and econometricians who produced careful research. Typical of the criticism consulting firms often face, however, some complained that the basic assumptions used in the WEFA research were distorted to guarantee a favorable analysis for its clients. Such criticisms are not uncommon (nor universal) for consulting firms.

Interest Groups and Nongovernmental Organizations (NGOs)

Corporate support for interest groups, including Washington, D.C.–based trade associations, grew after the mid-1960s as well. The number of corporations with Washington offices increased tenfold from 1961 to 1982 (Cigler and Loomis 1991,

11). Many of these offices created subsidiary research arms or incorporated research into their regular activities. Their work was often carried out by analysts with as much political as academic experience, and it was published in short, accessible formats.

The AARP is among the most active interest groups to develop a policy analysis unit. The AARP, which has more than 1,000 employees and its own postal code owing to the high volume of mail it produces, has a subsidiary, research-oriented policy institute. Housed within the AARP, the Public Policy Institute was started in 1985 and was staffed with forty-one analysts in 1999, mostly with degrees in public policy and law. The Public Policy Institute produces studies with relevance to the organization's mission, which is to defend and promote the interests of older Americans. Its studies may be released to policymakers and the public or may be kept only for internal organizational use. The AARP has the largest and most sophisticated research arm of any interest group. Other organizations tend to have more limited research staff or to make research a part of the responsibilities of their advocacy staff.

Public interest groups are as likely as traditional interest groups to have research arms, but they often have a greater dependency on research in their advocacy efforts. These non-corporate organizations, such as Ralph Nader's Public Citizen, depend greatly on research because they tend to have quite limited organizational budgets. With limited size and reach among the public, research is a more available and important currency for public interest groups to use with policymakers than, for example, campaign contributions, which are prominent in the arsenal of traditional interest group activities.

WHEN AND HOW ARE EXPERTS INFLUENTIAL?

By the end of the twentieth century, the United States had a rich variety of APAOs active within government and in civil society. A range of sources of support sustained the efforts of APAOs. The research and analysis of these organizations served a variety of purposes and audiences. Their influence varied as well.

In the end, the value of differentiating the many APAOs active in the United States lies in the extent to which these experts hold potential—and differing potential—for being influential in the policymaking process. I evaluate that potential in the rest of the chapter by reference to three questions: 1) How are experts and their products used in the policymaking process? 2) How do the uses of expertise vary based on its institutional sources (i.e., the location of experts) and the behavioral incentives its sources face? and 3) In what kinds of contexts and with what types of efforts do experts influence American policymaking?

The Uses of Policy Expertise

The policy process involves three stages: *Agenda-setting* is the period—from one month to twenty or more years—when policy proposals are generated and issues work their way toward becoming the priorities of policymakers. *Policy enactment* is the period when public officials—elected decision makers—are actually engaged in resolving issues by accepting or rejecting new legislation or regulation. The period of *policy implementation* begins once a law or regulation is enacted and refers to the administration of policies and programs and the tinkering that may be associated with efforts to ensure their effectiveness. Issues cycle through the three stages, with the boundaries between stages often difficult to distinguish.

Expertise plays active, important—but quite different—roles in each of the three stages of the policy process. As already noted, existing scholarship emphasizes the support and ammunition roles that expertise plays. It is in these capacities that expertise is often helpful during policy enactment (Shulock 1999). Expertise can serve at least three additional roles in the policy process, however—providing warning of impending problems, guidance on how to approach these problems, and assessment of how programs and policies work and might work better. Assessment is the work of experts during policy implementation, when their research might result in adjustments made in the administration of policies. That work contributes as well to agenda setting, when expertise also warns decision makers of possible crises and guides them—individually or in groups—toward policy solutions.

Different Kinds of Experts and Different Kinds of Expertise

If expertise serves a variety of purposes, experts also vary greatly in the kinds of expertise they produce. All types of APAOs are not equally engaged in the different stages of the policy process or active in producing expertise that fulfills each of the five roles mentioned. Table 1 illustrates the different stages of the policy process and the different types of experts, within and outside of government, most active in each stage. Within government, the legislative and executive branch research agencies serve statutorily defined roles that make one or more of the units active in each of the three stages of the policy process and as producers of expertise that may serve each of the five roles.

The CBO plays a critical and frequently influential role in estimating the public- and private-sector costs of new legislation. The CBO is required to provide cost estimates of legislation before it reaches a final vote in Congress. Its estimates are used as support and ammunition and as substantive guidance during enactment. The CBO's estimates are binding on Congress in its efforts to produce balanced budgets, with the consequence that, as Sheila Burke, former Senate

Majority Leader Robert Dole's chief of staff, points out, "Essentially, at the end of the day, we have to live by CBO estimates" (Rich 1999, 218).

Although not necessarily producing binding research, other government research agencies also have close ties to government officials, making them relevant with a variety of products at different points in the policy process. Their roles in the policy process range from agenda setting, where the OMB might be helpful to the president, to policy enactment, where the CBO's cost estimates are decisive, to policy implementation, where the GAO is active in evaluating government programs. With their statutorily defined roles and proximity to policymakers, the expert advisory organizations that exist in both branches of government share an ability to maintain relatively low public profiles in policy debates, low profiles that are often preferred by their government patrons.

Outside of government, sources of expertise similarly range from those active in agenda setting to those involved in policy evaluation. Rather than fulfilling roles prescribed by government, however, these experts and expert organizations define their own roles, usually making them consistent with the priorities of their patrons. Those intermediate APAOs reliant on government contracts, including contract research think tanks and FFRDCs, typically observe standards of neutrality and objectivity in research, maintain a relatively low public profile when promoting research, and are most active in the evaluation of government policies and programs.

By contrast, civil society–based APAOs active in agenda setting and policy enactment—advocacy think tanks, interest groups, consulting firms, and university-without-student think tanks—tend to observe a wider range of standards and often promote their research to achieve a higher profile. As a general matter, there are few incentives for experts not supported by the government to invest in policy evaluation. Evaluation research is time and resource intensive and produces work that rarely results in products directly suiting the needs or demands of policymakers most active in policy change. Instead, to have a chance of being influential with policymakers—mostly members of Congress, the president, and senior executive branch appointees at the national level—civil society–based experts produce research and information relevant to agenda setting and policy enactment. Academics, along with think tanks, particularly older think tanks not reliant on government support, tend to be active in agenda setting, and interest groups, consulting firms, and think tanks, especially the newer, more ideological and advocacy-oriented think tanks, are most active in policy enactment.

The Influence of Experts and Expertise

So when are experts influential? And what benefits some experts over others in achieving influence? Evidence about the visibility of experts in the news media

Table 1. APAOs and the Policy Process

	Agenda Development	Policymaking/Enactment	Policy Administration/Implementation
Venues	Presidential campaigns Following court decisions Areas of industrial or technological change	Executive Office of the President Congress Regulatory executive branch agencies	Executive branch agencies State and local governments Nongovernmental organizations
Types of research	*Expertise as warning and guidance* Scholarly and balanced Philosophically and ideologically appealing Lengthy, comprehensive formats	*Expertise as support and ammunition* Ideologically appealing Consistent with interests Short, accessible formats	*Expertise as assessment and guidance* Rigorous and quantitative Technical and nonideological Lengthy, comprehensive formats
Types of advice and expert organizations	Legislative research organizations Executive branch research organizations Academics/universities Federally funded R&D centers Contract research think tanks Consulting firms University-without-student think tanks Advocacy think tanks	Legislative research organizations Executive branch research organizations Interest groups and trade associations Advocacy think tanks University-without-student think tanks Consulting firms Academics Temporary executive branch task forces	Legislative research organizations Executive branch research organizations Contract research think tanks Federally funded R&D centers Academics/universities

Source: Developed by the author.
APAOs: alternative policy advisory organizations; R&D: research and development.

and as witnesses before congressional hearings begins to answer these questions. Table 2 provides counts of citations to a selection of twenty-six expert organizations received in the *New York Times*, the *Washington Post*, and the *Wall Street Journal* in 1998 along with counts of the number of times their staff testified before Congress in 1998.[1] Raw counts are provided along with values where the number of citations has been divided by the size of organizational budgets in 1998, to provide a sense for the extent to which visibility in these venues is a function of budget size.

Sources of expertise within government—especially the OMB, the CBO, and the GAO—generate substantial media and congressional visibility. The GAO makes particularly frequent appearances before congressional hearings, reflecting the GAO's contemporary emphasis on producing studies requested by members of Congress. All of the government units included in table 2 except the executive branch OPD, which is small and serves the president alone, receive substantial visibility in the news media and before Congress. This visibility reflects their statutorily defined roles more than the inherent quality of their products or the aggressiveness of their efforts with these audiences. The results illustrate well the importance of governmental APAOs in the U.S. policy process.

Among the expert organizations outside of government, those that are intermediate and most involved in evaluation research contracted with the government tend to have the least visibility. These include the FFRDCs, the university institutes, and the contract research think tanks, although the contract research think tanks receive more visibility than the former two. The university-without-student and advocacy think tanks receive substantially greater media attention. Many of these organizations, especially the advocacy think tanks, have well-financed media and public affairs divisions with the sole purpose of promoting the organizations' research findings. Among the university-without-student and advocacy think tanks, those in the selection of organizations that are older and based in Washington, D.C., receive more visibility in the news media and before Congress than newer ones based outside of Washington, D.C.[2] Besides think tanks, the selected interest groups received substantial visibility. Counts for interest groups do not distinguish between those citations related specifically to research versus general lobbying activity, however, so it is not appropriate to draw conclusions about the extent to which their research and expertise receive visibility.

Media and congressional visibility are, of course, not the equivalent of influence. Visibility may contribute to the influence of research and analysis with some audiences, and for many experts in many situations, visibility may be an end goal in itself—a way to attract new patrons, for example. But influence is more appropriately understood as instances where experts and their ideas become

Table 2. Newspaper and Congressional Visibility of Selected APAOs

	Visibility in the News Media		Visibility with Congress	
	New York Times Washington Post Wall Street Journal	Newspaper Citations/ Budget Size (US$ millions)	Congressional Testimony	Congressional Testimony/ Budget Size (US$millions)
Executive Branch Research Organizations (governmental)				
Office of Management and Budget	333	5.84	51	0.89
Office of Policy Development	6	1.50	0	0.00
Legislative Support Organizations (governmental)				
Congressional Budget Office	328	12.76	30	1.17
Congressional Research Service	87	1.22	25	0.35
General Accounting Office	477	1.36	278	0.79
Non-University Research Centers (federally funded)				
ANSER	7	0.12	0	0.00
MITRE Corp.	2	0.00	2	0.00
University-Based Research Centers (federally funded)				
Center for Health Services Research and Policy (George Washington University)	0	0.00	0	0.00
Center for Policy Research (Syracuse University)	0	0.00	0	0.00
Institute of Transportation Studies (University of California at Davis)	1	0.25	0	0.00
Think Tanks (nongovernmental)				
University-without-Student Think Tanks				
American Enterprise Institute	180	11.76	33	2.16
Brookings Institution	408	17.07	32	1.34

known among a set of policymakers and inform their thinking on or public articulation of policy-relevant information. By this understanding, the influence of APAOs is more variable and complex.

Within government, APAOs have the capacity to shape the policy agenda and determine the direction of final debate over issues. The CBO often plays a critical role during policy enactment, the final stages of an issue's consideration. During the universal health-care reform debates of 1993–1994, for example, the CBO was looked to for its calculations and estimates on alternative proposals. When President Clinton formally announced his health-care reform plan in September 1993, public and congressional attention immediately turned to the CBO to find out the budgetary implications of the bill. Both proponents and opponents of the president's plan viewed the estimates that the CBO produced as critical to mounting their case to defend or oppose the proposal. Within a short time, opponents, in particular, used the estimates, which calculated large new costs with the president's health-care plan, as ammunition to fight against it.

The CBO estimates served a substantive role as well, as members of the administration adjusted some features of the proposal to alleviate CBO concerns as the plan was translated into legislative language. Beginning with its estimates of the president's proposal in February 1993, the CBO produced eight full reports on health-care alternatives and scores of informal estimates related to specific proposal adjustments. Indicative of the agency's important role, every report the CBO produced resulted in a story in the *Washington Post* and, often, in the *New York Times* as well, and the CBO estimates prompted scores of changes—major and minor—to alternative health-care reform proposals. As one congressional staffer recalled, "I remember members of Congress in hearings often reading verbatim from [CBO] reports" (Rich 1999, 218).

The GAO plays little role in the policy enactment stage of the policy process, but its reports can be decisive in encouraging new congressional action, especially when their findings suggest inefficiencies or ineffectiveness in government programs. It is active and influential in policy evaluation. The CRS is actively relied on throughout the policy process by individual members of Congress, and it is frequently an important source of reference for the CBO and the GAO when they are completing studies and estimates.

In the executive branch, the OMB can be especially influential with the president during his efforts at agenda setting. The nature and extent of the agency's influence vary based on the personnel at the OMB and the general receptivity of a president to policy analysis. In the 1980s, President Reagan placed tremendous authority in the hands of his first OMB director, David Stockman. Stockman was instructed to construct the president's crucial first budget without assistance from executive branch agencies. Stockman's—and thus the OMB's—stature was substantial early in the Reagan administration, although the agency was influential more as a result of pursuing the new president's ideological objectives than from producing voluminous, rigorous analysis. The OMB's analytic capacities were largely restored in the 1990s. During the Clinton administration, the agency's influence varied with the technical complexity of issues and the strength of the bond of trust between the president and changing OMB directors. The same held for the CEA and the NEC.

The OPD, occasional task forces, and advisory committees had different amounts of influence in the 1980s and 1990s. The importance of the OPD varied with each president because the unit's staff are all political appointees. Presidents view the role and importance of the office in different ways.

Task forces and advisory committees likewise have variable influence. Like his predecessors, President Clinton used task forces in the 1990s as vehicles for developing alternatives and setting the agenda on issues of importance to him. The task forces tended to serve as much a political as policy purpose. They proved rather unsuccessful for President Clinton as vehicles for generating public and congressional support on issues as they headed toward policy enactment.

The influence of advisory committees in the United States is even more mixed than that of task forces. They tend to make contributions toward agenda setting on issues, often making recommendations to executive branch agency heads about administrative or regulatory changes. The receptivity of policymakers to their recommendations depends largely on conditions of the general political environment (the direction of winds of change) and on the potential political leverage of the members of the advisory committees.

Although their success is mixed, APAOs within government have a greater and more direct chance of being influential than APAOs based outside of government in the United States. Among nongovernmental APAOs, those that are intermediate or based in civil society with direct contractual relationships with governmental agencies—the FFRDCs, universities, consulting firms, and contract research think tanks—have the best chances of achieving substantive influence with policymakers. Their products are often highly technical and intended for narrow audiences where they serve as warning, assessment, and guidance. Their precise influence is difficult to track. An assessment of a military defense system, for example, may point out problems or make recommendations that take years—and repeated reinforcement—to reach Congress or the secretary of defense. Although slow and difficult to trace, such research, which is abundant in the United States, often has eventual consequence for public and policymakers' views on issues.

Many civil society–based APAOs, especially those not funded at all by the government, are interested in pursuing more immediate and easily traced influence. It is among these groups that there has been the greatest new growth in recent years and the most publicly visible activity. These APAOs—interest groups, consulting firms, advocacy think tanks, university-without-student think tanks, and some university institutes—tend to produce studies and reports intended for pending policy debates. Here APAOs provide some guidance for policymakers, but more often, they produce research that is used in a support and ammunition role by decision makers. Although these groups can produce work helpful to setting the agenda on issues, their general success at being influential is often more linked to the timing, accessibility, and desirability of their research than what may be its rigor or thoroughness.

DISCUSSION
AND RECOMMENDATIONS

In the end, experts are tremendously abundant and generally important actors in the American policymaking process. Some experts are more successful at securing visibility and influence than others. The types of experts influential in different stages of the policy process vary substantially. And the types of influence achieved by policy advisers are diverse. Those experts active in agenda setting and policy evaluation are most often those supported by or based within the government. They are also often the experts that generally seek to embody the promise of neutral expertise and careful assessment. The experts active in policy enactment may be those supported by or based within the government, notably the CBO. They are also often the experts based outside of government, concerned less with producing neutral or objective expertise than with the dynamic, often ideological debate over the appropriate role of government. These are the civil society–based APAOs that have emerged most recently in U.S. politics, including those with more interest- or ideologically based sources of patronage.

Overall, experts in many ways have the best opportunities to be substantively influential in the agenda-setting and policy evaluation stages of the policy process. Work directly commissioned or supported by government decision makers often has a rather direct path to policymakers' desks. And it can reach decision makers at points prior to when they form judgments about appropriate policy directions. At these points, the sources of expertise devoted to neutral, balanced, and rigorous analysis have an advantage in providing warning, guidance, and assessment.

The absence of the newer, more ideological, and marketing-oriented sources of expertise at these points is due less to their intentional exclusion than to their own preference to be active during final policy enactment, when their chances of securing high public profiles are greatest. Although there are notable exceptions, these APAOs tend to set their research priorities based on the agendas of

Congress and the president. Yet if and when these fastest growing segments of the APAO industry in the United States—in particular, advocacy think tanks and interest groups—decide to become more active in issue formation and program evaluation, there is reason to believe they may have some success.

In the densely populated environment of APAOs in the United States, especially outside of government, the marketing of expertise—at all stages of the policy process—can make a tremendous difference for whether the expertise of particular experts becomes visible and influential. Work commissioned by or supported by government decision makers may have a rather direct path to policymakers' desks, but it will likely fail to secure their attention unless promoted among them. In this regard, some experts are more aggressive and successful than others; some expert organizations have entire departments that serve as liaison with Capitol Hill and the news media, creating opportunities for experts to actively promote their ideas. Other advisory organizations, such as universities, usually do not provide such support.

The importance that marketing and promotion can carry in the United States suggests both a problem and an opportunity for those concerned with sustaining an important role for policy advisers at the beginning of a new century. The growing strength of these newer, more marketing-oriented sources of expertise is problematic insofar as it has contributed to a diminishing of the promise or regard in which experts and expertise generally are held in the United States. These newer sources of expertise may not achieve the greatest substantive influence, but they have emerged in great numbers and become noticeable among policymakers.

Moreover, to make their ideas influential, many different kinds of researchers—even including, in some instances, academics—have deliberately marketed their work in ideological terms and published it in ideological venues so that it might achieve a higher profile. Kent Weaver observes of the debate over welfare reform in 1996 that scholars often chose to publish their ideas leading up to the debate in political magazines such as the *American Prospect* and the *Public Interest*. He notes, "Although these publications may have helped to diffuse knowledge about policy research more broadly, they may also have had a less salutary effect: because many [of these] outlets . . . had ideological leanings, researchers who published in them may have undermined their perceived legitimacy as objective scholars with policymakers on the other side of the growing welfare ideology divide" (Weaver 2000, 164). These researchers were reacting to what have become almost behavioral requirements for nongovernmental APAOs to achieve visibility in a saturated organizational environment. The downside of having such an abundance of APAOs in the United States is that it is difficult for any one piece of research to gain recognition, and it can be difficult for policymakers to discern good research from bad.

What presents itself as a problem poses an opportunity as well to improve the potential for policy analysis in U.S. policymaking. First, researchers who adhere to careful and rigorous methods and are concerned by the perceptible decline in standards among experts generally in recent decades might take lessons from the more marketing-oriented and often ideological or interest-based APAOs. Weaver's warning notwithstanding, these concerned researchers might seek to produce and promote reports that rival in accessibility and marketing those from less rigorous sources. In the short term, such steps may improve the chances of their research being visible during policy enactment, and its rigor and objectivity may help to stem the decline in the reputation of experts generally.

Second and more important, those concerned with sustaining an important role for policy advisers in the United States might convene policymakers and their staffs in sessions to discuss the role of research in their decision making and the criteria by which they judge its accuracy and usability. In the context of such discussions—absent debate over particular policy issues—an honest and open dialogue might be possible in which both the producers and users of policy advice could express their expectations, hopes, and needs. An agency based inside of government, such as the CRS, might be the best convenor of such a session. The CRS is an agency viewed by many as nonpartisan and highly credible. In a country that benefits from its tremendous availability, such a forum would represent a small step toward improving the environment in which policy advice is provided and consumed.

NOTES

1. The organizations listed are illustrative rather than a representative sample. The findings in regard to the selected organizations in this analysis generally correspond to findings from more systematic analysis elsewhere (Rich forthcoming 2001; Rich and Weaver 2000).

2. These findings among the twenty-six selected organizations are confirmed in a more systematic analysis of think tanks that illustrates that older, bigger, and Washington, D.C.–based think tanks tend to receive greater media visibility than their counterparts (Rich and Weaver 2000). The same general findings hold among the selected think tanks in relation to congressional testimony, findings also confirmed with a larger sample in a more systematic analysis (Rich forthcoming 2001).

BIBLIOGRAPHY

Bimber, Bruce. 1996. *The Politics of Expertise in Congress: The Rise and Fall of the Office of Technology Assessment*. Albany, N.Y.: State University of New York Press.

Carson, Nancy. 1992. "Process, Prescience, and Pragmatism: The Office of Technology Assessment." In Carol H. Weiss, ed. *Organizations for Policy Analysis*. Newbury Park, Calif.: Sage Publications.

Cigler, Allan, and Burdett Loomis. 1991. *Interest Group Politics*, 4th ed. Washington, D.C.:

Congressional Quarterly Inc.

Deering, Christopher J., and Steven S. Smith. 1997. *Committees in Congress*, 3rd ed. Washington, D.C.: CQ Press.

Federal Advisory Committees. 1980. *Eighth Annual Report of the President*. Washington, D.C.: Government Printing Office.

Hall, Peter A. 1989. *The Political Power of Economic Ideas: Keynesianism across Nations*. Princeton, N.J.: Princeton University Press.

Hammack, David C., and Stanton Wheeler. 1994. *Social Science in the Making: Essays on the Russell Sage Foundation, 1907–1972*. New York: Russell Sage Foundation.

Havens, Harry S. 1992. "The Evolution of the General Accounting Office: From Voucher Audits to Program Evaluation." In Carol H. Weiss, ed. *Organizations for Policy Analysis*. Newbury Park, Calif.: Sage Publications.

Heclo, Hugh. 1975. "OMB and the Presidency—The Problem of 'Neutral Competence.'" *The Public Interest* 11(38): 80–98.

Light, Paul. 1995. *Still Artful Work*, 2nd ed. New York: McGraw-Hill, Inc.

Lindblom, Charles E. 1980. *The Policy Making Process*, 2nd ed. Englewood Cliffs, N.J.: Prentice Hall, Inc.

Malbin, Michael. 1980. *Unelected Representatives: Congressional Staff and the Future of Representative Government*. New York: Basic Books.

Radin, Beryl A. 1992. "Policy Analysis in the Office of the Assistant Secretary for Planning and Evaluation in HEW/HHS: Institutionalization and the Second Generation." In Carol H. Weiss, ed. *Organizations for Policy Analysis*. Newbury Park, Calif.: Sage Publications.

Rich, Andrew. 1999. *Think Tanks, Policy Making, and the Politics of Expertise*. Ph.D. dissertation, Yale University, New Haven, Conn.

———. Forthcoming 2001. "The Politics of Expertise in Congress and the News Media." *Social Science Quarterly*.

Rich, Andrew, and R. Kent Weaver. 2000. "Think Tanks in the National Media." *Harvard International Journal of Press/Politics* 5(4): 81–103.

Robinson, William H. 1992. "The Congressional Research Service: Policy Consultant, Think Tank, and Information Factory." In Carol H. Weiss, ed. *Organizations for Policy Analysis*. Newbury Park, Calif.: Sage Publications.

Schuck, Peter. 1995. "The Politics of Rapid Legal Change: Immigration Policy in the 1980s." In Marc K. Landy and Martin A. Levin, eds. *The New Politics of Public Policy*. Baltimore, Md.: Johns Hopkins University Press.

Seidman, Harold. 1998. *Politics, Position, and Power: The Dynamics of Federal Organization*, 5th ed. New York: Oxford University Press.

Shulock, Nancy. 1999. "The Paradox of Policy Analysis: If It Is Not Used, Why Do We Produce So Much of It?" *Journal of Policy Analysis and Management* 18(2): 226–244.

Smith, Bruce L. R. 1992. *The Advisers: Scientists in the Policy Process*. Washington, D.C.: The Brookings Institution Press.

Smith, James A. 1991. *The Idea Brokers: Think Tanks and the Rise of the New Policy Elite*. New York: The Free Press.

Waldmann, Raymond J. 1976. "The Domestic Council: Innovation in Presidential Government." *Public Administration Review* 36(3): 260–268.

Weaver, R. Kent. 1989. "The Changing World of Think Tanks." *P.S. Political Science and Politics* 22(3): 563–579.

———. 2000. *Ending Welfare As We Know It*. Washington, D.C.: The Brookings Institution Press.

Weiss, Carol H. 1989. "Congressional Committees as Users of Analysis." *Journal of Policy Analysis and Management* 8(3): 411–431.

Williams, Walter. 1990. *Mismanaging America: The Rise of the Anti-Analytic Presidency*. Lawrence, Kan.: University Press of Kansas.

———. 1992. "White House Domestic Policy Analysis." In Carol H. Weiss, ed. *Organizations for Policy Analysis*. Newbury Park, Calif.: Sage Publications.

Appendix A. Examples of APAOs in the United States

Organization	Mission	1998–1999 Budget	Sources of Support	No. of Staff	Profile of Research Personnel	Location	Year Formed	Areas of Research	Ideology
Executive Branch Research Organizations (governmental)									
Office of Management and Budget	"Assist[s] the President in overseeing the preparation of the Federal budget and supervis[ing] its administration in Executive branch agencies."	US$57 million	Government	504	Mostly M.A.'s and B.A.'s	Washington, D.C.	1921	Federal budget	Aligned with president
Council of Economic Advisors	"Analyzes the national economy and its various segments, advises the President on economic developments, recommends policies for economic growth and stability, appraises economic programs and politics of the Federal government."	US$3.8 million	Government	35	Mostly Ph.D. and M.A. economists	Washington, D.C.	1946	Economic policy	
Office of Policy Development	"Supports the National Economic Council and the Domestic Policy Council in carrying out their responsibilities to advise and assist the President in the formulation, coordination, and implementation of economic and domestic policy."	US$4.0 million	Government	31	Mostly M.A.'s and some Ph.D.'s	Washington, D.C.	1993	Economic and domestic policy	Aligned with president
Legislative Support Organizations (governmental)									
Congressional Budget Office	"Provide Congress with objective, timely, non-partisan analyses needed for economic and budget decisions and with the information and estimates required for the Congressional budget process."	US$25.7 million	Government	232	M.A.'s or Ph.D.'s in economics or public policy	Washington, D.C.	1974	Budget estimates	Nonpartisan

Continued on next page

Appendix A—continued

Organization	Mission	1998–1999 Budget	Sources of Support	No. of Staff	Profile of Research Personnel	Location	Year Formed	Areas of Research	Ideology
Congressional Research Service	"Provides confidential specialized nonpartisan research and policy analysis to Congress."	US$71.4 million	Government	747	Ph.D.'s in economics, political science, or public policy; J.D.'s; M.P.A.'s	Washington, D.C.	1914	To meet the demands of Congress	Nonpartisan
General Accounting Office	Investigative arm of Congress "charged with examining all matters relating to the receipt and disbursement of public funds."	US$349.7 million	Government	3,400 (2,100 are evaluators/ analysts)	Mostly M.A.'s and CPA's; a few Ph.D.'s	Washington, D.C.	1921	To meet the demands of Congress	Nonpartisan
Non-University Research Centers (federally funded)									
ANSER	"A public service research institute that provides analytic and technical support to federal agencies in the [aerospace area]."	US$60 million	Federal contracts	700	Mostly Ph.D.'s and M.A.'s in engineering, sciences, and social sciences	Arlington, VA	1958	Aerospace policy and engineering	No identifiable
MITRE Corp.	"Assists the United States government with scientific research and analysis, systems development, and systems acquisition."	US$520.9 million	Federal contracts	2,000 (plus 2,000 contract workers)	B.A.'s (more than 50%), M.A.'s, and Ph.D.'s in social sciences and engineering	Bedford, MA McLean, VA	1958	Defense policy and revenue collection policy	No identifiable
University-Based Research Centers									
Center for Health Services Research and Policy (George Washington University)	"Conducts sponsored health services research and policy analysis on complex health policy issues, [identifying, monitoring, and analyzing] emerging issues in federal and state health law and policy, [evaluating] the effects of changing federal policies on health care access, quality, and cost at the state and local levels."	US$4.75 million	Government, foundations, George Washington University	37	Mostly Ph.D.'s, J.D.'s, and M.P.H.'s	Washington, D.C.	1990	Health care	No identifiable

Name	Description	Budget	Funding Sources	Staff	Staff Type	Location	Year	Policy Area	Ideology
Center for Policy Research (Syracuse University)	"Conducts a broad range of interdisciplinary research and related activities in the areas of aging, disability, and income security policy; domestic urban and regional issues; public finance; and problems of economic development in less industrialized countries."	US$6.5 million	Government, foundations, Syracuse University	12 full-time, 25 affiliated faculty	Ph.D.'s and Ph.D. candidates in the social sciences	Syracuse, NY	1961	Social welfare and development policy	No identifiable
Institute of Transportation Studies (University of California at Davis)	"To serve the needs of society by organizing and conducting multidisciplinary research on emerging and important transportation issues, disseminating this research through conferences and scholarly publications, and enhancing the quality and breadth of transportation education."	US$4 million	Foundations, government	125	Ph.D.'s and Ph.D. candidates in the social sciences	Davis, CA	1991	Transportation policy	No identifiable

Think Tanks (nongovernmental)

University-without-Student Think Tanks

Name	Description	Budget	Funding Sources	Staff	Staff Type	Location	Year	Policy Area	Ideology
American Enterprise Institute	"Dedicated to preserving and strengthening the foundations of freedom through scholarly research, open debate, and publications."	US$15.3 million	Foundations, corporations, individuals	54 (researchers)	Mostly Ph.D. economists and political scientists; some M.A.'s with political experience	Washington, D.C.	1943	Social, economic, and foreign policy	Conservative
Brookings Institution	"Private nonpartisan organization devoted to nonpartisan research, education, and publication in economics, government, foreign policy, and the social sciences generally."	US$23.9 million	Endowment, foundations, corporations, individuals	230	Mostly Ph.D. economists and political scientists	Washington, D.C.	1916	Social, economic, and foreign policy	No identifiable (perceived as more liberal)
Hoover Institution	"Supports [through research, publication, and discussion] the Constitution of the United States . . . where the Federal Government should undertake no governmental, social, or economic action, except where local government, or the people, cannot undertake it for themselves."	US$22.1 million	Endowment, Stanford University, foundations, corporations, individuals	124 (researchers)	Mostly Ph.D. economists and political scientists; many are nonresident scholars	Palo Alto, CA	1919	Social, economic, and foreign policy	Conservative

Continued on next page

Appendix A—continued

Organization	Mission	1998–1999 Budget	Sources of Support	No. of Staff	Profile of Research Personnel	Location	Year Formed	Areas of Research	Ideology
National Academy of Social Insurance	"America's only private, non-profit, non-partisan resource center made up of the nation's leading experts on social insurance."	US$2.5 million	Foundations, government contracts, corporations, unions, individuals	14 full-time; 500 research-affiliated members	Mostly Ph.D. economists and public policy; most are nonresident contributors	Washington, D.C.	1986	Social policy	No identifiable
Contract Researchers									
RAND Corp.	"Mission is to improve policy and decision making through research and analysis."	US$128.4 million	Government contracts, foundations	600 (researchers) 1,000+ total	Mostly Ph.D. social scientists, engineers, and scientists	Santa Monica, CA	1946	Military, foreign, economic, and social policy	No identifiable
Urban Institute	"Sharpen thinking about society's problems and efforts to solve them, improve government decisions and their implementation, and increase citizens' awareness about important public choices."	US$52.6 million	Government contracts, foundations	365	Mostly Ph.D. social scientists	Washington, D.C.	1968	Social and economic policy	No identifiable
Cato Institute	"Nonpartisan public policy research foundation . . . [that] seeks to broaden the parameters of public policy debate to allow consideration of more options that are consistent with the traditional principles of limited government, individual liberty, and peace."	US$13 million	Foundations, corporations, individuals	89 full-time, 55 adjunct scholars	Half with advanced degrees; half with college degrees plus political experience	Washington, D.C.	1977	Social, economic, and foreign policy	Libertarian

Advocacy Think Tanks

Organization	Mission	Budget	Funding sources	Staff	Staff composition	Location	Founded	Policy areas	Ideology
Economic Strategy Institute	"Private, non-profit, non-partisan public policy research organization dedicated to assuring that globalization works with market forces to achieve maximum benefits rather than distorting markets, and imposing costs."	US$2.5 million	Corporations, 18 foundations		Combination of Ph.D.'s, M.A.'s, and B.A.'s; many with political experience	Washington, D.C.	1989	Economic and foreign policy	No identifiable
Heritage Foundation	"Mission is to formulate and promote conservative public policies based on the principles of free enterprise, limited government, individual freedom, traditional American values, and a strong national defense."	US$43.8 million	Individuals, foundations, endowment, corporations	150	Mostly M.A.'s and B.A.'s; many with political experience	Washington, D.C.	1973	Social, economic, and foreign policy	Conservative
Worldwatch Institute	"Nonprofit public policy research organization dedicated to fostering the evolution of an environmentally sustainable society . . . through nonpartisan research on emerging global environmental issues, the results of which are widely disseminated throughout the world."	US$3.0 million	Foundations, individuals	30	Mostly M.A.'s and B.A.'s; many with political experience	Washington, D.C.	1974	Environment	Liberal

For-Profit Research Facilities and Consulting Firms

Organization	Mission	Budget	Funding sources	Staff	Staff composition	Location	Founded	Policy areas	Ideology
Abt Associates	"Research-based consulting company [using] proven research techniques and analytical tools to gather information and transform it into knowledge [for our clients]."	US$125 million	Clients	900	Mostly M.A. and Ph.D. social scientists and engineers	Cambridge, MA	1965	Social policy and development policy	No identifiable
Mathematica Policy Research, Inc.	"Strives to improve public well-being by bringing the highest standards of quality, objectivity, and excellence to bear on the provision of information collection and analysis to our clients."	US$48 million	Clients	352 (180 researchers)	Mostly M.A. and Ph.D. social scientists	Princeton, NJ; Washington, D.C.; Cambridge, MA; Columbia, MD	1968	Health care, welfare, education	No identifiable

Continued on next page

Appendix A—continued

Interest Groups

Organization	Mission	1998–1999 Budget	Sources of Support	No. of Staff	Profile of Research Personnel	Location	Year Formed	Areas of Research	Ideology
Alan Guttmacher Institute	"To protect the reproductive choices of all women and men [by seeking] to inform individual decision making, encourage scientific inquiry and enlightened public debate, and promote the formation of sound public and private sector programs and policies."	US$5.8 million	Individuals, government, foundations, Planned Parenthood	51	Mostly M.A.'s	Washington, D.C., New York City	1968	Reproductive choices and health	No identifiable; started by and closely aligned with Planned Parenthood
AARP's Public Policy Institute	"A nonprofit, nonpartisan association dedicated to shaping and enriching the experience of aging for our members and for all Americans."	US$399.7 million	Foundations, membership, revenue	1,600 (41 in Public Policy Institute)	Ph.D.'s, J.D.'s, and M.A.'s	Washington, D.C.	1958 (PPI in 1984)	Domestic and economic policy affecting older people	No identifiable; represents concerns of older Americans
National Governors' Association	"The only bipartisan national organization of, by and for the nations' Governors. . . . Through NGA, the Governors identify priority issues and deal collectively with issues of public policy and governance at both the national and state levels."	US$11 million; CBP $6 million	States, federal grants, foundations, corporations	95 (45 in CBP)	Mostly M.A.'s	Washington, D.C.	1967	State and local issues—domestic and economic	No identifiable; bipartisan

Source: Information compiled by author from annual reports, IRS forms 990, organizational inquiries, and websites.
APAOs: alternative policy advisory organizations; ANSER: Analytic Services Inc.; AARP: American Association of Retired Persons; CBP: Center for Best Practices.

3 Japan

Yamamoto Tadashi

There is in Japan today a growing sense of crisis that something is fundamentally wrong with society. Some causes for the current intense public soul-searching are a decade-long recession, the inability of the government to deal with critical issues in the face of a rapidly graying society, and successive instances of corruption among government bureaucrats. Many Japanese feel that the model of development that served Japan so well during the country's "catch up and overtake the West" period after the Meiji Restoration of 1868 and throughout the reconstruction process after the end of World War II does not work in the present setting.

Under the earlier model of governance, a handful of elite government bureaucrats acted as the sole arbiter of the public good while society as a whole advanced in lock step. This system has become clearly ineffective and stifling because of society's diversification and pluralism in the face of the formidable forces of globalization. The emergence in recent years of an impressive number of civil society organizations in Japan has been, to some degree, a consequence of the public's disillusionment with the government bureaucracy. These nonprofit organizations (NPOs) and nongovernmental organizations (NGOs) are working to address the increasingly complex social needs not fully attended to by the government, such as care for the elderly, support for foreign workers, and environmental protection. The Great Hanshin-Awaji Earthquake of January 1995 was a galvanizing event for the development of civil society in Japan: The fact that 1.2 million volunteers rushed to the scene of the disaster to aid the victims was ample evidence that citizens could and were willing to take the public interest into their own hands (Yamamoto 1999).

With civil society organizations and the citizenry demanding a larger public space for themselves, the traditional state-centric system of governance has come under fundamental reexamination. The Prime Minister's Commission on Japan's Goals in the 21st Century—which submitted its report, *The Frontier Within: Individual Empowerment and Better Governance in the New Millennium*, in January 2000—recommended that the country undergo a change that can be characterized as moving "from governing to governance." The report argues for "establishing governance built up through joint endeavors, governance based on rules and the principle of responsibility and grounded in two-way consensus formation, rather than governance premised on one-way rule" (Prime Minister's Commission on Japan's Goals in the 21st Century 2000, 25). This changing nature of governance evident in Japan in recent years requires that the role of politicians change, and this chapter addresses the challenges that politicians in Japan face in representing the people in the implementation of policy decisions.

Indeed, the traditional pattern of policymaking in which government bureaucrats have played a predominant role has come under fire in recent years. The emergence of politicians as more active players in the legislative process, thus beginning to tip the power balance between themselves and bureaucrats in their favor, should be understood in this context. These politicians have begun taking legislative initiatives in areas where social needs clearly require addressing but where the government bureaucracy has constrained efforts to address them. They also have started proposing legislation that is designed to bring about structural reforms in many areas. Young members of the Diet, often labeled as the "new generation of policy tribes," have begun taking an active part in the legislative process. Yet, these politicians are not sufficiently equipped with the necessary support structure for conducting legislative activities. Alternate sources of policy ideas from outside the government bureaucracy are very much needed in Japan, and this chapter will examine ways to strengthen them. It is important to keep in mind, however, that the role of politicians in the governance of society is not well established as yet, and it is just as important to find ways to generate more intense public policy debate on the basis of multiple policy options and more active interaction among diverse actors in society centered around politicians. There is no guarantee, moreover, that politicians, once given greater power over the government bureaucrats in decision making in legislative affairs, will necessarily serve the broad public interest better. In short, Japan faces a major challenge of constructing a new system of governance, and guidance is needed particularly to strengthen the role of politicians in bringing about a more effective and responsive system of governance.

SIGNIFICANT CHANGES
IN THE LEGISLATIVE PROCESS

An Increase in the Number of Bills
Sponsored by Diet Members

Until very recently, close to 90 percent of legislation passed by the Diet was drafted by government bureaucrats and sponsored by the cabinet; sponsorship of bills by Diet members made up only 10 percent. This is not to say that Diet members have always been so legislatively reticent. Former Prime Minister Tanaka Kakuei was well known for his aggressive sponsorship of bills: thirty-six pieces of legislation between 1950 and 1962, including some key bills related to land development and living conditions (Nishikawa 2000, 142–143). But over the years, the number of bills sponsored by Diet members declined to such an extent that Doi Takako, when she was Speaker of the House of Representatives, established a private advisory commission to look into the matter. The report, "Ways to Reinvigorate Legislative Initiatives of Members of the Diet," was released in June 1996 (Doi and Kujiraoka 1996).

Because of these circumstances, the significant increase in the past few years in the number of legislative proposals sponsored by Diet members has been regarded as a positive development. In the ordinary session of the Diet from January 19, 1999, to August 13, 1999, sixty bills were sponsored by Diet members (as compared with 124 bills sponsored by the cabinet), an increase of ten from the previous year. Of the sixty bills sponsored by Diet members in the ordinary session, eighteen became law, as compared to 110 of the 124 bills sponsored by the cabinet; still, this was a significant increase in the number of bills sponsored by Diet members that passed the Diet. Moreover, some of the bills sponsored by politicians that have become law include some significant legislation that would not have materialized under the traditional bureaucracy-led legislative process. These bills include:

The NPO Law. The Law to Promote Specified Nonprofit Activities, or the NPO Law, enacted in 1998, substantially simplified the incorporation process for NPOs and NGOs. By this legislation, incorporation no longer required the approval of "competent authorities," which are the government agencies with jurisdiction over the area of the activities of the organization, thus decreasing the influence of the central government over the activities of NPOs and NGOs.

This episode of the passage of the NPO Law was dramatic in that politicians from different parties worked closely with NGO leaders during the legislative process instead of relying on the government bureaucrats (see Yamamoto 1999). This cooperation was further enhanced through the joint efforts of two groups newly established after enactment of the NPO Law. The Parliamentary League to

Support NPOs, formed with the bipartisan participation of more than 220 members of the Diet, and the Coordinating Committee on the Reform of the Tax and Legal Framework of NPOs/NGOs, established by civil society leaders, were instrumental in the passage in March 2001 of the Law Amending in Part the Special Tax Measures Law, which made it possible for NPOs incorporated under the NPO Law to receive tax-deductible donations (see "New Tax Bill Gives Partial Victory to NPOs" 2001).

The Financial Revitalization Bill. Passage of the Bill Concerning Emergency Measures for the Revitalization of the Functions of the Financial System, or the Financial Revitalization Bill, in 1998 was an extraordinary departure from the traditional legislative process. First of all, the major players in the process were younger members of the Diet who worked together across party lines. Typically in office for fewer than three years, they came to be known as the "new generation of policy tribes." In the drafting and markup of the legislation, they also worked independently of government bureaucrats. Second, the bill drafted by these younger politicians replaced an original bill drafted by the Ministry of Finance. Third, during the negotiations between the ruling coalition and the opposition over the markup of the bill, younger politicians, particularly those who were members of the Liberal Democratic Party (LDP), were again at center stage. They rejected the idea of their senior colleagues who had tried to establish the Financial Revitalization Commission within the framework of the Ministry of Finance. In the end, then-Prime Minister Obuchi Keizō shelved the cabinet-sponsored bill and accepted the opposition's legislation as the basis for markup.

The Dioxin Control Law. Enacted in 1999, the law, which called on the government to set standards for dioxin levels in the air, water, soil, and waste emitted from factories, was significant for its bipartisan sponsorship. In the traditional legislative process for such a cabinet-sponsored bill, any effort to set environmental standards having an impact on industry and agriculture would normally originate with the Environment Agency and would be expected to face vigorous opposition from ministries in charge of the affected sectors. According to Yamashita Eiichi, a member of the New Kōmeitō Party who played a leading role in the legislative process, the enactment of the very first law in Japan to control emissions of dioxin and dangerous chemicals would not have been possible if left to the government bureaucracy (Nishikawa 2000, 135).

A Change in Legal Environment and the Involvement of Politicians in the Policy Process

The growing participation of politicians in the legislative process has been accompanied by legislation that has accelerated the erosion of bureaucratic dominance in the policymaking process. These bills include:

The Freedom of Information Law. It has long been assumed that a fundamental source of the Japanese bureaucracy's power was its monopoly on access to information. The passage of the Law Concerning Access to Information Held by Administrative Organs, or the Freedom of Information Law, was finally enacted in May 1999 after years of debate, and it is likely to have a considerable impact on the governance of Japanese society.

Public pressure for greater transparency in government had been mounting as a result of a series of events. Most glaring was the disclosure of Ministry of Health and Welfare officials' having concealed documents related to the medical use of HIV-contaminated blood, which led to tragic consequences. There also have been a growing number of revelations of government officials' lavish wining and dining with public funds or government officials being lavishly entertained by interest groups.

The enactment of the Freedom of Information Law is likely to have a profound impact on the predominant role government bureaucrats had played in the policymaking process over the years by allowing politicians, civil society organizations, and citizens more opportunities to have access to information held by the government bureaucracy.

The Administrative Procedure Law. The law designed to minimize administrative discretion and realize rule-based administration was introduced by the government in 1992 under pressure from the United States in the U.S.-Japan Strategic Impediments Initiative, and enacted in 1994. However, the law was not effectively enforced due to several "loopholes" and escape clauses. In 1999, in an attempt to shore up the Administrative Procedure Law, the government introduced the "Public Comment Procedure for Formulating, Amending, or Repealing a Regulation" as a part of the Three-Year Program for the Promotion of Deregulation. The procedure provides opportunities for the public to send comments and requests directly to the government.

The Diet Revitalization Law. The predominance of bureaucrats in the legislative process in the past was not limited to the role they played in the drafting of bills—the bureaucrats' presence was felt in the Diet debate as well. Bureaucrats attended Diet committee meetings and were often called upon to respond for their ministers to questions by opposition party members. The Diet Revitalization Law, enacted in 1999, allows only ministers or deputy ministers to respond to questions in committee meetings in principle. Weekly debates between the prime minister and the leaders of the opposition parties were also instituted in January 2000, modeled after "Question Time" in the U.K. House of Commons.

Implementation of this law already has had a major impact on the Diet, particularly in the appointment of cabinet ministers and parliamentary vice-ministers. The prime minister cannot now follow the traditional seniority rule as a basis for cabinet or sub-cabinet appointments, and so tends to appoint those Diet members who are well versed in policy issues. Though this new trend will not be effective if the tenure of the cabinet and sub-cabinet members is limited to one or two years, as has been the case, it will further encourage politicians to spend time studying the policy issues and developing an expertise in particular policy issues.

ALTERNATIVE SOURCES OF POLICY ADVICE: ASSESSMENT OF CURRENT STATUS

Along with the more active, substantive involvement of politicians in legislative activities in recent years, there has emerged a distinct trend for more politicians to seek independent sources of policy advice outside the government bureaucracy. The role of government bureaucrats in the policymaking process has declined because of their inability to cope with pluralistic social needs, as evidenced by some clear cases of policy failures, and because of the enactment of specific legislation to curb their influence.

The cozy relationship between the governing LDP and the government bureaucracy, which lasted for thirty-eight years, came to an end with the start of coalition politics in 1993. During the era of high economic growth, which coincided with the LDP's dominance in politics, alternate sources of policy ideas were not sufficiently developed. The new political environment in Japan clearly calls out for a critical assessment of possible sources of policy ideas that can help politicians formulate policy initiatives or equip themselves with a better understanding of diverse policy options. Moreover, there is a growing awareness that there should be greater involvement of diverse actors in the policy debate and the legislative process in response to the growing diversification of interests within society and the increasing complexities of Japan's external relationships.

Resources Available
to the Legislative Branch

There are resources attached to the Diet designed to assist the legislative activities of members of the Diet. The Research and Legislative Reference Bureau of the National Diet Library has 167 staff members in ten research departments. They oversee general information related to legislation, especially as regards the laws and practices in other countries.

The House of Representatives (Lower House) and the House of Councillors (Upper House) both have research staff attached to their committees. Thus, the Lower House has eighteen standing committee research offices and three special committee research offices, while the Upper House has fifteen standing committee research offices and three special committee research offices. Ten researchers are assigned to each office, which is headed by a professional advisor. However, these researchers are not entirely free from bureaucratic influence as, currently, nine of the twenty-one professional advisors heading the research offices of the Lower House are seconded from government agencies. This is a significant reduction from 1997 when thirteen of the eighteen professional advisors were seconded from the bureaucracy ("Shuin, jimukyoku jinji" 2000).

In 1998, the Lower House established the Research Bureau as part of broader legislative reform. The bureau was charged with, among other functions, oversight of the efforts of the respective research offices, which had been independently linked to their specific committees. The Research Bureau coordinated the work of the research offices, making it possible for them to address policy issues that transcended the traditional jurisdictions of their committees. The Research Bureau was, in addition, authorized to undertake preliminary investigations of the administrative performance of ministries and agencies. In 1998–1999, ten preliminary investigations relating to public works and commercial activities of financial institutions were conducted. While the effectiveness of such preliminary investigations is yet to be seen, it is clear that the legislative hand has been strengthened.

The Lower House has a Legislative Bureau of seventy-five staff, and the Upper House a Legislative Bureau of seventy-three. The main function of these bureaus is to provide research support to Diet members sponsoring, or preparing to sponsor, legislation by verifying its constitutionality or checking for duplication or contravention of existing laws. The growing importance of the Legislative Bureaus is evident in their assistance to Diet members in drafting bills that they intend to sponsor. It is a comparable role to that performed by the Cabinet Legislative Bureau in connection with cabinet-sponsored bills. The Legislative Bureaus of the Diet, however, lack the professional expertise to deal with diverse issues, which may be due to the fact that they are divided into sections corresponding to the ministries. Legislative deliberations are contained within these sections, the senior posts of which are held by staff seconded from the ministries. The drawback of such a system is both the continued reliance on the bureaucracy and the limited opportunity to develop independent sources of ideas.

Legislative Assistants
to Members of the Diet

Under the Diet Law of 1963, provision was made for each member of the Diet to have two legislative assistants. In 1991, upon the recommendation of a council under the Speaker of the House of Representatives, Diet members were provided with another assistant.

A person qualifies to become a legislative assistant either by examination or by authorization of the Diet Secretariat after having served as Diet staff for many years. From 1993 to 1999, of the 1,802 persons to become licensed legislative assistants, only 261 were hired on the basis of examination. The remaining 1,541 assistants, who were authorized by the Secretariat, had been staff of Diet members for more than ten years but otherwise lacked any particular qualification to assist Diet members in legislative affairs.

Legislative assistants sometimes serve as critical points of contact: They receive suggestions and policy proposals from outside resources such as research institutions and NGOs, they take the proposals to the party research councils, and they deal with bureaucrats in the drafting of legislative proposals. The paucity of persons qualified to carry out such tasks is obviously a constraining factor in legislative competence. This may change as younger Diet members require the services of more professional staff, whose services have previously been relied on for more immediate concerns such as election campaigns.

Research Departments of Political Parties

Each major political party has a research department or a research council. These departments fulfill the important function of determining a party's policy position on issues raised in the Diet.

As the LDP has been the dominant party since 1955, obviously the Policy Affairs Research Council (PARC) of the LDP continues to play a critical role in Japan's policymaking process. It has seventeen divisions corresponding to each government agency, forty research committees to deal with broad policy issues, and fifty-nine special committees. PARC coordinates the party's policy positions and works closely with government bureaucrats and interest groups. Its influence is such that before any cabinet-sponsored bill is submitted to the Diet, the government bureaucrats must seek the agreement of the relevant PARC committees. In this sense, PARC is not a place where politicians go to seek alternative policy advice. Nor are its thirty staff members policy research experts but party operatives whose job is to organize the numerous meetings that take place under the auspices of PARC.

The situation is not much different for the research departments of the opposition parties. As of April 2000, the Democratic Party of Japan's Policy Research Committee had eighteen staff members, the New Kōmeitō's Policy Board had thirteen, the Communist Party's Policy Committee had twenty-nine, and the Liberal Party's Policy Board had four.

Given the lack of internal competence for generating policy ideas and initiatives, political leaders have voiced the need for their parties to develop think tanks of their own. The LDP has its think tank, the LDP Institute for Policy Research, established in 1982, but its main function has been reduced to staffing PARC. In fact, the current chairman of PARC is also a director of the LDP think tank, and the think tank's board is made up of party officials. Moreover, its ten senior research staff are seconded from major corporations, and normally they return to their corporations after two years at the think tank. Their function is largely limited to assembling policy-related data, although they will occasionally work with outside experts to generate policy ideas.

The Democratic Party of Japan has two closely related policy advisory organizations: The Shimin ga Tsukuru Seisaku Chōsa-kai (Citizen Policy Research Council) and the Shinku Netto Sentā 21 (Think Net Center 21). The Citizen Policy Research Council was established in 1997 to initiate legislation reflecting the citizens' public interests. This council aims to set policy agendas for resolving social issues such as achieving a more barrier-free public transportation system and a problem-free long-term care insurance system. The Think Net Center 21 was established in January 2000. Rather than focusing only on the study of mid-term and long-term policy agendas, the center is also seeking to develop networks with other think tanks and specialists.

In 1999, the Liberal Party launched a novel experiment with its establishment of the Center for Liberal Politics, which may be regarded as a virtual think tank in that it did not have an office but operated mostly through the Internet. The center had some 180 "research staff," recruited from party members who have run for office. They were assigned to eight policy discussion groups, and each group, including the party's Diet members, debated policy issues on Web forums and via e-mail. Proposals were submitted to the party's policy board for adoption as party policy. This virtual think tank also functioned as a means to attract and train candidates for office.

A think tank, in a stricter sense, of a political party seems to be elusive. In the case of the LDP, the leadership tends to rely on the bureaucracy for policy ideas, and, in fact, as suggested above, many legislative proposals are written by government bureaucrats in consultation with party leaders. Although some leaders have sought to commit more funds to development of the party's think tank, there never has been any consistent effort in this regard as the party leadership is rotated regularly. Other factors that may contribute to this state of affairs are a lack of job mobility for policy analysts, the principle of "revolving doors" (where bureaucrats become policy analysts and analysts become bureaucrats), and a traditional reliance on the bureaucracy for legislative process.

As the opposition, other parties have greater need for party think tanks as well as greater opportunity to submit alternative legislative proposals. Nevertheless, the lack of strong commitment by party leaders, the instability of party leadership, and the preoccupation with political maneuvering have worked against the establishment of internal apparatuses for policy analysis and proposals.

Think Tanks and NGOs

Whenever alternative sources of policy advice are discussed in Japan, the active role that think tanks play in the United States is cited. Indeed, think tanks in the United States play a central role, providing policy ideas to politicians as well as provoking public debate through the media and public education.

In Japan, the contribution of think tanks to the policy process has been limited by the dominant role of civil servants in the formulation of public policy. While studies show a large number of policy research institutes in Japan, they are substantially different from their counterparts in the United States and Europe. For one thing, many Japanese think tanks are for-profit.

According to a 2000 survey by the National Institute of Research Advancement (NIRA), Japan has 332 think tanks, or more than twice the number in 1988 when NIRA conducted its first survey of Japanese think tanks. Of these, 46.5 percent are for-profit institutes. The same survey found that almost 80 percent of research projects was contract research, while 17.3 percent was in-house and 3.1 percent conducted based on grants. The survey also indicated that think tanks are overconcentrated in Tokyo, with 54.2 percent of institutes centered in Tokyo and 78.9 percent of researchers belonging to these institutes (National Institute of Research Advancement 2001).

Another characteristic of Japanese think tanks is that they are closely associated with government agencies or major corporations and are often regarded as their subsidiaries. Because of this, the research activity is heavily client-oriented and therefore not designed to stimulate policy debate or assist politicians in formulating their positions. Even not-for-profit think tanks in Japan often come under government influence because they fall under the jurisdiction of agencies ("competent authorities") that require them to report their annual budget and planned activities. The climate for think tanks is, furthermore, bleaker for the fact that scholars and researchers, reflecting Japan's ivory tower–oriented intellectual tradition, tend not to be policy-oriented.

Because most think tanks are involved in client-oriented research, they have little interaction with politicians. Nor do they appear to have much desire to contribute to the public interest or to compete with other institutes in the intellectual marketplace. This contrasts sharply with the trend in the United States, where think tanks aggressively "market" their research products. According to researchers at NIRA, more than 40 percent of think tanks worldwide made "all" their research output available to the public, while only one institute in Japan did so; more than 75 percent of think tanks worldwide published "all or mostly all" of their research, while less than 50 percent in Japan did so (Nagata and Nakamura 1999).

One way think tanks in Japan do contribute to the public policy debate is through the constant visibility of their leaders in the media, at Diet hearings, on government commissions, and at public occasions. These leaders, who tend to have held senior positions in government agencies, have developed reputations as respectable thinkers in society. Among these leaders are Gyoten Toyoo, president of the Institute of International Finance; Fukukawa Shinji, president of Dentsu Research Institute; Kosai Yasushi, chairman of the Japan Economic Research Center; Owada Hisashi, president of the Japan Institute of International Affairs; and Ohba Tomomitsu, chairman of the Japan Center for International Finance.

Despite the limited contribution of think tanks to the need for alternative policy ideas, some innovative efforts have been made in recent years. Kōsō Nippon (Japan Initiative) was founded in 1997 by Katō Hideki after his resignation from the Ministry of Finance. Dependent on corporate and foundation support, Kōsō Nippon is an independent, not-for-profit, "think-and-advocate" tank whose goal is to make policy recommendations and to bring about their implementation. The organization maintains close contacts with members of the Diet, and it has made a large impact on Diet procedures, particularly in helping to eliminate the stipulation of "competent authorities."

The Tokyo Foundation was established in 1997 under the leadership of Takenaka Heizō, who has since been appointed minister of economic and fiscal policy by Prime Minister Koizumi Jun'ichirō. The foundation aspires to be a full-fledged, independent think tank, its policy research projects focusing on security alliances in the post–cold war era, the tax system and corporate behavior, and the administrative reform of the central government.

The foundation also makes an effort to disseminate results of its research through policy and research seminars. It holds regular "Intellectual Cabinet Policy Meetings," inviting leading policy experts to discuss key issues. It has sponsored international conferences and symposia, including the major meeting of the "Shadow G8 Summit" in April 2000, the Japan-Australia New APEC Initiative Workshop in 1999, and "Sustainability 21" in 1997. In 1999, it launched "Policy-Net" as a venue for politicians, government bureaucrats, policymakers, and policy researchers in universities and think tanks to exchange their views. In July 2000, it held a "Policy Summer Camp," bringing together representatives of policy study departments of universities.

Keidanren (Japan Federation of Economic Organizations), a powerful national organization with membership consisting of large corporations and industrial associations, established the 21st Century Public Policy Institute in 1997 with economist Tanaka Naoki as president. The primary focus of the institute is the private sector: that is, the initiatives and programs the private sector could implement to revitalize the Japanese economy. Aside from Tanaka, most of the institute's research staff is seconded from Keidanren or major corporations. Recent projects include normalizing the financial system, reform of the pensions and savings system, and a rethinking of the civil justice system.

The Japan Center for International Exchange (JCIE), a nonprofit, nongovernmental organization dedicated to strengthening Japan's role in international affairs, launched its Global ThinkNet Project in 1996 with funding from the Nippon Foundation. The concept of the project is to create a network-oriented think tank with resources that can be tapped within the country and around the world. The project consists of human resources development, joint policy research, conferences and workshops, publication of research, electronic information exchange, and interaction between policy research specialists and parliamentarians both in Japan and abroad.

NGOs, academics, and leading citizens have set in motion additional initiatives for alternative sources of policy advice in Japan. These groups usually operate with specific goals in mind, seeking to convince politicians of the need for certain policy. Shimin Rippō Kikō (Citizens' Initiative) was formed in 1997 as a collaboration of Gyōkaku Kokumin Kaigi (Citizens' Forum for Renewal) and Shimin Undō Sentā (National Center of Citizens' Movement). The 21st Century Policy Forum was launched in 1996 by Shindō Eiichi, a professor of social science at Tsukuba University, and a group of intellectual leaders for the purpose of making policy proposals on economic, legal, and foreign policy issues.

Private Advisory Councils for Political Leaders

Advisory councils are consultative organs to government agencies, the legal base for which is Article 8 of the National Administrative Organization Act. Advisory councils are categorized into two types by function. One type conducts inquiries into important issues and policy questions and submits policy recommendations. Another type adjudicates contradictory views of public policy and evaluates and authorizes professional standards and qualifications (Abe, Shindō, and Kawato 1994, 40–41).

While experts from the private sector, including business, trade unions, and professional groups, have been included in the councils, it is assumed that their role is not to provide alternative policy advice but to legitimatize policies to be adopted or to reflect the views of interest groups in the policymaking process. That these advisory councils are mostly staffed by government bureaucrats reinforces this perception. The councils are often portrayed as "helpless or willing tools of their parent agencies[;] they have been tarred as 'robots,' 'cheerleaders,' 'backers,' 'tunnel organizations,' and 'ornaments'" (Schwartz 1998, 54). At best, these councils are regarded as an effort by the bureaucracy to "counteract the diminished authority of the civil service after World War II and generate public trust in the impartiality and openness of the bureaucracy" (Abe, Shindō, and

Kawato 1994). Presently, there are 212 such advisory councils with 5,300 members. In 1999, the Administrative Reform Promotion Headquarters moved to reduce the number of councils to 93 and their members to 1,800 as part of its 2001 plan to streamline administrative organization.

While these councils have a tarnished image as advisory mechanisms, political leaders have found "private advisory councils," which are nonstatutory bodies without legal authorization, to be much more useful. These private councils invite the policy views of intellectual leaders and experts from the nongovernmental sector and are sometimes helpful in engineering public support for policies not favored by government bureaucrats.

Ōhira Masayoshi, when he became prime minister in 1978, established nine policy study groups, involving some two hundred intellectual leaders, business leaders, and elite bureaucrats. These study groups drafted such proposals as "A Plan for Pacific Rim Solidarity" and "A Design for Rural Cities," which have been discussed in official circles over the years. One unintended impact of Ōhira's study groups was that, when Nakasone Yasuhiro succeeded Ōhira as prime minister, he inherited many of Ōhira's scholars. Nakasone deepened his ties with them through the Second Provisional Commission on Administrative Reform, and relied on their help in preparing for the LDP's 1982 presidential primary. Many of the researchers who had gathered around Ōhira thus gravitated to Nakasone (Schwartz 1998, 106).

Nakasone was known for his frequent use of advisory councils, both official and private, to move his policy agenda though the Diet. A report of the Study Group on Economic Structural Adjustment for International Harmony, better known as the Maekawa Report after its chairman, was perhaps one of the best known reports of the private advisory councils. The private consultative bodies of recent years have already crossed the bounds of what the government calls private conferences or study groups and changed form to become semi-public bodies shouldering part of the official policymaking process (Schwartz 1998, 107).

The Prime Minister's Commission on Japan's Goals in the 21st Century, which operated under Obuchi, is an interesting model that merits analysis. Obuchi organized the group as a private commission in 1999, appointing sixteen private citizens from diverse fields of expertise as its members. Its mandate was to produce a report on desirable goals for the next generation of Japanese, thus encouraging broad national discussion. After ten months of deliberations, including consultations with experts in diverse fields, the commission submitted its final report to Obuchi in early 2000.

A singular characteristic of this commission was that, unlike most government commissions, there were no former government officials among its members and the drafting of the report was done by the members without relying on government

bureaucrats. The secretariat itself was unusual in that the staff director was seconded by JCIE, a nonprofit and nongovernmental organization. Perhaps because
the commission was addressing the long-term direction of Japan and was not concerned with short-term recommendations that could affect government agencies,
there was little intervention from the bureaucracy.

Even so, the report caused considerable debate. Recommendations calling for
a paradigm shift "from governing to governance," especially as regards "the methods and systems whereby citizens interact with society," and to "redefin[ing] and
rebuild[ing] the relationship between private and public space in civil society,"
met with criticism from the more conservative wing of the intellectual and political
communities (Prime Minister's Commission on Japan's Goals in the 21st Century
2000, 17–18). Among other controversial policy ideas were improving English-lan-
guage teaching to enhance Japan's global literacy, establishing a clear-cut immigration policy, and emphasizing individualism over a group-oriented approach.

Soon after the report was completed, Obuchi suffered a stroke from which he
never recovered, but politicians from different political parties have since reviewed
the report's analyses and recommendations with a view to sponsoring legislation.
One specific move emanating from the Democratic Party of Japan is to organize
a task force to make English the second official language of Japan.

PROSPECTS AND CHALLENGES FOR ALTERNATIVE SOURCES OF POLICY IDEAS IN JAPAN

The debate over governance in Japan has centered on moving away from the ineffective bureaucracy-led system. In this regard, there are opportunities for legislators to take a more proactive role in the legislative process as representatives of
their constituency. As the Prime Minister's Commission on Japan's Goals in the
21st Century points out, "the legislature and parties will have a key role to play in
dealing with policy issues in the period ahead, inasmuch as policy will increasingly concern issues such as social security, which involves choices among values"
(2000, 73).

The infrastructure to support the policymaking initiatives of elected politicians
is still very fragile, however. In particular, there are few alternative sources of policy
ideas for legislators to rely on outside the government bureaucracy. The situation is
serious because to create a new system of governance to replace the traditional
state-centric system is a daunting task—even as bureaucrats grow demoralized
and even cynical in the face of public criticism and legislation that undercuts their
monopoly on power. As discussed above, there is a multiplicity of challenges in
creating independent institutions for the provision of alternative policy advice,
building a funding base that circumvents control by the government agencies,

and recruiting competent policy experts to meet short-term requirements. There is as well the need to develop a stable supply of human resources by providing training and assuring a secure career path, to develop a market for policy advice among politicians, and to orient politicians in different ways of policymaking. While the tasks seem monumental, there are already stirrings of change that can be encouraged and enhanced. Even on a micro level, Diet members are finding that to be better versed in policy issues will be beneficial to their political careers.

Strengthening Policy Staff
Working for Diet Members

While strong policy staff of individual Diet members is important, staff is limited, and it is not possible for staff to have expertise on the many policy issues each politician has to deal with. Nor would it be necessary for each politician to develop a policy position where voting in the Diet is bound by parties. Nevertheless, strong policy staff can play a vital role in enabling politicians to participate more fully in the policy debate and in exploring diverse policy options.

For this reason, the quality of legislative assistants needs to be improved. Authorization by the Diet Secretariat on the lone basis of a lengthy tenure working for a Diet member should cease. Qualification should be paramount if quality is to be ensured. In addition, the Diet Secretariat should consider sponsoring programs such as regular briefing seminars or training seminars for the legislative staff.

Despite current constraints, an increasing number of Diet members, particularly those who are regarded as the new generation of policy tribes, are making innovative use of the legislative staff. These staff sometimes function as critical points of contact, bringing together resources from such diverse actors as NGOs and NPOs, academia, and the media to help Diet members take a more proactive legislative position.

Enhancing the Think Tank
Functions of Political Parties

Some political parties have established think tanks of their own, but their policymaking function is limited. The research councils or research departments of political parties do not have legislative staff with substantive knowledge of policy matters. In fact, in the case of the LDP, policy staff has been unnecessary as much of the substantive staff work for the drafting of bills has been done by bureaucrats working with politicians. Opposition parties have relied heavily on the legislative branch of the Diet for the drafting of bills.

Since the arrival of coalition government, policy consultation at the staff level has become critical, thus establishing the need for expertise within the party. It is important that party leaders commit to building a strong policy team within the party, recruiting credible policy experts to head such efforts. Legislative staff would be well utilized if their efforts were focused collectively on different policy issues. Collaboration is essential, as staff cannot function effectively alone. Financial support for building this policy capacity within political parties might be earmarked from public funds available to each party, or additional funds might be secured from the government budget specifically for this purpose.

Training Policy Specialists and Enhancing Their Interaction with Politicians

Involvement in politics has long been seen as inappropriate for scholars, and public policy has only recently become a bona fide academic discipline in universities. Today policy studies in universities abounds. According to the Ministry of Education, universities with a policy research department or a policy study center have jumped from two or three in 1995 to forty in 1999.

A growing number of young scholars have studied abroad at institutions such as the Kennedy School of Government at Harvard University and the School of Advanced International Studies at Johns Hopkins University, both in the United States. Senior Japanese politicians have begun to seek policy advice from these scholars, and although not many are doing so in a systematic manner, this trend has been established. Providing opportunity for further interaction between politicians and policy experts will benefit all. Continuing interaction will result in closer collaborative networks. In this regard, government funding should be made available for the training of social scientists in the same way that it is for natural scientists.

Strengthening Civil Society Organizations as Sources of Alternative Policy Advice

Awareness of the importance of civil society organizations in Japan is greater now, as evidenced by the passage of the NPO Law. What has not been sufficiently understood, however, is the important role played by independent policy research institutes. The lack of independence and the lack of funds of these policy research institutes account for their ineffectiveness in the policymaking process.

One definite step that can be taken to remedy the situation is the passage of legislation to make contributions to NPOs tax deductible; one victory in the movement to realize a more favorable tax environment for nonprofits was passage of the aforementioned Law Amending in Part the Special Tax Measures Law. Although more tax incentives for contributions will not automatically increase funding for independent think tanks, it will provide a base to build upon. Another step is the creation of a mechanism, outside the control of the government ministries, through which public funding would be channeled to policy research institutes.

Models for such mechanisms exist in other countries. In the United States, the National Endowment for Humanities, the National Endowment for Arts, and the National Endowment for Democracy rely on government funding, but their boards are independent, as are their decisions on making grants to private organizations, including think tanks. In Germany, political party foundations function similarly. Given the fact that private sources of funding for think tanks in Japan are so few, such models should be explored. While there are organizations in Japan that could channel public funds to private institutions, they are either under the control of government agencies or without grant-making capacity.

Interaction between politicians and NGOs and NPOs active in the environment, social security, and development assistance should be encouraged and facilitated. Such cooperative activities are mutually beneficial, as a growing number of politicians and leaders of NGOs and NPOs will attest. In the international sphere, NGO involvement in the policymaking process has been pronounced, with NGOs developing significant expertise in many areas. At the current stage of NGO development in Japan, the support of and collaboration with politicians should be of high priority.

Enhancing Cross-Sectoral Cooperation on Critical Issues

To seek alternative sources of policy ideas should not be seen as an effort to purge bureaucrats from the decision-making process. While excesses in the bureaucratic monopoly of legislative affairs have had undesirable consequences, to disregard the value of the bureaucracy, with its wealth of experience and expertise, is unproductive and unrealistic. Moreover, its technocratic knowledge of formulating policies can be relied upon once ideas are brought into the policy process.

It may also be in error to classify all bureaucrats as one, as young bureaucrats with innovative ideas are not uncommon. They too may be stifled in the institutional framework, but their knowledge can be tapped by politicians. As society faces more complex and diverse social issues, it is imperative that different resources be brought together to address them.

Accordingly, the worldwide trend toward greater cross-sectoral partnerships among politicians, government officials, policy experts from universities and research institutes, business, NGOs and NPOs, and the media should be encouraged and worked toward in Japan. These partnerships have resulted in effective responses to new challenges, and by their diverse coalitions they have introduced a competition of policy ideas. Such dynamism is yet to be seen in Japan, but it is a direction that, as participation in the public policy arena increases, Japan can aspire to.

BIBLIOGRAPHY

Abe Hitoshi, Shindō Muneyuki, and Kawato Sadafumi. 1994. *The Government and Politics of Japan.* Tokyo: University of Tokyo Press.

Asano Ichirō, ed. 1998. *Kokkai jiten, dai san-pan* (Encyclopedia of the Japanese National Diet, 3rd ed.). Tokyo: Yūhikaku.

Curtis, Gerald. 1988. *The Japanese Way of Politics.* New York: Columbia University Press.

Doi Takako and Kujiraoka Hyōsuke. 1996 "Giin-rippō no kasseika ni kansuru teigen" (Ways to reinvigorate legislative initiatives of members of the Diet). Reprinted in Ueda Akira and Igarashi Takayoshi. 1997. *Gikai to giin-rippō* (Legislation sponsored by the legislative assembly and its members). Tokyo: Kōjin-no-tomo-sha.

Iwai Tomoaki. 1989. *Rippō katei* (Legislative process). Tokyo: Tokyo Daigaku Shuppan-kai.

Kishimoto Kōichi. 1998. *Politics in Modern Japan.* Tokyo: Japan Echo Inc.

Nagata Naohisa and Nakamura Madoka. 1999. "Overview of Japanese Think Tanks." Paper prepared for GDN Bonn Conference, December 5–8. Unpublished.

Naikaku Hōsei Kyoku. 1999. "Saikin ni okeru hōritsu-an no teishutsu-seiritsu kensū" (Legislation data in the Diet: number of introduced and passed bills). <http://www.clb.admix.jp/5/bk/5_a.htm> (17 November 1999).

National Institute for Research Advancement. 2001. *Shinku tanku no dōkō* (Trends of think tanks in Japan). Tokyo: Sōgō Kenkyū Kaihatsu Kikō.

"New Tax Bill Gives Partial Victory to NGOs." 2001. *Civil Society Monitor*, no. 6: 1–3.

Nishikawa Shin'ichi. 2000. *Shirarezaru kanchō, Naikaku Hōsei-kyoku.* (Cabinet legislative bureau, unrevealed agency). Tokyo: Gogatsu Shobō.

Ōtake Hideo, ed. 2000. *Power Shuffles and Policy Processes: Coalition Government in Japan in the 1990s.* Tokyo: Japan Center for International Exchange.

Prime Minister's Commission on Japan's Goals in the 21st Century. 2000. "Overview." In *The Frontier Within: Empowerment and Better Governance in the New Millennium.* Tokyo: Office for the Prime Minister's Commission on Japan's Goals in the 21st Century.

Satō Seizaburō and Matsuzaki Tetsuhisa. 1986. *Jimintōseiken* (LDP administrations). Tokyo: Chuō Kōron-sha.

Schwartz, Frank J. 1998. *Advice and Consent: The Politics of Consultation in Japan.* Cambridge: Cambridge University Press.

"Shūin, jimukyoku jinji minaoshi" (Lower House reconsiders staff personnel system). 2000. *Sankei Shimbun* (8 May): 2.

Yamamoto Tadashi. 1999. "Emergence of Japan's Civil Society and Its Future Challenges." In Yamamoto Tadashi, ed. *Deciding the Public Good: Governance and Civil Society in Japan.* Tokyo: Japan Center for International Exchange.

4 United Kingdom

Diane Stone

T he government of the United Kingdom is typically regarded as an executive-dominated system. Parliamentary systems such as that in the United Kingdom are often portrayed as closed to external inputs. Some observers believe the decline of Parliament and the resulting concentration of power around the prime minister and the Cabinet have had the effect of insulating policymaking from outside sources. The convention of collective ministerial responsibility and an ethos of officialdom among Britain's powerful generalist civil service compounds this insulation. Indeed, the primacy of the central government among the institutions of the public sector is unequivocal.

The civil service, which represents approximately 2 percent of the entire U.K. workforce, is frequently portrayed as having a monopoly on advice and control over information. Civil servants carry out the work of the government under the direction of ministers and advise ministers on policy. As the U.K. civil service is nonpolitical, the civil servants remain when the ministers and the government change (Cabinet Office, quoted in Massey 1999, 10). Westminster traditions institutionalize the strength of the civil service. Nevertheless, twenty years of major reform throughout the public sector have had a significant impact on the size, shape, and responsibilities of the civil service.

Despite the influence of the civil service, for most of the past century the U.K. government has drawn on and gradually opened itself to alternative sources of policy advice and ideas. Today, the U.K. government consults a wide range of policy actors outside or on the margins of government. Although these sources of advice are based primarily within the United Kingdom, increasingly, policy advice is coming from and generated in transnational policy communities. As a mature democracy, the United Kingdom is characterized by a rich diversity of private policy advice as well as semiautonomous centers of policy advice. These organizations, ad hoc inquiries, and groups usually act as independent agents in seeking to promote policy ideas and recommendations, although they do not always act in isolation. These policy centers frequently create alliances with other bodies to influence government thinking.

The following section addresses the supply of and demand for alternative policy advice. The primary sources of alternative advice in the United Kingdom are numerous. Civil society organizations include policy institutes and think tanks; some interest groups, nongovernmental organizations (NGOs), and professional associations; and, on occasion, law firms, banks, and consultancies. An intermediate group of alternative policy advisory organizations (APAOs) with either a significant degree of independence or autonomy from government or private bodies in resource-dependent relations with the government include academic bodies such as university policy centers and funding councils, as well as the Monetary Policy Committee of the Bank of England (BoE). Alternative advice within the government comes from commissions of inquiry, parliamentary committees, policy units, and task forces established close to the prime minister, the Cabinet, or ministers or from nondepartmental public bodies (NDPBs). However, NDPBs cannot always be considered a source of alternative advice.

Commissions of inquiry, parliamentary committees, and NDPBs are part of the state architecture. Parliamentary committees are part of the government if not part of the executive. Although NDPBs and inquiries have greater autonomy, there are often subtle political pressures through the appointment processes, staffing by civil servants, and public funding allocations that cause such bodies to be mindful of government priorities. Instead of looking at institutions, the procedures by which alternative advice is drawn into government provide insight into the way in which advice influences policy. This claim rests on the particular constitutional structure of the United Kingdom, which does not have a single, written, codified constitution. Instead, the constitution rests on common law, statute law, and conventions. The flexibility and adaptability of the constitution have led to a multiplicity of practices and organizational forms.

This chapter does not generalize about the type of APAO that works best in the United Kingdom. The market for policy advice is too diverse and not structured solely around the formally defined institutions of power. At different junctures, and in different policy fields, some forms of policy advice work better than other forms. Furthermore, the advisory market has evolved considerably over the past century and continues to evolve with developments in information technology as well as the changing political and economic environment. In particular, the European Union (EU) has brought into play an additional range of sources of policy advice.

POLICY ADVISORY
ORGANIZATIONS IN THE UNITED KINGDOM

The sheer number of policy advisory organizations and the relatively high-quality output or product from the majority of these bodies suggest a vibrant industry. This is as much symptomatic of governmental demand and desire for advice as it is reflective of the health of British civil society in generating alternative policy perspectives.

There is a lack of appreciation of the range of social research in the United Kingdom and the locations in which it is carried out (Bulmer and Sykes 1998, 1). The focus tends to be on the academic social science product emanating from universities and institutes. Yet, empirical social research is organized predominantly outside academia.[1] It is beyond the scope of this chapter to address all sources of policy analysis. Although there is some discussion of central government research, the policy research produced by health authorities, market research firms, many volunteer sector organizations, and local government will not be outlined. What follows is a more modest overview of sources of policy research and alternative governance.

Alternative Policy Advice in
Civil Society and the Market

THINK TANKS
By international standards, the United Kingdom has a large community of think tanks and these organizations have recently attracted much scholarly attention. Estimates on the number of think tanks vary, but a recent survey identified ninety-seven think tanks in the United Kingdom (Day 2000).[2]

The oldest think tanks include the Royal United Services Institute for Defence Studies (RUSI, founded in 1831), which is para-statal; the Fabian Society (1884); the Royal Institute of International Affairs (RIIA, 1920; better known as Chatham House); and the National Institute of Economic and Social Research (NIESR, 1938). The Fabian Society is formally affiliated with the Labour Party, whereas the RUSI, the NIESR, and Chatham House are academic-type think tanks. After World War II, there was relatively significant growth of academic-type think tanks, including foreign policy, strategic studies, and development studies institutes such as the International Institute of Strategic Studies (IISS, 1958), the Overseas Development Institute (ODI, 1960), the Panos Institute (1986), and the Federal Trust (1945). Other prominent institutes include the Centre for Economic Policy Research (CEPR, 1983), the Institute of Fiscal Studies (IFS, 1969), the Policy Studies Institute (PSI, 1978), and environmental institutes such as the Institute for European Environmental Policy and Forum for the Future (1996).

EVOL
OF
THINK
TANKS

Most free-market think tanks emerged from the 1960s onward. These think tanks were stronger in their ideological advocacy. First among them was the Institute of Economic Affairs (IEA, 1955), followed by the more conservative Centre for Policy Studies (CPS, 1974), the Adam Smith Institute (ASI, 1977), the David Hume Institute (1985), the European Policy Forum (1992), and Politiea (1995). A crop of left-of-center think tanks emerged in the 1980s. These include Demos (1993), the New Policy Institute (1996), and the Institute for Employment Rights (1988). The liberal-market think tanks emerged as problems with the U.K. welfare state and nationalized industries were becoming increasingly apparent. During the 1970s and 1980s, these institutes were ardent critics of state intervention in the economy and society. The more progressive institutes emerged around a decade later to provide an intellectual counterweight.

Many of the ideological think tanks have strong sympathies with particular political parties but also maintain their distance. Increasingly, however, U.K. think tanks are affiliated with a political party, albeit not with the same strong formalized links that the Dutch and German institutes have with political parties. Think tanks with clear links to the Conservative Party include the Bow Group (1951) and the Conservative Policy Forum. New Labour-affiliated think tanks have emerged since the 1980s and include the Institute for Public Policy Research (IPPR, 1988), Catalyst (1998), the Smith Political Economy Unit (1996, now defunct), and the Foreign Policy Centre (1998). Nexus (1996, now defunct) has been described as a virtual think tank that brought together individuals from a range of organizations to debate the principles and priorities of the current government. The Social Market Foundation (1993) once had links with the former Liberal Party. Although such institutes are in tune with the needs of a particular political party, they also direct their activities to wider audiences in the media, bureaucracy, or business. Accordingly, it is best to describe them as politically affiliated rather than as political party think tanks.

A few of the new organizations (e.g., the Panos Institute and the Forum on Early Warning and Early Response [FEWER, 1996]) have characteristics and a campaigning style similar to those of interest groups. Other recent think-tank initiatives reflect the trends toward devolution and (EU) regionalism; examples in this vein include the reinvigorated Institute for Welsh Affairs (1987) and the short-lived Centre for European Reform (1996).

Many private think tanks undertake contract research. It is essential to an organization's survival, and the staff of many research institutes are often required to raise their own salary and to do so through contract work. Bodies such as the IFS, the NIESR, the ODI, the PSI, and the ASI all undertake a considerable amount of contract work for government departments as does the Family Policy Studies Centre (1983). However, in the context of U.K. political culture, it is difficult to classify such British think tanks as contract organizations. Although such funding is important, these institutes are also reliant on government grants and other forms of institutional support as well as corporate gifts, foundation grants, and public subscriptions. Contract research tends to be de-emphasized in favor of other organizational features such as policy research as a public good, to enlighten the educated public, or for political consumption.

INTEREST GROUPS, NGOS, AND PROFESSIONAL ASSOCIATIONS

The United Kingdom has a large population of interest groups, NGOs, advocacy organizations, professional associations, and other third-sector organizations that have developed an interest in policy. In the case of the largest organizations, internal research and policy analysis units have been established. Usually, this means only one or two individuals conducting policy research for an organization. In other cases, there has been significant investment in analytic capacity.

Trade unions, industry associations, and cause groups have increasingly recognized the power of policy knowledge. For example, in the first half of the 1980s when HIV/AIDS emerged, self-help groups formed in the absence of policy recognition of the problem. Bodies such as the Terrence Higgins Trust (THT), through its grass-roots activities, acquired considerable expertise in this policy field. As a new disease category, the AIDS policy community was relatively open to diverse groups interested in AIDS. AIDS policy lobbies grew around genito-urinary consultants and gay men who clustered around public health officials in the Department of Health. The biomedical gap, which was compounded by the lack of knowledge of the social and sexual activities that spread the disease, along with the evasiveness of the Thatcher government in responding to the problem, meant that local health authorities, gay support groups, medical professionals, and the Medical Research Council were the key actors. However, with the politicization of the issue in the late 1980s, the use of advice became more selective. Ministers deferred to professional medical advice and formalized advisory mechanisms with expert panels that increasingly marginalized HIV/AIDS support groups. Gay groups were not regarded as having the same stature and were not offering hard science but rather a mixture of psychology, sociology, and studies of social behavior. The Expert Advisory Group on AIDS was dominated by a certain type of knowledge, that is, clinical medicine. HIV/AIDS was defined as a medical problem, not as a social problem. Support groups were important in the early stages of advice and had some success in government lobbying from 1984. Once HIV/AIDS spread into the heterosexual community and became a wider health issue, policymaking became more centralized and elitist (Freeman 1992; Street and Weale 1992). Policy advice increasingly centered on the chief medical officer (CMO).[3] Consequently, this case suggests that the advisory influence of some interest groups can be time and issue contingent. In the late 1990s, however, the THT restructured to become the largest HIV/AIDS charity in Europe and in 1999 established a policy and research division. One of its first activities was to make a submission to the Special Standing Committee on the Immigration and Asylum Bill (http://www.tht.org.uk/).

By contrast, the Confederation of British Industry (CBI) is an established and recognized policy actor. The CBI, which engages in a considerable amount of policy work, claims its policy positions are "based on careful research, extensive consultation with members and continuous dialogue with and intelligence gathering in Whitehall departments and the European Commission" (www.cbi.org.uk/ndbs). Such position documents are primarily for the use of members and as a public expression of the CBI's general stance. However, such documents are of considerable use to the government in providing a business perspective.

Research departments have long been evident in trade unions (see Mutch 1999). Usually, trade union research departments focus on policy issues of relevance to the membership but in some cases unions take a wider remit. More important, the Trades Union Congress (TUC), as a leading association for the labor movement, has a long-established policy advisory capacity with a significant library in its main offices and, more recently, an extensive website that outlines its research-and-briefing activity (www.tuc.org.uk). For example, the TUC's views on the second round of the government's Comprehensive Spending Review for July 2000 can be found here along with its budget documents and reports from its Productivity and Partnership program.

To a greater extent than business groups and unions, many groups associated with broader social movements are connected to international networks. International environmental NGOs with branches in the United Kingdom generate policy analysis through both the international body and the local office. Friends of the Earth (FOE) is known as an NGO that initiates a number of environmental campaigns, but it also maintains an environmental data unit and provides research and policy development for decision makers. Indeed, the FOE claims to be the instigator of five acts of Parliament (www.foe.co.uk). Similarly, in a number of countries, Greenpeace employs people with political and business experience in its political and economic units (www.greenpeace.org).

Although professional associations are primarily concerned with the working interests of their members, a number of these associations, by virtue of the character of their membership, occasionally represent a source of alternative advice, especially the public-sector associations. For example, the Public Management and Policy Association (PMPA) draws together managers and policymakers from different disciplines of public service and provides a forum in which they can discuss public policy and management issues. The PMPA sponsors a number of events and programs with clear policy aims. Indeed, its broad mission is one that potentially enhances the operation of government, that is, to promote "joined-up" government across a fragmented public service where public service managers focus increasingly on specific professional or sectoral issues. The PMPA addresses the "big issues that affect the public services as a whole" (www.cipfa.org.uk/aims). Services, workshops, and publications are all geared to issues of direct interest to government operations. For instance, a workshop on institutional racism is one that aids governance and raises awareness and promotes norms of nondiscrimination. The Association of British Health-care Industries (ABHI) and the British Educational Research Association (BERA) are similar in seeking to disseminate their views to the state. By contrast, the Royal Economic Society (RES) is less forthright in this mission. One of the oldest economic associations in the world, the academic RES aims to "promote the encouragement of the study of economic science in academic life, government service, banking industry and public affairs" (www.res.org.uk/about). Its status as an APAO is probably the most tenuous of the organizations discussed here.

COMMERCIAL POLICY ADVICE

The business of policy advice is thriving in the United Kingdom. The so-called Thatcherite revolution of the 1980s that scaled back the reach of the state in society and the economy brought new advisory opportunities for the private sector. The new privatization policies required new thinking and practical advice on such matters as how to create and manage a stock flotation of a large public enterprise such as British Telecom. Indeed, one observer argues that, along with government departments, the City of London had far more impact on the shape of privatization in the United Kingdom (Heffernan 1996, 84) than the think tanks that first advocated privatization (Stone 2000).

Consultancies have been provided enormous opportunities by rapid changes in information technology, downsizing, and outsourcing. London Economic (now defunct), for example, claimed a strong capability in the analysis and design of economic incentives, applied in particular to regulatory and taxation systems. London Economics' understanding of policy issues had been tapped by public-sector institutions ranging from broadcasters and museums to transport businesses and environmental policymakers (www.londecon.co.uk). The large consultancies such as PriceWaterhouseCoopers, KPMG, and Andersen Consulting have government consulting divisions in their organizations that produce policy-relevant research, liaise with public servants, and advocate the adoption of a more managerial approach in government. With the advent of managerialism and its stress on exploiting the tools of financial management for efficient government, political executives and the senior officials of management consultancies have increasingly come in close contact with one another (Bakvis 1997; Saint-Martin 1999).

Intermediate Policy Advisory Organizations

APAOs that serve as intermediaries between the market and civil society on one hand, and the government on the other, are diverse and difficult to classify. Some, such as the Monetary Policy Committee (MPC) and the Royal commissions of inquiry, are close to the center of policymaking. Others, such as university policy research centers, are at considerable remove. Accordingly, this section starts with those bodies closest to and most dependent on the government and moves to the other extreme of bodies that could potentially be classified as market or societally based.

In mid-1998, the government gave the BoE operational responsibility for setting interest rates. The BoE's monetary policy objective is to deliver price stability (as defined by the government's inflation target). The key actor in this regard is the BoE's MPC (www.bankofengland.co.uk/mpc/). The MPC advises the governor of the BoE and the chancellor of the Exchequer on interest rate policy. The MPC's membership comprises the governor of the BoE, two deputy governors, two bank executive directors, and four full-time independent experts appointed by the chancellor. Although the government has certainly not privatized decision making, it can be argued that an important lever of macroeconomic policy is now one step removed with this development to enhance BoE independence.

RESEARCH COUNCILS AND ACADEMIA

The Economic and Social Research Council (ESRC) is a quasi-autonomous NGO (quango) that disperses research funding in the social sciences. Under its auspices, much policy research is undertaken. Indeed, a strong emphasis has emerged over the past decade and more of higher education reform to encourage greater relevance and interactions of universities and colleges with user groups in industry, government, and civil society. The mission of the ESRC is to "fund high quality research and training which meets the needs of users and enhances the UK's competitiveness, quality of life and the effectiveness of public services and policy" (www.esrc.ac.uk/themes). As a consequence, much research sponsored by the ESRC constitutes policy analysis of a direct or indirect nature.[4]

The ESRC's research centers and programs are good examples of such policy analysis. The Centre for the Study of Globalisation and Regionalisation at the University of Warwick is essentially a university-based quasi–think tank albeit with a more scholarly character than the private British think tanks. The Constitution Unit based at University College London is more private in character with a mix of

Leverhulme Foundation funding, ESRC support, and other grants. The Constitution Unit is an independent body composed primarily of lawyers and political scientists examining devolution and constitutional change in the United Kingdom. The unit issues press releases, organizes conferences and seminars for academics and civil servants, and provides experts for parliamentary testimony (see www .ucl.ac.uk/constitution-unit/). The recent changes to the U.K. constitutional architecture with devolution have created new opportunities for the unit and the legal fraternity more generally.

The new ESRC Future Governance program is more disaggregated in structure than the centers (which are based in one institution), setting up research projects and networks on a particular theme across the country, in this case, lesson-drawing and the potential for policy transfer (Stone 1999). The ESRC has just established an evidence-based policy initiative that will incorporate a national coordinating center for specialist research groups and will liaise with the Centre for Management and Policy Studies (CMPS). Other funding councils include the Biotechnology and Biological Sciences Research Council, the Medical Research Council, and the Biology and Biological Sciences Research Council, all of which have responsibility for providing analytical and research support to the government. Toward this end, the councils fund some policy evaluation and review.

Alternative Advice within Government

Where this section began with independent or private think tanks, it closes with this overview of the alternative advice landscape with some of their functional equivalents within government—that is, command papers, parliamentary committees, NDPBs, policy task forces, and the Policy Unit. Although these institutions are not independent of the government, they do exert some autonomy. A central rationale for creating these bodies was to draw inside government expert analysis from outside sources.

COMMAND PAPERS

Command paper is the collective name given to different types of papers prepared by the government and presented to Parliament. It includes some white papers, some green papers, reports of Royal commissions, and reports of some major committees of inquiry. These papers are presented to Parliament with the words "presented to Parliament by command of His/Her Majesty," hence the term *command papers*. Frequently, part of the process of gathering evidence and compiling reports involves drawing on the knowledge and recommendations of experts and other witnesses.

Theoretically, commissions of inquiry and other formal public inquiries operate with some degree of independence from the government. The reasons are several. Often an inquiry deals with a highly politicized issue where the conduct of the state is at issue and an internal inquiry would be deemed as lacking sufficient detachment and objectivity. One example is the Stephen Lawrence Inquiry, which investigated the brutal killing of a young black man by a gang of white youths, focusing specifically on police handling of the incident. In other circumstances, an investigative body is established to provide advice on a qualitatively new area of policy development where there has been, to date, relatively little state intervention or policy innovation. On other occasions, inquiries are initiated to question existing policy orthodoxy, recommend reforms, address potential new directions, or establish the future parameters of policy in a particular field of government activity that is languishing, under pressure, or presenting problems of management and policy implementation. Many such inquiries have been significant in marking new departures in policy and undertaking long-term planning.

On the latter score, the Royal Commission on the Reform of the House of Lords (2000) was established to make recommendations about the role, composition, and functions of the United Kingdom's second chamber, the House of Lords. Accordingly, its recently submitted report and recommendations are of relevance to the general theme of this chapter. One of its recommendations for the new second chamber was that "it should bring a range of different perspectives to bear on the development of public policy." To that extent, enhanced powers to scrutinize secondary legislation and EU business might allow the House to play more of a legislative support role. Similarly, the extent to which it provides a range of alternative advice is dependent on the composition of the House.

Commissions of inquiry are also used to address long-term policy concerns. They are considered useful for matters requiring partisan detachment and expert input. The use of Royal commissions of inquiry as a tool of policy analysis and reform depends on the character of the government in office. Under Margaret Thatcher during the 1980s, none were established. Both the Major and Blair governments have made greater use of this tool. These bodies may take a number of years to complete their investigations, and it is rare for more than two or three to report in a year. In most cases, these are temporary entities that are terminated once they have reported to Parliament.

PARLIAMENTARY COMMITTEES

Parliamentary select committees represent another device to draw in external sources of advice and expertise. Significant reforms were undertaken to the committee structure in 1979 not only to provide more effective scrutiny of government but also as a means of contributing to greater openness in government (House of Commons 1998). The committees are empowered to take evidence from ministers, parliamentarians, and civil servants. Although not a frequent occurrence, they can also call witnesses from the public when necessary. These committees have the power to insist on the attendance of witnesses as well as the authority to produce papers and other materials. The specific issue of inquiry, the external deadlines, and the extent of oral evidence determine whether an inquiry will last for several months leading to a report to the House or consist of a single day's oral evidence to be published without a formal report.

The select committees are mechanisms to ensure the accountability of ministers to Parliament. Accordingly, these committees are mostly composed of backbenchers. Support staff for the committees are provided by the House of Commons and usually include one or more clerks (with administrative and secretarial assistants). Full-time specialist assistants are usually appointed (House of Commons 1998). These committees have no direct budgetary or legislative powers.

Compared with U.S. legislative committees, the U.K. committee structure is poorly staffed and resourced. The reasons are interlinked. The first-past-the-post electoral system creates single-party majoritarian governments alternating between the two largest political parties—Labour and the Conservatives. Combined with strong political party discipline, the committees usually reflect the composition of the houses of Parliament and are thus dominated by the party in office. Their alternative advisory capacity is undermined to the extent that deliberations reflect party policy preferences. The intervention of the whips in committee membership weakens the independent influence of individual members of Parliament (MPs) and Lords vis-à-vis Cabinet ministers. As one observer notes, from government "there is a degree of resistance to investigations which may embarrass government as well as a general wish to resist extensions of select committee activities which may become disruptive to the work of departments" (Peele 1995, 174).

NONDEPARTMENTAL PUBLIC BODIES

Often known as quangos, there are four types of NDPBs: executive, advisory, tribunal, and boards of visitors. Advisory NDPBs are usually established by ministers to advise them and their staff on matters of concern to their portfolio. Some Royal commissions are categorized as advisory NDPBs. For example, the British Government Panel on Sustainable Development was established in 1994 to advise the government on strategic issues arising from the Sustainable Development Strategy and other post-Rio reports on climate change, biodiversity, and forestry. It is an advisory body consisting of a small group of individuals appointed on the basis of their "wide knowledge and practical experience" in the area. Sir Crispin Tickell is the convenor of the panel—an individual long associated with environmental think tanks. The panel is not a policy research unit itself and is "not expected to conduct analytical studies or write detailed reports, which would duplicate the detailed work of others, but draws upon the experience of these bodies and the detailed work of others" (www.open.gov.uk/panel-sd/panel/intro.htm). In other words, the panel is a mechanism to channel external sources of analysis into government when compiling government position papers as well as an expert body to monitor government progress in responding to recommendations. From February 2000, this panel was subsumed into the Sustainable Development Commission.

NDPBs are usually supported by staff from within the sponsoring department, that is, civil servants. NDPBs do not incur expenditures of their own account (Massey 1999, 12). The arm's-length relationship with government allows a considerable degree of autonomy. English Heritage, for example, is the U.K. government's official adviser in England on all matters concerning heritage conservation. Yet, it also has significant authority in other areas regarding the protection of historic sites. In general, concerns have been expressed regarding the exploding number of these organizations, including questions about their accountability and effectiveness. However, they can also be used as a mechanism for accountability.

Recently, the use of special advisers (also known as spin doctors) came to the attention of the Neill Committee on Standards in Public Life, which is an NDPB reporting to the prime minister. The Neill Committee was charged generally with the task of examining concerns about the standards of conduct of all holders of public office. As such, the work of the committee contributed to departmental efforts to ensure better government and high ethical standards within the civil service and NDPBs. Ministers appoint special advisers although they may only number one or two in each office. The Neill Committee recommended curbs on the use of these publicly funded spin doctors, expressing concern that they undermine the traditional neutrality of the civil service. Since the election of the Blair government in 1997, the number of advisers has doubled to seventy-four at a cost of £4 million (*Financial Times* 13 January 2000, 4). Power accrues to these nonelected individuals who are collectively said to undermine the roles and responsibilities of ministers' private offices and add impetus to the centralization of political control around the prime minister and the Cabinet. For example, the development of the Policy Unit has reflected a shift in core executive power dependencies. "Whereas in the past the Prime Minister was dependent on colleagues and Departments for advice and information, he or she now increasingly relies on advisers within the PM's Office" (Smith 1999, 173).

GOVERNMENT POLICY UNITS
The salience of long-term planning at the center of government has been enhanced by the establishment of bodies such as the Central Policy Review Staff (CPRS), which is widely known in Britain as *the* think tank. At the time of its

creation in 1971, the CPRS was considered an innovation in the machinery of government. However, it was preceded by other developments. During World War II, the crisis situation meant that alternative and additional advice could not be met entirely by the central government. Accordingly, a few private policy research organizations were brought inside the ambit of government. For example, the wartime mobilization of Chatham House saw one of its operational units, the Foreign Research and Press Service, transformed into the Foreign Office Research Department (FORD). Its contribution to the war effort was "the provision of raw material in the form of historical background studies and surveys of factors that might come to play a part in the future" (Thorne 1978, 9). Prior to World War II, the dividing line between Chatham House as a private organization and the official world was relatively clear. However, during the exceptional circumstances of war and the mobilization of propaganda and research organizations, Chatham House represented a valuable source of information and was drawn inside the ambit of government. The line between the private and governmental sectors was redrawn during the war and remained blurred immediately after the war with the consolidation of a strong relationship between Chatham House and the Foreign and Commonwealth Office (FCO). Today, the links are much weaker.

The CPRS was established as a small multidisciplinary staff within the Cabinet Office to provide advice to the Cabinet and then Conservative Prime Minister Ted Heath (Willetts 1987). Although a central government body, it was designed to draw in some external expertise. As a coordinating body with oversight of departmental activity, it challenged the authority of senior civil servants and ministers. However, one reason the CPRS was abolished in 1983 was because its long-term policy research interests and motivations clashed with the needs of the ministers and the Cabinet to respond to short-term political realities (Blackstone and Plowden 1988, 201). This appears to be a common fate for such entities in other countries as well (Andeweg 1999). External sources of advice are not subject to such pressures in the same degree. Similarly, the demise of the CPRS was partly due to the reforming zeal of the incoming Thatcher government. The press notice on the CPRS termination indicated the CPRS was no longer needed as the Cabinet had developed its own capacity for long-term analysis, the Cabinet Office Secretariat's role had been extended, and a policy unit had been expanded in the Prime Minster's Office (Blackstone and Plowden 1988, 180).

The Policy Unit, established shortly before the announcement of the closure of the CPRS, has better withstood the pressures from ministers and competing departments. It is far less part of the bureaucratic machinery given its formal attachment to the Prime Minister's Office at No. 10 Downing Street.[5] The role of the Policy Unit is to provide expert advice to the prime minister on policy issues and government-wide objectives. The Policy Unit contains a mix of civil servants and special advisers and is currently headed by David Miliband, who was previously based in the think-tank world. It is often regarded as more partisan than the CPRS and lacking the capacity to undertake the large-scale, long-term projects sometimes undertaken by the CPRS. Appointments to the Policy Unit are political and staff serve the prime minister. By contrast, the CPRS served the Cabinet as a whole.

A new development at the center of government is the formation of the CMPS in the Cabinet Office. The CMPS was established incorporating the Civil Service College and adding a strengthened capacity for corporate training and development of present and future leaders of the civil service. The CMPS also provides a knowledge and research management capability for No. 10 Downing Street and the wider civil service, accessing knowledge and lessons learned elsewhere in government. As it was only created in 1999, it is too early to discern its roles and functions. A former head of the ESRC, Ron Amman, is its first director.

Another priority of the current Labour government is to facilitate joined-up government—that is, to promote greater coordination across departments and agencies. For example, the Social Exclusion Unit was created in December 1997. Most of its work is based on specific projects, which the prime minister chooses following consultation with other ministers and suggestions from interested groups. The Social Exclusion Unit is staffed by a mixture of civil servants and external secondees. They come from a number of government departments and from organizations with experience in tackling social exclusion—the probation service, housing, the police, local authorities, the volunteer sector, and business. The Social Exclusion Unit reports directly to the prime minister and is located within the Cabinet Office. Other units attached to the Cabinet include the Women's Unit, the Policy Innovation Unit, and the Regulatory Impact Unit. Accordingly, these units cannot be considered APAOs in terms of their structural position and given the status of the Cabinet as a government department. Yet, these units occupy ambiguous territory at the center of government. In preparing reports, they draw extensively on research, external expertise, good practices, and promising ideas developed elsewhere. Members of the Social Exclusion Unit visit and consult widely with local authorities, business, the volunteer sector, other agencies, and people who have direct experience of social exclusion (http://www.cabinet-office.gov.uk/seu/index/march).

SUMMATION

Although largely illustrative, the above discussion reflects the great diversity of policy analysis, social research, and advocacy entrenched in U.K. political culture. Britain is characterized by all types of policy advisory organizations albeit with local features and peculiarities. There is a substantial population of think tanks—

university-like, advocacy-oriented, and those affiliated with political parties. NGOs and consultancy and professional associations sit uneasily with the APAO definition, but a greater balance is being given to policy research and advice in some of these organizations with the establishment of policy research units. Rather than blue-ribbon commissions, there are ad hoc commissions of inquiry and advisory NDPBs convened to address specific policy issues. Permanent advisory bodies are an established part of the U.K. bureaucratic structure with numerous expert panels and advisory committees attached to or coordinated by government departments. By comparison with U.S. legislative committees, U.K. parliamentary committees are weak, resource poor, and understaffed, a consequence of legislative support being provided by the civil service via government departments. Accordingly, central government review bodies in the Cabinet or attached to the Prime Minister's Office have played a more preeminent role. Instead of contract researchers in profit-making contract research organizations, resort to consultants (based in universities, law firms, think tanks, and consultancies) is the more apparent and wider phenomenon.

Policy Focus of U.K. Advisory Organizations in an Era of Globalization

It is difficult to generalize on the policy focus of the United Kingdom's various advisory organizations. To an extent, it is feasible to distinguish between single-issue organizations and those with a broad brief. For example, commissions of inquiry are created to address a specific issue. Similarly, there are single-issue think tanks such as the IFS. Of course, interest groups focus on their area of concern.

Most of the older think tanks in the United Kingdom—those created before the 1970s—have a relatively wide policy focus. Three decades ago, it would have been feasible to categorize many of these organizations as having either a domestic or an external (foreign policy/strategic/overseas development) focus. Today, globalization and regionalization have led to a more complicated equation. Institutes that once focused only on domestic questions of health, education, or fiscal policy are increasingly addressing issues such as the impact of transnational pension funds on the provision of care for the elderly, the export of education services, and international capital flows.

Some bodies acquire tasks as a consequence of the government ratifying international agreements. For example, the Women's National Commission (WNC) was given authority by the government in 1969 to represent the views of women in response to a resolution adopted by the UN Economic and Social Council. As an advisory NDPB, it has an official remit: to ensure by all possible means that the informed opinion of women is given due weight in the deliberations of government and in public debate on matters of public interest that may be considered of special interest to women. Where the WNC is less research based and more outward looking to the community, the Women's Unit is focused more on the central government. The unit coordinates work across departments, adding energy and momentum, and supporting ministers across Whitehall in its efforts to promote women's interests (http://www.cabinet-office.gov.uk/womens-unit/). Margaret Jay and Tessa Jowell provide ministerial representation for the Women's Unit. Their role is to ensure that the voices of women are heard throughout government, including the Cabinet and Parliament. One area of involvement of the Women's Unit was the introduction of the national minimum wage as this initiative benefited low-income workers, the majority of whom are women. The Women's Unit also undertakes and applies social research to social policy.

One of the most apparent developments over the past three decades following Britain's entry to the European Community has been much greater emphasis on the European dimension of policymaking. Virtually all policy advisory organizations have factored EU issues into their research agendas and have hired EU specialists in recognition of the impact of the EU on national policy. Indeed, there are a number of private institutes and government agencies with a specific EU remit. EU-wide policy communities have drawn experts and advisers beyond their national constituencies into wider policy domains such as the Common Agricultural Policy and around the European Commission (Sherrington 2000). New sources of advice are emanating through the EU whereby, in some circumstances, EU policy advice actors impinge on the British nation-state. For example, the Forward Studies Unit of the European Commission has as its primary objective to generate ideas for internal commission consumption but has gradually altered its focus over the past five years to engage with national policy communities in efforts to legitimize the European project. "Part of its original remit was to establish relations with other research institutes in member states. This has primarily developed informally, although *Carrefours* or symposiums are held, at which the Forward Studies Unit can exchange ideas with other research institutes, government and political parties, business and interest groups" (Sherrington 2000).

This transfer of ideas is not restricted to the EU. Through the International Public Service Unit (IPSU) attached to the Cabinet, advice is exported to other countries in what could be described as a policy transfer (Stone 1999). Established in 1996, the IPSU helps to promote and export U.K. expertise in public-sector reform and public administration. It does this by coordinating visits to the Cabinet Office for overseas guests and supporting a wide range of overseas projects, mainly on behalf of the Department for International Development and the British Council (www.official-documents.co.uk/document/cm42/4221/4221-02.htm). In general, globalization has implications for policy advisory organizations. Actors within the nation-state can be partnered with another set of actors in an alliance to influence government thinking and policy in more than one country. For example, the Institute for European Environmental Policy is a confederation of three autonomous institutes, one of which is based in London. Regional dynamics and globalization cannot be ignored. Such structural changes in the world's political economy have altered the evolutionary course of development of alternative sources of advice in many countries.

Staffing and Funding

The staff of a think tank, a university policy institute, or the research arm of an NGO or professional association are its strength. It is paramount that these organizations maintain financial stability and credibility so that the future career prospects of its staff are not endangered, hence triggering a flight of intellectual resources. In think tanks, university institutes, and NGOs, salary structures for policy researchers are reasonable but do not compare with the private sector or the benefits often attached to governmental research positions. Furthermore, it is unusual to find tenured research staff. Staff are generally attracted for reasons other than pecuniary reward. Often, they are committed to the values represented by the organization.

In the United Kingdom, the individuals attracted to think tanks are usually well-educated middle-class professionals. The in-house capacity of think tanks varies considerably. Although there are no think tanks as large as the Heritage Foundation or RAND Corp. in the United States, the older think tanks such as the NIESR, Chatham House, the IFS, and the IISS have a sizable in-house research capacity. Working for such institutes also has some status attached to it. The newer think tanks tend to be leaner. Some, such as the CEPR, function as a network institute with a strong base in Europe and a small permanent staff in London. Many institutes are reliant on volunteer labor in the absence of adequate funding. Some institutes are cross-subsidized by universities when academics undertake research work under the banner of an institute. NGOs are probably even more dependent on the research support of members and supporters in academe, the media, and government. By contrast, the large consultancies can attract economists and public-sector specialists with attractive salary packages.

In university policy research institutes, the minimum professional credential of staff is usually a doctorate. The size of these institutes varies significantly, sometimes padded by the number of associate researchers who are teaching faculty in the cognate departments of the university. The personnel of university policy institutes are more homogenous—academics. By contrast, think-tank staff or consultants usually come from more diverse backgrounds. The previous work experience of former senior public servants, international civil servants, or retired politicians is used to enhance the analytic skills of an institute or a firm. The phenomenon of people moving in and out of government into think tanks is known as the revolving door and, although less pronounced than in the United States (where the term originates), it remains apparent.

Professional associations are reliant on the volunteer efforts of their membership with only a small salaried executive staff to administer the association. However, a leading association such as the CBI has significant resources. The CBI has more than eighty policy professionals working on its committees (www.cbi.org.uk/ndbs). The credentials of staff in professional associations are usually closely related to professional experience. In the United Kingdom, degree inflation has meant that in most associations, staff members in executive and policy positions increasingly have graduate degrees. In trade unions also, researchers are usually postgraduates, sometimes with limited hands-on experience in the industry or trade that they represent. Professionalization among third-sector organizations generally has brought a ratcheting up of staff qualifications.

NDPBs are usually staffed by civil servants. For example, the WNC is supported in its work by a secretariat of staff who are civil servants seconded to serve the commission as an independent organization. About half of the staff of the Policy Unit at No. 10 Downing Street are civil servants on secondment. The remainder come from diverse backgrounds in business, academia, and think tanks or from a trade union, media, or political party background. In 1998–1999, the Prime Minister's Office had a staff complement of 123 at a cost of £8.5 million (http://www.official-documents.co.uk/document/cm42/4221/4221-02.htm). Few civil society APAOs can match such expenditure levels (table 1).

Depending on the individual concerned, the career structures of policy researchers of one organization can be intertwined with the interest group or NGO world, the university system, a political party, a consultancy, or the civil service. For example, the consultancy firm London Economics was established by a former IFS think-tank director and deputy director, two London School of Economics professors, and a former chief economist of the European Bank of Reconstruction and Development. Staff movements outlined in the 1999 KPMG annual report indicate that a former chairman of KPMG International, Colin Sharman, entered the House of Lords; the parliamentary adviser to the firm, Lord Bassem, was appointed parliamentary undersecretary of state at the Home Office; and a leading partner, Digby Jones, became director-general of the CBI (http://www.kpmg.co.uk/). The Policy Unit at No. 10 Downing Street under Blair overlaps considerably with the civil service and with Labour-affiliated think tanks. The same intermeshing with the think-tank world was true of the Policy Unit when the Conservatives were in power. An association such as the RES has a membership that overlaps significantly with university departments as well as think tanks and the civil service. Academics serve on parliamentary committees or the boards of NDPBs, usually in a part-time capacity. An increasingly frequent occurrence in the careers of advisers is some kind of international experience either within the EU, international NGOs, or international organizations such as the World Bank, the World Health Organization, or the United Nations. In short, there are many opportunities for individual advisers to become involved in policy communities and interact with ministers and bureaucrats, although some disdain such involvement where they are critical of or opposed to current policy.

The U.K. social research industry is relatively fragmented, and there is considerable difficulty in estimating turnover. The *Directory of Social Research Organisations in the United Kingdom* estimates as many as 20,000 individuals engage in social research as their primary activity with expenditures of £600 million per annum (Bulmer and Sykes 1998, 4). This chapter takes a much narrower perspective on policy research organizations with only a proportion of this sum being expended directly on analysis for governance. Commissions of inquiry and NDPBs are funded by the U.K. state. Some comparative data indicates that more than £350 million was spent in 1998–1999 on research commissioned by government departments (Strategic Policy Making Team 1999, para. 7.6).

Most university policy centers are state funded, although there is considerable pressure on the university system as a whole to generate additional private sources of funding. Increasingly, these institutes are able to recoup funds from major international foundations, through the EU, or via the private sector. As the privatization of U.K. higher education proceeds, the distinctions between private and publicly funded policy research become increasingly blurred. In 1999–2000, the ESRC awarded more than £63 million of grants to researchers and postgraduate students throughout the United Kingdom. The other six research councils have larger budgets. For example, the Natural Environment Research Council (NERC) uses a budget of about £220 million a year to fund scientific research in its own laboratories and in universities. About 2,700 people are employed in NERC establishments and a further 1,800 are funded annually through a variety of research and training awards in university departments and other outside bodies. The Engineering and Physical Sciences Research Council is the largest of these bodies. Most of the research funds are allocated for pure or basic research with only a small amount for policy research.

Funding sources for independent think tanks are usually more diverse than for the organizations above. Usually their funding is a mix of membership income (e.g., Chatham House, the Fabian Society, and the CPS), foundation grants, government research funds, corporate sponsorship, and earned income. Policy research institutes cannot rely on membership dues or sales of publications and services to cover operating costs. Philanthropy, corporate support, and government

Table 1. A Select Overview of Private Policy Advisory Organizations

	Established	Budget	Staff	Notes
Think tanks				
Centre for Economic Policy Research (CEPR)	1983	£2,373,000	27	
Centre for Policy Studies (CPS)	1974	£300,000	6 full-time, 2 part-time, 80 external	
Demos	1993	NA	12	
Family Policy Studies Centre (FPSC)	1983	£0.37 million total income	9	
Federal Trust	1945	NA	8+ research fellows	
Foreign Policy Centre (FPC)	1998	NA	9 full/part-time + external research associates	
Forum for the Future		£0.85 million income	4	
Forum for Early Warning and Early Response (FEWER)	1996	US$400,000*	6 (+ 3 overseas)	International body
Institute for Public Policy Research (IPPR)	1988	£1.24 million income	17	
Institute of Economic Affairs (IEA)	1955	£1.1 million	16	
Institute of Fiscal Studies (IFS)	1969	NA	30 researchers	
International Institute of Strategic Studies (IISS)	1958	£3.5 million	38	2,500 membership
National Institute of Economic and Social Research (NIESR)	1938	£1,696,000†	41	
Overseas Development Institute (ODI)	1960	£5.5 million*	50 research/directorate + support	
Panos Institute	1986	£1.79 million total income		
Royal Institute of International Affairs (RIIA)	1920	£3.5 million*	70	a.k.a. Chatham House
Royal United Services Institute for Defence Studies (RUSI)	1831	£2 million	22+ part-time	Based in Whitehall
Foundations				
Esmee Fairbairn	1961	£652million in funds	13	
Joseph Rowntree	1904	£6 million in grants		

Nuffield	1943	£5.2 million in grants		Medical charity
Wellcome	1936	£600 million in grants		
Consultancies				
KPMG	1987	£1,037.8 in fees*		Merger in 1987
London Economics	1986	NA	NA	NA
Research Councils/Academic				
Centre for the Study of Globalisation and Regionalisation (CSGR)	1996	£386,106	12 full-time + associates	
Constitution Unit	1995	NA	10 permanent	
Future Governance	1999	£3.53 million over 5 years	30 projects	
Institute of Development Studies (IDS)	1966	NA	48	University of Sussex
Medical Research Council (MRC)	1913	£470 million†		Scientific research
Policy Studies Institute (PSI)	1979	£2 million*	30	University of Westminster
Learned Societies & Professional Associations				
Association of British Health-care Industries (ABHI)	1989	£756,000*	13	
British Educational Research Association (BERA)	1974	£50,000	1	
Public Management and Policy Association (PMPA)	1998	NA	NA	Managed by CIPFA
Royal Economic Society (RES)	1890	NA	NA	3,300 members
Social Policy Association (SPA)	1971	NA	Voluntary	
Interest Groups & Nongovernmental Organizations				
Confederation of British Industry (CBI)	1965	NA	260 (200 in London)	
Greenpeace	1977	£4.5 million	70 full-time	
Trade Union Congress (TUC)	1868	£13,741,000	200	6.7 million members
Friends of the Earth (FOE)	1971	£0.35 million total funds	36	80% funds from individuals

Sources: Charities Information Direct accessed at <http://www.caritasdata.co.uk/home.htm>. Websites and e-mail queries.

Note: Data is for 1998–1999 unless indicated otherwise. Figures are approximate.

CIPFA: Chartered Institute of Public Finance and Accountancy.

* 1999–2000
† 1997–1998
‡ 1996–1997

contracts are essential to their survival. Large donations from individuals are rare and think-tank directors generally bemoan the lack of a strong philanthropic tradition in the United Kingdom. Nevertheless, most think tanks (aside from the CPS, the New Policy Institute, and the Fabian Society) are registered charities. As such, they benefit minimally from indirect taxpayer contributions. Few think tanks have an endowment. However, ownership of facilities provides long-term security for an institute as well as cultivating an image of stability and security. It tends to be the older institutes that possess land and buildings, whereas the newer institutes occupy leased offices. Both the Fabian Society and Chatham House generate revenue from rent. However, Chatham House, a building listed by the National Trust, involves considerable sums in upkeep and modernization.

Taking a long-term perspective, the pattern of funding has changed. The funding and provision of policy advice and research is less dominated by the U.K. state. The ethos of the new public management (NPM) and the trend toward outsourcing has allowed alternative organizations to benefit and to dilute the elitist and centralized character of U.K. decision making. The culture has changed. Consultancy work has a greater degree of legitimacy than in the past. The changing balance between local and central government and the policy functions of NDPBs have meant that sources of advice are increasingly decentralized and often outsourced to independent bodies. The corporate sector is more willing to fund alternative sources of advice, and, to a limited extent, changes to charity law in the past twenty years have given a little impetus to the funding of policy research. Over the past thirty years, more EU funding has become available.

Despite the fluctuations of funding and uncertainties in the policy environment brought on by electoral cycles, international developments, and reform initiatives, APAOs are tenacious organizations. Although some think tanks have closed or merged to form a new entity, many more have been born alongside NGOs with stronger research capacities. Institutional mortality among civil society and market APAOs is evident but not overwhelming. Instead, a number of other developments are notable. The dormancy of an organization is one phenomenon. Reinvention (as opposed to closure) is another in a few bodies that have seen weak leadership, declining membership, or dwindling support. For example, the PSI was formed through a merger of two institutes, but in the 1990s it encountered funding difficulties and was merged into a university as a research body with considerable autonomy. Similarly, mergers of consultancies have taken place. Among intermediate and government APAOs, organizational mortality is also evident alongside institutional innovation. Commissions of inquiry, for example, are usually established as temporary bodies. Although the CPRS was shut down, new specialized units are now doing similar work in the orbit of the

Cabinet. Notably, the growth of APAOs in civil society and the marketplace has been complemented by similar growth within government.

Conduits of Advice

In policy advice delivery, the product mix differs according to the particular actor and sometimes the policy field or issue. Professional associations, think tanks, and pressure groups use media such as newsletters, journals, workshops, and annual conferences to broadcast their message as well as delegations and public campaigns to spread ideas. Websites have become an increasingly important device for providing information. Ministers and MPs are lobbied by interest groups, lobbyists, consultants, and professional associations. Charitable organizations are prevented by their legal status from engaging in public advocacy on anything other than issues directly associated with their mission. In any case, think tanks and university centers usually disdain such activity. There are many routes to make policy advice publicly accessible. However, ensuring that such analysis or advice reaches those with decision-making authority and, furthermore, that the advice is actually used, is a far more difficult task to achieve and equally difficult to demonstrate.

Formal structures such as parliamentary committees and inquiries represent institutional targets for advisory bodies external to government. Yet, the parliamentary committees are not a means of access to decision makers or a guarantee of influence as they are subject to political party controls in their deliberations. Furthermore, the route of access is top-down; expert advice is invited. In the case of inquiries, sometimes a green paper is first produced as a discussion document prior to a final document, the white paper, which outlines or recommends new directions in government policy. Inquiries invite submissions of written evidence and sometimes receive other submissions from interested parties and experts as well as convene public hearings.

Commissions of inquiry have an automatic route of bureaucratic and political access in that they are usually required to submit a report to Parliament and, as part of the state apparatus, can take advantage of access to resources and personnel. In instances where an inquiry takes years to undertake its investigation, the advice sought from relevant parties in the public domain may well be out of date. This is especially the case when an election ushers in a new political party. A further problem with inquiries is that they are frequently restricted by their terms of reference. Rarely do they have the power to enact decisions or implement their recommendations. Instead, they report to Parliament and are dependent on Parliament to institute new legislation or reform existing policy programs. For a variety of political reasons, governments frequently choose to ignore the findings of an inquiry, water down the recommendations, or, yet again, delay in responding to the findings. However, for all their flaws, these permanent and ad hoc inquiries and NDPBs are important parts of the machinery of state for drawing in public, professional, and expert perspectives on specific policy issues or matters of public concern. Although many external actors seek additional informal routes of policy access and sometimes bypass the institutional mechanisms of policy analysis, inquiries, parliamentary committees, and other policy review structures have an important role as a form of public symbolism indicating that the government is addressing a policy matter seriously. Accordingly, these external actors often attract considerable media attention.

Consultancies, law firms, or other commercial enterprises that have been contracted by central or local governments to review some aspect of policy have a clear route of access to decision makers and will consult with the contracting agency as necessary prior to submission of their final product. A number of organizations have established relationships with the U.K. government. The CBI, for example, claims "unparalleled access to decision-makers in Whitehall, Westminster and Brussels." As is well known in business, academic, and bureaucratic circles, the CBI is often consulted informally before the government drafts new legislation (www.cbi.org.uk/ndbs). Through its pole position as a representative body for business, the CBI cannot be ignored by any U.K. government. In general, however, relevant interest groups and associations are incorporated into policy discussions through numerous departmental committees and panels.

Academic institutes are more often focused on workshops, conferences, and the publication of books or scholarly articles to disseminate policy-relevant ideas. The current structure of incentives imposed by the Research Assessment Exercise (RAE)—the government-sponsored evaluation by discipline of university research capacity and quality—as well as the norms and standards of excellence in the social science disciplines, means that university policy research has a strong scholarly character. In many cases, it will not be of immediate policy relevance (*Times Higher Education Supplement* 17 December 1999, 17). Furthermore, such institutes are pulled in the direction of teaching priorities and in general are less well structured (in the absence of public affairs offices) to promote policy research and propel ideas into policy. Even so, a respectable number of individuals associated with such institutes are well connected to political and bureaucratic actors and are increasingly co-opted into policy deliberations.

Think tanks fall between the university approach and the more commercial approach of law firms and consultancies. The location of private-sector think tanks is markedly different to that of university policy institutes. Whereas university institutes are geographically dispersed throughout the United Kingdom, the vast majority of think tanks and consultancies are in London. Moreover, many of the think tanks are concentrated in the Division Bell area of Westminster. This positioning suggests that proximity to the centers of power is important in pressing forward policy recommendations. Furthermore, the annual conference of the London School of Economics in conjunction with the *New Statesman*—which is structured to cater to the needs of policymakers—is timed to launch the political season. It is one public forum that convenes the U.K. policy communities.[6]

IMPACT OF ALTERNATIVE SOURCES OF POLICY ADVICE

Determining the relevance, impact, or influence of alternative sources of advice can be a subjective exercise. The criteria or indicators are multiple. An organization may have huge impact with the media but little or no input into policy development. There is much anecdotal evidence about the input of individual organizations into U.K. policymaking. However, even though, for example, Margaret Thatcher was known to read think-tank pamphlets late at night (Hames and Feasey 1993, 234) and Tony Blair patronizes academics and think tanks, it cannot be proved that think-tank policy recommendations thereby percolated into actual policy. Consulting alternative sources of policy advice does not mean that advice will be incorporated in decision making. Furthermore, in those instances where ideas or policy recommendations from outside government are seriously considered, they are invariably modified and adapted by internal bureaucratic dynamics and other political considerations.

Long-term policy impact is equally difficult to prove. Changing the climate of opinion or shaping public thinking cannot be attributed to one set of organizations. Nevertheless, the free market think tanks are frequently identified as a key source of ideas and thinking that helped undermine the Keynesian policy paradigm. Another set of think tanks, in conjunction with some of the United Kingdom's leading social scientists in universities, is now credited with helping to outline the parameters of the third way (Giddens 1998). This is in tandem with the Blair government's patronage of the concept.

Independent think tanks have some short- to medium-term impact on government in that they have become a stepping stone in the careers of a number of actors now inside government. The trajectories of David Miliband and Geoff Mulgan are cases in point. Miliband was a founder of the IPPR and spent a number of years there before becoming the director of the Policy Unit at No. 10 Downing Street. Mulgan was the cofounder of Demos and, like Miliband, moved to the Policy Unit after the Labour Party acquired office. From mid-2000, Mulgan began directing the Policy Innovation Unit of the Cabinet Office. Similarly, David Willetts was director of studies at the CPS in the late 1980s and early 1990s before his election as a Conservative MP. Likewise, Graeme Mather was director of the IEA before establishing a new think tank, the European Policy Forum, and becoming a Euro-MP. The young graduates in the circle of the Foreign Policy Centre are said to be Labour Party wannabes. In other words, think tanks and other civil society APAOs can serve as political training grounds, grooming emerging political leaders in policy debates prior to an opportunity arising for them to move into the formal political sphere.

Like think tanks, the policy analyses of trade unions, business associations, and NGOs are recognized as having a valid place in the public debate of policy issues. Although both the CBI and the TUC were drawn directly into policymaking under Conservative and Labour governments in the 1960s and 1970s, this corporatist link was dissolved during the Thatcher and Major years. Nevertheless, there is a range of permanent advisory committees to advise the civil service with expert information. No government can afford to ignore such interests, yet rather than a tripartite arrangement structuring the flow of information into government, more fluid arrangements of policy communities exist bringing in more diverse sources of advice. In decision making, however, these organizations confront a competitive environment of ideas and proposals. Sometimes political leaders clearly favor one perspective or group and at other times ignore or give lip service to the value of alternative policy perspectives. The influence of trade unions in policy has declined over the past three decades: They have neither the power once institutionalized within the Labour Party nor the power they once wielded over the economy. NGOs (especially those with international recognition) and think tanks, by contrast, have become more noticeable in the public eye as a result of their policy advocacy or campaigns in terms of political patronage and in the amount of scholarly attention they receive. Unlike consultancies, these groups have media impact—think-tank experts and NGO executives are frequently called on by journalists for expert commentary—and to that extent could be said to help shape the climate of opinion.

The impact of external APAOs in the United Kingdom is multidimensional, competitive, and in constant flux. There are no fixed points of policy impact. The influence of any set of organizations is not constant; rather, it ebbs and flows for individual bodies as well as their counterpart organizations. The rising political status of think tanks and NGOs is possibly a reflection of the malaise and declining membership in the trade union movement and political parties. Individuals are redirecting their energy and talent through new institutional arrangements. Greater use of private policy advisory organizations—think tanks, consultancies, and contract researchers in universities—is also symptomatic of the broader NPM movement and a culture of privatization.

APAOs inside government arguably have much greater impact. Those in the Policy Unit have the ear of the prime minister. The recommendations of Royal commissions are often the precursors of legislative changes. Various other units and commissions in the orbit of the Cabinet are predominantly staffed and supported by civil servants who have a clear route of access to the Prime Minister's Office.

ENVIRONMENTAL AND ORGANIZATIONAL CONSTRAINTS ON ALTERNATIVE POLICY ADVICE

A well-known argument about parliamentary systems is that they are portrayed as closed compared with the U.S. presidential system. Claims of the decline of Parliament and the concentration of power with the prime minister, the Cabinet, and the bureaucracy are said to insulate policymaking from outside influences. The convention of collective ministerial responsibility and an ethos of officialdom compound the insularity of policymaking creating a "predisposition for secrecy."

Politicians often do not have the time or the inclination to think beyond the next election. They are driven by immediate political concerns in "a 'pressure cooker' environment" (Seymour-Ure 1987, 177). Incorporating long-term policy analysis in the political process is problematic. Furthermore, there are multiple sources of policy advice competing for the attention of the prime minister and ministers. Departmental policy advice, advice from the Cabinet Office, political party advice, political advice from policy units, the recommendations of parliamentary committees, and outside advice are all potentially conflicting sources of advice. A report of the Cabinet Office Strategic Policy Making Team identifies a further set of constraints: "There is a danger of 'overload' compounded by a shortage of people with the skills needed to act as an 'intelligent customer' for research and to understand or interpret available information." The team identifies two issues in need of attention: "the need to improve [a] department's capacity to make [the] best use of evidence; and the need to improve the accessibility of the evidence available to policy makers" (1999, paras. 7.9-7.10).

The favored source of advice is subject to a variety of factors such as a leader's personal preferences and the avenues of access to that leader (Weller 1987). Governments can also be characterized by "closed advice circuits," whereby advisers and decision makers share values and policy approaches that effectively exclude alternatives from consideration. While Thatcher was in office, access to government was relatively closed. Thatcher was dismissive of the "chattering classes" in universities and intellectual circles. Her personal style of leadership was to rely on those who shared her values. Under John Major, access was opened to a greater extent to consult the interests of relevant parties (Holliday 1993). The Blair Labour government has also maintained channels of communication although there are clearly different preferences for think tanks, academics, and other advisory organizations than those favored by Conservative governments.

Too much info

There are systemic difficulties faced by alternative advisory organizations in their interaction with government that limit their potential for influence. As some question and challenge policy orthodoxy, they can be politically and bureaucratically dysfunctional. By elaborating on policy options, increasing the number of alternatives, and outlining possible problems, these policy research bodies potentially overwhelm the collective decision-making processes, disrupt established programs, undermine consensus, and question the legitimacy of a government's chosen policy. They provide the rhetorical weapons for opposition groups. Identifying flaws in policies or promoting superior policy design does not endear these organizations to politicians or bureaucrats.

In addition to the external political culture, other constraints are found within APAOs themselves. University policy centers are geared to more scholarly pursuits. Often, the product is not in a usable format for decision makers or is not effectively communicated to the relevant policy actors. Nexus hoped to facilitate the influence of a network of academic-based policy thinking representing center-left political thought. It failed due to financial constraints; the perception of too-close links to new Labour, which frightened off some academic support; and, ironically, the lack of political access and communication with the new government (*Times Higher Education Supplement* 17 December 1999, 17). Consultancies are sometimes regarded as profit-oriented organizations that will tailor a report to suit the fee. They lack credibility and the scholarly authority sometimes associated with academic experts and think tanks. A number of smaller organizations lack authority and status as policy advice organizations either because they are recently established, have adopted inappropriate marketing or advocacy approaches, or lack the organizational skills to effectively target policymakers. Internal feuding, funding crises, or other disruptions also undermine policy relevance. For example, the current dilemmas of Chatham House have seriously tarnished the reputation of this establishment body within foreign policy circles.[7] Issues of sustainability are crucial to the capacity for policy impact.

The changing culture of U.K. public administration wrought by the NPM provides improved prospects for some organizations of access to more funding through contract research. However, bodies that are truly external to the governmental structure—independent think tanks, university centers, pressure groups—face considerable structural constraints to policy influence. Only a few find the opportunity to represent their ideas by participating in consultative exercises. Royal commissions, advisory NDPBs, and parliamentary committees have more promising routes of influencing policy. It is those bodies closest to the Cabinet that are most likely to have the greatest bearing on decision making, but it is difficult to categorize them as APAOs as they are at the core of government.

PROSPECTS

Compared with the U.S. system, the British constitutional architecture does not provide as wide a range of points of access for alternative sources of public policy advice. This does not mean that the structure of the British government presents an impenetrable exterior to outside sources of advice. Royal commissions and discussion papers have increased opportunities and demand for policy analysis in the past. Although the partial revivification of the committee system in Parliament has not presented a strong source of demand for external advice and analysis, the political culture of the United Kingdom is such that, for purposes of political legitimacy, governments must consult with societal actors. As the number of research institutes grows, university centers become more policy oriented, and as the research units of interest groups become more professional, the decision makers in bureaucracies and political parties become more conscious of, and open toward, them. Of relevance is the current rhetoric of the incumbent Labour government. The concept of a third way involves steering a course between the state and market ideas of organization and incorporating greater involvement of societal actors in the delivery of public goods. This implies an engagement with alternative sources of policy advice. However, the gradual opening to such advice began much earlier with the Thatcher government's reforms to the civil service.

The ethos of the NPM has meant that purchasing policy advice outside government is a more frequent occurrence (Boston 1994). The NPM is a term associated with a policy discourse and a set of practices concerning privatization, outsourcing, making government more businesslike, economic rationalism, managerialism, and a move away from the provision of public services by a single provider in favor of competitive, multiple provider structures. The NPM has encouraged the growth of quangos, whereas programs such as the Private Finance Initiative have brought the private sector into public-sector projects. This mix represents a change in the character of U.K. governance—from process, with the civil service monopolizing the advice, to output, whereby policy analysis and advice can be sought more widely.

Of considerable importance is the so-called hollowing out of the U.K. state with a transferring of functions to the EU, a fragmentation of central government under the NPM, and the increasing involvement of new actors in policy formulation that undermines the capacity of the central government to steer the system. This concept suggests that the capacity and coherence of core agencies and actors of the executive (e.g., the Cabinet; key departments such as Treasury, Trade, and Industry; senior civil servants) are being eroded, thereby adding to the complexity of government. Three tendencies are in play: The core executive is losing or conceding its capacity (1) to societal actors, (2) to other state agencies, and

(3) to suprastate entities (Saward 1997, 20). If this theory is accepted, then the opportunities for alternative providers of policy research, analysis, and advice have improved and will likely continue to improve in the United Kingdom. Privatization has fundamentally altered the structure and functions of the state with both private entities and new regulatory bodies outsourcing or generating their own policy analysis.[8] The emasculation of local government under Conservative governments was paralleled by the creation of alternative local agencies (quangos) to deliver policy. In particular, the creation of Next Steps executive agencies, which remain a part of government departments but are hived off from policy formulation and evaluation to be delegated to undertake specific tasks, separated implementation from core policymaking departments. This decentralization, along with the more recent development of devolution, creates additional institutional arenas of governance within the United Kingdom. Whether one agrees that hollowing out is occurring or that the state is being reshaped and redesigned, these transformations improve the prospects for alternative providers of advice.

Although the institutional architecture, the dominance of the civil service as a source of policy advice, and the strength of political party discipline suggest that the British policymaking system is closed, this chapter highlights the informal dimensions of policy formulation. In practice, there has long been a strong tendency to include societal groups in decision making through informal policy communities (Rhodes 1997). The policy community concept refers to all actors or potential actors from both inside and outside government who share a common policy focus and who, over time, succeed in shaping policy.[9] These communities are said to emerge and consolidate around specific policy fields or subsystems such as education, tax, or security policy and revolve around relevant institutions such as specific ministries or government agencies. In the United Kingdom, policy communities have consolidated. APAOs external to government will likely be accorded insider status if they share the central values and attitudes of the policy community. They have important information and analytic resources to exchange with other participants in a policy community. A mixed economy of policy advice has become the norm. This does not mean that policy communities are open to the public. Indeed, there are valid questions and concerns regarding the accountability of such arrangements for they undermine political responsibility by excluding public scrutiny and participation. Nevertheless, although the U.K. bureaucracy remains the dominant provider of policy analysis, the legitimacy of external sources of advice is not questioned but explicitly recognized as representative of stakeholders. Moreover, the development of policy units and new research capacity is not to be viewed as a dynamic that will squeeze out or marginalize intermediate and civil society APAOs. Capacity at the center, as well as within government departments, is needed to absorb the alternative policy research. Expansion of the idea that policymakers are intelligent customers for policy research augurs well for British APAOs.

Finally, globalization and regionalization have created opportunity structures for transnational policy communities. This trend is especially apparent at the EU level. With international treaties and regimes, systems of international reporting and monitoring by expert bodies have been instituted. The requirement for transparency advocated by many international organizations has improved access to information and data, further expanding opportunities for advisory organizations, which also find themselves in demand as evaluators of transparency.

RECOMMENDATIONS AND CONCLUSION

The general recommendation that emerges from this overview is the need for APAOs to be sensitive to multilevel forms of governance, the multisectoral implications of policy, and the multiple sources of advice. First, much policy in the United Kingdom is now made with reference to the EU. APAOs with EU expertise could contribute to the good governance of the United Kingdom not only through the research and monitoring of EU-wide developments but also through the collaborative arrangements and relationships they build with counterpart institutes on the continent. In this regard, there is considerable potential for cross-national lessons. Second, centers of alternative advice outside government may need to better accommodate the constraints on bureaucrats and politicians in absorbing alternative sources of research, evidence, and advice. Government may not always be able to determine the quality of competing sources of alternative advice particularly when there is a cacophony of conflicting advice. In such circumstances, a ministry or the Cabinet may default to trusted sources close at hand rather than to what may be the best available range of advice. Accordingly, where there is such intense competition to gain the attention of Cabinet ministers, key political advisers, and senior civil servants, the reputation for sound analysis and relevant solid policy research will be important in creating or sustaining a route of expert access to government.

The industry for alternative policy advice is thriving in the United Kingdom. Accordingly, there is competition and clamor for political attention from outside the formal policy process. One recommendation for APAOs outside government would be for less growth of new think tanks and more consolidation of existing organizations alongside new collaborative arrangements. In particular, developing a solid reputation for quality analysis founded on rigorous standards is necessary to maintaining a good working relationship with government. Sloppy or substandard policy research not only undermines individual organizations but also detracts from the reputation of other organizations. This is not to suggest that there is no political space for new institutes, but rather that new development should be aimed at providing quality policy research and ideas rather than as a vehicle for the career aspirations of new generations of policy entrepreneurs. One noteworthy development is the extent to which extant organizations develop new kinds of relationships—partnerships with the state and with international organizations as well as alliances and networks with other nonstate actors in the policy advice business.

Alliances and partnerships, often through policy communities, represent a well-trodden avenue of policy relevance and impact for organizations inside and outside government. Different levels of governance and policy sectors are connected by networks. "As British government creates agencies, by-passes local government, uses special purpose bodies to deliver services and encourages public-private partnerships, so networks become increasingly prominent among British governing structures" (Rhodes 1996, 658).

APAOs function in this context. In the future, governance will increasingly be about managing networks. This sentiment is reflected in the current Labour government's concerns about coordination and its rhetoric on joined-up government. APAOs that provide advice on coordination across departments and policy sectors, that have professional and policy research links with counterparts in international organizations and with other EU members, and that can traverse networks to pull together the best information on overall government priorities have the necessary capabilities to advise government. It is within this context that the diverse and abundant ecology of APAOs will become a key feature in effective governance.

NOTES

1. A recent survey of social research identified ten main sectors of social research: central government, quangos (or NDPBs), consultancies, health authorities and trusts, higher education, independent institutes, local government, market research, professional associations and trade unions, and volunteer organizations and charities (Bulmer and Sykes 1998).

2. Links to think tanks not discussed here can be found at <http://www.keele.ac.uk/depts/por/ukbase.htm#parliament>.

3. The CMO, which is under the Department of Health, is the government's principal medical adviser and head of the Medical Civil Service. The CMO is the professional head of all medical staff, with responsibilities in the Department of Health and the National Health Service Executive. The CMO also provides medical advice to other parts of the government. The CMO is positioned to provide medical advice on the widest possible range of matters affecting the nation's health and, as such, has direct access to ministers in all departments.

4. A historical analysis of the ESRC's predecessor, the Social Science Research Council created in 1965, suggests that the link between social research and its uses for societal planning have been a key to the public funding of research in the postwar era (see King 1997).

5. The Prime Minister's Office is the prime minister's private office handling the entire management of No. 10 Downing Street. It consists of a private office, a section for appointments and honors, the Policy Unit, a press office, and a political office that manages relations between No. 10 and the party of the government.

6. This conference is designed for those who "make, influence or implement policy." Its target audience is business leaders, economists, corporate affairs directors, local authority leaders, government relations directors, public relations offices, public-sector managers, research staff, councillors, city analysts, regulators, banks and finance organizations, trade associations, civil servants, think tanks, policy advisers, members of public bodies, trade unions, volunteer organizations, campaign organizations, embassies, academics, and members of the press.

7. A new director was appointed in 1998 and again in 2001 to turn Chatham House around. However, Chatham House has been riven by internal feuding, low staff morale, and high-level dismissals that have seriously undermined organizational effectiveness.

8. These bodies include Ofgem (Office of Gas and Electricity Marketing), Ofwat (Office of Water Services), Oftel (Office of Telecommunications), and Ofrail (Office of the Rail Regulator). These are government departments that are independent of ministerial control. Aside from regulating their relevant industries, they advise the government on industry developments. For example, Ofwat plays an important role in monitoring EU directives and regulations on environmental and drinking water and advising the government on compliance.

9. The policy community framework was developed in the U.K. and European context. The American idea of iron triangles—closed, exclusionary, and tight networks of sectoral policymaking—has generally been regarded as inappropriate in the U.K. context.

BIBLIOGRAPHY

Andeweg, Rudy B. 1999. "Advising Prime Ministers." *Public Money and Management* April–June: 13–17.

Bakvis, Herman. 1997. "Advising the Executive: Think Tanks, Consultants, Political Staff and Kitchen Cabinets." In Patrick Moray Weller, Herman Bakvis, and R. A.W. Rhodes, eds. *The Hollow Crown: Countervailing Trends in Core Executives.* London: Macmillan.

Blackstone, T., and William Plowden. 1988. *Inside the Think Tank: Advising the Cabinet 1971–1983.* London: Heinemann.

Boston, Jonathon. 1994. "Purchasing Policy Advice: The Limits to Contracting Out." *Governance* 7(1): 1–30.

Bulmer, Martin, and Wendy Sykes. 1998. "Introduction: The Present State of Professional Social Research in the United Kingdom." In Martin Bulmer, Wendy Sykes, and Jaqui Moorhouse, eds. *Directory of Social Research Organisations in the United Kingdom,* 2nd ed. London and New York: Mansell.

Common, Richard. 1996. "The Epidemiology of Public Policy: Accounting for the Spread of the New Public Management." Paper presented at the Conference on Policy Transfer, University of Birmingham, October.

Day, Alan. 2000. "Think Tanks in Western Europe." In James G. McGann and R. Kent Weaver, eds. *Think Tanks and Civil Societies: Catalysts for Ideas and Action*. New Brunswick, N.J.: Transaction.

Freeman, Richard. 1992. "The Politics of AIDS in Britain and Germany." In P. Aggleton, P. Davies, and G. Hart, eds. *AIDS: Rights, Risk and Reason*. London: Falmer Press.

Giddens, Anthony. 1998. *The Third Way: The Renewal of Social Democracy*. Cambridge, U.K.: Polity Press.

Hames, Tim, and Richard Feasey. 1993. "Anglo-American Think Tanks Under Reagan and Thatcher." In Andrew Adonis and Tim Hames, eds. *A Conservative Revolution: The Reagan-Thatcher Decade in Perspective*. Manchester, U.K.: Manchester University Press.

Heffernan, Richard. 1996. "'Blueprint for a Revolution'? The Politics of the Adam Smith Institute." *Contemporary British History* 10 (Spring): 73–87.

Holliday, Ian. 1993. "Organised Interests after Thatcher." In Patrick Dunleavy, Andrew Gamble, Ian Holliday, and Gillian Peele, eds. *Developments in British Politics*. London: Macmillan.

House of Commons. 1998. "The Post-1979 Departmental Select Committee Structure." House of Commons Library Research Papers No. 6 (revised July 1998). London: House of Commons.

King, Des. 1997. "Creating a Funding Regime for Social Research in Britain: The Heyworth Committee on Social Studies and the Founding of the Social Science Research Council." *Minerva* (35): 1–26.

Massey, A. 1997. "Management, Politics and Non-Departmental Public Bodies." *Public Money and Management* 17(2): 21–25.

——— . 1999. *The State of Britain: A Guide to the UK Public Sector*. London: Public Management and Policy Association.

Mutch, A. 1999. "Unions and Information, Britain 1900–1960: An Essay in the History of Information." *International Review of Social History* 44: 395–417.

Peele, Gillian. 1995. *Governing the UK*. Oxford, U.K.: Basil Blackwell.

Rhodes, R. A.W. 1996. "The New Governance: Governing Without Government." *Political Studies* 44(4): 652–667.

——— . 1997. "Foreword." In Walter J. M. Kickert, Erik-Hans Klijn, and Joop F. M. Koppenjan, eds. *Managing Complex Networks: Strategies for the Public Sector*. London: Sage Ltd.

Royal Commission on the Reform of the House of Lords. 2000. *A House for the Future: A Summary*. London: HMSO.

Saint-Martin, Denis. 1999. "The New Managerialism and the Policy Influence of Consultants in Government: An Historical-Institutionalist Analysis of Britain, Canada and France." *Governance: An International Journal of Policy and Administration* 11(3): 319–356.

Saward, Michael. 1997. "In Search of the Hollow Crown." In Patrick Moray Weller, Herman Bakvis, and R. A.W. Rhodes, eds. *The Hollow Crown: Countervailing Trends in Core Executives*. London: Macmillan.

Seymour-Ure, Colin. 1987. "Institutionalization and Informality in Advisory Systems." In

William Plowden, ed. *Advising the Rulers*. Oxford, U.K.: Basil Blackwell.

Sherrington, Philippa. 2000. "Shaping the Policy Agenda: Think Tank Activity in the European Union." *Global Society* 14(2): 173-189.

Smith, Martin. J. 1999. *The Core Executive in Britain*. London: Macmillan.

Stone, Diane. 1999. "Learning Lessons and Transferring Policy Across Time, Space and Disciplines." *Politics* 19(1): 51-59.

———. 2000. "Non-governmental Policy Transfer: The Strategies of Independent Policy Institutes." *Governance: An International Journal of Policy and Administration* 13(1): 45-70.

Strategic Policy Making Team. 1999. *Professional Policy Making for the Twenty-First Century* (Cabinet Office report). <http://www.cabinet-office.gov.uk/index/guid cons.htm> (September).

Street, John, and Albert Weale. 1992. "Britain: Policy-Making in a Hermetically Sealed System." In Donald. L. Kirp and Ronald Bayer, eds. *AIDS in the Industrialized Democracies: Passions, Politics and Policies*. New Brunswick, N.J.: Rutgers University Press.

Thorne, Christopher. 1978. "Chatham House, Whitehall and Far Eastern Issues: 1941-45." *International Affairs* 54(1): 1-29.

Weller, Pat. 1987. "Types of Advice." In William Plowden, ed. *Advising the Rulers*. Oxford, U.K.: Basil Blackwell.

Willetts, David. 1987. "The Role of the (UK) Prime Minister's Policy Unit." *Public Administration* 65(4): 443-454.

5 Brazil

Amaury de Souza

The demand for policy expertise in Brazil has soared over the past two decades. In part, this phenomenon reflects the growing complexity of government and the need for expert advice and technical knowledge to deal with a dizzying plethora of emerging issues. After a long period in which government activism, centralization, and the bureaucratic pattern of policymaking were taken for granted, institutions and public policies are undergoing fundamental change. In the past ten years, the government has embarked on an ambitious attempt to liberalize trade and finances, privatize state industries, streamline the civil service, and reduce budget deficits, touching off intense competition among think tanks, research-oriented nongovernmental organizations (NGOs), and consultancy firms to provide policy analysis and advice. Pressures for the government to become more responsive and accountable to society have also increased. Outside policy organizations have helped to articulate the views of the individuals, social groups, and organized interests most directly affected by the outcomes of the policy process.

Yet the growing opportunities for alternative policy advisory organizations (APAOs) to serve the government are also indicative of its inability to retain a significant in-house policy capability. The increasingly complex demands placed upon the government in recent years have served to highlight the central bureaucracy's appalling lack of technical and managerial qualifications. Tight fiscal constraints, the control of government agencies by clientelistic interests, and a series of

The author wishes to thank Antonio Octávio Cintra, Flávio Freitas Faria, Helio Zylberstajn, João Paulo dos Reis Velloso, José Fernando Cosentino, Luiz Carlos Bresser Pereira, Marcílio Marques Moreira, Miguel Fogel, Ricardo Henriques, Ricardo Paes e Barros, Roberto Martins, Sérgio Abranches, and Vilmar Faria, who shared their experiences as policymakers and advisors and offered useful suggestions and comments. However, they bear no responsibility for the views expressed in this work. All translations from Portuguese-language sources are by the author.

misguided reform initiatives have disrupted bureaucratic careers, dispersed technical expertise, and sapped morale. Early retirement packages have also created strong financial incentives for senior and other experienced civil servants to leave. The irony, then, is that the need for new sources of policy advice has increased precisely when the government has most lacked the capacity to use it effectively.

Effective governance and policy capacity have been gradually restored since 1994. President Fernando Henrique Cardoso's overwhelming victories in two consecutive presidential elections have afforded him an inordinately high degree of autonomy in macroeconomic policymaking, while privatization and civil service reform have begun to address crucial issues related to the size and reach of the public sector. The "reform of the state" program was initiated in 1995 to "make public administration more efficient and modern, focusing its attention on serving the needs of the citizenry" (Pereira 1999, 131). In addition to increasing the competence and efficiency of the central bureaucracy, the program seeks to privatize "nonexclusive state services," such as universities, hospitals, research centers, and museums, and to delegate managerial authority to quasi-autonomous NGOs, or quangos, dubbed "social organizations." If successful, the Brazilian equivalent of a "new public management" policy is likely to significantly alter the current pattern of interaction between policymakers and APAOs.

Policy capacity concerns "the intellectual dimension of governance" (Bakvis 2000, 73), and the issue at hand is the extent to which the government is able and willing to draw on external sources of policy analysis and advice to replace at least part of the capacity that has been lost. Public-sector reform has also brought to the fore important supply-side constraints. While the availability of qualified personnel has increased nationwide, low salaries and poor career prospects have depleted the human resources of many policy research institutes, including the governmental think tanks that remain the most influential policy advisors. Despite their recent proliferation, many research-oriented NGOs encounter even greater difficulties in recruiting qualified policy staff as they strive to secure adequate funding. The need to balance the supply of and demand for policy expertise rises in importance as the fiscal crisis recedes and budgetary surpluses once again allow the government to define and pursue new goals.

THE INSTITUTIONAL AND POLITICAL
ENVIRONMENT OF ALTERNATIVE POLICY ADVICE

APAOs are a recent phenomenon in Brazil. Such organizations appeared after World War II as the complexity of government increased, with the central authorities taking the lead in creating a modern public sector and launching an ambitious program of state-led industrialization. External advice giving, however, was affected by technocratic policymaking and the articulation of societal interests by corporatist structures.

State building under President Getúlio Vargas (1930–1945) led to a steady expansion of the scope and size of government. A growing demand for technically trained personnel was triggered by the creation of new ministries and specialized agencies, the replacement of patronage appointments with a merit-based civil service, and increased government intervention in the economy. State building also raised the prominence of the presidency relative to Congress, while external input to policymaking was largely shaped by corporatism. To guarantee the political stability required for industrialization, labor and business were coaxed into a corporatist representational system that provided them with generous funding and privileged access to the policy process in exchange for compliance with government guidelines (Schmitter 1971).

The rise of technocrats as the principal architects of economic policy acted as a counterweight to organized interests' influence over policy, however. Since the late nineteenth century, scholarly authority and intellectual argument had turned a group of outstanding thinkers into major agenda builders. Their self-proclaimed ability to interpret reality in an objective and impartial manner won an active role for social scientists in public affairs, creating the cultural foundations for the rise of technocracy decades later (Lamounier 1995). The creation of central advisory councils, such as the Federal Foreign Trade Council (CFCE, Conselho Federal de Comércio Exterior), and the support provided by an enlarged professional staff turned the Office of the President into the effective center of policymaking. Staffing policy positions with appointed officials with an academic background and a reputation for expert knowledge helped to strengthen links between the government and emerging think tanks.

From the 1950s through the early 1970s, during the height of optimism about the government's capacity to lead economic growth, the basic model for governance seemed to require little fundamental change. An intense economic policy debate took place throughout this period between two major epistemic communities, that is, networks of "experts who seek to translate their beliefs through a common policy project into public policies and programmes" (Stone 1996, 86). Such epistemic communities formed distinct subgroups within Brazil's larger macroeconomic policy community and found expression in emerging think tanks (Loureiro 1997). The "structuralists," who advocated state-led industrialization and protection of domestic industry, were concentrated in government think thanks, such as the National Bank of Economic Development (BNDE, Banco Nacional de Desenvolvimento Econômico), created in 1952 and later renamed the National Bank of Economic and Social Development (BNDES, Banco Nacional de Desenvolvimento Econômico e Social), and the Roberto

Simonsen Institute (IRS, Instituto Roberto Simonsen), established in 1948 by the São Paulo State Federation of Industrialists (FIESP, Federação das Indústrias do Estado de São Paulo). The "monetarists," who opposed state intervention and favored the adoption of free-market policies, held their ground at the Brazilian Institute of Economics (IBRE, Instituto Brasileiro de Economia), established in 1951 as an independent research institute of the Getúlio Vargas Foundation (Fundação Getúlio Vargas) (Loureiro 1997). The growing importance of policy expertise led organized labor to set up the Inter-Union Department of Statistics and Economic and Social Studies (DIEESE, Departamento Intersindical de Estatística e Estudos Sócio-Econômicos) in 1955. The highly influential Superior War College (ESG, Escola Superior de Guerra), a think tank that advocated the military's involvement in the country's development, was established in 1949. The ESG's intellectuals elaborated the conceptual body of theses and doctrines about national security and development that became the guiding principles for the military regime that seized power in 1964. The military game plan sought to nurture a new civilian elite able to implement military principles in government and society. The coalescence of military and development tasks allowed the ESG to instill its security doctrines into a civilian elite of technocrats through training programs tailored by the military. Until the 1980s, the ESG retained a major advisory role to successive military governments.

In the early 1960s, economic instability and growing ideological polarization pushed novel advocacy think tanks to center stage. The Superior Institute of Brazilian Studies (ISEB, Instituto Superior de Estudos Brasileiros) was established in 1957 as a policy research institute attached to the Ministry of Education. Adding the political dimension of nationalism to the structuralist defense of state-led growth, the ISEB rapidly achieved an influential role in public debate. At the other extreme of the ideological spectrum, business groups and the ESG's military intellectuals sponsored a free-market think tank, the Institute for Economic and Social Research (IPES, Instituto de Pesquisas Sociais), to wage a battle of ideas. Although many professionals who were later appointed to top policy-making and advisory positions under the military were originally affiliated with the IPES, it disappeared along with the ISEB in the post-1964 period.

Seeking to enhance the government's capacity to promote rapid economic growth, the military undertook changes at the federal level that were consequential for the policymaking process. Beginning in the 1950s, the central bureaucracy was gradually bypassed by a parallel structure of more autonomous and decentralized public agencies. Rather than streamline the central bureaucracy, each incoming administration opted for creating new decentralized public agencies in order to avoid outdated control procedures, gain more autonomy in the management of public funds, and pursue its policy objectives in a more agile and independent manner. Although the bureaucracy still retained some power, the rapidly increasing number of regulatory agencies, public foundations, and public-sector companies played an increasingly significant role in the making of public policy. Successive military governments pushed the decentralizing tendency even further. Most state-owned companies and virtually all public foundations were established in the 1970s. In the politically rarefied atmosphere of authoritarian Brazil, these semiautonomous agencies were often captured by private interests and turned into pathways for privileged access to the policy process.

Institutional autonomy and fragmentation did not necessarily compromise policymaking at the federal level, however. Technocrats retained power as designers of macroeconomic policies by building sets of personal and political alliances through which they could secure their careers and achieve success in the implementation of policies (Schneider 1991). Interpersonal networks and highly flexible career paths allowed the civil service elite to circulate very rapidly among different public agencies, think tanks, and the private sector, functioning as "revolving doors" that ensured the continuous flow of qualified personnel in and out of government. The executive branch drew on such organizations as the BNDES and the IBRE to staff a large number of policy positions. The IBRE alone contributed three finance ministers (one of whom also served later as minister of planning), two central bank governors, and numerous officials in technical and advisory bodies (Chacel forthcoming). Other policy research institutes, such as the Institute of Applied Economic Research (IPEA, Instituto de Pesquisa Econômica Aplicada), created in 1964, and the Institute for Economic Research Foundation (FIPE, Fundação Instituto de Pesquisas Econômicas), linked to the University of São Paulo and chartered as a foundation in 1972, also functioned as conveyor belts between policy networks and the executive branch as well as between these networks and the external environment of societal interests and demands. This flow of senior staff kept the policy process relatively open to external input, expanding the range of policy options available to ministers and their staffs and providing fresh views beyond the formal channels of information and advice.

In the 1960s and 1970s, authoritarian rule was the primary impetus in the creation of a new generation of independent think tanks that often provided political refuge for dissidents (De Truitt forthcoming). In 1969, social scientists who had been forced out of the University of São Paulo, among them the current president of Brazil, created the Brazilian Center for Analysis and Planning (CEBRAP, Centro Brasileiro de Análise e Planejamento). Helio Jaguaribe, one of the founders of ISEB, established the Institute for Political and Social Studies (IEPES, Instituto de Estudos Políticos e Sociais) in 1979. The Center for the Study of Contemporary Culture (CEDEC, Centro de Estudos de Cultura Contemporânea) was created in

1976, and the Institute for Economic, Social and Political Studies (IDESP, Instituto de Estudos Econômicos, Sociais e Políticos de São Paulo) in 1981. Another important research organization, the University Research Institute of Rio de Janeiro (IUPERJ, Instituto Universitário de Pesquisas do Rio de Janeiro), was set up in 1969. Independence from the government and universities, academic credentials, and a commitment to scholarly standards of research set these organizations apart from traditional research institutes and gave their activities a distinctive academic flavor. Institutional and project funding provided by foundations and international assistance agencies allowed them to play an important role in developing policy research and setting the intellectual climate nationwide. Despite the military's suspicion of academic think tanks, they were soon able to sell contract research to federal and state governments, thus ensuring alternative sources of financial support (Levy 1996, 107).

The real boom in APAOs however, occurred in the mid-1980s. A recent survey conducted by the Brazilian Association of Non-Governmental Organizations (ABONG, Associação Brasileira de Organizações Não Governamentais) shows that 57 percent of its member organizations were created between 1980 and 1989 (ABONG 1998). The transfer of power to a civilian government in 1985 and the approval of a new constitution in 1988 greatly expanded the opportunities for civil society organizations to influence the public agenda, although the transition to democracy did not result in the immediate creation of new conduits of policy advice. The demand for external policy advice also increased as Congress won back most of the prerogatives that had been lost under the military. The new APAOs differed from their predecessors in significant ways. In contrast to the scholarly character of academic think tanks, the new institutes acted more as advocates and policy innovators. The Liberal Institute (IL, Instituto Liberal) was in many ways the prototype for Brazilian free-market think tanks. Created in 1983, the IL built extensive links with the business sector, politicians, public officials, academia, and the media to influence broader thinking about the role of private markets and the need to reduce government intervention in the economy. Other policy institutes were more of the "think and do" variety. They focused primarily on issues of human rights, education, and poverty and provided technical assistance to grass-roots and community-development programs. Established in 1981, the Brazilian Institute for Social and Economic Analysis (IBASE, Instituto Brasileiro de Análises Sociais e Econômicas) defined as its mission the building of a radically democratic society guided by the ethical values of liberty, equality, diversity, solidarity, and participation. The drafting of the 1988 constitution also provided an opportunity for business associations to emerge as intellectual brokers between organized interests and the government, although their fragmentation precluded the pursuit of broader policy decisions (Weyland 1998). The National

Confederation of Industry (CNI, Confederação Nacional da Indústria), a corporatist organization created in 1938, assumed an important role in defining sectoral proposals and getting them onto the policy agenda by disseminating ideas and research findings, forging alliances with other groups, and servicing their information requirements. The same drive to influence policy led to the creation of the Institute for Industrial Development Studies (IEDI, Instituto de Estudos do Desenvolvimento Industrial) in 1989 by leaders of São Paulo industry.

In the following decade, changing public attitudes at home and abroad shaped a new public agenda. Environmental institutes and NGOs were the quintessential APAOs of the 1990s. They belonged to what Diane Stone characterizes as a "third wave of development" (2000, 157) in which think tanks developed a global and regional focus on research and action, reflecting the growing importance of transnational policy communities. The decision to hold the 1992 United Nations Conference on Environment and Development (the Earth Summit) in Rio de Janeiro further strengthened links among Brazilian environmentalists and transnational think tanks and networks. The Brazilian Foundation for Sustainable Development (FBDS, Fundação Brasileira para o Desenvolvimento Sustentável), for instance, was formed in 1991 to conduct research and promote the view that economic development should be made compatible with environmental protection. Concern with ethical issues and the belief that civil society should handle social issues without the intervention of government were other distinctive elements of the public agenda of the 1990s. The IBASE's successful national mobilization of volunteers for the 1993 Campaign Against Hunger effectively raised the issue of poverty to the public agenda. Similarly, the Ethos Institute of Business and Social Responsibility (Instituto Ethos Empresas e Responsabilidade Social), an advocacy think tank formed in 1998, seeks to promote socially ethical business practices and the achievement of an economically prosperous and equitable society.

The 1988 constitution encouraged greater participation by civil society in policy decisions while it aggravated the problems of governance. By restoring the principles of "a highly centralized, hierarchical, and rigid public administration" (Pereira 1999, 122), the constitution paved the way for a bureaucratic retrenchment that stifled hiring practices, deprived government agencies and public foundations of autonomy, and created a system of job tenure that made it nearly impossible to hold civil servants accountable. To make matters worse, the constitution also mandated a radical devolution of revenue and authority to states and municipalities, weakening the executive branch's capacity to deal with pressing economic and social issues. "Lacking the resources and, in all but a few isolated sectors, the competence required to carry out its expansive portfolio of tasks," notes Philippe Faucher, "the bureaucracy lost its capacity to implement governmental policies"

(1998, 109). Persistently high inflation and sluggish economic growth rates reflected the declining capacity of government to deal with the fiscal crisis.

An antiinflation program called the Real plan was successfully implemented in 1994. Curbing inflation dramatically increased President Cardoso's capacity to push constitutional amendments through Congress and to roll back the fiscal devolution and state spending patterns of the previous decade. Of Cardoso's constitutional reforms, the initiatives to streamline the public sector and reform the civil service are most directly relevant to APAOs. The downsizing of government through the privatization of state assets, the creation of new channels of access to policymakers, and the introduction of competitive provision of public services are some of the innovations that are likely to enhance the role of alternative sources of advice and expertise.

THE CURRENT STATUS OF ALTERNATIVE SOURCES OF POLICY ADVICE

The structure of the Brazilian government offers multiple points of access to policymakers. As in the United States, presidentialism, the separation of powers, and a decentralized federation foster competition, and can even breed rivalries, among branches and levels of government. Although such conflicts often transcend reasoned argument, political actors tend to seek expert advice to support new policy stances or to defend existing positions.

Policymaking in a presidential system, however, varies substantially in the extent to which specific constitutional provisions affect the powers of the president and the incentives facing legislators (Shugart and Haggard 1997). For example, Brazilian presidents have considerable lawmaking powers. They can issue new laws by executive decree (or "provisional measures") in practically any policy area, allowing them to shape the legislative agenda and to obtain legislative outcomes even when they lack a disciplined majority in Congress. The concentration of policy functions in the hands of the federal executive is the key to the demand for policy expertise. The disposition of the president and his ministers to step beyond their immediate staff in search of counsel is also affected by other factors, however. Consensus on reforms is thin, making central authorities overzealous of their policy direction as well as defensive toward policy proposals that diverge from the official line. Deep-seated suspicion of corporatist tripartite participation arrangements also reinforces the inclination to insulate certain policy areas from pressures from vested interests even if that means limiting the range of policy options under consideration.

Appendix A provides an overview of alternative sources of policy advice within and outside of government in Brazil.

Alternative Policy Advice
within the Executive Branch of Government

There are numerous advisory councils at the federal level, a few of which report directly to the Office of the President. Such bodies have been in existence since the 1930s to provide the executive branch with the policy expertise needed for decision making.

PERMANENT ADVISORY COUNCILS

Not all advisory councils have the same composition and functions, and a few bodies that carry that designation would hardly qualify as sources of advice independent from the line bureaucracy. The need to insulate policymakers behind an institutionally autonomous body has led some councils simply to shed a previous advisory function. The National Monetary Council (CMN, Conselho Monetário Nacional) is now a central macroeconomic policymaking forum. Back in 1964, when it was established, the CMN was composed of sixteen members, including two representatives from corporatist business and labor organizations, and functioned as the "prime institutional locus for bargaining" over policy (Lafer 1975, 91). Since 1993, it has been reduced to the minister of finance, the minister of planning, management, and budget, and the central bank governor, a powerful triad known as the president's "economic team."

Policy coordination is at a premium, given that the executive branch comprises twenty ministries and seven secretariats with ministerial portfolios. In 1995, the Cardoso administration tried to deal with this problem by creating "policy chambers" to coordinate policymaking and implementation in areas that involved several ministries, such as public-sector reform, foreign trade, and social policies. For that reason, many advisory councils were set up primarily to coordinate policy activities across executive-branch agencies, although they also provide forums for the expression of views from individuals and organizations outside government. A case in point is the National Science and Technology Council (CNCT, Conselho Nacional de Ciência e Tecnologia).

Corporatist councils have traditionally provided a formal setting to bring labor and business representatives into negotiation with the government over policy. One example is the National Social Security Council (CNPS, Conselho Nacional de Previdência Social). Corporatist councils can have important policymaking powers, as do the trustees of the Workers' Relief Fund (FAT, Fundo de Amparo ao Trabalhador). A third and more innovative type of advisory council is exemplified by the Solidaristic Community Council (Conselho da Comunidade Solidária). It seeks to establish new interfaces between public officials and civil society organizations and to provide an open space for building a consensus policy agenda. Similar councils exist in the Ministries of the Environment and Agrarian Development.

National Science and Technology Council

Established in 1975, the CNCT was designed to assist the president with expert advice on matters of scientific and technological development. It was originally set up as the advisory board of a major federal funding agency, the National Council for Scientific and Technological Development (CNPq, Conselho Nacional de Desenvolvimento Científico e Tecnológico). In 1996, it was reorganized and granted a broad mandate to assist the president in developing science and technology policies in the context of economic and social development goals. The CNCT is composed of the ministers of science and technology, planning management, and budget, foreign relations, finance, and education and the chairman of the joint chiefs of staff, as well as seven eminent figures in science and technology appointed by the president. It exerts a modest influence over policy decisions.

National Social Security Council

The CNPS was created in 1991 to assess and approve social security policies as well as to oversee the management of the social security apparatus in order to improve the delivery of services. By law, social security councils at all levels of government are required to promote a decentralized form of management through tripartite representation. The CNPS is composed of six government officials, six representatives from labor federations and the Brazilian Confederation of Retired Persons, and three representatives from business confederations, in addition to the minister of social security, who presides over the council.

Solidaristic Community Council

This council aims to implement an ambitious antipoverty agenda in close consultation with NGOs and policy experts in order to find solutions to pressing social problems. Established in 1995, it is composed of ten cabinet members and twenty-one representative individuals from civil society appointed by the president. The council is presided over by the first lady, Ruth Cardoso, a respected anthropologist with extensive contacts with NGOs. The council is expected to advise executive-branch officials on social policy priorities and directions, to mobilize and strengthen civil society organizations, and to act as a catalyst for joint policy initiatives in the social area. The council's operational arm, the Executive Secretariat, reports directly to the president's chief of staff and is empowered to coordinate the activities of various government agencies and to shield social programs from budget cuts. The council has developed innovative methods to target the poor and to promote policy accountability through the active participation of local communities in the design and implementation of local programs. It has a small permanent staff and contracts research to academic and contract research think tanks as well as research-oriented NGOs.

BLUE-RIBBON AND TEMPORARY ADVISORY COMMISSIONS

Praise of temporary advisory commissions as significant sources of policy advice often disguises considerable skepticism about their practical results. A frequent criticism is that creating a commission is the best way to postpone action while appearing to be at work on a problem. The track record of temporary advisory commissions is disappointing. President José Sarney (1985–1989) appointed a blue-ribbon commission headed by the jurist Affonso Arinos to prepare a constitutional draft. The result was a detailed blueprint for major institutional and political reform that among other things sought to strengthen Congress and the party system by recommending that Brazil adopt a parliamentary system of government. Out of fear that the congressional opposition might use the recommendations to shorten his term of office, the president quietly shelved the commission's report.

Alternative Policy Advice within the Legislative Branch of Government

Advising Congress can be more difficult than advising the government. Political party fragmentation and the multiplicity of regional and functional constituencies tend to make Congress less receptive to broad policy issues than to narrow sectoral concerns that guarantee electoral support to individual legislators (Kingstone 1998). While Congress continues to need policy expertise to discharge its legislative responsibilities, the demand for alternative sources of policy advice has been restricted, since the locus of national policymaking remains in the executive branch.

CONGRESSIONAL PROFESSIONAL STAFF

Congress has established a permanent professional staff that provides legislators with information that can often rival that possessed by the bureaucracy. The congressional staff was originally organized by the military in the 1970s to serve the bureaucracy, however, not to respond to the needs of legislators or political parties. Congressional committees were expected at the time to enable legislation initiated in the executive branch rather than to design policies. Strict adherence to objective, neutral advice provided cover to the congressional staff, allowing it to forgo a more active role in initiating policy (Baaklini 1992).

The congressional professional staff is organized into three main bodies. The Senate Data Processing Center (PRODASEN, Serviço de Processamento de Dados do Senado) provides Congress with a highly effective information-gathering and -processing system. The Legislative Support Service (AL, Assessoria Legislativa) was set up in 1972 to assist Congress in policy formulation and enactment. Congressional committee staffs, as well as individual legislators, refer routinely to the AL for information and research as well as advice and assistance in drafting legislation. The AL receives some 18,000 requests for research and analysis annually, and its staff takes pride in providing impartial and objective information and advice to legislators, regardless of party or ideological persuasion. The Budget and Financial Review Service (AOFF, Assessoria de Orçamento e Fiscalização Financeira) was established in 1979 to assist and advise Congress in general and the congressional budget committee in particular in matters related to the federal budget. The new multiyear program budget has enhanced the AOFF's role, since congressional committee members lack the expertise to deal with it. Both the AL and the AOFF have been able to attract and retain qualified personnel, and their staffs include a large number of people with master's degrees or doctorates in economics, law, and the social sciences.

CONGRESSIONAL COMMISSIONS OF INQUIRY (CPI)
CPIs, or Comissão Parlamentar de Inquérito, have been the principal manifestation of a more assertive mood in Congress. They are granted broad investigative and quasi-judicial powers by the constitution. It was evidence unearthed by a CPI that led to the impeachment of President Fernando Collor de Mello in 1992. Since CPIs can deal with practically any issue, they afford legislators an opportunity to enhance their public profile. Predictably, corruption and other issues of great public impact have taken the lead. A CPI's travails can on occasion influence policymaking. In 1999, for example, a CPI formed in the Senate to look into charges of corruption in the judicial branch helped to focus attention on a reform bill before Congress.

FEDERAL AUDIT TRIBUNAL (TCU)
The TCU, or Tribunal de Contas da União, and similar audit courts that exist at all levels of government perform the same functions as the General Accounting Office in the United States. Created in 1890 to oversee the use of public monies, the TCU has undergone major changes in the past half century. In its current form, it is empowered to audit government expenditures and to advise policymakers regarding the legal status of proposed expenditures and the efficient use of public funds. The predominance of political appointees among top-ranking TCU officials, however, has discredited its advisory role, even though it is properly staffed to provide sound policy advice.

APAOs Outside Government
The Brazilian government relies extensively on outside expert advice and technical judgment to carry out its duties. There are many potential sources of advice

outside government. The focus here is on think tanks, or independent public policy research organizations that "attempt to influence policy through intellectual argument and analysis rather than direct lobbying" (Stone 2000, 155). Brazil has a relatively small but active community of think tanks, in which government-linked institutes play a highly visible role.

CONTRACT RESEARCH THINK TANKS

Contract research institutes are notoriously difficult to define as a discrete category of think tank, but a common feature is the relative sway that funding agencies have over their research agendas. Policy research institutes and public foundations working independently within line ministries are important sources of expert advice to the government. These think tanks are funded in large part by line-item appropriations of the federal budget, by contracts with government agencies, or, more often, by a combination of both. The IPEA and the BNDES stand out as top research organizations in the macroeconomic policy area. Although the IPEA reports to the Ministry of Planning, Management, and Budget, it has traditionally enjoyed substantial freedom to set its own research priorities (Chacel forthcoming). Its mission is to function "as if it were the critical conscience of the government within the government." The BNDES is a development bank that has played a crucial role in developing managerially sound policies for economic growth, industrial restructuring, and the privatization of state assets, as well as long-term strategic visioning and planning studies. Both the IPEA and the BNDES have served as important points of intersection for the activities of epistemic communities. Although free-market liberal economists were behind the creation of the IPEA, since 1966 the institute has housed an economic training center staffed by Keynesian economists linked to the United Nations Economic Commission for Latin America. The dynamics of this intellectual coexistence have resulted in many innovative policy initiatives over the years, especially in the areas of income distribution and poverty.

Other policy research institutes partly funded by the government are the National Institute of Educational Research (INEP, Instituto Nacional de Estudos Pedagógicos), founded in 1937, and the Institute for Research on International Relations (IPRI, Instituto de Pesquisas em Relações Internacionais), founded in 1985. The INEP was established to assist the government in the development and evaluation of educational policies. It conducts nationwide evaluation surveys of student performance and monitors the quality of educational programs from the elementary school to the university level. Although it has lost most of the influence it had in the 1960s and 1970s, the ESG promotes training programs, organizes conferences and study groups, and sponsors networks in which military and civilian personnel jointly conduct development and strategic studies. Other government-funded research institutes, usually chartered as public foundations, are found at the state level. The Joaquim Nabuco Foundation (FJN, Fundação Joaquim Nabuco) was created in 1949 to study developmental issues in the northeastern and northern regions of Brazil. The João Pinheiro Foundation (FJP, Fundação João Pinheiro), established in 1969, conducts policy-relevant research on regional and sectoral development strategies. The Foundation for Administrative Development (FUNDAP, Fundação do Desenvolvimento Administrativo), created in 1974 in the state of São Paulo, conducts research and develops training programs in public-sector management performance and effectiveness.

Contract research think tanks funded mostly by corporations include the Center of Foreign Trade Studies Foundation (FUNCEX, Fundação Centro de Estudos do Comércio Exterior), created in 1976 to contribute to the expansion of Brazil's foreign trade. Consultancy firms, such as Booz Allen & Hamilton and McKinsey, have moved in swiftly to fill the space left empty by the undersupply of research and advice by established think tanks and take advantage of the opportunities arising from the privatization of state assets and the restructuring of government functions and activities. These firms have recruited several former senior officials and built the capacity to provide the policy expertise that the government needs. Over the past decade, they have played an increasingly important role in helping the government to make informed choices in a number of policy areas.

ACADEMIC THINK TANKS
Intellectual credibility, research orientation, and scholarly tenets of validity make academic think tanks resemble a "university without students" (Weaver 1989, 564). Independent research institutes, such as CEBRAP, get their funding mostly from foundation grants and contract research. Other research institutes are embedded in universities but derive a sizable part of their funding from grants and contract research with the government, corporations, and international agencies. The IBRE is traditionally identified with the monetarist school of neoclassical economics and serves as a hub from which a free-market epistemic community propagates its policy views. In other academic tanks, such as the Institute of Economics of the Federal University of Rio de Janeiro (IE-UFRJ, Instituto de Economia da Universidade Federal do Rio de Janeiro) and the Institute of Economics of the State University of Campinas (IE-UNICAMP, Instituto de Economia da Universidade Estadual de Campinas), there is a predominance of neo-Keynesian thought not infrequently tinged with Marxist analysis. The rise of a globalized economy inspired the creation of the Getúlio Vargas Foundation's Center for the Study of the World Economy (CEM, Centro de Estudos da Economia Mundial) in 1990 to carry out research and public debate on issues

related to globalization and its impact on Brazil. The Institute of Advanced Studies (IEA, Instituto de Estudos Avançados) of the University of São Paulo was formed in 1986. The IEA conducts multidisciplinary research and debate on a variety of topics related to culture and science. Created in 1963, the Department of Economics of the Pontifical Catholic University of Rio de Janeiro (PUC-RIO, Pontifícia Universidade Católica do Rio de Janeiro) does not fit neatly into the definition of an academic think tank. It is primarily a discipline-based research organization involved in undergraduate and graduate training. Several faculty members, however, have had enormous sway over antiinflation policy design, such as the 1986 Cruzado and the 1994 Real stabilization plans, and many have been appointed to top policymaking posts.

The National Institute of Higher Studies (INAE, Instituto Nacional de Altos Estudos), created in 1987, has been referred to as "probably the purest form of a think tank in Brazil" (Chacel forthcoming). The INAE is a nonprofit and nonpartisan institution funded by public and private corporations and international foundations, such as the Ford Foundation and the Tinker Foundation. Its core activity is the annual National Forum, which assembles top government officials including the president and several ministers, members of Congress and other politicians of all persuasions, business and labor leaders, and academic and think-tank intellectuals to debate pressing issues in several policy areas. Discussions are open to the general public and the proceedings are published in book form. The National Forum also provides an open space for policy communities to engage in lively intellectual exchange as well as to smooth the rough edges of disagreement. Since the first National Forum in 1987, it is possible to observe an increasing convergence of elite thinking on major policy issues.

ADVOCACY THINK TANKS, INCLUDING RESEARCH-ORIENTED NGOS

Historically, interest-based APAOs had to operate within the rigid confines of corporatist structures. Since the 1980s, advocacy think tanks have thrived as corporatist interest groups have gradually lost most of their privileged access to policymaking. The research arms of the more established policy actors, such as the CNI, have been transformed into full-fledged advocacy think tanks with considerable expertise and financial resources. Organized labor's DIEESE has also been engaged in advocacy directed at influencing economic and labor policies. Although many advocacy think tanks are engaged in the production of policy research, they are more likely to act as brokers that use research findings produced elsewhere to support their policy views.

Not all business-affiliated advocacy tanks share a common policy outlook. On the contrary, they often compete to influence policy in line with different and sometimes even opposed sets of core beliefs. Free-market liberals have been the driving force behind the influential think tanks created in the 1980s and early 1990s, such as the IL, the more scholarly Fernand Braudel World Economy Institute (Instituto Fernand Braudel de Economia Mundial), and the Atlantic Institute (IA, Instituto Atlântico). Meanwhile, the advocacy of government activism on behalf of domestic industry has been the unifying theme of the IEDI. Extensive privatization and the implementation of market-oriented reforms by the government have blurred the lines of disagreement among advocacy think tanks. The new business leaders who created the Ethos Institute of Business and Social Responsibility in 1998 tend to support more pragmatic policy stances while they champion socially responsible business practices.

A thin line separates advocacy think tanks from public-interest NGOs. Advocacy think tanks and research-oriented NGOs take a much more direct marketing approach in seeking to influence policy (De Truitt forthcoming) than the more traditional academic and contract research think tanks. Rather than disseminate their policy views primarily among policymakers, they target specific audiences, put out policy briefings, sponsor one-day meetings and workshops, and value policy experience and contacts over academic credentials in recruiting staff.

Advocacy think tanks and NGOs have also been highly innovative in building public support for their policy positions. They have turned exposure in the media into a major pursuit. Lobbying for popular causes in Congress also enables NGOs to raise issues to the level of the public agenda and then to the level of policy. The groundbreaking "grass-roots lobbying" organization is the Inter-Union Department of Congressional Assistance Services (DIAP, Departamento Intersindical de Assessoria Parlamentar), created in 1983 by a group of lawyers connected to the labor movement. Other NGOs that have chosen to increase their influence by lobbying legislators and the government include the Institute of Socio-Economic Studies (INESC, Instituto de Estudos Sócio-Econômicos), founded in 1979, and the Institute for Social Policy Studies, Training and Consulting (POLIS, Instituto de Estudos, Formação e Assessoria em Políticas Sociais), established in 1987. While advocacy think tanks and NGOs have a research component to their activities, the NGOs tend to combine research and grass-roots activities as part of their advocacy work. The Institute for the Study of Religion (ISER, Instituto de Estudos da Religião), for example, has conducted public-opinion studies on crime and violence and helped organize an antiviolence movement, the Viva Rio, which gathers business associations, government agencies, and civil society organizations.

Participation in transnational networks is another common feature of advocacy think tanks. The Ethos Institute of Business and Social Responsibility maintains close collaborative links with several like-minded international institutions, such as the Conference Board and the World Business Council for Sustainable Development. Transnational linkages are even more important for research-oriented NGOs, in that they provide a steady flow of information, ideas, and experience across national frontiers as well as access to funding. The Institute for Society, Population and Nature (ISPN, Instituto Sociedade, População e Natureza) and the Institute of Amazon Man and Environment (IMAZON, Instituto do Homem e Meio Ambiente da Amazônia), whose core theme is sustainable development, are connected to global institutions, such as the World Wide Fund for Nature (WWF), and to several worldwide research networks. International advocacy is also facilitated by access to transnational networks, allowing local organizations to mobilize opinion on a global scale on issues that the government has treated as marginal to its own agenda. The Brazil Network on Multilateral Financial Institutions–Rede Brasil (Rede Brasil sobre Instituições Financeiras Multilaterais) is a nonprofit, nonpartisan public-interest network supported by some fifty civil society organizations whose common objective is to monitor and evaluate government policies and projects financed or technically supported by multilateral financial institutions, such as the World Bank, the Interamerican Development Bank, and the International Monetary Fund. Rede Brasil advocates societal participation in policymaking and seeks to coordinate NGO advocacy activities aimed at the Brazilian government and multilateral institutions.

POLITICAL PARTY THINK TANKS
In sharp contrast to other think tanks, there is no dearth of funding for party-affiliated institutes. The law that created the Political Party Fund requires that at least 20 percent of total revenues destined for parties be spent on the establishment and maintenance of party institutes devoted to political research, education, and indoctrination. Keeping contact with legislators and the rank and file and disseminating party materials generally take precedence over policy research and analysis. Only two party institutes have developed some capacity to deal with policy matters. The Tancredo Neves Institute for Political and Social Studies (ITN, Instituto Tancredo Neves de Estudos Políticos e Sociais), created in 1985, is affiliated with the Liberal Front Party. The institute has a busy agenda of workshops and meetings and has published several book-length blueprints for policy reform. The ITN also contracts out policy research and advice on a variety of issues, operating as a dissemination outlet for the brokerage activities of free-market advocacy think tanks.

Policy research and expertise are equally valued at the other extreme of the ideological spectrum. The left-wing Workers' Party created the Perseu Abramo Foundation (Fundação Perseu Abramo) in 1996 to propagate the party's political and ideological views and to help preserve its history. In the past few years, the foundation has developed an in-house opinion research capability and become more actively engaged in policy issues. As the leading opposition force in the country, the Workers' Party has traditionally drawn on sympathetic think tanks and research-oriented NGOs for policy analysis and advice, seeking to operate as a shadow cabinet of sorts. It has also set up a professional staff of its own to assist legislators in designing and enacting legislation.

Staffing and Funding

The performance of APAOs hinges on a combination of qualified staff and adequate organizational systems and practices. Most academic and contract research think tanks, as well as top consultancy firms, are staffed with a sufficient number of high-quality research personnel, usually with master's or doctorate degrees, and have adequate support staffs. Such organizations are able to reinforce their institutional knowledge by recruiting policy analysts and researchers with the requisite expertise and skills and by retaining some of the most talented people recruited. Advocacy think tanks, especially those linked to corporatist interest organizations, tend to maintain smaller in-house staffs and to contract out policy research and analysis more often.

The limitations imposed by their resource levels create a skill gap in many APAOs, however. In terms of staff numbers, these APAOs tend to be small to middle-sized and to rely to a significant extent on trainees and part-time research personnel who generally hold outside jobs at universities or governmental agencies. The quality of policy advice has been adversely affected by the proliferation of NGOs with minuscule staffs and insufficient expertise. Competing for human resources in a limited pool of qualified personnel leads poorly funded NGOs, especially of the "think and do" variety, to hire people who are too young and inexperienced, thus undermining their status as sources of policy expertise.

Lack of a stable funding base is the foremost constraint for many APAOs. The federal government and to a lesser extent the state governments have thus far been important sources of funding. As the age of government activism ebbs, however, the resources available are increasingly allocated from a stable or shrinking funding base, leading policy organizations in and outside government to scramble for alternative sources of sustainable funding. A case in point is the Getúlio Vargas Foundation, a private foundation that was included in the federal budget until recently. In 1995, budgetary appropriations were converted into funds for research contracts. At present, only 10 percent of the foundation's needs are covered by federal funds, compared with more than 70 percent in the past (Chacel forthcoming).

Academic and contract research think tanks have access to research funds provided by the CNPq, created in 1951, and the Research and Project Financing Agency (FINEP, Financiadora de Estudos e Projetos), a public corporation created in 1967 with the mission of promoting technological development and innovation. At the state level, a great deal of policy research is conducted under the auspices of the Research Foundation of the State of São Paulo (FAPESP, Fundação de Amparo à Pesquisa do Estado de São Paulo), established in 1962. Project-based research funding does not enable APAOs to maintain an adequate core of professional and support staff, however. Ownership of facilities and the tax-exempt status granted to nonprofit policy organizations are positive elements in the funding equation. Organizations that obtain funding mainly from foreign sources are not necessarily in better financial shape, since the institutional funding that helped to set up the academic think tanks of the 1970s and 1980s is no longer available.

The prospects for the financial sustainability of smaller APAOs are even worse, and their predicament is aggravated by a lack of fund-raising expertise and of proper financial management and control systems. Nearly 70 percent of the NGOs surveyed in 1998 reported that funding was their most pressing concern. The same survey shows that 81 percent had annual revenues below US$500,000, with some 36 percent grossing US$100,000 or less. Only 7 percent had budgets of US$1 million or more (ABONG 1998). The same is true of environmental NGOs. Most of the 1,035 organizations surveyed in 1996 had an annual budget below US$100,000 (WWF and Mater Natura 1996). Membership dues, individual donations, income from the sale of products and services, and grants from international agencies are some of the funding sources available to them. Signals about their future are mixed at best. Philanthropic giving has increased substantially, but donors still favor charitable activities over research and advocacy. Meanwhile, contribution levels have shrunk since 1997, since individual donations are no longer tax deductible (Sadek and Debert 1998).

THE IMPACT OF
ALTERNATIVE SOURCES OF POLICY ADVICE

Assessing the impact of expertise on the policy process in Brazil reveals a paradox. The dramatic shift in macroeconomic policy orientation in recent years has been attributed to policy prescriptions emanating from a highly visible group of economists affiliated with university research institutes. Arguments for the potency of policy advice, however, are contradicted by indications that economic think tanks are often frustrated by the government's lack of responsiveness to their policy proposals. Specifically, the case for influence stems largely from the government's success in curbing high inflation from 1994 onward. The antiinflation policy was designed by faculty members of PUC-RIO, whose earlier theoretical work had sought to explicate the inertial components that gave inflation its own momentum. What is often overlooked is the extent to which these scholars' ability to influence the policy process resulted from a sense of urgency spurred by rising inflation and economic stagnation. As Stone notes, conditions of uncertainty are likely to bolster the impact of epistemic communities, "as expertise is at a premium" (1996, 89). Many scholars were also appointed to top policymaking positions, from which they were able to implement their own policy blueprints and ward off pressure for change from competing policy communities. In this sense, their ability to shift a policy paradigm can hardly be generalized to the influence of APAOs as a whole.

It is generally accepted that the ability to influence policy varies at different stages of the policy process. Some policy organizations stand a better chance of influencing policy by helping to shape public attitudes on certain issues, while others may be able to play a significant role in the policy-formulation or -implementation stages. Yet agenda setting seems to be in every APAO's brief despite the fact that a great deal of time and effort are required to move new issues onto the policy agenda. Even under favorable circumstances, policy influence results from a complex interaction between APAOs' ability to change public thinking about major issues and their ability to spot windows of opportunity and engage the attention of policymakers. Seen in this light, most organizations can expect to have a modest policy influence at best, especially in competitive advice-giving contexts. The 1993 constitutional revision represented a major opportunity for APAOs to reach a wider audience and seek to influence the congressional policy agenda. The IEA, for instance, sponsored a high-level group of experts to draft a comprehensive proposal for constitutional reform. The congressional revision effort ended in "hyperactive paralysis" (Lamounier 1994, 86), however, since legislators and policy advocates overloaded the congressional agenda while making no significant decisions.

Policy formulation and implementation require the kind of analysis and advice that advocacy and contract research think tanks and the congressional professional staff are better positioned to provide. In tendering policy advice, proximity to the government may give a competitive edge. Executive-branch agencies with considerable powers of policy formulation and implementation, such as the Ministry of Finance and the central bank, are relatively closed decisional arenas. The effort to insulate these agencies from external pressure creates a reluctance to hire outsiders for policy work, giving government-linked research institutes an advantage over other APAOs unless they lack the required policy expertise. Major policy reforms initiated by the government in the past few years, including the privatization of state assets, have required the support of dense networks of policy expertise that cut across the public-private divide, pooling expert knowledge resources from government agencies, independent think tanks, and consultancy firms.

Some APAOs have been able to exert a lasting effect on public policy by taking advantage of exceptional opportunities. Environmental think tanks, for example, succeeded in having a chapter on the environment included in the 1988 constitution by deftly advocating new policy stances (Hochstetler 1997, 206). Social policy communities that advocated major changes in welfare and health-care policies, however, failed to overcome the opposition of self-serving "iron triangles" of narrow legislative interests and government agencies and their clients (Melo 1993). Growing congressional assertiveness has also opened up new opportunities for think tanks to bring their expertise to bear on substantive policy matters. Legislators have recently defied the government's resistance to overhauling the tax system before the public accounts are balanced. A tax-reform bill drafted by a congressional committee has polarized the policy debate, with one group of think tanks pitted against another as they argue over fiscal and economic implications. Intellectual ammunition for reform-minded legislators has been provided by advocacy and academic tanks such as the CNI and the FIPE.

The public sector's rapidly growing demand for policy and program evaluation expertise has thus far failed to attract a significant number of APAOs outside government. One hurdle is that policy evaluation requires expert and detailed knowledge of implementation and service-delivery structures. Government-linked think tanks have had the upper hand in this area. The annual assessment of educational performance conducted by the INEP helps to correct course in formulating educational policies. Similarly, the IPEA has suggested new departures for poverty-eradication and income-redistribution policies by focusing on policy implementation. IPEA-sponsored studies have shown that significant slippage occurs in various social policy delivery chains, such as health-care and unemployment insurance, so that the benefits fail to reach the ultimate targets, the poor.

PROSPECTS AND RECOMMENDATIONS

A complex set of forces that reflects the changing economic environment and increasing demand for civil society participation is continuously at work to generate new public agendas. The emerging features of governance will depend on the institutional processes that translate pressing public agendas into new policy responses.

Demand-Side Opportunities
and Constraints

Beset by an intractable fiscal crisis, Brazil's federal government has found its policy capacity greatly diminished in the past fifteen years. Loss of technical and managerial expertise has gradually dissolved a culture of planning, programming, and analysis and stalled the development of techniques and practices for following up, evaluating, and correcting course in policy implementation (Abranches 1992, 139). Effective governance has been gradually restored since 1994, but fiscal austerity and public-sector restructuring have taken a heavy toll on the civil service. The federal payroll has been virtually frozen for the better part of the past five years, making it difficult for the government to retain qualified personnel. Many senior policy analysts have opted for early retirement, while constraints on recruitment have continued to hinder the renewal of policy expertise in government. Fiscal constraints have also thinned the professional staffs of government-linked think tanks, and some organizations now depend on the work of a few "policy stars" to maintain a high public profile.

It is debatable, however, whether policy capacity should be restored to what it was under a more activist government. The use of outside sources of expertise to regenerate policy capacity is more consistent with current efforts to streamline government operations and introduce competition into the provision of services through public bidding and outsourcing. Nevertheless, a core policy staff should be retained to direct, contract out, and oversee the production of policy research and analysis. Senior policy advisors and managers should be able to use expert advice effectively, sift factual information and elaborate the implications for policymaking, formulate and develop policy proposals, and present compelling arguments and feasible options to policymakers. There is a dearth of government officials with the required profile, and existing training programs in public policy analysis are unlikely to meet the demand for qualified personnel. Some agencies provide on-the-job training for junior staff, while others have sought to strengthen policy capacity by recruiting experienced senior personnel through appointment to commissioned positions (or DAS, Comissão de Direção e Assessoramento Superior). Such appointments have actually created a thriving market for talented personnel at the federal level "in which ministers of state and high-level public managers with available DAS positions dispute among themselves for the best of the government's civil servants" (Pereira 1999, 130).

The low visibility and accessibility to policymakers of many APAOs set a limit on their potential contribution. There is a need for policy units that can act as brokers, identifying and contracting suppliers of policy expertise and providing them with information regarding the government's policy research needs. These units should also be capable of conducting their own research. That should have been the mission of the short-lived National Policy Review and Evaluation Secretariat established in early 1999 within the Office of the President. Building shared research agendas is another promising strategy. The Ministry of Agrarian Development's newly created Agrarian and Rural Development Study Group (NEAD, Núcleo de Estudos Agrários e Desenvolvimento Rural) was designed to bring together internal policy staff and outside experts from international agencies and academic and government-linked think tanks to address the ministry's policy research needs.

Resistance to outside advice, however, has grown in some quarters. Although the bulk of government personnel is modestly qualified at best, the upper echelons of the civil service are staffed with well-trained and analytically sophisticated appointed officials who are reluctant to accept outside advice on matters that lie within the purview of their agencies. Many are professional economists who share with their key officials strong beliefs about macroeconomic management and efficiency. A long history of influence on policymaking by narrow interests and corporatist organizations also tinges their perception of outside advice as inherently interested.

Supply-Side
Opportunities and Constraints

New policy agendas are shaped not only by social demands but also by factors that enable organizations to act as major initiators of policy. While much is being made of the relevance of APAOs as a means of improving governance, there are unaddressed questions regarding their functioning and performance. It is apparent that APAOs in Brazil make less than optimal use of the opportunities available to them. Many factors account for this, but an important one is lack of scale. The landscape of policy organizations underwent fundamental changes in past years, creating a wide gap among APAOs in terms of analytical and advisory capabilities as well as of access to the policymaking process. Most organizations, especially the "think and do" NGOs, are too small and carry little weight in the marketplace of ideas. The managerial skills and organizational resources that enable professional staffs to turn out high-quality policy work and the marketing and entrepreneurial competence that allows them to act on policy issues in a timely fashion are noticeably absent in many organizations. Unrealistically ambitious lists of priorities and activities are common. Instead of focusing on a few policy areas, research agendas typically span a wide range of domestic and international issues. The quality of research is another reason for concern, since it reflects the deep inequality in the distribution of intellectual capital among APAOs. Despite a shortage of people with adequate training in public policy analysis, organizational reputation works in favor of the more established think tanks by increasing their ability to recruit and retain more skilled and experienced policy analysts. Smaller and less well staffed organizations, on the other hand, often undertake projects of questionable quality and policy relevance, and their work tends to be short on research and heavy on advocacy.

Although there is no easy solution to these problems, some recent initiatives may provide new opportunities for policy organizations. Networking is a means of scaling up APAOs' activities, and hence augmenting the supply of policy analysis and advice. NGOs already make extensive use of information systems to enhance communication and collaboration with other organizations. The IBASE was one of the first Internet providers in Brazil. A communication network called the Third Sector Information Network (RITS, Rede de Informações para o Terceiro Setor) was set up recently to assist NGOs to coordinate activities. Networking can also be used as a strategy for catalyzing the formation of intellectual capital. The IPEA has set up the Public Policy Research Network (Rede IPEA, Rede IPEA [Instituto de Pesquisa Econômica Aplicada] de Pesquisas) to entice academic and contract research think tanks to pool their research capabilities and share their findings with the government. The Rede IPEA seeks to improve socioeconomic databases, conduct studies with a focus on development, and promote debate on policy options.

Greater managerial and financial flexibility can be granted to government research institutes by allowing them to provide educational and scientific research services as quangos. Such "social organizations" are required to sign a management contract with specified performance targets in exchange for being authorized by Congress to receive funds from the federal budget (Pereira 1999, 10–12). The National Laboratory of Synchrotron Light (LNLS, Laboratório Nacional de Luz Sincroton) was the first agency to switch from bureaucratic to "public nongovernmental" control, and the Institute for Pure and Applied Mathematics (IMPA, Instituto de Matemática Pura e Aplicada) is expected to follow suit. The government can also induce the formation of NGOs to fill a gap in the market or strengthen those already in existence (Tendler 1997). Recent legislation allows the transformation of private nonprofit organizations into "public interest civil society organizations" (OSCs, Organizações da Sociedade Civil de Interesse Público), which are also authorized by Congress to be funded through budgetary appropriations.

Such possibilities present difficult dilemmas. There is an intense debate as to whether government funding compromises the autonomy of advocacy groups. Rather than work directly within the structures they intend to influence, many NGOs wish to keep a critical distance from the government and seek to shape the public agenda by reaching a wider audience. Another concern is that the incorporation of APAOs into the policy process will turn them into adjuncts of the state and erode the boundaries between government and civil society. More generally, it is feared that the involvement of NGOs in public-service delivery will create rigidity in budgetary allocations and increase federal spending responsibilities.

Recommendations

APAOs can contribute to improving governance by strengthening the policy capacity of government through the provision of expert advice and technical judgment. Rather than efforts to restore the bureaucratic pattern of policymaking, the extensive use of outside sources of advice while preserving a small in-house policy capacity appears to be a more suitable design for today's policy environment. Priority should be placed on assigning adequate policy resources to the "strategic core of the state" (Pereira 1999, 132), which comprises the president, his cabinet, and the upper echelons of the civil service with policymaking responsibilities. In particular, a policy review unit reporting directly to the Office of the President should be created to coordinate policy analysis and advice to the president and to assist him in making policy decisions. The new unit should consist of a small core of policy experts acting as brokers and capable of directing, contracting out, and making effective use of outside sources of advice. Executive-branch agencies should build up a critical mass of seasoned policy staff to provide interfaces with APAOs and to ensure the quality of policy research and advice.

Creating open arenas where the government can share policymaking authority with elements of civil society is another important contribution to improved governance. The involvement of APAOs in the policy process through public-private partnerships and shared research agendas should be encouraged in order to give expression to a plurality of views, identify relevant policy options, and grant legitimacy to the policy agenda. Such arrangements have raised concern over blurred lines of accountability and responsibility in the policy process, however. An effective monitoring mechanism requires transparency in transactions, full disclosure of interests, a clear definition of the expertise required to gain entry, and rules for the alternation of participants over time. As stressed by two senior presidential advisors, NGOs should "set the standard for any discussions of public issues" (Faria and Graeff 2000, 38).

On the supply side, a series of incentives should be created to augment the supply of policy analysis and advice. Innovative arrangements, such as networking and collaboration with the government in research projects, may help to improve the infrastructure of policy organizations and provide greater scale to their activities. Developing learning capacity should take precedence over setting up costly structures for information storage and retrieval. APAOs should also address staffing and organizational issues as well as the many ancillary activities of their mission, including fund raising. Domestic funding agencies and transnational policy organizations, such as Oxfam, can help APAOs to establish clear priorities, build up adequate organizational governance and fiscal management, and ensure the quality and range of their programs and services.

To improve APAOs' long-term funding prospects, philanthropic giving should be encouraged through changes in legislation that increase tax incentives for individual and corporate contributions to nonprofit organizations. Incentives should also be provided to expand the supply of training programs in public affairs and public-policy analysis.

BIBLIOGRAPHY

ABONG. 1998. *ONGs: Um Perfil* (NGOs: A profile). São Paulo: Associação Brasileira de Organizações Não Governamentais.

Abranches, Sérgio. 1992. "O Estado" (The state). In Helio Jaguaribe, ed. *Sociedade, Estado e Partidos na Atualidade Brasileira* (Society, state, and parties in contemporary Brazil). Rio de Janeiro: Paz e Terra.

Baaklini, Abdo. I. 1992. *The Brazilian Legislature and Political System.* Westport, Conn.: Greenwood Press.

Bakvis, Herman. 2000. "Rebuilding Policy Capacity in the Era of the Fiscal Dividend: A Report from Canada." *Governance* 13(1): 71–103.

Chacel, Julian. Forthcoming. "Think Tanks in Brazil: The Case of Instituto Brasileiro de Economia as an Illustration." In James G. McGann and R. Kent Weaver, eds. *Think Tanks and Civil Societies: Catalysts for Ideas and Action.* New Brunswick, N. J.: Transaction.

De Truitt, Nancy Sherwoo. Forthcoming. "Think Tanks in Latin America." In James G. McGann and R. Kent Weaver, eds. *Think Tanks and Civil Societies: Catalysts for Ideas and Action.* New Brunswick, N. J.: Transaction.

Faria, Vilmar, and Eduardo Graeff. 2000. *Progressive Governance for the 21st Century: The Brazilian Experience.* Brasília: Senior Advisory Body, Presidency of the Republic. <www.planalto.gov.br/seculo21.htm>

Faucher, Philippe. 1998. "Restoring Governance: Has Brazil Got It Right (at Last)?" In Philip Oxhorn and Pamela K. Starr, eds. *Markets and Democracy in Latin America.* Boulder, Colo.: Lynne Rienner.

Hochstetler, Kathryn. 1997. "The Evolution of the Brazilian Environmental Movement and Its Political Roles." In Douglas A. Chalmers et al., eds. *The New Politics of Inequality in Latin America.* New York: Oxford University Press.

Kingstone, Peter R. 1998. "Constitutional Reform and Macroeconomic Stability: Implications for Democratic Consolidation in Brazil." In Philip Oxhorn and Pamela K. Starr, eds. *Markets and Democracy in Latin America.* Boulder, Colo.: Lynne Rienner.

Lafer, Celso. 1975. *O Sistema Político Brasileiro* (The Brazilian political system). São Paulo: Editora Perspectiva.

Lamounier, Bolívar. 1994. "Brazil at an Impasse." *Journal of Democracy* 5(3): 72–87.

———. 1995. "Intellectuals and Political Life in Twentieth Century Brazil." In Benno Galjart and Patricio Silva, eds. *Designers of Development: Intellectuals and Technocrats in the*

Third World. Leiden: Research School.

Levy, Daniel C. 1996. *Building the Third Sector: Latin America's Private Research Centers and Nonprofit Development.* Pittsburgh, Penn.: University of Pittsburgh Press.

Loureiro, Maria Rita. 1997. *Os Economistas no Governo* (Economists in government). Rio de Janeiro: Editora Fundação Getúlio Vargas.

Melo, Marcus André. 1993. "Anatomia do Fracasso: Intermediação de Interesses e a Reforma das Políticas Sociais na Nova República" (Anatomy of failure: Intermediation of interests and social policy reform in the new republic). *Dados* 36(1): 119–163.

Pereira, Luiz Carlos Bresser. 1999. "From Bureaucratic to Managerial Public Administration in Brazil." In Luiz Carlos Bresser Pereira and Peter Spink, eds. *Reforming the State: Managerial Public Administration in Latin America.* Boulder, Colo.: Lynne Rienner.

Sadek, Maria Tereza, and Guita G. Debert. 1998. *Terceiro Setor: Uma Avaliação da Legislação* (Third sector: An appraisal of the legislation). São Paulo: Instituto de Estudos Econômicos, Sociais e Políticos de São Paulo.

Schmitter, Philippe. 1971. *Interest Conflict and Political Change in Brazil.* Stanford, Calif.: Stanford University Press.

Schneider, Ben R. 1991. *Politics Within the State: Elite Bureaucrats and Industrial Policy in Authoritarian Brazil.* Pittsburgh, Penn.: University of Pittsburgh Press.

Shugart, Matthew Soberg, and Stephan Haggard. 1997. "Institutions and Public Policy in Presidential Systems." Center for the Study of Democracy Research Paper, University of California at Irvine.

Stone, Diane. 1996. *Capturing the Political Imagination: Think Tanks and the Policy Process.* London: Frank Cass.

———. 2000. "Think Tank Transnationalisation and Non-Profit Analysis, Advice and Advocacy." *Global Society* 14(2): 154–172.

Tendler, Judith. 1997. *Good Government in the Tropics.* Baltimore, Md.: Johns Hopkins University Press.

Weaver, R. Kent. 1989. "The Changing World of Think Tanks." *PS: Political Science and Politics* 22(3): 563–578.

Weaver, R. Kent, and James G. McGann. 2000. "Think Tanks and Civil Societies." In James G. McGann and R. Kent Weaver, eds. *Think Tanks and Civil Societies: Catalysts for Ideas and Action.* New Brunswick, N. J.: Transaction.

Weyland, Kurt. 1998. "From Leviathan to Gulliver? The Decline of the Developmental State in Brazil." *Governance* 11(1): 51–75.

WWF and Mater Natura. 1996. *Cadastro Nacional Ecolista de Instituições Ambientalistas* (National register of environmentalist institutions). Curitiba: Mater Natura—Instituto de Estudos Ambientais.

Appendix A. Alternative Sources of Policy Advice in Brazil

Organization	Mission	Year Formed	Location	Areas of Research	Sources of Support
Executive-Branch Policy Advisory Organizations					
National Social Security Council (CNPS)	"To deliberate over policies and the management of the social security system"	1991	Brasília	Social security	Government
National Science and Technology Council (CNCT)	"To advise and assist the president in the formulation and implementation of science and technology policies, to propose goals and priorities, and to evaluate policy implementation"	1975	Brasília	Science and technology	Government
Solidaristic Community Council	"To provide advice on government policies and social priorities, to foster the development of civil society organizations by acting in partnership with the government, and to promote the coordination of government agencies for the eradication of hunger and poverty"	1995	Brasília	Poverty and social policy	Government
Legislative-Branch Policy Advisory Organizations					
Legislative Support Service (AL)	"To provide legislators with relevant and objective information and help analyze policies and draft legislation"	1972	Brasília	According to the demands of Congress	Government
Budget and Financial Review Service (AOFF)	"To provide Congress with objective analyses of economic and budget decisions"	1979	Brasília	Federal budget	Government
Federal Audit Tribunal (TCU)	"To oversee and review the receipt and disbursement of public funds"	1890	Brasília	Federal budget	Government
Contract Research Think Tanks					
National Institute of Educational Research (INEP)	"To conduct research and assist in the formulation and implementation of educational policy"	1937	Brasília	Education	Government, contract research

Continued on next page

Appendix A—continued

Organization	Mission	Year Formed	Location	Areas of Research	Sources of Support
Joaquim Nabuco Foundation (FJN)	"To produce and disseminate knowledge and promote scientific and cultural activities to foster the development of Brazilian society, principally in the northern and northeastern regions"	1949	Recife	Economic and regional development	Government, contract research, grants
Superior War College (ESG)	"To contribute to the improvement of Brazilian society through research and debate on democratic political-strategic options that may help to solve national problems"	1949	Rio de Janeiro	Development and national security	Government
National Bank of Economic and Social Development (BNDES)	"To provide long-term funding for projects that contribute to the country's development"	1952	Rio de Janeiro	Economic and sectoral policy, industry, foreign trade	Government
Institute of Applied Economic Research (IPEA)	"To function as if it were the critical conscience of the government within the government, debating policy options and helping to correct policy implementation"	1964	Brasília, Rio de Janeiro	Economic issues, income distribution, poverty	Government, contract research
João Pinheiro Foundation (FJP)	"To conduct applied research, consulting, human resource development, and technical support activities"	1969	Belo Horizonte	Regional planning and public-sector management	Government, contract research
Oswaldo Cruz Foundation (FIOCRUZ, Fundação Oswaldo Cruz)	"To produce, absorb, and disseminate scientific and technological knowledge on health through the integrated development of research, teaching, information, and technology activities in order to provide strategic support for the Unified Health System"	1970	Rio de Janeiro	Health care	Government, contract research
Foundation for Administrative Development (FUNDAP)	"To improve organizational, managerial, and performance standards of the public sector and to propose more effective forms of government intervention"	1974	São Paulo	Public-sector management	Government, contract research
Center of Foreign Trade Studies Foundation (FUNCEX)	"To contribute to the development of Brazil's foreign trade"	1976	Rio de Janeiro	Foreign trade	Contract research, grants

				International relations	Government, corporations, grants
Institute for Research on International Relations (IPRI)	"To contribute to the increasing effectiveness of Brazilian foreign policy"	1985	Brasília	International relations	Government, corporations, grants
Academic Think Tanks					
Brazilian Institute of Economics (IBRE)	"To produce and disseminate ideas, data, and information in order to contribute to the country's social and economic development, international integration, national ethical standards, and responsible governance"	1951	Rio de Janeiro	Economic issues, prices and inflation, foreign trade	Contract research, grants
Department of Economics, Pontifical Catholic University of Rio de Janeiro (PUC-RIO)	"Dedicated to research and teaching in economics"	1963	Rio de Janeiro	Economics	University, contract research, grants
University Research Institute of Rio de Janeiro (IUPERJ)	"A center for graduate research and teaching"	1969	Rio de Janeiro	Social and political issues	University, contract research, grants
Brazilian Center for Analysis and Planning (CEBRAP)	"An independent nonprofit research center dedicated to the study of Brazilian society"	1969	São Paulo	Economic, social, and political issues	Contract research, grants
Institute for Economic Research Foundation (FIPE)	"To debate and influence the making of decisions in the public sector"	1972	São Paulo	Economic issues, prices and inflation	University, contract research, grants
Institute for Political and Social Studies (IEPES)	"A higher social sciences study and research center devoted to the analysis of Brazilian development and international relations with emphasis on Latin America and to the discussion of contemporary human and world problems"	1979	Rio de Janeiro	Social and political issues	Contract research, grants
Center for the Study of Contemporary Culture (CEDEC)	"To conduct research on Brazil and the consolidation of its institutional profile as a space to debate a plurality of views regarding today's main theoretical and practical issues"	1979	São Paulo	Social and political issues, culture	Contract research, grants
Institute for Economic, Social and Political Studies (IDESP)	"Dedicated to research and the promotion of public debate in order to contribute to the consolidation and improvement of representative democracy and economic modernization with maximum social equity"	1981	São Paulo	Social and political issues	Contract research, grants

Continued on next page

Appendix A—continued

Organization	Mission	Year Formed	Location	Areas of Research	Sources of Support
Center for the Study of Public Policy (NEPP, Núcleo de Estudos de Políticas Públicas)	"To conduct multidisciplinary research to follow up, monitor, and evaluate public policy"	1982	Campinas	Public policy	University, contract research, grants
Institute of Economics, State University of Campinas (IE-UNICAMP)	"To promote teaching and research in economics"	1969	Campinas	Economic, labor, and agricultural policy	University, contract research, grants
Institute of Advanced Studies (IEA)	"To conduct multidisciplinary research on issues of science and culture"	1986	São Paulo	Science and culture	University, contract research, grants
National Institute of Higher Studies (INAE)	"Operates as an independent, nonpartisan, and pluralist agent of civil society dedicated to promoting a dialogue among public and private national leaders seeking to find ways toward the country's economic, social, political, and cultural development as well as to orient the making of relevant decisions to achieve it"	1987	Rio de Janeiro	Economic, social, and political issues	Corporations, grants
Center for the Study of the World Economy (CEM)	"To encourage research and debate on different issues related to the opening of the economy and Brazil's competitive integration into the external environment"	1990	Rio de Janeiro	International economy	Contract research, grants
Institute of Economics, Federal University of Rio de Janeiro (IE-UFRJ)	"To carry on a tradition of excellence in teaching, thinking, and the provision of specialized services in economics"	1996	Rio de Janeiro	Economic and industrial policy	University, contract research, grants
Advocacy Think Tanks, including Research-Oriented NGOs					
National Confederation of Industry (CNI)	"To promote and support the country's development in a sustainable and balanced manner with respect to its social, economic, and spatial dimensions"	1938	Rio de Janeiro	Economic issues, industry, foreign trade	Corporations
Roberto Simonsen Institute (IRS)	"To create and disseminate ideas to support the right of free initiative"	1948	São Paulo	Economic issues, industry, foreign trade	Corporations

Organization	Mission	Year	Location	Focus	Funding
Inter-Union Department of Statistics and Economic and Social Studies (DIEESE)	"To conduct research, communication, training, and support activities regarding issues related to the world of work"	1955	São Paulo	Employment, income, cost of living	Labor unions, contract research
Institute for the Study of Religion (ISER)	"To support networks, institutions, and initiatives that seek to strengthen civil society and to promote citizenship rights through the production of information and the training of intermediate groups"	1971	Rio de Janeiro	Human rights and public safety	Contract research, grants
Institute of Socio-Economic Studies (INESC)	"To lobby for popular movements in Congress and to provide policy-oriented articulation, assistance, and education"	1979	Brasília	Human rights and international issues	Contract research, grants
Brazilian Institute for Social and Economic Analysis (IBASE)	"To build a radically democratic society guided by the ethical values of liberty, equality, diversity, solidarity, and participation"	1981	Rio de Janeiro	Human rights, economic issues, poverty	Contract research, grants
Liberal Institute (IL)	"To conduct research on and to disseminate free-market liberal ideas"	1983	São Paulo, Rio, Porto Alegre	Free-market ideas	Corporations, individuals
Inter-Union Department of Congressional Assistance Services (DIAP)	"To lobby in order to turn into law principal, majority, or consensual working-class demands"	1983	Brasília	Labor issues	Labor unions
Institute for Social Policy Studies, Training and Consulting (POLIS)	"To promote radical urban democracy and to strengthen civil society and social movements to attain sustainable and democratic city management"	1987	Brasília	Human rights and economic and international issues	Grants, sale of services
Fernand Braudel World Economy Institute	"To study the ways and conditions of strengthening market forces as a means of survival in the face of rapid change in the world economy"	1987	São Paulo	Free-market economy and global integration	Corporations, grants
Institute for Industrial Development Studies (IEDI)	"To formulate and implement an industrial development policy as part of a national project to expand the share of Brazilian industry in world production, to increase the production of high-value-added goods and the continued growth of national wealth, and to improve standards of living in order to build a more just and egalitarian society"	1989	São Paulo	Industrial and economic policy	Corporations

Continued on next page

Appendix A—continued

Organization	Mission	Year Formed	Location	Areas of Research	Sources of Support
Institute of Amazon Man and Environment (IMAZON)	"To promote the sustainable development of the Amazon through research, dissemination of information, and training"	1990	Belém	Environment and land use	Contract research, grants
Institute for Society, Population and Nature (ISPN)	"To contribute to the attainment of economic growth with social equality and environmental protection"	1990	Brasília	Environment and economic growth	Contract research, grants
Brazilian Foundation for Sustainable Development (FBDS)	"To help implement environmental treaties through research projects, the identification of new environmental technologies, and human resource training in environmental issues"	1991	Rio de Janeiro	Environment	Contract research, corporations, grants
Atlantic Institute (IA)	"To disseminate modernization proposals inspired by democratic and liberal economic ideals"	1993	Rio de Janeiro	Free-market ideas	Corporations, individuals
Socioenvironmental Institute (Instituto Socioambiental)	"To defend social and human rights regarding the environment and the cultural heritage of mankind"	1994		Environment	Contract research, grants
Ethos Institute of Business and Social Responsibility	"To disseminate business social responsibility, implement policies and practices that meet high ethical standards, and act in partnership with the community"	1998	São Paulo	Business social responsibility	Corporations
Political Party Think Tanks					
Tancredo Neves Institute for Political and Social Studies (ITN)	"To propagate free-market liberal thinking"	1985	Brasília	Economic, political, and social issues	Government (through the Political Party Fund)
Perseu Abramo Foundation	"An organ oriented toward research, the development of party doctrine, and political education"	1996	São Paulo	Party political history and doctrine and opinion research	Government (through the Political Party Fund)

Source: Information compiled by author from annual reports, organizational inquiries, and websites.

6 Germany

Martin W. Thunert

There is little doubt that the demand for expert advice in politics, business, and society as a whole is on the increase in Germany. Politics, in particular, requires a constant flow of new ideas and concepts if it is to master the urgent and complex problems that face it today. Alternative policy advisory organizations (APAOs) are playing an increasing role in advising leaders in the public and private sectors on the strategic choices before them. Consequently, the policy advice industry in Germany has become much more diverse and complex since the 1980s and so have its clients.[1] Gone are the times when the federal government (Bundesregierung), the Federal Assembly (Bundestag), and large corporatist actors such as labor unions and employer associations were the only patrons of external advice. Today, governments and public sector agencies on all different levels of government—from the European level down to the municipal level—as well as diverse interest groups, small business associations, labor unions, and, more recently, grass-roots organizations, nongovernmental organizations (NGOs), and lobbies are using policy experts and research in developing their own positions on public policy questions.

THE POLITICAL AND CULTURAL ENVIRONMENT OF APAOS IN GERMANY

Germany is a parliamentary democracy with a strong tradition of cabinet and, arguably, "prime ministerial" government (chancellor democracy), a tradition-conscious civil service, and party domination of policymaking. Strong party discipline allows political parties to present a united front within parliament, and most maintain sizable in-house research capacities to assist in the formulation and analysis of legislation. On the federal level, a permanent career civil service staffed with senior bureaucrats and having powerful internal policymaking capacities traditionally has been suspicious of too much dependence on external advice. Leadership in policy development is not only shared between the Chancellery and the ministries, but is heavily confined by the federal structure of the political system, by the Federal Constitutional Court, and by the European Central Bank (replacing the German Central Bank, or Bundesbank, as the guardian of price stability), and by power relationships within the governing coalition and the ruling party. Thus, compared to the U.K. prime minister, for example, the German chancellor seems to act in a more restrictive leadership setting (Niclauss 2000, 69). His role is to lay down policy guidelines and direct the business of government.

Another crucial variable that shapes the opportunities for and constraints on Germany's APAOs is federalism. Germany became a nation-state only in 1871. Today, the country is composed of sixteen states (*Länder*), some of which rest on age-old regional identities and traditions, while others were designed more recently as administrative units. Despite strong regional subcultures, however, German federalism follows a cooperative pattern rather than the dual or competitive model of American or Canadian federalism. Fiscal revenues are shared and redistributed between the federal, regional, and local levels to comply with the constitutional mandate to approach an equality of living conditions throughout the country. Governmental responsibilities are defined mostly on a national level, then become functionally decentralized, and are often carried out at the state and local levels, or under the joint jurisdiction of the national and state governments, but rarely result in competition between the *Länder*. Participation by the *Länder* in national politics is strong and is carried out through the second legislative chamber, the Federal Council (Bundesrat), which is a parliament of state executives rather than a directly elected body. In areas such as culture, education, research, and the administration of justice—areas where *Länder* jurisdiction is paramount and *Länder* autonomy is strongest—federalism works through intergovernmental bodies.

German federalism is thus an executive-dominated, interlocking system of shared, but functionally decentralized, responsibilities. Important governmental bodies such as the Constitutional Court and other high courts, the Bundesbank, or the Federal Court of Audit are not located in the nation's capital, but are scattered throughout the country. The same is true for important components of the national media (few, if any, newspapers or magazines of national importance are published in Berlin or Bonn), and in particular for the scientific and business infrastructure. The German landscape of APAOs reflects these dual traditions of functional decentralization and cultural autonomy. This does not mean, however, that advisory bodies outside the capital concentrate primarily on issues of regional importance. Rather, functional decentralization is above all an attempt to ensure some regional input into national or transnational discourses on policymaking.

Cultural and mental predisposition, as well as the legacy of German history, are other important variables for understanding the role and self-image of policy experts and advisory bodies in Germany. Postwar German political culture was shaped by a consensus orientation on the basic tenets of the German "social state." Moreover, the (technocratic) ideal of "nonideological pragmatism" among many members of APAOs can also be attributed to the exceptionally strong scholarly disposition (*Wissenschaftlichkeit*) that can be found among many policy experts in Germany. Most members of the policy advice industry are reasonably proud of their scholarly reputations, their research profiles, and the soundness of their academic work. For example, more than 70 percent of German think tanks surveyed by this author in the late 1990s believed these qualities to be their major assets. This strong scholarly disposition is reinforced by a negative attitude toward partisanship. To have a sharp partisan or ideological profile is seen neither as desirable nor as an advantage in the policy advice market. William Wallace correctly explains the prevailing search for consensus and the unusually high respect for impartial research by pointing to "Germany's broken history." The reestablishment of democratic government in West Germany after the Second World War brought with it an active concern to encourage informed and reasoned debate through state support at a level far stronger than has been thought necessary in either the United Kingdom or France (Wallace 1994, 152).

Stages of APAO Development

Between the founding of the Federal Republic in 1949 and the mid-1960s, the federal executive branch was the sole recipient and the exclusive patron of external policy advice. There was no concerted effort to organize policy advice across departments or between the core executive and the ministries. Most policy planning was carried out on the ministerial level in mutual isolation from other departments or from the core executive. Departments would commission the occasional report from policy experts, none of which was made public. The advice-giving process was strictly confidential and excluded the public almost completely (Reinecke 1996). Consultative bodies that included policymakers, bureaucrats, and academic experts emerged first in the mid-1950s in areas of overlapping federal and state jurisdiction—especially in the fields of education and science policy. Thereafter, the German APAO industry underwent at least five stages of postwar development. Each stage opened a window of opportunity for APAO growth and expansion, and each has left a long-lasting organizational legacy.

The first opportunity arose in the early 1960s, when the executive realized that

Germany, in contrast to other countries in the North Atlantic Alliance, was insufficiently able to base its decisions on sound research and information, especially in the areas of foreign, security, and economic policy. The establishment of the Council of Economic Experts and quasi-ministerial think tanks in security policy and international affairs, as well as the emergence of strong public sponsorship of economic research, are the organizational legacies of this particular period.

The second window, which was possibly the largest, opened in the late 1960s, when societal actors—above all the student movement—demanded an end to executive hegemony in politics. This was also a time when the legislatures became more assertive and when confidence in scientific, functional, and technocratic approaches to governance, coupled with a strong belief in the superiority of social science methods, were paramount. Planning bureaus, legislative support organizations—including study commissions and their external aids such as the Social Science Research Center Berlin (WZB, Wissenschaftszentrum Berlin für Sozialforschung)—and "countercultural" think tanks such as peace research institutes date from this era.

In the third stage, the energy crisis, the environmental movement, and the "limits to growth" mood of the late 1970s encouraged the distrust of mainstream expertise, the inclusion of "alternative" experts and nonexperts in consulting processes, and the establishment of assessment bodies and auditing agencies. That was followed in the 1980s by a fourth stage, which brought institutional consolidation and maturation of existing APAOs, as well as a few specialized newcomers such as the think tank called the Wuppertal Institute for Climate, Environment, and Energy (Wuppertal-Institut für Klima, Umwelt und Energie) and the Office of Technology Assessment (Büro für Technikfolgen-Abschätzung), a federal advisory bureau.

Finally, the most recent stage was precipitated by the end of the cold war and was further intensified by the effects of German unification, including the transfer of the capital to Berlin and the redistribution of funds among state-sponsored research organizations. These events, combined with the impact of globalization and European integration, led to a (partial) reassessment and readjustment of Germany's internal and external policy research infrastructure and to a new debate about the appropriate role of external and alternative policy advisory organizations.

It is likely that future discussion on APAOs in Germany will shift from the issue of institutional sustainability to issues of public visibility and policy influence. If this prediction proves to be accurate, the future challenge for these organizations will no longer lie primarily in seizing the right moment for organizational growth and institutional expansion, but in improving the awareness of expert advisors of windows of opportunity for public visibility and policy influence. In short, APAOs would be well advised to assume the role of policy entrepreneurs, capitalizing on the opening of policy windows.

CURRENT STATUS OF ALTERNATIVE SOURCES OF POLICY ADVICE

Internal Resources Available to the Executive Branches

There is no uniform system of advisory structures across all levels and sectors of the German government. Ministers, and even more so the chancellor, play a rather selective role in the process of policy development. Federal ministries are run relatively independently within the broad policy guidelines of the chancellor. Policies are drafted in the ministries first, before being presented to the cabinet. The chancellor and his inner circle of senior civil servants and advisors are unable to control the activities of the ministries on a day-to-day basis. Accordingly, senior staff in the Federal Chancellor's Office are as much there to monitor the ministries as they are to design policy.

EXECUTIVE CONSULTATIVE BODIES WITHIN THE FEDERAL EXECUTIVE BRANCH

Within the federal executive, there are numerous consultative bodies, including scientific advisory boards, specialized interdepartmental committees, ministerial working groups and planning bureaus, and ad hoc consultants. In the mid-1990s, Axel Murswieck (1994, 110) counted 294 advisory bodies with a combined staff of 2,875 answering to the ministries of the federal government. Only a fraction of these staff members are external policy experts. Most of these consultants and advisory bodies work for the line organizations of their ministries and provide informative rather than strategic advice to their clients. For example, the scientific advisory boards at the Ministries of Finance, Economics and Technology, and Economic Cooperation and Development deal with specific problems pertinent to the agenda and jurisdiction of the corresponding ministry and are composed of external academic experts and some practitioners. Although their reports are published, they rarely receive attention outside the ministries.

More recently, planning bureaus—especially in the Foreign Office—have increased informal exchanges with external experts. In addition to several thousand civil servants working in-house for information-generating units, the federal government also spends substantial funds (33 million–40 million euros, or roughly US$29 million–US$35 million) for out-contracted consulting and research (Murswieck 1993). Taken together, these internal structures of governmental policy advice reflect the interests of the senior bureaucrats within the ministries and strengthen their position vis-à-vis not only the legislature and the general public, but also the core executive.

CENTRAL EXECUTIVE REVIEW AGENCIES AND POLICY PLANNING UNITS OF THE FEDERAL GOVERNMENT

In the late 1980s, when Renate Mayntz studied the organizational and procedural arrangements designed to assist ministers and the chancellor with policy and strategic advice, she concluded that "in West Germany there are hardly any advisory staffs outside the regular ministerial bureaucracy which serve the top executive directly" (1987, 5–6). Although this description is still accurate in quantitative terms, change has been slowly emerging in qualitative terms. Compared to the United States, for example, the number of political appointees is quite small.[2] However, lacking a more flexible structure to appoint armies of special advisors, the politicization of the uppermost reaches of the bureaucracy, as well as devices such as "external recruitment for top positions" and "early political retirement" may serve as functional equivalents (Bakvis 1997). These externally recruited deputy ministers, parliamentary state secretaries, and directors are almost always partisans of particular policies, if not of specific political parties and their factions. Their continual preoccupation with pressing political matters, their likely inexperience, and their sometimes uneasy relationship with the career civil service clearly limit their advisory roles in long-term policy planning and in performing as a counterweight to the line bureaucracy.[3]

The Chancellery, headed by a chief-of-staff (with the rank of a secretary of state), is there to assist the chancellor in the fulfillment of his duties. While a good deal of responsibility for policy development is accorded to the key ministries such as Finance, Labor and Social Affairs, Health, Defense, and the Foreign Office, the Chancellery serves as a coordinator and conflict manager between ministries and among the partners in the coalition governments that have become the rule in Germany. Today, the Chancellery employs a staff of approximately 450 (Niclauss 2000, 68). Besides serving as a secretariat for cabinet committees and the Chancellor's personal office, the Chancellery has prominent political importance as a center for government policy coordination.

Similar to the situation in the federal ministries, a distinction is made at the Chancellery between the policymaking level and the operating or working level. The policymaking level includes the chancellor, the chief-of-staff, the ministers of state (deputy ministers), the heads of directorates, two working staff, and representatives of the chancellor's personal office. The operating units are either "mirror" units, which are responsible for the policy area of a single ministry, or "cross-sectional" units, whose responsibilities cut across several ministries or jurisdictions (Niclauss 2000, 68).[4]

Starting in 1967, several attempts were made to incorporate a policy planning and review unit into the core executive, working alongside but somewhat autonomously from the line organizations of the civil service. A Policy Planning Bureau (Planungsstab) composed of three civil servants, three external academics, and two other staff members, and having a broad mandate to address long-term strategy as well as more immediate concerns, was created in 1967 under Chancellor Kurt Georg Kiesinger (1966–1969). It failed for four reasons: lack of support from and dialogue with the chief executive; lack of cooperation with line directorates within the Chancellery; resistance from line ministries; and lack of corporate identity and team spirit among the staff members (Krevert 1993, 91–93).

The Planning Bureau was revamped as a formal policy coordinating and review directorate under Chancellor Willy Brandt (1969–1974) and his chief-of-staff, Horst Ehmke, in 1969. It had two main functions: to coordinate policy and to plan long-term policy projects (Müller-Rommel 2000, 93). The new planning unit was supposed to act as a moderator and coordinator at the apex of an interdepartmental policy planning alliance, employing state-of-the art "scientific" planning, programming, and budgeting techniques. Due to both a supportive chief-of-staff and an equally committed planning director, the new directorate operated quite successfully at first, but soon aroused resentment among certain ministries (which were suspicious of a strong Chancellery in the first place) and met resistance from departmental civil servants. A lack of political backing from the decision-making level—i.e., a lack of willingness to accept the results of policy planning as binding recommendations—led to a downgrading of the planning directorate to a unit responsible for data collection and speech writing (Müller-Rommel 2000, 93; Krevert 1993, 180–181). The Chancellery therefore remained, above all, a "multi-purpose administrative body" (Murswieck 1993, 88).

Some chancellors have used the political and administrative potential of the office better than others. When looking for external advice, chancellors have often turned to kitchen cabinets and other ad hoc advising structures. Such informal mechanisms are often a function of personal style and are thus not well suited to drawing general conclusions. With Chancellor Helmut Schmidt (1974–1982), kitchen cabinets coincided with the formal structures of a highly professional Chancellery, whereas under the longest-serving chancellors, Konrad Adenauer (1949–1963) and Helmut Kohl (1982–1998), these circles tended to include more outside forces. Participants were often drawn from the party or from banks and business associations, but also included sympathetic journalists and an occasional academic generalist. Schmidt and Kohl (the latter in his post-unification terms) utilized flexible advisory structures like "situation meetings," "extended consultation circles," and cross-cutting "working groups." Neither chancellor was particularly well disposed toward formally institutionalized planning and review bureaus or directorates. In the last years of the Kohl era, a consensus seemed to emerge among reform-minded experts, politicians, corporate leaders, and management consultants that innovative leadership for the modernization of Germany would require a strengthening of the policy capacity of the core executive, not by creating new bureaucratic bodies, but by utilizing intelligently the available knowledge resources and new means of communication.

It is still too early to give a conclusive account of incumbent Chancellor Gerhard Schröder's advisory arrangements. Advisory structures surrounding his government reflect the fact that he is, above all, a pragmatic politician. Most of the time, Schröder is a consensus-seeker with a strong preference for external advisory structures that feature bipartisan blue-ribbon commissions, stakeholding groups in tripartite arrangements, and action-oriented rather than intellectual leaders. At other times, he seems to favor radical breaks with the past, both in terms of policy and political strategy. The following examples of advisory arrangements at the Chancellery reflect Schröder's pragmatic approach to governing.

Creating a Narrative for Governance

After he was sworn in as chancellor, Schröder brought in Bodo Hombach as chief-of-staff, an individual who clearly belonged in the "political type" category of chiefs-of-staff (Müller-Rommel 2000, 92). As a strategist and former political consultant, Hombach was instrumental in coining Schröder's election slogan, the "New Middle," and was one of the few advisors trying to fill this German version of the British so-called "New" Labour Party's "Third Way" with substantive content. Working closely with key policy advisors from the Labour government under Tony Blair, Hombach and his small team in the Chancellery were searching for an overarching narrative not just to pull together government priorities in Germany, but to give coherence to a new centrist and social democratic approach to policymaking across Europe. The preliminary result of this attempt was a joint British-German declaration entitled "The Way Forward for Europe's Social Democrats," drafted by Hombach and his British counterpart Peter Mandelson. The manifesto called for a radical reform of the two nations' pension and welfare systems and criticized European center-left parties and governments for being too slow to adapt to economic globalization. It was announced by Schröder and Blair on June 8, 1999, in London—immediately before the elections to the European Parliament, where both leaders' parties performed poorly in their respective countries. The declaration received a frosty reception from Germany's Social Democratic Party (SPD) and among social democrats on the Continent. It was largely ignored in the United Kingdom and was officially shelved in Germany, but some of Schröder's domestic policy measures in Germany—especially in economic and fiscal policy—are nonetheless consistent with the general thrust of that document.

Hombach's endeavors represent an informal way of converting sections of the Chancellery into a policy-developing think tank. His strategy to create an intellectual, policy-oriented power center in the Chancellery, thereby bypassing party think tanks and party structures as well as the SPD parliamentary delegation, was too bold, too provocative, and too nonbureaucratic to succeed instantly. On the other hand, he communicated successfully to the chancellor that, despite a pragmatic case-by-case approach to governing, some vision or set of bigger ideas—as the New Middle was meant to be—should serve as the blueprint for policy coordination and should guide the course of governance. After several rounds of rather informal consulting sessions with public intellectuals, the notion that Germany should develop into a less state-centered "civil society" (*Bürgergesellschaft*) has become the chancellor's preferred framework for determining long-range government priorities.

Domestic Policy Coordination: Alliance for Jobs, Training and Competitiveness

Hombach, who was replaced in July 1999 as chief-of-staff by Frank Walter Steinmeier (who represents the administrative type), also left his mark on another consulting arrangement at the core executive, which seems more in line with Germany's bureaucratic and cultural traditions: the Alliance for Jobs, Training and Competitiveness (AfJ, Bündnis für Arbeit, Ausbildung und Wettbewerbsfähigkeit).[5] A more institutionalized form of providing external advice to the core executive, the Alliance for Jobs is a tripartite arrangement between the federal government (as represented by senior staff of the Chancellery and cabinet members) and employers' associations and trade unions (as represented by their leaders), designed to address structural tensions in the German labor market through a range of reform initiatives. As such, the AfJ, which originated as a trade union initiative and was adopted by Schröder during his campaign as a policy response to high unemployment, represents a continuation of the postwar German tradition of seeking consensual solutions to economic difficulties. As a result, we might expect the AfJ to be characteristic of interest-group-driven and corporatist consultative arrangements.[6] To be sure, similarities in the institutional arrangements between the AfJ and earlier tripartite arrangements based around peak-level negotiations are inevitable. On closer inspection, however, the AfJ reveals signs of a new approach to a seemingly traditional consulting and negotiating arrangement: In addition to a Steering Group, the institutional framework for the AfJ comprises a Benchmarking Group. Both are under the leadership of the Chancellery, while nine additional working groups are under the leadership of various ministries.

The Benchmarking Group is the section of AfJ where external policy experts play an important role. One member is the director of the Cologne Institute for

Business Research (Institut der deutschen Wirtschaft Köln), the main think tank of the Confederation of German Employers' Associations (BDA, Bundesvereinigung der Deutschen Arbeitgeberverbände). A second is the director of the Institute of Economic and Social Research (Wirtschafts-und Sozialwissenschaftliches Institute) of the German Federation of Trade Unions (DGB, Deutscher Gewerkschaftsbund), while others are from universities or academic think tanks. The Benchmarking Group has the task of comparing the AfJ with other international examples of labor market policies and other negotiating arrangements, as well as considering the broader political and socioeconomic implications of the AfJ's work. While the inclusion of the Benchmarking Group is a distinct innovation from earlier tripartite consultative arrangements, the group's own aspiration of membership in the AfJ Steering Committee was not met.

The experience of the Benchmarking Group has been mixed. By addressing the specific issue of unemployment within the context of a large number of international socioeconomic debates and from a holistic perspective, the group proved to be an ambitious project, reminiscent of the Labour Party's desire for strategic "joined-up" government. It has been complicated, however, by difficulties—similar to those experienced by earlier attempts to establish central review and policy planning bureaus—in coordinating information-sharing between various ministries and the core executive. The experience of the Benchmarking Group has also demonstrated the narrow limits for research-based independent policy advice in interest-driven consulting arrangements. In May 1999, a report produced by two prominent and fairly independent academics of the group, Wolfgang Streeck and Rolf Heinze, was leaked to the news magazine *Der Spiegel*. The report focused on the low-wage employment sector and suggested that a combination of progressive tax cuts and wage subsidies—loosely based on the U.S. Earned Income Tax Credit for the working poor—would be a means of creating employment opportunities. Representatives of both labor and business gave the report a frosty reception, not just because it was leaked to the press, but because it was seen as a proposal for a deregulated service sector with little relevance to the industrial sector, which both of the nongovernmental sides in the AfJ represent. The report clearly undermined the credibility of the Benchmarking Group within the AfJ framework (Silvia 1999; Timmins 2000), but has increased its standing among the wider public.

Transnational Policy Coordination:
Modern Governance in the 21st Century
After the government had moved from Bonn to Berlin in the summer of 1999, a policy planning directorate known as Directorate 5 (Abteilung 5) became fully operational in the Chancellery. It has the features of a policy unit, is headed by a

policy-minded civil servant, Wolfgang Nowak, and is much more focused on policymaking than was the planning directorate under the Kohl government. According to the official government directory (Erb 2000), the main tasks of the new directorate are planning the legislative term, identifying policy priorities, evaluating and benchmarking new approaches and models to governance and problem solving, analyzing economic and technological trends, interpreting polling results and opinion research, and preparing content for important speeches and publications.

The most publicized activity to date of Directorate 5 in the field of policy coordination and advice giving was the planning and organization of an international summit on "Modern Governance in the 21st Century," which brought fourteen heads of reform-oriented, center-left governments to Berlin on June 2–3, 2000.[7] The conference was intended to provide information about various ways in which participating governments and countries could shape their responses to the key issues of the new economy and globalization, the future of governance and the administrative state, and new approaches to state–civil society relations. During the conference, the 14 chief executives were able to rely on the expert advice of some 150 academic advisors (each country was given a maximum of 10–12 experts) who helped define the essential themes of the reform summit and drew up a communiqué. The German delegation of experts comprised a number of directors and key staff of well-known German think tanks, one head of a corporate think tank, some policy-oriented journalists, and a small number of corporate executives. Similar to the benchmarking methods used in business administration and economics, politicians and experts reflected on various approaches to similar policy problems in order to learn from the experience of others. Furthermore, the experts had the opportunity to sound out the idea of building global networks of thinkers and academic research institutions. Such networks will have the task of furthering the work done in Florence and Berlin and of highlighting options for policy action.

In addition to the governance summit, several ad hoc advisory bodies with the participation of policy researchers and public intellectuals have been set up around the Chancellery, whose task it is to provide Schröder with visions as well as policy recommendations on issues such as the new economy and new approaches to state–civil society relations. Those efforts have resulted in several high-profile articles and magazine contributions on these issues authored by the chancellor.

CENTRAL EXECUTIVE REVIEW AGENCIES AND POLICY PLANNING UNITS OF THE *LÄNDER* GOVERNMENTS

The most ambitious attempt to date to incorporate a policy unit staffed with both external academics and civil servants on the state level was carried out between 1989 and 1993 in the premier's office of the state of Schleswig-Holstein, under Premier Björn Engholm of the SPD. After four years of operation, this unit—named Denkfabrik (think tank, or, literally, "think factory")—was abolished by Engholm's successor, Heide Simonis (ironically, from the same party) and replaced with a more managerial controlling unit.

The reasons for Denkfabrik's demise are complex. It was staffed with three outsiders and four insiders and was composed of three units that addressed Schleswig-Holstein's options in three key areas: its role in the EU common market, its role in the Baltic region, and its potential as a location for high-tech industries. Between 1989 and 1992, twenty-one out of fifty specific recommendations made by the EU unit were implemented. On the other hand, in 1989, on the eve of the fall of the Berlin Wall, the proposals of the Baltic Sea unit were ahead of their times. A policy window for implementing some of those proposals only fully appeared in the mid-1990s, when the dynamic potential of the newly opened Baltic region, which had been hit so hard by the cold war, became more visible. Moreover, the Denkfabrik met the usual bureaucratic obstacles within the line bureaucracy. Its activities were constantly scrutinized by a skeptical opposition in the state legislature. The medium- and long-term nature of its work did not correspond well to the overall mood of a poor, high-deficit state like Schleswig-Holstein. In addition, the unit did not fit well into the managerial approach to policymaking of the early 1990s, which also was clearly the new premier's personal policy style.

Generally speaking, attempts to create innovative central executive review structures on the state level have not been particularly successful and one should not have illusions about the policy capacity of the state governments. Only some of the larger states—especially Bavaria—maintain significant in-house research capabilities and interfaces with external advice.

Internal and External Resources
Available to the Legislative Branch

With at least 656 members, of whom 328 are elected in the constituencies and an additional 328 via lists of candidates drawn up by the political parties in each state, the German Bundestag is today the largest parliament among Western democracies. From the late 1960s on, the Bundestag became increasingly interested in establishing its own sources of political advice. Undoubtedly, some of the changes made in the early 1970s were carried out under the reformist spirit of the first term of a Social Democratic/Liberal government (1969–1972) and under the pressure of a more self-conscious civil society. But it is equally true that they occurred at a point in time when every political party represented in the Bundestag had experienced the role of the opposition, lacking the resources that the executive and the government majority in a parliamentary system enjoy.

The work of the Bundestag is largely determined by the parliamentary groups, or party caucuses, known as *Fraktionen*, and their executive committees. They are the key centers of political power and the main driving force in the work of the Bundestag. It is in these parliamentary groups that the political parties agree on the positions they then present to the Bundestag and to the general public. The logic of parliamentary government requires—and the public expects—unity on issues from parliamentary groups, and especially from the governing parties. Each parliamentary group sets up a number of working groups to prepare the ground for decisions subsequently taken by the group as a whole, and appoints spokespeople to the Bundestag committees. Permanent committees are a mirror image of the executive branch. The work of the Bundestag committees is largely prepared and steered by the parliamentary groups. As the bulk of the Bundestag's work—carried out by parliamentary groups, working groups, permanent committees, and subcommittees—takes place behind closed doors and therefore goes unnoticed by the larger public, it is not always easy to determine the access points for nonbureaucratic policy advice. Advisory resources can be broken down into three categories: (1) resources for the Bundestag as a whole and its committees; (2) support services for parliamentary groups, members of parliament (MPs), and committees; and (3) resources for individual MPs.

RESOURCES FOR THE BUNDESTAG
AS A WHOLE AND ITS COMMITTEES
Hearings
The committees may and do invite experts and representatives of interest groups to attend their nonpublic meetings. In order to obtain information on a subject under debate, the committees also hold public hearings, attended by experts from outside the Bundestag, who are often policy experts from interest groups. The committees make extensive use of their power to convene such hearings. Occasionally, but not on a regular basis, public hearings are broadcast on television and the proceedings are published in a Bundestag series.

Legislative Policy Analysis Unit: Office of Technology Assessment
Unlike the United States' General Accounting Office, there is no auditing agency working exclusively on behalf of the Bundestag. There is no equivalent to the Congressional Budget Office either. However, the Congressional Office of Technology Assessment, which was abolished by the U.S. Congress in 1995 (Bimber 1996), inspired the creation of a similar body at the Bundestag committee level, also named the Office of Technology Assessment (TAB, Büro für Technikfolgen-Abschätzung).

In November 1989, the Bundestag decided to institutionalize technology assessment in parliament. They followed a recommendation given in an earlier report of the Study Commission on Technology Assessment and created a new instrument for gathering information and assisting parliamentary decision making. The Bundestag gave its Committee on Education, Research, and Technology Assessment the task of initiating technology impact analyses and seeking ways to translate their findings into practical policy. The committee was authorized to commission external bodies of experts to conduct advisory and consulting work in the area of technology assessment. While the steering committee would be made up exclusively of MPs, the new external office would be an academic body of scientists and researchers.

In 1990, the Institute for Technology Assessment and Systems Analysis (ITAS) at the Karlsruhe Research Center assumed responsibility (for a five-year renewable term) for conducting technology assessment. TAB is a unit of ITAS, but is physically located at the seat of the Bundestag in Berlin. Organizationally, it is a combination of in-house consulting agency and contract research institute. TAB works directly on behalf of its parent Bundestag committee and prepares analyses on such issues as ways to reduce the load on the transportation system. TAB's mandate is to conduct technology assessment, monitor activities, and advise the Bundestag of its findings, with the purpose of providing the parliament with the information it needs for active policymaking in the fields of science and technology. In this way, TAB has followed the U.S. Office of Technology Assessment model.

Legislative Study Commissions

A distinction must be made between committees of inquiry (*Untersuchungskommissionen*) and study commissions (*Enquete-Kommissionen*). Whereas the former are composed entirely of members of the Bundestag and follow an investigative mandate, the latter comprise both MPs and external experts. Study commissions are intended to establish a more permanent, institutionalized, and transparent relationship between practitioners and experts. They were also established to enhance the institutional standing of the parliament vis-à-vis the executive.[8] Their task is to gather as much relevant information as possible on a given subject, thereby providing legislators with a basis for decision making on complex issues. Their topics of inquiry are chosen by a bipartisan panel of MPs on the basis of the importance of a particular subject for the long-term development of society and politics. Very narrow or short-term policy issues are never the focus of their attention. During the period 1998–2002, five legislative study commissions are under way, focused on the themes "The Globalization of World Economics," "The Future of Civic Engagement," "Demographic Change—Challenges of an Aging Society," "Sustainable Energy Supply under Conditions of Globalization and Liberalization," and "Law and Ethics of Modern Medicine."

Study commissions are composed of approximately eleven or twelve MPs, selected according to the current balance of parliamentary representation, plus a similar number of external experts nominated by parliamentary parties. (Hence, their composition reflects the political cleavages and the partisan balance of power in the Bundestag.) Experts appointed to the study commissions enjoy the same rights as the MPs. The reports presented to the Bundestag by study commissions do not end with recommendations for decisions by the Bundestag plenary. Rather, if the Bundestag is to make a decision on them, proposals contained in the reports must be adopted by the plenary or by the federal government and introduced in the Bundestag in the form of a motion or a bill. More often than not, commissioners argue and vote along party lines about the content of the final report. Because of the long-term nature of their topics of inquiry, final reports of study commissions are said to be more influential among the public at large and among certain expert communities than among decision makers.

The commissions have immediate legislative impact only in the rarest of cases (e.g., technology assessment) and they rarely initiate legislation. Since the study commissions do not deal with immediate policy concerns from the government's legislative agenda, this is not surprising. On the other hand, when bills touching on a study commission's subject come up for authorization and are being read in the Bundestag, recommendations and reports of the relevant commission often provide the intellectual background for policy deliberations in the Bundestag committees. Study commissions have also strengthened member MPs' policy knowledge and policy capacity, as well as their political standing. This is particularly relevant for opposition MPs. Some MPs use membership in these commissions to enhance their public profile and to demonstrate that they are interested and competent in the intellectual dimension of governance. These MPs sometimes go on to serve as deputy ministers or in similar policy-oriented functions. For their part, experts often leave their term on study commissions frustrated about their poor leverage, but with a more realistic view of the utilization of scientific knowledge in politics. In addition, study commissions have sharpened the Bundestag's teaching and informing functions, as reports and high-profile expert hearings often stimulate debate among academics and the broader public (Euchner, Hampel, and Seidel 1993, 25). In some cases—especially in the areas of technology assessment and science policy—study commission reports have contributed to enhancing the legitimacy of governmental policy decisions among the electorate.

SUPPORT SERVICES FOR PARLIAMENTARY GROUPS, INDIVIDUAL MPS, AND COMMITTEES

Members of parliament are granted an annual allowance of up to 88,491 euros to hire staff under private law employment contracts. It is up to individual MPs to define, in line with their specific needs, the qualifications staff should have and the tasks they are expected to perform. Many of the personal staff, of whom there are currently 4,000 in total, work on a part-time basis; around 40 percent work in the constituency offices. Personal staff tend to encompass three main functions: administration, communication, and advising. Less than 20 percent of personal staff are acting in an advisory role. On the operational level of the Bundestag, policy expertise is concentrated in the leadership staff of parliamentary groups. The parliamentary groups employ a total of some 800 staff members, whom they pay through grants from the federal budget. These staff are partly specialist advisors and partly administrative support personnel (Murswieck 1993).

Each of the Bundestag's twenty-three permanent committees, as well as committees of inquiry and study commissions, has a small secretariat at its disposal—provided by the Bundestag administration—which offers mostly technical, administrative, and organizational assistance for their work. Since the other tasks of committee secretariats include advising the committee chairman, as well as maintaining contact with the ministries, parties, parliamentary groups, and interest associations, one can assume that purely informative policy advice is provided by the secretariats at random. Another staff of eighty supports the Bundestag Petition Committee, which responds to citizens who exercise their right to address requests and complaints to the Bundestag.

SUPPORT SERVICES FOR INDIVIDUAL MPS:
THE BUNDESTAG REFERENCE AND RESEARCH SERVICES

In a parliamentary democracy like Germany, institutionalized legislative support services are perhaps most important for MPs from opposition parties and for individual backbenchers of the ruling parties, who may be cut off from the information flow among the power centers in the executive, the leadership of parliamentary groups, and key committee chairs.

The Bundestag Reference and Research Services is one of three directorates-general within the Bundestag administration. It provides the backup that MPs require in terms of specialized information and documentation when dealing with legislation and other policy issues. The staff of approximately 400 includes librarians, archivists, information specialists, and a small minority of policy experts. In existence since 1951, the institution underwent a number of organizational changes but has maintained a reputation for providing federal MPs with the most interest-free, nonbureaucratic, nonpartisan, factual, and scientific information they can get in the capital. In its early stages, the research services were divided into a more policy-oriented committee service, answering directly to committees, and an information-oriented reference service that concentrated on conducting archival work and running a parliamentary library. (With 1.2 million books and 11,000 journals, the library is one of the largest of its kind.)

Even after its bureaucratic consolidation in the late 1960s, the division of labor between committee services and documentation services was upheld informally, but another dimension was added, the Specialized Research Services (SRS). In line with the overall Bundestag administration growth rates, the services' staff grew by roughly 30 percent in the early 1970s and became slightly more activist in offering their products, although they still kept a low public, and even parliamentary, profile. The main form of advising individual MPs is through studies and reports conducted by the SRS. Members can request the SRS—which employs a staff of sixty academically trained experts, many of whom hold a law degree—to provide specialist information on any issue relevant to federal policy. In response to such requests, the SRS prepares some 2,000 studies each year. In addition to complying with requests from MPs, the individual research sections of SRS also have an extensive range of information services they provide on their own initiative, including studies on topics of general interest, background notes on new issues, and summaries of important judicial decisions. To meet demand, 12,000 copies of these studies are distributed each year.

The Bundestag Reference and Research Services continues to be an important source of information for individual MPs. In the German parliamentary system of government, the services' staff does not help MPs legislate—they do not compete with the executive line bureaucracy in drafting legislation, nor do they evaluate or improve private MP bills. When they do move beyond information collection and selection, these reference and research specialists summarize and analyze policy-relevant information in response to MPs' information needs, and provide them with concise and clearly structured expositions, without catering to their clients' partisan needs.

SUPPORT SERVICES FOR THE BUNDESRAT AND RESOURCES ON THE *LÄNDER* LEVEL: STATE-BASED STUDY COMMISSIONS

The consultative needs of the Bundesrat, which is a parliament of state executives and not a directly elected chamber, are served by the premiers' offices and the intergovernmental affairs ministries of its member states.

Most *Länder* legislatures institutionalized legislative study commissions ten to fifteen years after they had been set up on the federal level. While study commissions on the federal level are an integral part of parliament and a well-known institution inside and outside the Bundestag, *Länder* study commissions are not as well established and are much less visible. Their legal basis and their composition are not uniform across the country. In a few cases, state-based study commissions lack any independent status and are reduced to legislative support units; in others, parliamentarians dominate and the role of experts is reduced to serving as witnesses before hearings. Another factor is the relative weakness of *Länder* legislatures vis-à-vis their executive branches and within the German federal system in general. It is no coincidence that the oldest *Länder* study commissions were established in the city-states of Hamburg and Berlin, where the premier is much weaker than in the more spacious states. In quantitative terms, however, there have been more state-based study commissions than federal ones (Euchner, Hampel, and Seidel 1993).

Resources Available to All Branches and Levels of Government and to the Public

PERMANENT INDEPENDENT ADVISORY BODIES

In contrast to the scientific advisory boards mentioned above, there are several bodies that have a legal basis independent of ministerial decrees.

German Council of Economic Experts

The German Council of Economic Experts (SRW, Sachverständigenrat-Wirtschaft) consists of five academic economists, who are usually university professors. They are appointed for an overlapping term of five years by the federal government. The experts work only part-time in this advisory position. Although the law which created the council in 1963 prescribes its independence from both the government and interest groups, by tradition one of the members is considered to be an informal representative of the trade unions and another that of employer and manufacturing associations. The mandate of the council is to provide the government with the views of five senior academic economists—dubbed the "five economic wise men"—on economic policy in the Federal Republic. At the same time, the council helps to transmit economic thinking to a wider audience. The SRW Law mandates that the council submit an annual report on the state of the German economy by November 15 of each year. The report—usually several hundred pages in length—is published by the government printing office. The federal government is then obliged by law to respond to the report within eight weeks in the form of its own annual economic report. Institutionally, the council is located with a small research staff at the Federal Statistical Office in Wiesbaden. As Otto Singer notes, "Its independent status prevents the Council from advising the government directly. Its advice therefore mainly concerns the general direction of economic policy" (1993, 83). In other words, it is not within the official mandate of the council to give explicit policy recommendations or to propose specific policies that could be binding to the federal government. Its official mandate is analytic rather than prescriptive. In reality, however, the council's report contains indirect recommendations in that it discusses several policy options, dismissing some and supporting others.

The Monopolkommission *(Monopolies Commission)*
This commission is comprised of five experts, mainly with backgrounds in commercial law and economics, who analyze the processes of concentration in the economy with regard to potential distortions of competition. The commission is mandated by law to prepare a biannual report for the federal government, which has to be published and must provide specific proposals for legal action against constraints on corporate competition. While members of the Council of Economic Experts and the Monopolies Commission are formally nominated and accepted by the German president, political considerations and interventions by business groups and labor unions are a common feature of the selection process.

German Council of Environmental Advisors
In 1971, the Social-Liberal government under Willy Brandt, with suprapartisan support, inaugurated a new administrative and scientific framework for the conduct of environmental policy, called the German Council of Environmental Advisors (SRU, Der Rat von Sachverständigen für Umweltfragen). The federal government assumed new responsibilities in the areas of air pollution, noise pollution, and waste management policies. The Federal Environment Office was created as an administrative body, while ministerial responsibilities remained divided across several departments. This structure was maintained until 1986, when the Federal Ministry for Environment, Nature Conservation, and Nuclear Safety was created in the wake of the Chernobyl nuclear disaster, and SRU was placed under its jurisdiction, although still maintaining its independence.

SRU was meant to provide scientific guidance for environmental policy in a broad area of policy subfields. Based on the Council of Economic Experts model, SRU was provided with a specific mandate to give policy recommendations. It is the task of SRU to identify environmental problems, prepare the ground for political decisions, analyze policy options and their likely consequences, and propose preventive measures (Merkel 1997). Until 1990, SRU was staffed with twelve academic experts who served a three-year term, and who were almost exclusively drawn from the disciplines of law, economics, and the environmental, technical, and natural sciences. In 1992, in an effort to streamline the administrative aspects of the council, SRU was reduced to seven members serving four-year terms. At the same time, SRU was mandated to expand its counseling role and to reduce its devotion to basic research. Environmental experts from the social and administrative sciences, as well as from the humanities (particularly the field of ethics) were included, signaling the expectation of a more holistic approach to environmental issues. SRU publishes a biannual *Environmental Report* (Umweltgutachten), which is presented to the government and to the general public.

JOINT FEDERAL-STATE ADVISORY COUNCILS

Article 91b of the Basic Law is the basis on which the federal and state governments can cooperate in the promotion of research and educational matters. This area of overlapping jurisdiction has a number of advisory councils made up of academic experts and small administrative staffs. The Science Council (Wissenschaftsrat), for example, was established as an advisory body by the federal government and the *Länder* in 1957. Its two jointly appointed commissions make recommendations and statements on developments in higher education and other research establishments with regard to content and structure. The council exerts considerable influence on both the substance and the structure of science and research in Germany. Its evaluation of extramural institutes and its statements on the universities in East Germany provided the basis for a reorganization of the science landscape after reunification in the early 1990s.

TEMPORARY BLUE-RIBBON COMMISSIONS AND TASK FORCES

Temporary blue-ribbon commissions and task forces have been booming recently in Germany as well as on the European Union level. They come in different shapes and fulfill different functions: Most blue-ribbon commissions on the federal level answer to ministries or to the cabinet, especially if their mandate is in line with departmental boundaries. Task forces often deal with more cross-cutting issues and are appointed by the Chancellery. For the most part, however, the two are indistinguishable, and the statements in this section should be taken to apply to both. Blue-ribbon commissions have been appointed in recent years on the structural reform of the armed forces, on the future of the pension system, on the reform of the Bundesbank structure, on higher education and university professors, and on immigration, integration, and asylum. The core executive has appointed a task force dealing with the regulation of corporate takeovers.

In contrast to study commissions, the blue-ribbon commissions reflect the policy preferences of the government or of important societal and bureaucratic interests influencing the government's agenda. The commissions are expected to report within a period of between twelve and eighteen months and to make specific recommendations for legislation. Some even draft an early version of a bill. Although temporary commissions differ in terms of "issue salience" and membership, they tend to follow a similar pattern: The higher an issue ranks on the list of governmental and/or societal priorities, the higher the public profile of the commission. The most important commissions are chaired by and staffed with a number of senior elder statesmen. This was the case on the European Union level as well with the so-called Three Wise Men Commission on EU Reform (1999–2000). At the national level, the Commission on Common Security and the Future of the Bundeswehr (1999–2000) was chaired by former Federal President

Richard von Weizsäcker, and the Immigration Commission (created in July 2000) by former Bundestag President Rita Suessmuth. Other frequent members in a leading role are well-known corporate leaders, business tycoons, leaders of employers' associations and trade unions, civil society representatives, and senior management consultants. Academic experts—usually from academic think tanks or policy-oriented university departments—tend to be less visible and seem to serve only in a supporting role. During a commission's operation, academics become more influential as providers of and conduits for further commissioned research and hearings.

To give a recent example, the Immigration Commission is composed of twenty-one members who are supported by a secretariat of ten seconded civil servants from various federal ministries. The actual work of the commission is conducted in flexible study groups, which invite expert opinions from relevant individuals from the immigration policy community, members of which in turn have already begun to lobby the commission. The commission was given a specific deadline—the summer of 2001—for producing its final report and recommendations, which it delivered on July 3, 2001.

It is difficult to generalize about the functions and the impact of temporary commissions and short-term task forces. If their political and bureaucratic patrons have a clear-cut vision of the direction of policy, these commissions and task forces are often used to legitimize departmental policy preferences with "scientific" arguments. Sometimes the likely policy preferences of the minister are even reflected in the composition of the members. Although some blue-ribbon commissions and temporary task forces are installed to serve the policy preferences and political goals of senior government politicians and/or the cabinet, they often develop a dynamic and a life of their own and do not always fit neatly into the government agenda—nor into the agenda of the opposition parties. Because of their high level of publicity—usually a consequence of the "celebrity status" of their chairperson—the recommendations of blue-ribbon commissions stimulate public debate, create issue awareness, and mobilize societal support for specific courses of action, and thus they may have a medium-term impact even if they are ignored by the government and the ruling coalition parties in the short-term.

Commissions play a different role when their mandate affects society as a whole and/or when policy preferences are blurred and being contested not only along party lines, but within parties, coalitions, and societal groups. In these cases—for instance on the issue of immigration—temporary commissions may be used as a device to buy time, but more importantly to help develop an "expert consensus" before the governing parties begin framing a detailed bill. Governing "by commission" has become a trademark of the consensus-seeking and reform-minded Schröder government. In order not to be upstaged by too much consensus and agenda-setting power of blue-ribbon commissions, parties (particularly opposition parties) have begun to create their own partisan commissions and task forces (e.g., on immigration) within the party organizations. Although it is too early to conclude that, as in Sweden, such temporary commissions and task forces have become an integral, regularized part of the policymaking process, the current trend points in that direction.

Certain *Länder* governments have long recognized the flexibility and the prestige of temporary blue-ribbon commissions. A high-profile blue-ribbon commission on "Questions Regarding the Future," which examined the future of work, entrepreneurship, and the welfare state, was appointed jointly by the *Länder*-premiers of Bavaria and Saxony between 1995 and 1997. Despite its *Länder* origins, the mandate of the so-called Future Commission was by no means restricted to issues of regional importance. Its purpose in addressing questions related to the labor market and employment policy was to emphasize the national role, as well as the independent policy capacity of *Länder* premiers. The Future Commission was masterminded and run by a formally independent think tank, the Bonn Institute for Economic and Social Research (known as IWG Bonn), and maintained a secretariat in the nation's capital rather than either of the states' capitals. It was staffed with experts and civil servants and was given the opportunity to meet with the Bavarian and Saxon cabinets on several occasions. Its final report went beyond any existing consensus on the future of the European social model and advocated a more "Americanized" social model—including a greater reliance on entrepreneurship, privatization of state services, and the strengthening of the voluntary (third) sector. Although the report received a rather strong, but frosty, public reception, it has been used as a template for policy change by market-oriented politicians and state governments ever since. Subsequently, a small number of other states have followed the Bavarian and Saxon example and created similar—although less visible—commissions to determine their policy options in several policy areas.

Think Tanks

In Germany, as elsewhere, "think tank" is an imprecise and elusive term covering many different types of organizations scattered across the country. Germany has a long-standing tradition of state-sponsored "applied basic research," especially in economics, but hardly a vigorous legacy of independent policy analysis and research. It is therefore necessary to use "think tank" in its broadest sense: nonprofit private and public organizations devoted to examining and analyzing policy-relevant issues, and producing research outputs such as publications, reports, lectures, and workshops that in most cases are targeted to identifiable audiences with the hope of influencing decision making and public opinion. Recent estimates of the number of think tanks (or their functional equivalents) operating in Germany vary, ranging between seventy and ninety institutions (Day 2000). If one broadens the definition to also include various church-sponsored academies (which sometimes serve as part-time think tanks) or university research centers, the number easily exceeds 100.

More than half of the German policy research institutes were founded in the past twenty-five years, although many of the largest and best-funded think tanks date from pre-1970. Compared to other countries—especially to the United States—the percentage of government-financed institutes is very high. There are about a dozen large nonuniversity institutes that have annual budgets of US$5 million–US$14 million and employ between thirty and eighty research staff. They receive funding from the federal government or the *Länder*, from research bodies such as the Max Planck Society and the Fraunhofer Society, as well as from contract research. The important role of state governments as sponsors and financiers of think tanks reflects Germany's federal structure.

By and large, the German think tank landscape fits into the mold of international think tank typologies (McGann and Weaver 2000), although the sector of private and advocacy-oriented policy research institutes is less developed than in Anglo-American countries. It is also sometimes hard to distinguish between research-oriented think tanks ("universities without students") and institutions of basic research touching on policy-relevant questions. It is equally difficult for members of this diverse group of think tanks to recognize that they may belong to a clearly identifiable community. See table 1 for a breakdown of types of think tanks in Germany.

Table 1. Types of Think Tanks in Germany (as percentage of all think tanks)

Academic think tanks	50% or more
Contract research institutes	10–15%
Advocacy institutes	30–40%
Party think tanks	10–15%

Source: Author's survey.
Note: Organizations may fall under more than one category.

ACADEMIC THINK TANKS

Academic think tanks are by far the largest group of think tanks in Germany. An even larger number of institutes professes to adhere to the ideal of an independent research institute engaged in applied basic research. Academic think tanks can be divided into the following categories:

(1) Created by government, but working independently within public sector guidelines
(2) Nonuniversity ("Blue List") institutes
(3) University-affiliated centers of applied policy-relevant research

(4) Academic think tanks with considerable private funding

The federal government created two large research bodies in the area of international affairs in the 1960s—the Foundation for Science and Politics (SWP, Stiftung Wissenschaft und Politik), inspired by the RAND Corporation of Santa Monica, California, and the Federal Institute for Russian, East European and International Studies (BIOSt, Bundesinstitut für Ostwissenschaftliche und internationale Studien). Between the 1970s and the 1990s, state governments became important sponsors of academic think tanks, sometimes with a strong advocacy bent. Scandinavian think tanks such as the Stockholm International Peace Research Institute (SIPRI) and the Peace Research Institute Oslo (PRIO) served as the operative models for state-based peace research institutes founded by Social Democratic *Länder* governments in Frankfurt (the Peace Research Institute Frankfurt, or HSFK PRIF) and Hamburg (the Institute for Peace Research and Security Policy at the University of Hamburg). North Rhine–Westphalia launched the Science Center North Rhine–Westphalia, an umbrella organization of four state-based research institutes, which attempts to combine the concepts of an academic advanced studies center with that of a pragmatic think tank. Other examples of such state government–initiated institutes include the Wuppertal Institute for Climate, Environment and Energy, the Bureau for Future Studies (Sekretariat für Zukunftsforschung), and the Bonn International Center for Conversion, all of which have gained a reputation beyond Germany's borders.

The largest group of academic think tanks are the so-called Blue List institutes.[9] This diverse group of eighty-three nonuniversity research institutes, most of which receive financial assistance from the federal government and the states on a fifty-fifty basis, undertake applied research of supraregional importance. Among these Blue List organizations, a group of six large economic research institutes with a combined staff of approximately 400 economic researchers are the most policy-oriented.[10] The joint funding of these economic think tanks through the national and state governments not only reflects Germany's federal structure, but expresses the desire to encourage competing views on economic policy and on Germany's economic development. Twice annually, experts of these six economic research institutes issue a Common Report predicting the short- and medium-term performance of the German economy. The six expert institutes are meant to arrive at joint conclusions, but the opportunity to express dissenting views in the form of minority opinions is given. In recent years, four of the six institutes have usually concurred in the majority opinion based on the assumptions of neoclassical economics, while one or two institutes—generally, the German Institute of Economic Research (DIW Berlin, Deutsche Institut für Wirtschaftsforschung) and the Rhine-Westphalia Institute for Economic Research (RWI)—have been noted for their adherence to neo-Keynesian paradigms. The Common Report receives the attention of the media as well as of the government, the Bundesbank, interest groups, and other actors in the economic policy community. It influences the public debate about the legitimacy of government economic policy more than it influences policy decisions (Scholz 1997, 15).

Other Blue List institutes that conduct work of some policy relevance, but which have a less deliberate policy orientation, include the WZB, which was founded in 1969 at the suprapartisan initiative of federal members of parliament and was inspired by the Brookings Institution in Washington, D.C., and the German Overseas Institute (DÜI, Deutsches Übersee-Institut), an umbrella organization that incorporates a group of Hamburg-based area studies institutes. Most member institutes of other scientific associations, such as the Max Planck Society for the Advancement of Science, are too devoted to long-term, basic research to be regarded as policy-oriented think tanks. Among the notable exceptions are individual researchers and research units at the Max Planck Institute for the Study of Societies in Cologne, at the Center for European Economic Research in Mannheim, or at the Fraunhofer Institute for Systems and Innovation Research (ISI, Institut Systemtechnik und Innovationsforschung) in Karlsruhe.

Many German think tanks are affiliated with universities or operate in a semi-academic environment like the Center for Applied Policy Research (CAP) at the University of Munich—one of the largest institutes of its kind. CAP is somewhat unusual for a university-based research institute as it draws a substantial amount of its core funding from governmental (European Union) and private sources (e.g., the German Marshall Fund and the Bertelsmann Foundation). Another Munich-based academic research center, the Center for Economic Studies (CES), operates as the academic arm of the more "pedestrian" Ifo Institute for Economic Research, which belongs to the Blue List. In most cases, it is not easy to draw a line between academic research and policy-oriented work. Two notable recent additions to the field of university-affiliated academic think tanks are the Center for European Integration Studies (ZEI, Zentrum für Europäische Integrationsforschung) and the Center for Development Research (ZEF, Zentrum für Entwicklungsforschung) in Bonn. Founded in the mid-1990s, both academic think tanks received substantial government grants to compensate Bonn for the loss of its status as Germany's capital.

Finally, there are at least two major exceptions to the rule of government-created and publicly financed academic think tanks. One is the German Society for Foreign Affairs (DGAP, Deutsche Gesellschaft für Auswärtige Politik). More recently, it uses the German Council on Foreign Relations as its official English name. DGAP was founded in 1955 in Bonn as an independent, nonpartisan, nonprofit organization. The models for this oldest German think tank dealing with international affairs were the Council on Foreign Relations in New York and the Royal Institute of International Affairs at Chatham House in London. The DGAP's goals, its organizational structure as an elite network-cum-research institute, and its mode of financing are indeed strikingly similar to that of the older Anglo-American flagship institutes.

The second exception is the Bertelsmann Foundation, which emerged in the 1990s as a heavyweight player in privately funded policy research, with resources matching or exceeding those of the largest government-funded institutes. Boasting a constantly expanding staff of more than 200, this operating foundation organizes and carries out projects in close cooperation with partners in public and private scientific institutions. Members of the foundation have increasingly sponsored and organized expert meetings for the Federal President and the Chancellery. Some of the foundation's units, such as the Center for Higher Education Development (CHE), operate like think tanks, whereas others specialize in running specific programs.

Finally, while having a more limited research capacity than the Bertelsmann Foundation, a growing number of other corporate foundations, such as the Thyssen Foundation, Körber Foundation, and the Quandt Foundation, and academies like the Burda Academy of the Third Millennium, Protestant and Catholic academies, the Einstein Forum, and the American Academy, are becoming catalysts for policy-relevant ideas by organizing and sponsoring dialogue activities that bring together experts and practitioners.

CONTRACT RESEARCHERS

Almost all publicly funded research institutes look for additional "third funding" to finance project research (Weilemann 2000, 171). Hence, the number of think tanks receiving a considerable portion of their revenue from some kind of contract research is quite high. However, contract research rarely defines their institutional purpose entirely. Contract research is a territory that nonprofit think tanks must share with for-profit think tanks, such as the Swiss-based Prognos Group, and increasingly with large commercial management consulting firms.

ADVOCACY THINK TANKS

Not only in the United Kingdom and North America, but also increasingly in Germany, there exists a whole range of institutions that do not restrict their activities to seemingly objective scientific research, but see themselves primarily as advocates for specific solutions to public policy problems or for their own political worldview (*Weltanschauung*). It would be a grave mistake to believe that all of these special interest think tanks are academically questionable. Nevertheless, they are sometimes less oriented toward producing disinterested research or maintaining high academic standards than one might wish them to be.[11]

Interest-based policy research organizations affiliated with the German Federation of Trade Unions, the Confederation of German Employers' Associations, the Protestant and Catholic Churches, or certain single-issue interest groups (e.g., the Taxpayers' Union) are among the oldest think tanks in Germany, dating back to the 1950s and 1960s. The 1970s and 1980s saw the emergence of a small number of more independent advocacy-oriented think tanks, often founded by entrepreneurial academics or politicians. In 1977, for example, with the help of corporate seed money, Kurt Biedenkopf, a prominent maverick politician from the Christian Democratic Union and later the premier of Saxony, and the economist Meinhard Miegel founded the previously mentioned IWG Bonn—a miniature version of the American Enterprise Institute. In the same year, Germany's first environmental think tank, the Öko (Ecology) Institute, opened its doors in Freiburg. Hans Filbinger, a former conservative state premier from Baden-Württemberg with a questionable record in the Wehrmacht, created his legacy institute, the right-wing Weikersheim Study Center, in the early 1980s. In 1982, a group of market-oriented academics set up the Frankfurter Institute Foundation for Market Economy and Political Policy and its research council, the Kronberger Kreis. A small number of market-oriented institutes such as the Institute of Independent Entrepreneurs (UNI, Unternehmerinstitut) and the Ludwig Erhard Foundation have followed suit.

The decision to convert the Frankfurter Institute from a loose dialogue forum into a full-fledged advocacy think tank in the 1990s was influenced by the success of the Heritage Foundation and the Cato Institute in the United States, as well as by the free-market think tanks in the United Kingdom. The products of this institute, which will move to Berlin in 2001 to enhance its visibility among policymaking circles, closely resemble those of American advocacy tanks. While policy briefs and one-pagers are not yet the dominant product of German advocacy institutes in general, their activities are clearly more devoted to marketing, communication, and convocation than most of their more academic counterparts. Advocacy tanks align themselves with sympathetic actors—from governmental bodies, national newspapers, business firms, or the nonprofit sector—within advocacy coalitions. They market value-driven policy recommendations through op-ed pieces, one-day conferences with prominent keynote speakers, other educational activities targeted to tomorrow's elites, and appearances on the television news.

A large and well-funded academic, party, and interest group research sector has limited the space and the resources available for free-standing, specialized, advocacy-oriented think tanks. Despite such unfavorable circumstances, however, some of the smaller free-standing advocacy institutes such as IWG Bonn and the Frankfurter Institute continue to do rather well.

POLITICAL PARTY–AFFILIATED THINK TANKS

The fourth distinct group of think tanks is the party-affiliated think tanks, or "political foundations," as they prefer to be called. These organizations are more prominent and better funded in Germany than nearly anywhere else. The semi-official status of political parties in the Basic Law (Article 21) and the desire not to channel various educational, research-oriented, and international activities directly through the party system, but also not to keep them outside the influence of political parties, has resulted in a huge—albeit shrinking—amount of public funds (approximately 390 million euros in 1998) flowing into political foundations. Today there are six such foundations (see table 2), each of which is related to one of the parties represented in the Bundestag. When their associated party is in government, the foundations are often perceived as semiofficial bodies by many outside observers, but that certainly is an overstatement.

It is difficult to distinguish potential think tank functions from the other activities of party foundations. Think tank activities may account for up to 15 percent–20 percent of a party foundation's budget. The remainder is given in tied grants for development aid, student scholarships, civic education, and archival work. Most foundations host in-house academies, research and consulting units, or study groups that focus on foreign policy, on economic and domestic policy, or on empirical social research, thereby fulfilling the typical think tank functions.[12]

Neither the policy expertise nor the think tank functions of political foundations are uniform. International networking with like-minded civil society organizations is one of their most important functions and their most common denominator. Apart from that activity, political foundations may differ in their institutional and policy priorities. For example, during the 1990s, the Konrad Adenauer Foundation merged several smaller institutes into a large Department of Political Research, equipped with powerful empirical research tools and a particular expertise in local government and security policy (Weilemann 2000, 179–186). During the early and mid-1990s, when the Free Democratic Party was in government, that

Table 2. German Political Foundations

Foundation	Date Established	Party
Friedrich Ebert Foundation	1925	Social Democratic Party (SPD)
Konrad Adenauer Foundation	1964	Christian Democratic Union (CDU)
Hanns Seidel Foundation	1967	Christian Social Union in Bayern (CSU)
Friedrich Naumann Foundation	1958	Free Democratic Party–The Liberals (FDP)
Heinrich Böll Foundation	1996	Green Party
Rosa Luxemburg Foundation	1998	Party of the Democratic Socialism (PDS)

party's liberal Friedrich Naumann Foundation was good at "flying kites," testing the ground for new and generally more radical (i.e., libertarian) ideas than the party establishment initially was ready to accept in the party platform. Today, the party platform is very much in line with some of those libertarian ideas.

The health of the political foundations' in-house think tanks depends on the willingness of the foundation leadership to sponsor think tank activities and on the availability of suitable policy entrepreneurs and experts for the job. All too often, important posts (especially abroad) are given to deserving but retired or even failed politicians. (Again, the Adenauer Foundation would make an excellent case study in this respect.) Power relationships within the party and the foundation, between the foundation and those in the parliamentary and the government party, as well as the overall funding and staffing situation are other important variables for the success of these think tanks. On the other hand, the public funding laws governing the party foundations, in combination with public distrust of politicians and partisan politics, may prompt the foundations to officially hide possible behind-the-scenes partisan consulting activities from the wider public and to make political foundations appear as civil society organizations acting in the public interest. Despite the close personal and ideological links to their "mother party," the foundations are not always willing external affairs instruments of the party leadership or extended arms of the party's in-house research departments. Conversely, pragmatic party politicians often ignore the findings and recommendations of the party think tanks in favor of the views of more politically powerful interests or in favor of the preferences expressed through opinion polls and focus groups.

Other External Sources of Policy Advice

A more recent phenomenon is the presence of management consultants in government and public sector agencies—especially in the areas of health and social services, as well as in education. In as far as policy implementation is policymaking and therefore a highly political activity, it is too shortsighted to see management consultants solely through the lens of technocratic aid. The more governments of all political spectrums wish to make government and the public sector business-like and managerial, the more they will rely on management consulting firms (Saint-Martin 1998). In 1998, a consortium of several large consulting firms under the leadership of Arthur D. Little actually asked for a "mandate" from the Bundestag to "turn around Germany Inc." (Andersen Consulting et al. 1998). The politicians politely declined. In addition to management consultants, chief economists and research departments at large commercial banks and at corporate think tanks of such multinationals as DaimlerChrysler and Deutsche Telekom have become more prominent advisors in recent years.

186 | Martin W. Thunert

Main Features of
APAOs in Germany

FOCUS OF CONCERN

Most of the larger academic institutes, the party think tanks, as well as a significant number of advocacy tanks produce their research in-house. The same applies to a few permanent advisory bodies such as the Bundestag Research Services or the Council of Economic Experts. The latter can rely on the work of the Federal Bureau for Statistics, to which it is formally attached. Legislative study commissions and blue-ribbon commissions, as well as quasi-ministerial think tanks and most academies run research secretariats but rely heavily on externally recruited expertise. Most German think tanks and many other APAOs are neither single-issue institutes nor full-service institutions (although the Bertelsmann Foundation and the larger party think tanks, such as the Konrad Adenauer and Friedrich Ebert Foundations, are possible exceptions); the majority can be classified some-where in between. Economic and financial issues are paramount, followed by the environment, technology policy, social issues, and labor issues. European integration research, including "European Central Bank–watching" is booming, while foreign policy, including research on defense, peace, and human rights, follows at some distance. Professional associations and interest groups such as unions and the employers' associations are involved in research on employment policy, secondary and vocational education, and health care.

FINANCES

The most important source of income for APAOs in Germany is still the state—primarily at the national and regional levels, but increasingly at the European Union level as well. Governments on all levels continue to be willing to finance APAOs, especially think tanks, task forces, and blue-ribbon commissions, as witnessed by the recent founding of institutes for European integration and development policy studies in Bonn. Research institutes for peace studies, human rights, and conflict research have also received an upswing in funding from the Federal Ministry of Education and Research. Increasingly, however, the core funding of organizations—which advisory organizations and research institutes prefer because it gives them maximum discretion—has been reduced in relation to project funding. Many of the generously core-funded public APAOs, especially the party foundations, suffered budget and staff cuts in the second half of the 1990s.

In the past, the availability of state funding made up for the relative absence of a strong philanthropic tradition of funding for independent policy institutes. This is going to change, albeit only slowly and gradually. In the 1990s, some operating and grant-giving foundations such as the Thyssen Foundation and the German Marshall Fund began shifting their funding priorities from basic academic research to applied and policy-oriented work, and thus play a bigger part in financing the policy advice industry.

LOCATION

While the operating mode of German federalism is highly cooperative and centralized, in terms of geography, Germany's policy research infrastructure is highly decentralized. Think tanks and experts external to the federal government (with the exception of foreign and security policy) are by no means assembled in the capital, but rather are spread across the country with regional concentrations in Berlin, Munich, Frankfurt, Cologne-Bonn, the Ruhr area, Stuttgart, and Hamburg-Kiel. This wide scattering of locations is a result of Germany's unique federal structure, of the important role played by the *Länder* in the financing and foundation of think tanks, of their close attachment to the (equally scattered) academic world, and of the structure of the German media landscape. Very few of the think tanks' most important mouthpieces—i.e., national newspapers and magazines—are headquartered in the German capital.

STAFFING

Academic experts serving in senior administrative and governmental positions have been the exception rather than the rule in postwar Germany. Some of the most notable exceptions include Ludwig Erhard, the father of Germany's postwar "economic miracle" and co-founder of the social market economy, who served as chancellor between 1963 and 1966, and Karl Schiller, a Keynesian economist, who held a so-called super-portfolio as joint minister for finance and commerce in the Brandt government in the early 1970s. In addition, there has been some exchange between large economic research institutes such as the Kiel Institute of World Economics (IfW, Institut für Weltwirtschaft) and the German Institute of Economic Research on the one hand, and the position of deputy minister or director in the Ministries of Finance and Commerce.[13]

As far as external recruitment and external advisory relations are concerned, official advisory bodies consult with economists, legal experts, and natural scientists far more often than with political scientists or historians. Recruitment at most external APAOs has followed academic patterns. Many senior staff at academic think tanks, for example, hold doctoral degrees, with most being in economics, followed by political science/international relations, and the natural or applied sciences. Senior positions at academic think tanks, such as research director, often require qualifications similar to a medium-level or even senior professorship at a university.

In the past, many of the older and larger academic institutes offered a high degree of job security through semitenured research positions. In the 1990s, however, job security for new appointments was cut back drastically, even at some formerly cushy institutes with tenured positions. This was partly a result of overall budget constraints, but also a reflection of the directors' desire for more flexibility in creating new research groups and as a way to avoid the bureaucratization of the think tanks. The revolving door phenomenon that allows people to move freely in and out of government, however, is still extremely rare in Germany. The career paths of the staff of APAOs are largely separate from the ministries and are more closely linked to academic career paths, although more recently there have been some important exceptions, especially in economic and environmental policy.

Despite certain career path rigidities, a career in an academic think tank is still somewhat attractive for qualified young people, especially those with degrees in the social sciences or humanities. On the other hand, and due to the decentralization of the industry, the social capital of young people working for a spell in a think tank (for a very modest salary) as part of a career progression in related fields such as journalism, media, academia, politics, or management consulting, is still underdeveloped in Germany, although it may emerge over the next decade in Berlin.

IMPACT OF
ALTERNATIVE SOURCES

This section attempts to cast some light on the underexplored relationship between German APAOs and their target audiences both in government and among the wider public. It is almost impossible to measure empirically and accurately how much APAOs contribute to the preparation, introduction, and realization of policies, for it is seldom the case that positions taken by politicians or policies that are adopted and implemented are unambiguously attributable to the influence of individual experts or specific knowledge-based organizations. Usually the only thing that can be measured objectively in this respect is the activity level and the public visibility of institutes, organizations, and individual experts, but this is not done as systematically in Germany as it is in the United States. As a result, the following remarks on APAO influence should be treated as hypotheses and educated guesses in need of further testing, rather than as conclusive findings.

Conditions of Influence:
Stages of the Policymaking Process and the Role of Expertise

The potential of APAOs to influence the policymaking process depends a great deal on such variables as the policy field (closeness or openness of policy communities in a given policy field), the institutional source and the location of the advice-giving organization (closeness to government or closeness to civil society), and the stage of the policymaking process. I will concentrate here on the latter variable.

External influence is likely to occur at three stages of the policymaking process: first, the agenda-setting and problem-definition stage; second, policy selection and policy enactment; and third, policy implementation and evaluation. Policy-relevant knowledge fulfills different roles at different stages of the process. Expertise appears as warning and guidance during the first stage, as support and ammunition in the second, and as assessment in the third. Few if any German APAOs are active at every stage of the policymaking process, nor does their expertise fulfill every one of these roles. Table 3 illustrates the intensity of activity, visibility, and thus possible influence of different APAOs at each stage.

In-house advisory bodies, executive advisory boards, and interdepartmental committees have very little direct long-term agenda-setting influence, but have a greater influence on policy detail in terms of proposal selection and revision. Some of these bodies act as managers or supporters of external advisory sources as well as information brokers and therefore their influence varies according to their brokerage and knowledge-management skills. These bodies may also be used by the government for performance review or for the justification of policy choices.

The reverse is true for legislative study commissions, which have a much higher potential to offer warnings or guidance that change politicians'—as well as the public's—understanding of a particular policy problem, but have a low degree of actual involvement in policy enactment or the assessment of policy details. The study commissions tend to be agenda setters in cross-cutting problem areas and in policy fields with a low institutionalization of advice giving. They often provide basic, policy-relevant knowledge in new problem areas without policy history.

The impact of legislative support organizations varies. Lacking an organization such as the Congressional Budget Office, it is difficult for Bundestag support agencies to play a proactive role. Their potential impact in supporting MPs and parliamentary groups on short-term agenda setting and on policy enactment depends mainly on the political clout of their parliamentary clients. Temporary blue-ribbon commissions and task forces have a strong guidance function and their mandate permits them to provide specific policy recommendations. Commissions are often a result of atmospheric agenda change rather than its cause, and they tend to affect the nexus of short-term agenda setting and policy selection. However, commissions and task forces are often dissolved before their proposals grind through the legislative process and are assessed by other experts and bureaucratic actors. Therefore, their direct impact on policy enactment and implementation is rather low, unless their proposals are adopted by strong bureaucratic or legislative actors. Commissions may also be used by governments to buy time in solving a tricky problem or to broaden the support base for a particular course of action.

Table 3. Policy Impact of APAOs

Type of APAO	Impact on Agenda Setting and Problem Definition	Impact on Policy Selection and Enactment	Impact on Policy Implementation and Evaluation
In-house advisory bodies	*	**	***
Legislative study commissions	**+	*	*
Temporary blue-ribbon commissions	***	**+	*
Independent advisory councils	**+	***	**
Academic think tanks (and members thereof)	**	**	**
Contract research organizations	**_	**	***
Advocacy think tanks (and members thereof)	***	*	*
Party-affiliated think tanks	**	**	**
Commercial consultants	*	**	***
Individual experts	***	**+	*+

Sources: This table reflects (a) surveys and interviews conducted by the author and others that have yielded data that can help illustrate especially how think tanks and academic experts decide on their strategies and target groups; and (b) an internal survey conducted by the Federal Court of Audit among the ministerial recipients of external policy advice in the field of foreign policy (Federal Court of Audit 1996).
* low visibility and potential influence
** medium visibility and potential influence
*** strong visibility and potential influence
+ and – indicate current trends

Independent advisory councils have a strong potential to provide warnings about impending problems and to provide guidance on to how to approach those problems. Often these warnings are based on a critical assessment of existing policies and offer recommended courses of action. Their main currency is the institutionalization of their advisory role in key policy fields such as economic, environmental, or health policy, but they have little opportunity to act as policy entrepreneurs after their reports are published. However, individual council members—in most cases, respected academics—have become increasingly active in marketing the policy recommendations of their reports.

Academic think tanks have a moderate but consistent influence on each stage of the policymaking process, but their role in providing warning, guidance, and support is perhaps their strongest asset. Their academic status gives their warnings more credibility than those of quasi-interests, and, in turn, academic credibility enhances their usefulness as sources of information and analyses.

Advocacy think tanks and party think tanks in particular are stronger in early stages of the policymaking process—particularly medium-term agenda setting—than are academic think tanks, but their overall influence is more intermittent. Some independent advocacy think tanks have cautiously started to adopt the strategies of their U.S. counterparts to provide ammunition and support to advocacy coalitions during policy selection and enactment. Party think tanks can become powerful agenda-setting resources, especially when their party is in the opposition and their access to governmental advisory sources is rather restricted. Legal regulations prevent political foundations from becoming too closely involved in political strategy or in the drafting of party manifestos. As agenda setters they rather guide and reshape the understanding of broader policy questions—particularly in the area of foreign policy—for their party and even beyond. They are often more principled and forward looking than party politicians.

Finally, it should be noted that while the sole influence of contract research organizations should be on policy assessment, some for-profit organizations have stepped beyond a purely passive approach. A number of them have begun producing unsolicited policy evaluations and proposals.

DISCUSSION AND RECOMMENDATIONS
Demand-Side Opportunities and Constraints

Guidance to governance in Germany can take many forms. The contents and forms of advice giving differ with respect to the inherent dynamism of each policy area. In dynamic and potentially innovative areas, such as media policy or biogenetics, advisory structures need to be more flexible, focused, and timely, since the pressure for decision making in hitherto uncharted policy territories is high. In long-established and more predictable policy areas, governments and advisors can rely on past experience and the timetables of long-standing—and in most cases institutionalized—consulting relationships.

The advisory needs of decision makers are not uniform across branches of government or agencies, nor across time. Governments and other decision makers may expect the following from APAOs:
- Provision of basic knowledge in highly dynamic and undiscovered policy fields;
- Continuous factual updates as the basis for the reauthorization or the implementation of laws;
- "Scientific" and philosophical justification of courses of action already taken;
- Buying time for either problem avoidance or more thorough decision making;
- Ammunition for interagency and interdepartmental rivalries;
- Ammunition for self-promotion and public relations exercises, such as the

publishing of annual reports;
- Critical performance review;
- Early warning.

It is a healthy feature of the German advisory system that most advisory bodies are—at least officially—granted independence from governmental directives. The legacy of German history during the Nazi period and during the era of communist dictatorship in East Germany, when experts served as mere executioners of governmental directives, will help to uphold a high degree of sensitivity against direct governmental control of the consulting process in the near future. Arguably, expert advisers involved in the consulting process are less independent from the interference of political parties and large vested social groups. Many members of formally independent advisory bodies are being nominated according to party and interest group loyalties, such as the experts serving on the legislative study commissions.

Historically, many senior politicians such as Chancellors Adenauer and Schmidt treated independent bodies of expert advisers, especially those which directed their deliberations and results toward the general public, with suspicion. They regarded them as a "fifth power" that unduly imposed constraints on elected politicians' room to maneuver (Kloten 1989, 55). While the rising complexity of issues before decision makers has contributed to nearly universal acceptance of the need for advice, an inherent uneasiness about advisory bodies remains, especially among senior politicians. This uneasiness has two aspects: First, many APAOs—especially those serving government departments—have specifically defined mandates in particular policy areas. This often prevents them from taking a more holistic view. Instead, they become mere suppliers of specialized factual information. Senior politicians, especially Cabinet members, can rarely afford such "departmental blindness." They cannot ignore strategic considerations in policymaking. Secondly, unlike politicians, advisory bodies are not compelled to make compromises between competing demands and therefore their policy recommendations are often too "radical" or "academic" for the taste and needs of most decision makers, who are bound by the realities of everyday politics. Politicians who expected expert bodies to act as a moderating and rationalizing force in the decision-making process have often been in for a surprise. It is therefore not uncommon that politicians, regardless of party affiliation, approach advisory bodies with a pick-and-choose strategy and show a preference for expert advisors who combine a knowledge of detail with a strategic vision of the big picture.

THE POLITICS OF POLICY ADVICE

The majority of APAOs have little control over the way their expertise is utilized, especially by their actual and potential clients. APAOs with a heavy dependence on contract research do not even control their own research agendas. Expertise is not a disinterested and detached resource to political or even to bureaucratic actors. Nor do they consider a certain item of policy-relevant knowledge legitimate if it is only technically credible. Empirical studies in the United States have demonstrated that political actors do not understand policy analyses, policy studies, or other forms of expert information in isolation from the people and institutions that produce them (Bimber 1996). If the conclusions of policy analysis collide with the political objectives of political actors, more often than not the latter prevail. In the cases of political foundations, internal governmental advisory bodies, and quasi-interests, this is quite obvious. Selected topics must correspond to the political goals of their "mother organizations" and experts are chosen who are in line with that thinking.

It is regrettable but only natural that interest groups and politicians use expert analyses and reports for their own purposes. To give an example, the autumn edition of the *Common Report* that is produced by six economic think tanks and the *Annual State of the Economy Report* put out by the Council of Economic Experts are published within two weeks of each other between late October and mid-November of each year. The analysis of the economic situation more often than not differs between the two reports, or even within each report since the *Common Report* publishes minority opinions if agreement cannot be reached. Political decision makers use the differences in the diagnoses of economic performance for their own purposes, picking out those facts and statements that correspond to their own views.

In the worst cases, expert opinions are used to confirm politically biased opinion (Scholz 1997, 16–18). After the fall of the Berlin Wall in 1989–1990, most economic advisors—from the chairman of the Bundesbank to the Council of Economic Experts and to individual academics—advised then Chancellor Kohl against a premature monetary union between West Germany and a still independent German Democratic Republic. Most of their predictions regarding the fragile state of the East German economy proved to be correct. Kohl went ahead with the monetary union as a preliminary step for political union for purely political and, some may say, historical reasons. Consciously or unconsciously, external experts provide arguments for politicians who are engaged in trying to make seemingly objective decisions, but who are at the same time politically motivated and value oriented in their actions.

This situation often causes APAO staff to be caught on the horns of a dilemma. On the one hand, they earn their living from the fact that politicians, parties, and similar associations are anxious to receive not only objective expert advice but also advice that flatters their own political point of view. On the other hand, it is risky in the long run to an expert's or a think tank's public credibility to position himself/itself too closely to specific political groups by offering ingratiating advice and providing ideological ammunition. Even though policy advice in general cannot be strictly separated from political advice (Murswieck 1993, 87), most external advisors—especially those with an academic background—shy away from providing a mix of both, resorting instead to purely scientific advice. The strong dependence of the German policy research community on the state has accentuated their tendency to present a scientific front and to sacrifice general comprehensibility to academic standards. Those external advisory organizations that have no problem with having a reputation for being strongly value-oriented or for following specific interests are few and far between. This reluctance of many academics to become involved in the politics of policymaking, however, is one reason why politicians often resort to the advice provided by organized interests, who have no such inhibitions.

FROM POLICY TO POLITICS

Politicians in elected office increasingly depend on, and thus ask for, a mixture of policy advice and political consulting. A survey conducted among policymaking civil servants in the premiers' offices on the state level, which was echoed by similar studies on other levels of government, showed that marketing and communication expertise (e.g., public relations, polling, "spin" skills, etc.) are deemed as important as, and sometimes more important than, detailed policy expertise (Mielke 1999). This type of political consulting knowledge sells better and offers a better result for many politicians.

Despite these tendencies in the uses of expertise, however, politicians in senior positions are not equally receptive to external advice. Whether and how alternative sources of advice are sought and utilized depends on the incumbents in high office, their policy styles, and their policy preferences. As the experience of various planning bureaus inside the Chancellery, as well as the case of the Schleswig-Holstein Denkfabrik, demonstrate, it depends a great deal on the personality and the preferences of the chief executive and/or the chief-of-staff as to whether a department or agency prefers advice from a policy-creating think tank or from an accounting office.

In 1995–1996, the president of the Federal Court of Audit conducted a report on the coordination and rationalization of federally funded research on Eastern and international affairs (Federal Court of Audit 1996). The report was based on a survey among senior civil servants in key federal ministries, who were asked to report on their utilization of research provided by federally funded international affairs research institutes. Among the responses were criticisms regarding the usefulness and the policy relevance of such research. According to this key audience in government, high-caliber staff of academic think tanks are too inclined to indulge in theoretical abstraction and to write and speak in a vocabulary that does not travel well in the worlds of political decision making or business. Research is not timely and sometimes out of synch with the foreign policy agenda of both governments and nonstate actors. Some policy institutes are seen as too academic, detached, and uninvolved, providing avalanches of information rather than strategic recommendations. The report led to a consolidation of federally funded foreign policy research institutes and to their relocation to locations of closer geographical proximity to their target audiences in Berlin.

While the actors on the receiving end of policy advice in Germany are neither uniform nor always clear in articulating their specific advisory needs, and sometimes appear captured by reform-averse organized interests, it is equally true that the strong forces that are mentioned in the introductory chapter of this volume are pushing toward an increasing demand for policy-relevant expertise in Germany. In addition, there are some other "pull-factors" that are peculiar to the German case: Senior civil servants and ministerial bureaucracies educated in law are not always skilled in or trained for making decisions on complex cross-cutting issues in areas such as international finance, biogenetics, international security, or European integration. Moreover, in the new capital of Berlin, politics has shifted gears and has become a much faster and more media-driven affair than was the case in cozy and quiet Bonn. The number of actors in government and civil society demanding expertise has never been higher. Last but not least, after the end of the cold war, a reunited Germany is assuming a much more prominent international role both within Europe and beyond.

With this broadening and increasing demand, the key question for the future of the "ideas industry" in Germany is whether the demand can be met by existing supplies. From a supply-side perspective, most German APAOs are not limited by a lack of funding or by insufficient qualifications of their staff, but by external structural factors that cannot be changed easily and by an underdeveloped awareness of their potential role as policy entrepreneurs.

Supply-Side
Constraints and Opportunities

FROM DETACHED EXPERT TO POLICY ENTREPRENEUR

A high level of state funding has shielded the German APAO industry in general and large think tanks in particular much better from political business cycles and fashion trends in the marketplace of ideas than their counterparts in the United Kingdom, for example (Weilemann 2000, 172–173). But this very "autonomy" from the business of policymaking and the marketing of ideas has made many German institutes and their products less relevant to the immediate and short-term needs of policymakers and the larger public than some potential clients outside academia (and even some of their own staff) wish them to be.

Nonetheless, a new generation of recently appointed think tank directors, policy-oriented academics at university-based research centers and in consulting bodies, as well as younger researchers, is slowly changing the political culture of APAOs in Germany. This new generation does not treat applied policy-oriented research with the same suspicion as it was treated twenty or thirty years ago. One may even state that the validity of the once widely held equation that excellence in basic research implies policy irrelevance and vice versa is now being called into question. Some of the new think tank directors—especially in economic and foreign policy research institutes—challenge their staff to produce more internationally competitive, cutting-edge research, to venture into thinking the unthinkable, and to become more policy relevant and audience oriented at the same time.

Whether this is too ambitious a challenge for the German APAO community remains to be seen. Clearly, the path followed by parts of the American think tank industry in the 1980s and 1990s, sacrificing academic credibility for short-term political influence and public visibility, is not a path that large chunks of the German community of policy experts are willing to follow, nor should they. Instead of becoming more politically biased in their research, policy experts and their organizations should attempt to become more assertive and proactive in controlling their agendas and in using the public agenda-setting process for their purposes instead of relying on politicians to pick and choose from their analyses. In short, policy experts and their institutes ought to become policy entrepreneurs and assume the role of strategic advisors, whenever this is possible. This recommendation is based on responses to this author's questionnaire, in which a sizeable majority of respondents from think tanks admitted that marketing and public relations are areas where improvement is necessary and urgent. What is needed is independent, semidetached involvement.

"Policy entrepreneurs" are advocates for a particular understanding of a problem or for the prominence of an idea, or they may be lobbyists for specific proposals and solutions. They are willing to invest resources such as time, reputation, and even money in the hope that their values will affect the shape of public policy (Kingdon 1984, 129). Until fairly recently, in most European countries including Germany, such leadership came from the government and from the political class itself rather than from the private sector or from knowledge-based actors. While the Bertelsmann Foundation and a few other foundations certainly are notable exceptions, Germany did not see major initiatives to create APAOs from the private sector in the past. The privatization of policy expertise has by no means reached British, let alone American, proportions. But there are indications that this pattern is about to change—especially on the European Union level and in policy areas such as international finance and tax policy. These indicators include the proliferation of think tanks and individual expert entrepreneurs, often in the form of university-based, for-profit consulting firms in Brussels or at the national level.

POLICY ENTREPRENEURSHIP AND POLICY WINDOWS

In order to have an impact on the political agenda-setting and decision-making processes in any given country, APAOs, like other actors such as pressure groups, party activists, or NGOs, must operate and plan their activities in accordance with some notion of which issues are likely to emerge on governmental agendas and which are not. They must also come up with some notion of how to best gain access to agenda setting and to subsequent stages of the policy process. According to John Kingdon (1984, ch. 7 & 8), who developed a full-fledged theory of the agenda-setting process on the federal level in the United States, policy entrepreneurs inside and outside government play a key role in taking advantage of agenda-setting opportunities to move issue items onto formal government agendas. These opportunities or policy windows arise when policy entrepreneurs are able to recognize when and how the problem stream (characteristics of issues) combines with the politics stream (characteristics of political institutions and circumstances) and with the currents of the policy stream (policy solutions). In short, policy entrepreneurs play a key role in coupling policy problems and specific policy solutions with political opportunities. Successful issue-opportunity linkage management by policy entrepreneurs does not guarantee the successful entrance of an item onto the "official" political agenda. Real success requires the opening of a policy window.

Individual exceptions notwithstanding, German APAOs have not fully realized their potential to assume the position of external policy entrepreneurs. The distance of many German think tanks from the world of agenda setting and policy-making, for example, is reflected in the admission of at least half of the institutes surveyed by this author that their knowledge of the needs, operating procedures, and inner workings of their audiences and target groups is inadequate and fragmentary at best.

In most cases, policy windows are opened and policy advice is sought by new governments, whereas governments with longevity prefer administrative routine. Administrative routine becomes triumphant over policy innovation unless a government or public sector agency feels challenged or is new. After the consolidation of power, administrative personnel are recruited over policy entrepreneurial staff. It is therefore crucial for entrepreneurial APAOs to maximize their visibility and influence during the opening of institutionalized policy windows before and after critical elections on both the federal and regional levels (between ten and sixteen such elections are held in Germany over a four-year period) as well as around crucial meetings, elections, power shifts, or appointments at the European and international levels.

To give one example, in 1998 Germans for the first time in their fifty-year-old democratic history voted into power two opposition parties instead of merely ratifying the change of coalition partners. Despite the opening of such a major institutionalized political window, the interaction and communication between APAOs and the incoming Social Democratic Schröder government did not proceed very well in the beginning. Few APAOs prepared the new government with realistic and pragmatic blueprints for reform, nor had the government itself developed a coherent governing philosophy within which, or in opposition to which, APAOs could locate specific policy proposals. There were, of course exceptions. Both the Institute for Peace Research and Security Policy and the Center for Applied Policy Research published "to-do" lists in international and European affairs for the new Schröder government, while researchers at the Max Planck Institute for the Study of Societies in Cologne helped to turn the attention of Social Democratic policy elites to international approaches in employment and labor market policy.

Two years into the legislative term, it had become clear that in the governmental orbit, task forces, temporary commissions, and networks of experts with some affinity to either the government and/or expertise in the most important issues (e.g., the future of pensions) were the winners of this most recent window opening. At least in terms of visibility and media coverage, legislative support organizations and party think tanks have not been able to keep pace in terms of participation in policy debate and development. In terms of media visibility, the political clout of legislative support agencies has suffered from the trend toward executive dominance of German politics. The executive branch, and the Chancellery in particular, have been rather inventive in creating flexible advisory structures that suit their changing needs. By comparison, MP's offices are too understaffed to fulfill the task of managing an ever-increasing amount of information. Legislative Study Commissions are often paralyzed by party politics and operate beyond the reach of executive control. With their long-term approach to the "study" of policy-relevant issues, the commissions easily become out of synch with a media culture focusing on immediate decision making and office holders who are forced to execute what British historian Arnold Toynbee once described as "one bloody thing after another." Only the Bundestag Research Services have assumed a more proactive role in recent years, providing unsolicited factual information to a larger audience than ever before.

Outside the orbit of government, think tanks and civil society–based APAOs, which have modernized their mission statements and adjusted their research agendas to new challenges, which are able and willing to enter into temporary partnerships with governmental agencies and public/private networks, which produce timely and digestible research, and which are not afraid to market their products in nontraditional ways and venues (i.e., outside the academic world), have been rewarded at least with visibility, if not with influence.

Concluding Suggestions

OVERALL CONDITIONS AND FUNDING

Overall conditions for the growth and sustainability of APAOs in Germany have been good—in some respects very good—ever since the (western part of the) country became a consolidated democracy with a high GDP in the 1960s. APAOs in Germany operate on a solid and predictable legal base, although tax laws introduced in the late 1990s that offer incentives to create civil society APAOs could and should have been promoted much earlier. The cultural norms toward individual and corporate philanthropy should be improved. It must be demonstrated to potential philanthropic donors that devoting resources to civil society APAOs is worth their while. As long as the view prevails that independent policy-relevant research is the sole responsibility of the state, Germany will not be able to establish and maintain a more up-to-date and sustainable infrastructure of independent APAOs. The overall financial situation of most German APAOs at the present, however, is satisfactory. Some of the publicly funded research institutes—especially those in economic, environmental, and security policy—are among the best-funded in the world. The Bertelsmann Foundation is certainly one of the wealthiest operating foundations, addressing a wide array of policy issues. Still, imbalances in the distribution of available public funds across policy fields and types of APAOs should be addressed.

WHAT GOVERNMENTS SHOULD CONSIDER

Governments seem to prefer advisory arrangements over which they can exert some kind of control. (Control here does not mean direct control over research results, but rather over research agendas and the timing of research reports.) Governments prefer to remain flexible, creating ad hoc bodies that suit their needs rather than setting up more permanent bodies. But experts and advisory bodies should not be treated as mere bearers of policy-relevant knowledge external to the policymaking process who can be called upon on demand. Instead, political decision makers and their bureaucratic staff in the civil service should seek to involve APAOs in issue networks and other policymaking structures. This would require both parties to assume new roles: Experts would no longer be distant bearers of relevant knowledge, but would assume some kind of responsibility for their recommendations. Political decision makers and civil servants would have to engage in difficult and time-consuming research. Instead of withholding information from advisory bodies, the administration would have to reveal to the experts some insider knowledge, their internal codes of operation, and their political strategies.

Given the holistic and cross-departmental nature of many policy issues, advisory structures at the apex of power (i.e., in the Chancellery and/or the Cabinet, as well as in the premiers' offices in the *Länder*) should be strengthened and expanded. At the federal level, such an advisory body could be built upon existing units such as Directorate 5 of the Chancellery. It could also take the form of an advisory council located outside of existing structures. Regardless of the administrative shape, this body should help to identify fundamental issues, to sharpen the chief executive's eye for conceptual conformity of policies, and to find politically feasible solutions. Such a unit should also help to evaluate recommendations made by other advisory councils and expert bodies specifically from the perspective of executive and political leadership.

Finally, legislative study commissions should be opened to the civil society sector by including representatives of nongovernmental organizations in addition to MPs and academic experts. These commissions could thus serve as a bridge between a parliament that is dominated by party MPs representing territorial units and a civil society that is organized in functional sectors.

WHAT ADVISORS SHOULD CONSIDER

German APAOs that circulate within the governmental orbit will continue to operate in an institutional environment where the legislature does not play an independent legislative role and where a strong element of executive dominance over policymaking will remain. Nevertheless, the business of executive policymaking is changing rapidly and offers new opportunities to external knowledge-based actors of various sorts. One has to recognize and accept the fact that most, if not all, research institutions, consulting bodies, and individual advisors inside and outside of government will continue to pursue their own separate missions. The challenge, however, is to make them, or networks among them, devote some of their efforts and resources to creating shared policy research and planning initiatives. A common space should be created—to which participating members of consulting networks devote a certain amount of time and human resources—to engage in agenda sharing, the creation of knowledge partnerships, professional exchanges, and the promotion of linkages across the academic, policy-research, and policy-planning communities. It remains unclear, however, what degree of institutionalization these new approaches require.

Research and expertise are highly specialized, whereas problems in need of solutions or management are often cross-cutting and multidisciplinary. External advisory bodies should not copy departmental boundaries of academic research institutions such as universities or academies of basic research. Moreover, it is necessary for external advisors—i.e., the "ideas industry"—in Germany to become aware that institutes and less institutionalized advisory groups and individuals belong to a community of policy advisors, in the same way that political consultants are aware of their communal ties.

Finally, external advisory bodies cannot and should not rely primarily on solicited and commissioned research, but should consider their own priorities in setting the public policy agenda via the media, old and new. They should see themselves as actors focused on the interface between two different streams—policy and politics—and should attempt to adjust their work to the potential opening of policy windows, as far as these are predictable.

WHAT THINK TANKS SHOULD CONSIDER

Despite the impressive size of individual institutes, there are still too few interdisciplinary think tanks that are capable of integrating researchers from various backgrounds dealing with cross-cutting policy issues. Institutes that operate in the border areas between academia, market and trend research, and political consulting, and that take an unorthodox, cross-sectional approach to problems, are still too few and far between. There is a severe lack of institutes capable of combining visionary courage with depth of expertise.

Classical think tanks and foundations must slim down their organizations and make them more flexible if they are to respond more swiftly to rapidly changing policy concerns. They need to be more aware of the fact that the research they are conducting is not purely academic but forms the basis of political decision making. The guild of policy advisors and political consultants must bring forth more than theoretical wisdom. And those that seek their advice can do their part to see that supply is brought more in line with demand. Integration of think tanks into the institutionalized channels of policy advice giving is significantly more advanced in economic and social policy, the environment, and technology than it is in foreign policy and national security, or in the broad field of basic political principles. There are constant calls for more interchange of personnel and thus of ideas between business, education, politics, and the media, but such calls seldom result in practical change. More working groups, planning teams, and policy units in the top echelons of politics would greatly accelerate such an exchange of personnel and ideas.

THE FUTURE GEOGRAPHY OF APAOS:
BERLIN AS AN APAO CAPITAL ?

Finally, the question as to the proper place of APAOs in political consulting in Germany remains open. Those who offer policy-relevant advice and those who seek it are a very heterogeneous and scattered group. Berlin is not yet the capital of think tanks and political dialogue in Germany to the same extent that London is in the United Kingdom, or even that Washington, D.C., is in the United States. Although Berlin has acquired nearly all federal executive and legislative consultative bodies, as well as important institutes in foreign policy and national security, for those in other policy areas such as finance, business, and area studies, proximity to the stock exchange in Frankfurt, to the European Commission in Brussels, or to regional capitals and economic centers is at least as important as having roots in Berlin. But decentralization has its price. In London, 90 percent of British think tanks are located in the Westminster area, close to the media and the headquarters of important national organizations and political parties, not to mention the country's financial and business center and the head offices of the major nonprofit organizations. In addition, the British think tanks maintain close ties with the most important universities in Greater London, such as the London School of Economics. Such an intensive, vital and efficient consulting cosmos—for the best advice is often given unofficially, by word of mouth—has yet to be created in Berlin on such a scale. Will such an intellectual milieu, close to the world of politics, in which various types of APAOs play a prominent role, ever be created in Berlin? Only time will tell.

NOTES

1. It should be noted at the outset that the words "policy" and "politics" are indistinguishable in the German language. Therefore, the distinction between political consulting and policy advice is not an easy one semantically in Germany. Both activities can be referred to by the German term *"Politikberatung."*

2. In the Chancellery, for example, out of a staff of 400–450, only a little over 5 percent are political appointees (Müller-Rommel 2000, 85).

3. Wolfgang Filc is a professor of economics and an expert in international finance at the University of Trier. Between November 1998 and May 1999, he headed the international finance directorate in the German Ministry of Finance under Minister Oskar Lafontaine. He served as an externally recruited top bureaucrat and kept a diary of his experiences at that job. Even though Lafontaine and his senior political staff were the most ideological stewards of German financial policy in recent memory and an advocacy coalition at its very best, Filc's detailed account of his expert advisory role is rather sobering. Access to the minister was infrequent and restricted to ceremonial occasions, policy was rarely discussed among the senior staff, and Filc's staff, which was composed exclusively of career civil servants, mistook his open, discursive leadership style as a sign of indecision and bureaucratic weakness (Filc 1999).

4. The "mirror" sections of the Chancellery reproduce in miniature format the structure of the federal government as a whole. They enable the chancellor to monitor ministerial compliance with his policy guidelines.

5. An older Alliance for Jobs under Chancellor Helmut Kohl lasted from 1995 to 1996,

but was abolished by the chancellor due to irreconcilable differences with the trade unions over certain policy issues, such as sick pay.

6. Given the parameters of this chapter, this is not the place to discuss whether the AfJ is an appropriate response to the competitive pressures facing the German economy.

7. The conference was a follow-up to a similar meeting of six heads of reform-minded, center-left governments that took place in Florence in November 1999, under the title "Progressive Governance for the 21st Century." The countries represented in these two meetings were Argentina, Brazil, Canada, Chile, France, Germany, the United Kingdom, Greece, Italy, the Netherlands, New Zealand, South Africa, Sweden, and the United States.

8. Legislative study commissions do not affect the right of the federal government to appoint expert commissions of its own.

9. In 1975, the federal government and the *Länder* governments enlarged the Framework Agreement on the Promotion of Research to include independent research institutions of supraregional importance and national scientific interest, and institutions performing service functions. Those qualifying for this financial assistance were listed in an implementing agreement in 1977 which was printed on blue paper—hence the name "Blue List Institutes." In 1995, this group was officially named the Wissensschaftsgemeinschaft Gottfried Wilhelm Leibniz, or Scientific Association Gottfried Wilhelm Leibniz (*Education and Science* No. 4, 30).

10. The six large institutes—the German Institute of Economic Research in Berlin, the Kiel Institute of World Economics, the Munich-based Ifo Institute for Economic Research, the Rhine-Westphalia Institute for Economic Research in Essen, the Institute for Economic Research (HWWA) in Hamburg, and, more recently, the Halle Institute for Economic Research—are complemented by some state-based economic research institutes, such as those in Hannover and Bremen. The newer Mannheim-based Center for European Economic Research also aspires to full Blue List status.

11. In the large academic think tanks too, the value-oriented political preferences of individual experts tend to result in unambiguously biased recommendations.

12. In 1996, the Greens recognized the Heinrich Böll Foundation (HBS) as their official political foundation on the federal level. HBS's forerunner, Stiftungsverband Regenbogen (Rainbow Foundation), was a loose federation of three independent foundations closely attached to the feminist, environmental, and peace movements of the 1980s. As far as policy research is concerned, neither the Böll Foundation nor the Rosa Luxemburg Foundation (Party of the Democratic Socialism) has been able to catch up with the other political foundations. Two in-house think tanks, the Feminist Institute and the Green Academy, are being created at HBS.

13. See Kloten (1989) on the role of economists in the German government until reunification.

BIBLIOGRAPHY

Andersen Consulting, Arthur D. Little, Schitag Ernst & Young, Young & Rubicam. 1998. *Modell Deutschland 21, Wege in das nächste Jahrhundert* (Model Germany 21: Pathways into the new century). Reinbek: Rowohlt.

Bakvis, Herman. 1997. "Think Tanks, Political Staff and Kitchen Cabinets: Advising the

Executive." In Patrick Moray Weller, Herman Bakvis, and R. A. W. Rhodes, eds. *The Hollow Crown: Countervailing Trends in Core Executives.* Basingstoke, U.K.: Macmillan.

———. 2000. "Country Report: Canada. Rebuilding Policy Capacity in the Era of the Fiscal Dividend." *Governance* 13(1): 71–104.

Bimber, Bruce. 1996. *The Politics of Expertise in Congress. The Rise and Fall of the Office of Technology Assessment.* Albany, N.Y.: State University of New York Press.

Day, Alan J. 2000. "Think Tanks in Western Europe." In James G. McGann and R. Kent Weaver, eds. *Think Tanks and Civil Societies: Catalysts for Ideas and Actions.* New Brunswick, N.J.: Transaction.

Erb, Hans-Jörg, ed. 2000. *Handbuch der Bundesregierung, 14. Wahlperiode* (Federal government directory, 14th legislative term, February 2000). Darmstadt: Neue Darmstaedter Verlagsanstalt.

Euchner, Walter, Frank Hampel, and Thomas Seidel. 1993. *Länder-Enquete-Kommissionen als Instrumente der Politikberatung* (State-based legislative study commissions as instruments of policy advice). Baden-Baden: Nomos.

Federal Court of Audit. 1996. "Die Präsidentin des Bundesrechnungshofs als Bundesbeauftragte für Wirtschaftlichkeit in der Verwaltung: Gutachten über die Koordinierung und Rationalisierung der Aktivitäten im Bereich Ostforschung, Bonn" (President of the Federal Court of Audit: Report on the coordination and rationalization of federally funded research into Eastern and international studies). Unpublished report.

Filc, Wolfgang. 1999. *Mitgegangen, Mitgehangen: Mit Lafontaine im Finanzministerium* (With Lafontaine in the Ministry of Finance). Frankfurt: Eichborn.

Janning, Josef. 1996. "Anforderungen an die Denkfabriken" (What is expected from think tanks). *Internationale Politik* 9(Sept.): 51, 65–67.

Kingdon, John W. 1984. *Agendas, Alternatives, and Public Policies.* Boston: Little Brown Co.

———. 1994. "Agendas, Ideas and Policy Change." In Lawrence C. Dodd and Calvin Jillson, eds. *New Perspectives on American Politics.* Washington, D.C.: Congressional Quarterly Press.

Klaiber, Klaus-Peter. 1996. "Zielvorgabe: Aktualität, Praxisnähe und Durchsetzbarkeit" (Objective for policy advisors: Topicality, project orientation and assertiveness). *Internationale Politik* 9(Sept.): 51, 63–64.

Kloten, Norbert. 1989. "West Germany." In Joseph A. Pechman, ed. *The Role of the Economist in Government: An International Perspective.* Hemel Hempstead, U.K.: Harvester Wheatsheaf.

Krevert, Peter. 1993. *Funktionswandel der wissenschaftlichen Politikberatung in der Bundesrepublik Deutschland* (The changing functions of policy advice giving in Germany). Münster/Hamburg: LIT-Verlag.

Mayntz, Renate. 1987. "West Germany." In William Plowden, ed. *Advising the Rulers.* Oxford, U.K.: Basil Blackwell.

McGann, James G., and R. Kent Weaver, eds. 2000. *Think Tanks and Civil Societies: Catalysts for Ideas and Actions.* New Brunswick, N.J.: Transaction.

Merkel, Angela, ed. 1997. *Wissenschaftliche Politikberatung für die Umwelt* (Policy advice giving for the environment). Bonn: Analytica.

Mielke, Gerd. 1999. "Sozialwissenschaftliche Beratung in den Staatskanzleien" (The role of social-scientific consultation in the state chancelleries of the federal states). *Forschungsjournal Neue Soziale Bewegungen* 12(3): 40–48.

Müller-Rommel, Ferdinand. 2000. "Management of Politics in the German Chancellor's Office." In Guy Peters, R. A. W. Rhodes, and Vincent Wright, eds. *Administering the Summit: Administration of the Core Executive in Developed Countries.* New York: St. Martin's Press.

Murswieck, Axel. 1993. "Policy Advice and Decision-Making in the German Federal Bureaucracy." In Guy Peters and Anthony Barker, eds. *Advising West European Governments: Inquiries, Expertise and Public Policy.* Edinburgh: Edinburgh University Press.

———, ed. 1994. *Regieren und Politikberatung* (Governance and policy advice giving). Opladen: Leske & Budrich.

Niclauss, Karlheinz. 2000. "The Federal Government: Variations of Chancellor Dominance." In Ludger Helms, ed. *Institutions and Institutional Change in the Federal Republic of Germany.* London: Macmillan.

Petermann, Thomas. 1990. *Das wohlberatene Parlament. Orte und Prozesse der Politikberatung beim Deutschen Bundestag* (The well-advised parliament: Locations and processes of policy advice-giving). Berlin: Edition Sigma.

Peters, Guy, and Anthony Barker, eds. 1993. *Advising West European Governments: Inquiries, Expertise and Public Policy.* Edinburgh: Edinburgh University Press.

Plowden, William, ed. 1987. *Advising the Rulers.* Oxford, U.K.: Basil Blackwell.

Reinecke, Wolfgang. 1996. *Tugging at the Sleeves of Politicians. Think Tanks—American Experiences and German Perspectives.* Gütersloh: Verlag Bertelsmann Stiftung.

Saint-Martin, Denis. 1998. "The New Managerialism and Policy Influence of Consultants in Government: An Historical-Institutionalist Analysis of Britain, Canada and France." *Governance* 11(3): 332–353.

Schick, Rupert, and Wolfgang Zeh. 1999. *The German Bundestag—Functions and Procedures.* Rheinbreitbach: NDV.

Schlecht, Otto, ed. 1995. *30 Jahre Sachverständigenrat zur Begutachtung der gesamtwirtschaftlichen Entwicklung* (The Council of Economic Experts at 30). Krefeld: Sinus Verlag.

Scholz, Lothar. 1997. "The Think-Tank Landscape in Germany: A Look behind the Mirror." Paper presented at a conference on "Think Tanks in the USA and Germany. Democracy at Work: How and Where Do Public Decision-makers Obtain Their Knowledge?" University of Pennsylvania, Philadelphia, Pennsylvania, 18–20 November 1993.

Silvia, Stephen. 1999. "Every Which Way But Loose: German Industrial Relations Since 1980." In Andrew Martin and George Ross, eds. *The Brave New World of European Labour: European Trade Unions at the Millennium.* Oxford: Berghahn Books.

Singer, Otto. 1993. "Knowledge and Politics in Economic Policy-Making." In Guy Peters and Anthony Barker, eds. *Advising West European Governments.* Edinburgh: Edinburgh University Press.

Stone, Diane, Andrew Denham, and Mark Garnett, eds. 1998. *Think Tanks across Nations: A Comparative Approach.* Manchester: Manchester University Press.

Thunert, Martin, 2000. "Players Beyond Borders? German Think Tanks as Catalysts of

Internationalization." *Global Society* 14(2): 191–212.

Timmins, Graham. 2000. "Alliance for Jobs and Prospects for Social Partnership in Germany." Paper presented at the Political Studies Association of the U.K., 2000 Annual Conference, at the London School of Economics, 10–13 April 2000.

Vieregge, Henning von. 1990. "Die Parteistiftungen: Ihre Rolle im politischen System" (The party foundations: Their role in the political system). In Göttrik Wewer, ed. *Parteienfinanzierung und politischer Wettbewerb: Rechtsnormen-Realanalyse-Reformvorschläge* (Party financing and political competition: Legal framework, analysis, and reform). Opladen: Westdeutscher Verlag.

Wallace, William. 1994. "Between Two Worlds: Think Tanks and Foreign Policy." In Christopher Hill and Pamela Beshoff, eds. *Two Worlds of International Relations: Academics, Practitioners and the Trade in Ideas*. London: Routledge and London School of Economics.

Weilemann, Peter R. 2000. "Experiences of a Multidimensional Think Tank: The Konrad Adenauer Stiftung." In James McGann and R. Kent Weaver, eds. *Think Tanks and Civil Societies*. New Brunswick, N.J.: Transaction.

7 India

Kuldeep Mathur

That the character of a political system is key to the way public policy is deliberated, formulated, and implemented is a widely accepted notion. The two extremes of an open and a closed political system are associated with distinctive and opposite policy processes. Theoretically speaking, a closed political system is more likely to have a policy process that is centralized, secretive, and unresponsive; whereas an open political system is likely to be allied with a policy process that is decentralized, consultative, and responsive. The characteristics associated with a closed political system, however, are not limited to authoritarian regimes and may persist in new democracies in the developing world (Robinson 1998). There may also be variations of policy processes as a political system evolves from a formal democratic system to a more meaningful, participative democracy.

India is an example of a political system undergoing such an evolution. In 1950, democracy was introduced to India with the formal institutions of elections, political parties, and a Parliament. A parliamentary system of government created in the image of its colonial ruler, the United Kingdom. Through the years, India's democratic institutions have grown to give fuller representation to the country's people, providing them with a greater voice in determining public policy. But India's particular politics and national aspirations have contributed to its forging its own democratic identity, making it a little different from the U.K. model.

This chapter attempts to delineate the way that India's public policy processes have evolved. In the early years of democracy, consensus over development policies was widespread, and formulation of these policies was based on rational economic and technocratic criteria. Specialists and experts, who were incorporated into government institutions, played a major role in the deliberative process. This consensus began to break down with the end of the Nehruvian years, and the period from 1966 to 1980 was marked by turmoil. Economic difficulties beset the country, and democratic institutions were suspended. With the return to power of Indira Gandhi in the 1980s, government started down a path of liberalization, which gained momentum under the regime of Rajiv Gandhi and subsequently with a series of economic reforms put in place in 1991. Policy processes at the time were a reflection of these political and economic changes.

In the last decade, a market for alternative policies and forums to articulate competing public choices has emerged. The development strategy espoused during the administrations of Jawaharlal Nehru and Indira Gandhi had neither alleviated poverty nor strengthened the country industrially. Disparities in wealth had grown further, and politics grew to be dominated by demands for equality, justice, and development. Public discourse began to focus on what had gone wrong and what instead should be done. Research institutes that had operated within familiar paradigms began to suggest different formulations. Even government committees, which had relied exclusively on in-house advice, sought policy advice from elsewhere. Nongovernmental organizations (NGOs) that advocated new options and means of implementation caught the imagination of the people.

The frustration that technicians and professionals had known was transformed into an idealism centered on NGOs. Many young people forsook lucrative careers to pursue work in the fields of education, health, and environment. The result was the emergence of research-based institutions and grass-roots organizations, both of which have gained but slow acceptance in the government's policy-making process. Why slow? Nongovernmental organizations have grown at a speed that governmental institutions have not been able to keep up with. The major hurdle has been the structure and role of bureaucracy, which now includes at least a few more individuals interested in change.

Even so, political leadership has not adequately responded to the demands of long-term policymaking. One reason is that political parties and members of Parliament have little professional or research support that could help them articulate alternative choices. Another is, after the decline of the Congress Party, coalition politics has led to the rise of regional parties and sectional interests. There has been no emergence of a national perspective in the last decade, and policy has been a secondary consideration to a politics of survival.

DEMOCRACY AND GOVERNANCE

With its size and heterogeneity, India is not an easy country to govern. In area as well as population, many Indian states are larger than sovereign nations. India has a federal system of government, but in contrast to the United States, which has a population of 280 million divided among fifty states, India has a population of 950 million in twenty-two states. The border areas in the northeast and northwest have continued to be trouble spots since independence in 1947. As a result, national unity has always dominated the policy concerns of the government, but a consequence of such thinking has been hesitant decentralization and reluctant opening up of the decision-making process.

India's adoption of a democratic parliamentary system of government with universal adult enfranchisement occurred at a time when its literacy rate was 35 percent and more than half its population was living below the poverty line. Much of the government's effort since then has been to equip its people to exercise their franchise effectively—by raising the literacy rate and reducing the level of poverty. The discourse on democracy also centered on the core Western liberal concepts of individual rights, freedom, and equal opportunity, and it is in this context that claims of the failure of Indian democracy are often heard. The wanting quality of public life and the state's incapacity to meet the demands of the people are attributed to the pathology of India's political system.

Indeed, India faces a paradox. On the one hand, incidence of social conflict has risen, the economy has undergone difficulty, and democratic institutions are continuously under pressure by the tide of protest and violence. Democracy in India, on the other hand, seems to have deepened and widened its reach. The proportion of the socially and economically deprived who exercise their right to vote has risen. If there is turbulence at the electoral level, one reason is that the participatory base of the electorate has expanded since the 1990s (Yadav 1999).

This kind of democratic experience has severely strained the system of governance. Difficulties were compounded by the pattern of economic development in the country. Some regions have done much better, while others with large populations have lagged behind considerably. Economic growth and the removal of poverty were the goals of policy, but as population growth has continued to hover at 2 percent–2.5 percent per year, the rate of per capita income growth has been a little less than that, thus having little impact on poverty levels. Illiteracy rates have come down, but less than half the population is still unable to read or write. The dilemma of increased political participation within a system of limited economic benefits is the major challenge for policymakers as India enters the second millennium.

STATE AND BUREAUCRACY

India's development experience is embedded in a highly expanded role of the state. In Nehru's vision of planned development, the state occupied a preeminent position. It was the agency that would be instrumental in providing to society the public goods from which everyone would benefit. The state would occupy

210 of Kuldeep Mathur

commanding heights in the economy, producing goods and services when the private sector could not or where the private sector created inequities. Accordingly, India became a highly interventionist state that pursued welfare and socialist objectives by itself becoming an entrepreneur and by controlling and regulating the private sector. This has had the effect of creating a public sector with a huge army of employees whose interest lay in its self-perpetuation and in the acquisition of as much benefit as possible from the economy. As L. I. Rudolph and S. H. Rudolph argue, "the state sector that burgeoned and flourished on the way to socialism began to acquire and vest interests. Means began to become ends. Those in the pay of state firms became the beneficiaries of monopoly profits and administered prices; petty bureaucrats and senior officials became the beneficiaries of rents, the petty and grand larceny made possible by administrative discretion in the application of rules" (1987, 62–63). Thus, the feeble development record of the Indian state could be explained in terms of the pulls and pressures of various groups that had subordinated the state to their interests (Bardhan 1984).

Faith by policymakers in the ability of the state to undertake the enormous task of development had stemmed from the perceived strength and efficiency of the bureaucracy that the British had left behind. At a time when other developing countries were struggling to establish a professional and career-based civil service, the standing of the Indian Civil Service (ICS) was exceptional. It had served the colonial masters well, and in the initial years of independence, it had provided tremendous support to the integration of the country, quelling riots that followed upon partition. It had quickly assumed the role of upholding the law of the new sovereign state. These civil servants together with their successors, the Indian Administrative Service, also became great supporters of the Nehruvian policy of state-led development. As a result, the legacy of British administrative structure has remained untouched, even when questions of its suitability have been raised.

A powerful metaphor for the ICS was "the steel frame," which signified the service's endurance in the maintenance of law and order in the face of local pressures to the contrary. Another was that of guardianship, which suggested how the ICS worked in the public interest. In everyday life, it imparted a sense of superiority to the civil servants who believed in their heaven-born status to rule over common man. Significantly, the ICS tradition also resulted in the celebration of the generalist and the amateur, who were placed in positions of authority to filter and process specialist and technical advice. This role came naturally to them because of their perceived monopoly on understanding and working for public interest, and it is this legacy that has shaped and circumscribed the Indian administrative system in the independence era (Potter 1986). Little in the way of administrative reform has since occurred.

In actual practice, the economic strategy that relied on the state for development translated into an unprecedented expansion in the public sector. Public enterprises were initially limited to manufacturing in the basic industries and the defense sector, but gradually, starting with the administration of Indira Gandhi, their role expanded. Banks were nationalized, and hotels and services that interacted directly with citizens were subsumed by the state. At the same time, the traditional functions of government, including regulation of the private sector, were also expanding, making the role of the bureaucracy in Indian society all-pervasive. Bureaucrats became arbiters of public interest, refusing the advice and consent of citizens—so much so that one aspect of the democratic struggle in India has been to make government more responsive to the needs of citizens.

It would not be entirely correct, however, to depict the bureaucracy with a single stroke of the brush. There are some members of the Indian bureaucracy who stand today as a progressive force working for greater decentralization, democratization, and the widening of the consultative process.

In the past decade, whether by emulation or innovation, country after country has embarked on reform in the administration of government. Reform is stylish today. On the one hand, changes in technology, particularly information technology, have necessitated changes in management. But on the other, under the terms of globalization and liberalization, international financial agencies have called for internal structural reform. While administrative changes may be profoundly domestic concerns, the fact that they are part of a new, more comprehensive package opens them up to external pressure and influence. For example, the International Monetary Fund (IMF) and the World Bank, which funded NGOs for the implementation of development programs, have pushed strongly for reducing fiscal deficits by downsizing the government and cutting down on subsidies.

In contrast to earlier decades, when government leadership initiated change, now it is the society and victims of ham-handed administration who are demanding administrative reform. As decentralization is effected, democracy in the country has deepened, even as local institutions like the *panchayats* (village-level government created through constitutional amendment) have been subject to frustration and anger with the functioning of the state.

In the give and take, the government itself expressed concern about the need to be more open and responsive. In 1997, it established a working group to examine the feasibility of a full-fledged right-to-information act. The president of Common Cause, an NGO active in consumer issues, was named chairman of the group. Other members included lawyers and heads of government agencies, including railways and telecommunications. When the group had done its work, it issued a public report recommending enactment of a freedom-of-information bill.

This experience seems to have established a precedent, leading to organized pressure from below for government reform. NGOs have acted as catalysts in this movement. *Jan sunwais* (public hearings) are now held regularly. These hearings were initiated by Mazdoor Kissan Shakti Sangathan (Labour Peasant Unity Organization), an organization of rural laborers and farmers, giving people an opportunity to demand accountability from the government, to expose corruption, to focus on specific issues concerning decentralization, and to build grassroots democracy (*The Hindu* 12 December 1999).

HISTORY OF THE
PLANNING PROCESS

The leadership of the national movement for government reform spearheading the struggle for independence before 1947 was by and large urban professionals and intellectuals who identified the future of India with the developments in the West. Of particular significance was the perception of the role science and technology played in transforming society. Nehru was further impressed by the strides Soviet Russia had made through judicious planning and the rational use of resources, and he envisioned India quickly attaining the levels of economic development achieved by Western nations through industrialization and modernization. Rational allocation of resources, industrialization, and modernization became key words in the vocabulary of development during this period. A corollary element in this thinking was the principal role the state would play: It would initiate development and the market would function under its overall direction. The private sector was willing to accept these terms, for which there was broad national consensus based on agreement among the leaders of the Congress party, industrialists, and technocrats and bureaucrats. Because the discussion required knowledge not only of economics but also of science and technology, expert advice was needed. In 1950, the Planning Commission was created for this purpose.

The commission, as a body of technical experts, was granted a certain degree of autonomy in decision making. Its power and prestige flowed from Nehru's own patronage and the fact that he assumed chairmanship of the group. Over the next decade, the economic development of India was thus placed in the hands of about twenty men, most of whom were civil servants, with some representing private interests as well (Khilnani 1997, 81).

In quick succession, professional economists and technocrats came to dominate all public discussion on economic development, and the Planning Commission became the exclusive theater for formulation of economic policy. The Cabinet and Parliament were merely informed of the decisions made by these experts. By the time of the Second Five-Year Plan (1956–1961), political decisions made by the commission were camouflaged in technical terms to insulate them from public scrutiny (Khilnani 1997, 86).

Another way of ensuring the influence of the group in executive decisions was to create a link between the Planning Commission and the bureaucracy. The Cabinet secretary, who is the top bureaucrat in the country and to whom all the secretaries of the ministries are accountable, was named the secretary to the Planning Commission in 1950. This practice was discontinued in 1964 when a separate secretary to the Planning Commission was appointed. This interlocking of offices had the effect of making the advice of the Planning Commission tantamount to a command.

As a result, experts and technocrats who worked within government rose in power and influence. If an expert chose not to join the government, the government was pleased to support his research if it was policy oriented. In the period prior to 1964, the government established and funded several institutes involved in such research. Examples included the National Council of Applied Economic Research, the Institute of Applied Manpower Research, the National Council of Education Research and Training, the National Institute of Education Planning and Administration, the National Institute of Family Planning and Health (now Welfare and Health), and the Indian Institute of Public Administration. These institutes, which maintained close links with government and the Planning Commission, brought in academics to monitor and evaluate development programs. The data of their research provided direct input in the government's formulation of public policy.

Research organizations that generated alternative points of view were few. So there was neither need for the government to seek advice elsewhere, nor need for it to consult its citizenry. For the government knew best. Whatever dissent there may have been came from the Gandhians, but their voice did little in countering the prevailing influence of the modernizers.

In the post-Nehruvian period, beginning in 1964, by which time the Planning Commission had lost its glamour, the link between the Planning Commission and the bureaucracy was cut. Lal Bahadur Shastri established his own secretariat and created a group of experts who could serve as alternative sources of advice. During his administration, as well as that of Indira Gandhi's, the prime minister's office was staffed by career economists, and thus was the government's dependence on the Planning Commission diminished. Shastri's arrangement continues today with trained economists being replaced by civil servants.

GROWTH OF RESEARCH INSTITUTIONS

The Planning Commission's support of extra-governmental research was funded through its Research Planning Committee (RPC). But the commission's work

214 | Kuldeep Mathur

came under a cloud when a plan holiday was declared during 1966–1968 and formulation of the Fourth Five-Year Plan was postponed. During this period, the funds administered by the RPC were transferred to an autonomous body that was enjoined to fund research institutes and sponsor independent research. This body was the Indian Council of Social Science Research (ICSSR).

Promotion of research in social sciences was the major objective of the council. It did this mainly by (a) keeping track of literature, research, and trends in social science research in the country; (b) inviting new research proposals from scholars; and (c), among other functions, conducting seminars, training, and workshops for India's young social scientists. Sponsoring institutes outside the university system has been a major function of the council, the purpose being to encourage multidisciplinary and policy-oriented research.

Today there are twenty-seven research institutes spread throughout the country supported by the ICSSR. Each institute decides its own direction of research, which spans a wide spectrum of subjects related to agriculture and rural development, industrial structure and growth, income distribution and poverty, employment and wages, interregional differences in development, education, health, nutrition, women, energy, technology, the environment, and social, cultural, and institutional aspects of development.

The ICSSR supported only nine institutes until 1974, after which the number increased gradually. The reason for this was the need for regional orientation that could be brought to bear in policy. Through a funding program that required institutes located outside Delhi to secure matching funding from state governments, regional involvement in the policy process was assured. And conversely, state governments found these research institutes to be a source of advice and expertise for their own programs.

Usually, the initiative for the establishment of a research institute was taken by individual scholars or public figures who enjoyed the support of state government or the central government. The prestige of the institute and the access it had in governmental circles depended largely on the influence of the founder. In addition, it was the academic standing of the founder that attracted other university scholars to the institute. Part of the appeal of these institutes was the research facilities, which universities could ill-afford. The drawback was that while many scholars joined these institutes, universities suffered. Recently, however, with the ICSSR unable to maintain good research facilities and high salaries, the situation has begun to change.

The ICSSR gave block grants as well as project funds (see table 1). Over the years, block grants have dwindled, even as state governments have matched them and shared in the capital cost of land and buildings. The institutes that have endured are those that have been successful in securing additional funding.

Table 1. Research Institutes Supported by ICSSR, 1997–1998

Research Institutes	Research Projects		Staff Strength		ICSSR Grants
	Completed	Ongoing	Faculty	Others	(Rs million)
A. N. Sinha Institute of Social Studies, Patna	5	4	36	33	2.34
Centre for Economic and Social Studies, Hyderabad	12	13	14	21	1.42
Centre for Policy Research, New Delhi	17	16	41	38	1.55
Centre for Research in Rural and Industrial Development, Chandigarh.	4	19	-	-	1.73
Centre for the Study of Developing Societies, New Delhi	8	27	17	24	5.27
Centre for Social Studies, Surat	9	6	-	-	1.53
Centre for the Study in Social Sciences, Calcutta	3	27	15	42	4.01
Council for Social Development, Hyderabad	10	14	10	11	1.02
Centre for Women's Development Studies, New Delhi	4	10	10	30	1.84
Gandhian Institute of Studies, Varanasi	8	11	-	-	2.46
Giri Institute of Development Studies, Lucknow	7	11	22	27	2.57
G. B. Pant Social Science Institute, Allahabad	5	9	15	42	2.68
Gujarat Institute of Development Research, Ahmedabad	5	4	-	-	1.12
Indian Institute of Education, Pune	2	5	4	19	1.46
Centre for Multi-Disciplinary Research, Dharwar	2	9	-	-	0.77
Dr. Baba Saheb Ambedkar National Institute of Social Science, Mhow	3	7	8	-	0.64
Institute of Development Studies, Jaipur	2	13	-	-	2.55
Institute of Economic Growth, New Delhi	22	-	36	67	2.93
Institute of Public Enterprise, Hyderabad	3	4	-	-	1.51
Institute of Social and Economic Change, Bangalore	29	36	45	90	3.48
Institute for Studies in Industrial Development, New Delhi	-	2	3	10	2.45
M P Institute for Social Science Research, Ujjain	3	7	5	5	5.08
Madras Institute of Development Studies, Chennai	7	4	17	27	2.45
N. Choudhary Centre for Development Studies, Bhubeneshwar	9	9	13	21	3.41
O K Das Institute of Social Change and Development, Guwahati	2	4	3	10	0.86
Sardar Patel Institute of Economic and Social Research, Ahmedabad	5	4	13	57	2.90

Source: Data collected through various annual reports of the Indian Council of Social Science Research.
ICSSR: Indian Council of Social Science Research.

Another purpose that these institutes provided was the inclusion of noneconomic social sciences in the formulation of policy. Most institutes carried names underlining the multidisciplinary nature of their interest. Thus if there was the Centre of Development Studies at Trivandrum and the Madras Institute of Development Studies, there was also the Institute of Social and Economic Change at Bangalore and the Sardar Patel Institute of Social and Economic Research at Ahmedabad. Yet, it was eminent economists like V. K. R. V. Rao, K. N. Raj, Malcolm Adisesasiah, and D. T. Lakdawala who led most of these institutes, and despite expectations to the contrary, the major research projects were dominated by economists. As studies focused on the evaluation and impact of government programs, input from other social scientists was necessary, and the character of the institute faculty changed.

How the government responded to the findings of these research institutes depended on the influence of the leadership of the relevant bureaucracy. If the leadership were members of important government committees, they could act as policy brokers, promoting the research findings of the institutes and mobilizing funds for further research. As the cast of leaders changed, however, the connections between the institutes and government became tenuous. Today, for the most part, these institutes do not command the status they once did. Those established after 1989 are struggling.

In a study of research conducted under sponsorship of the ICSSR, Myron Weiner acknowledged the wide variation in quality. But he stressed that "though these institutes have not yet made a conspicuous impact on public debates over policies, several have made state governments—at least some officials, if not politicians—aware of the value of research for policy and programme development and for assessing the consequences of governmental interventions" (Weiner 1982, 315).

It is difficult to assess the actual role these research institutes play in the policy process. Perhaps, as the director of one institute pointed out, the main function of these institutes has been in the generation of ideas. A politician or a bureaucrat will sometimes act upon ideas proffered, he recounted, but ideas required constant repetition, like the chanting of a mantra, in order to make an impact. Politicians, in his view, were more receptive to change than bureaucrats.

Bureaucrats, as noted by a member of another institute, need a lot of convincing, which is time-consuming. Once a bureaucrat is convinced, he is transferred. With his replacement, a new round of convincing begins.

Bureaucrats alone do the processing of the research; the researcher is not involved. What is or is not accepted for policy formulation—and why—is not to be known. As ideas have diverse and multiple sources, it is difficult to identify a specific study that has made a difference to policy. This has had a disheartening effect on staff at these institutes. A long-time ICSSR administrator laments that "today neither policy relevance nor excellence in research are the identifying features of these institutes."

It is due to this increased awareness that a number of institutes outside the gambit of the ICSSR have emerged. Some have partial central government support; others have raised funds through endowments from state governments. Still others have received support through international sources. Most do not depend on a single source of funding. Institutes that have caught the public eye as promoters of alternative policies include the National Institute of Public Finance and Policy, the Centre for Science and Environment, the Tata Energy Research Institute, and the Institute of Social Sciences. Common among these institutes is the fact that, apart from conducting research, they play an important advocacy role by publicizing their studies in the media and holding seminars for policymakers. The director of the Tata Energy Research Institute defined his role by asserting that the institute "has generated a wealth of information and data and it is our job to bombard policy-makers through letters, workshops and individual meetings. I think the challenge starts from here" (*ExpressNewsline* 24 February 2000).

The National Institute of Public Finance and Policy was established by a leading advocate of liberalization, who had been a member of the Planning Commission after a stint on the research staff of the IMF. The National Institute has a close relationship with government, its faculty members serving on special committees as they conduct the relevant research. Under the leadership of its founder, R. J. Chelliah, the institute played a prominent role in shaping the economic reforms introduced in 1991.

The Centre for Science and Environment has had a critical influence on environmental policy. It publishes a journal of state-of-the-art studies and crusades against policies that will lead to environmental degradation. Its influence in reducing air pollution in Delhi has been clear.

TEMPORARY
BLUE-RIBBON COMMISSIONS

Dominated by a generalist civil service, the Indian government has little provision for experts or technocrats. Wherever there is, the circumstances adhere to the philosophy of experts on tap, not on top. As such, within ministries there are no specialized units that keep a long-term perspective in mind.

To fill this need, the Administrative Reforms Commission in 1969 recommended the establishment of policy units within each ministry. Little came of this. The result is, when there is need, the government appoints a blue-ribbon commission, which is responsible for generating new ideas for framing policy. These commissions usually consist of well-known experts, technicians, economists, and social scientists; they might also include retired civil servants. But apart from preparing a report, these commissions have no role in the formulation of policy, and no role in the implementation of policy. Government decides whether to make the commission's report public or to confine it to the archives or, actually, to use it for policy purposes.

The Education Commission of 1964–1966 offers a case study of how government functions in seeking policy advice. The 1948–1949 University Education Commission and the 1952 Secondary Education Commission had each looked at the state of education within their specific purview, but never had a governmental committee or commission considered education on a more basic level, despite the country's low literacy rate. Thus, the Education Commission of 1964–1966 became the first comprehensive effort after independence to assess the country's educational system. It was also charged with responsibility to suggest a national education system for the country.

Membership of the Education Commission was large, drawing upon educational expertise both in India and abroad. In the course of its work, the commission traveled the length and breadth of the country, holding discussions and seminars, visiting schools, colleges, and universities. There were two conferences with student representatives. All told, more than nine hundred people were interviewed, and notes and memoranda sent to the commission numbered about 2,450. In addition, the commission met international consultants, including Edward Shils and Lord Lionel Robbins.

After two years, the Education Commission completed its labors and submitted its report in June 1966. In January, following the death of Shastri, in whose tenure the commission had been appointed, Indira Gandhi had become the prime minister. Even so, there was continuity as M. C. Chagla was retained as the education minister in the new cabinet. When the report was submitted, he held a press conference and made its recommendations public for debate and discussion. Copies of the report were distributed to state governments, the Vice-Chancellors' Conference, the Central Advisory Board of Education, and members of both houses of Parliament, which represented different political parties. The expectation was that, after comments were received, the government would issue a statement on education policy.

Elections were announced in early 1967, however, so the process of consultation continued until a new government under Indira Gandhi was installed in March. Triguna Sen, who had been a member of the Education Commission, was named education minister. Although Sen was committed to implementation of the report, he lacked a political base (Naik 1982, 31). When he lost the political support of the prime minister, he found it difficult to carry the state governments, among other constituencies. Undaunted, Sen proceeded to appoint a committee comprised of members of Parliament representing all hues of political opinion. His hope was that, based on the report of this parliamentary committee, a draft for national education policy could be formulated and put before Parliament.

Discussions in this parliamentary committee were contentious; the wide differences in opinion could be gauged from the fact that no fewer than nine of the thirty members wrote minutes of dissent amounting to twenty-three pages of a report twenty-six pages long. Discussions in committee had centered on but a few issues such as selectivism in admissions, special funding for universities, and the medium of instruction. Most larger issues were ignored (Naik 1982). Still, Sen made the report of this parliamentary committee available to wider debate. The education policy document that finally emerged was a considerably watered down version of the recommendations made by the Education Commission in its original 1966 report.

Through subsequent education ministers, the recommendations of this report were kept alive, but even the pretence of future implementation was dropped as the country moved on to more immediate concerns, such as the war in Bangladesh and national elections, during the 1970s. The report, however, has become the standard by which all education policy is now measured. Even after the New Education Policy was adopted in 1986, it continues as a source of ideas for policymakers.

The recommendations of the Education Commission were dealt a blow by politics. Nonetheless, the report contributed a wide range of ideas that raised the level of discussion, and this contribution refused to go away even though the government did not accept many of its significant recommendations. It may be said that, after all, the report has been quite influential—its effect on policy has just been a slow, ongoing trickle.

The Administrative Reforms Commission, which was appointed during the same time, underwent a similar political experience and met a similar fate. This reinforces the notion that such blue-ribbon commissions yet serve as a storehouse of ideas whose influence on government is imperceptible. Usually, bureaucrats will pick up an idea here or there, and that idea is piecemeal then incorporated into policy. In the example of the two commissions here, the entrenched educational and administrative systems proved to be too strong, and at the time most recommendations and ideas for change battled unsuccessfully with the politics of survival of the government and the status-quo self-interest of the bureaucracy.

STATUTORY COMMISSIONS

The Indian constitution has provision for several statutory commissions. One such, the National Commission for Scheduled Castes and Scheduled Tribes

(NCSC&ST), was established by the 65th Constitutional Amendment of 1990 as a national advisory body on all policy matters related to the development of deprived sections of society. The function of this commission is to monitor the implementation of government policies, to inquire into complaints with respect to the deprivation of rights, to safeguard these deprived communities, and to recommend measures to make policies more effective (National Commission for Scheduled Castes and Scheduled Tribes [NCSC&ST] 1997).

All members of the NCSC&ST, who serve a three-year term, come from a political background, even though the government in its notification stipulated that experts in the fields of social anthropology, social work, and other social sciences might be included. No experts have been appointed. The commission does, however, employ an academic, who heads a unit of professional staff that conducts studies, surveys, and evaluations.

Reports of the NCSC&ST are submitted to the president, who in turn sends them to Parliament for discussion and debate. To date, Parliament has not found time to discuss any recommendations made by the NCSC&ST, let alone implement them. This experience is not unique to the NCSC&ST. It is the case with most statutory commissions, even when political leaders sit on them.

Due to heightened national and international interest, one particular statutory commission seems to have been successful in getting its recommendations not only heard but actually implemented. This is the National Human Rights Commission (NHRC), established in 1993 to advise the government and to respond to complaints of human rights violations. The NHRC was created as the result of the campaign for human rights waged by NGOs both national and international. While the Indian constitution reflects all articles included in the Universal Declaration of Human Rights, the provisions could be enforced only through a long drawn-out judicial process, complicated by the fact that evidence was to be gathered by the very agencies accused of violations. Hence, the establishment of the NHRC as an autonomous body. The commission was given proactive powers of inquiry, investigation, and review. It was also empowered to recommend action against any public servant or agency involved and, if necessary, appeal to the Supreme Court for action.

The NHRC has its own staff, headed by a senior police officer, and the authority to utilize the services of any person or investigative agency of central or state government. Elaborate processes have been devised to ensure its autonomy. A retired chief justice of the Supreme Court chairs the commission, which is comprised of two other retired justices and two persons of eminence in public life with interest in human rights. The president appoints NHRC members on the advice of a committee headed by the prime minister and that includes the leader of the opposition in Parliament. A fixed tenure of five years helps to ensure the independence of the commission.

Obviously, in contrast to the NCSC&ST, NHRC has been effective in its goals. The reason lies not only in the broad significance of its work but also in the monitoring of its progress by NGOs and activist groups.

PARLIAMENTARY COMMITTEES

In recent years, the role of Parliament in providing input to policy through discussion on financial proposals of government has seriously eroded. First, members of Parliament do not have research assistance, but, moreover, their primary focus is on the political considerations of their constituency. During the period 1985–1995, Parliament held discussions on financial proposals of only a few ministries—seven, to be specific. The demands for grants for as many as eleven ministries received no detailed discussion; often in this period, more than 85 percent of the budget was passed without discussion (Shastri 1998, 185–186)

In view of this state of affairs, Parliament in 1993 set up standing committees for most of the ministries. These committees consist of members from both houses of Parliament, and the chair is chosen by proportional party representation. Usually, highly regarded parliamentarians are chosen to lead the committees, even if they belong to the opposition. Every committee has a maximum of forty-five members, and each member of Parliament serves a two-year term on at least one committee.

The hope was that standing committees would provide a forum for discussion of financial proposals and for more thoughtful opinion on the policy issues involved. Here legislators could consider technical matters that Parliament, as a whole, had not the time to discuss. Ostensibly, legislative oversight would be ongoing in a setting where members could avail themselves of expert testimony, initiate studies, issue reports, and examine draft legislation as a prelude to legislative action or postponement (Rubinoff 1996, 727).

Despite the establishment of these committees, legislators have expressed continuing dissatisfaction with the limitations of their role in government. In interviews (Rubinoff 1996), parliamentarians complain of inadequate resources at their disposal as compared with those available to the executive branch. One expected result of such lack is that the committees' in-depth studies have yielded perfunctory reports that the government and the media give no weight to.

Another issue is that ministers have no incentive to take these standing committees seriously as long as they do not have to testify before them. With sessions closed to the public and only secretaries—that is, civil servants heading the ministries—required to appear, busy cabinet ministers can easily choose not to participate in committee activities. Further, since secretaries are not confirmed by Parliament and enjoy permanency of tenure through constitutional provision, they are not accountable to the parliamentary system. Their arguments have often overwhelmed legislators lacking alternative sources of ideas. All of this does not bode well for the role of these committees in effective policymaking (Rubinoff 1996).

The work of the legislature does not stop at approving the financial outlays at the start of the year. It includes the examination, after the year is over, of audit reports of the comptroller and auditor general, to determine if public money was spent appropriately. The Public Accounts Committee and the Committee on Public Undertakings, both of which are viewed as watchdogs of democracy, have oversight of these fiscal matters. Unfortunately, this responsibility is not taken seriously; often, fiscal examination is delayed by several years. "As far as it has been possible to find out, the central Public Accounts Committee has not yet given its report about even the Bofors audit which is sometimes credited with bringing down the government of Rajiv Gandhi" (Joseph 2000, 2999). It seems that financial irregularities uncovered by the comptroller and auditor general are of little interest to either parliamentarians or the media.

Parliamentarians also face a bottleneck of information. That is, because they lack research staff, policy ideas coming from diverse sources sometimes go by the board. Only politically volatile and visible issues will catch their attention. This lack of expertise, it goes without saying, has hurt the workings of the standing committee system.

In India, there is little tradition of research cells that provide support to legislative activities. Parliament has a rudimentary staff that can collect relevant data or refer to important sources, and there is a well-equipped library. The actual research, however, or the study of policy implications from available data is left to the legislators themselves. Not many are inclined to do this, and even if they did, most do not have the capability. The tendency instead is to stick to politically visible issues. The result is that these committees fall short of the role that congressional committees play in the United States, even if that is their model. (See Mathur and Jayal 1992 for discussion on drought policy in Parliament; see also Jain 1985 for similar discussion on electronics policy.)

In general, one might dare say that Parliament has lost its sheen. There is general apathy among its members, absenteeism has assumed alarming proportions, and defections for money and office have been a common phenomenon (Kashyap 2000, 138). Frequently, debates turn into unruly fighting matches, and pandemonium prevails on the floor of the House. The result is that, as regards the formulation of public policy, Parliament as the voice of the people has been ineffectual.

Nor do representatives come to office prepared for their role in policy. Political parties have no research organization that can frame alternative policy ideas. It is left to the individual legislators to seek out such opinions from professionals and academics whom they may know. It bears repeating that most of this is of an ad-hoc nature, generated only through personal volition and personal contacts.

One reason parliamentarians do not demand research support is that they may not consider their role as lawmakers very important. In contrast, their constituency demands are so strong that they ignore them only at the peril of losing the next election. For a constituency, a member of Parliament is an intermediary it has installed to sort out difficulties or roadblocks. Concerns run the full gamut—from municipal problems, to securing employment, to getting the gas and telephone connected, even to jumping the queue for air and rail tickets. "The MP [Member of Parliament] may be an acknowledged authority on constitutional law, foreign relations or defence. But this will hardly please his constituents. The clogged drains and bad roads will in all probability seal his fate" (Prakash 1995, 50).

EMERGENCE OF NGOS

With the adoption of economic reform policies in 1991, there came explicit recognition of the role of markets and NGOs in the life of India. The Eighth Five-Year Plan (1992–1997) reexamined the role of government and stressed the importance of a participatory democracy. Development had to be made a people's movement. If people's institutions could be created and held accountable to the community, then, the plan suggested, a great deal could be achieved in such areas as education (especially literacy), health, family planning, land improvement, land use, minor irrigation, watershed management, recovery of wastelands, afforestation, animal husbandry, dairy farming, fisheries, and sericulture. In contrast to the Second Five-Year Plan of 1956–1961, which stipulated that "the state had to take on heavy responsibilities as the principal agency speaking for and acting on behalf of the community as whole," the Eighth Plan made a strong plea for an increased role for the voluntary sector (Mathur 1996, 24–40).

Organized voluntary action in India has a long history. In the first half of the twentieth century, the struggle for independence was a galvanizing factor in the growth of voluntary agencies. Mass mobilizations and political campaigns were undertaken during this period, and Gandhi's "constructive work," which began in the 1920s, spoke to dimensions of economic and social reform. This would be a model for voluntary agencies to go by. In the post-independence period, many of these Gandhian organizations were led by public figures who did not, or could not, join the ruling Congress government. These organizations worked closely with government for the development of handicrafts and cottage industries, credit and other cooperatives, and educational institutions. Official institutions such as the Central Social Welfare Board, the Khadi and Village Industries Commission, and the People's Action Development India were established in the

1950s and 1960s to promote and fund similar voluntary social work organizations (Khan 1997, 5).

Since that time, voluntary organizations have grown further as educated and professional people joined the ranks of voluntary agencies in large numbers. The NGOs that came into being kept close linkage with professional research institutions like the Tata Institute of Social Sciences, the Institute of Rural Management, the Indian Social Institute, and the Centre for Women's Studies. The accomplishments of several NGOs brought recognition to their principals, and government began to incorporate these NGOs into official agencies. Sanjit (Bunker) Roy of the Social Work and Research Centre (SWRC), Tilonia, became adviser to the Planning Commission during Rajiv Gandhi's tenure as prime minister, and Ela Bhatt of the Self-Employed Women's Association (SEWA), Ahmedabad, was nominated as a member of the Upper House of Parliament and appointed chairperson of the National Commission on Self-Employed Women.

There is no complete inventory of development NGOs in India. As Ghanshyam Shah notes, "Our guess, based on available directories of NGOs, our own studies on NGOs in Gujarat and West Bengal and discussion with NGO activists, is that there are around 15,000 development NGOs in the country" (1991, 6). Niraja Jayal (1999) estimates that NGOs active in rural development alone can range from ten thousand upwards and are probably between fifteen thousand and twenty thousand. Most are registered under the Societies Registration Act, which gives them legal entitlement to raise funds from government and nongovernment sources, and binds them to rules of financial scrutiny by the government as well as their own membership. Any NGO group of five or more people can present its memorandum of association, which is a statement of activities, to the local authority. Once registered, the association is a legal entity. It has been estimated that NGOs currently receive around Rs9 billion–Rs10 billion in foreign funding; during the Seventh Plan government funded NGOs with Rs1.5 billion.

Traditionally, NGOs have worked with local groups providing services, supplementing efforts of government in delivering services, and enabling communities to organize to procure services and access entitlements. Their scope is limited, and whatever engagement they have with state or other groups is to facilitate their primary task of working for their constituency. An assessment of their performance or role in development, however, is of less interest here than their means of influence on policy.

NGOs, by their nature, wish to make an impact on society. If their projects are replicated by the state, this impact can be felt nationwide. Thus, NGOs often seek to establish feasibility for wider application by replicable models. But NGOs also attempt to influence policies and practices directly rather than through example.

For instance, in the concerns of poverty, participation, democratization, and equity, Indian NGOs have organized advocacy in fields as diverse as informal, unorganized sector and child labor; affirmative action and protection for the disabled; women's issues; environment, forests, and issues such as displacement and rehabilitation; health; judicial reform; participatory management and governance; consumer rights; technology; shelter and the urban poor; and work space (Khan 1997, 13). Successful policy changes, like the adoption of joint forest management and the representation of women in local institutions, have come about through advocacy as well as social action promoted by NGOs. There is bound to be some overlapping in the process of influence.

Grass-roots NGOs may engage in policy advocacy by protesting and organizing campaigns or by joining networks or issue-based coalitions. Azeez Khan (1997), in a volume published by the Society for Participatory Research in Asia (PRIA), documents the activities of five such NGOs. One, which campaigned for a comprehensive law for construction labor, had a national perspective. Others were concerned with changes at the state or local level.

In influencing national policies, the role of research institutes that have become nodal institutions for creating networks or coalitions is very important. The role of Walter Fernandes (1995) of the Indian Social Institute, for example, was critical to formulation of the alternative draft of national rehabilitation policy. Initially, a research paper addressing the problems of displaced persons was circulated among activist NGOs working in the field. The NGOs responded by organizing meetings to discuss the paper and to identify principles on which rehabilitation policy should be based. A database was created, and alternatives to displacement projects were proposed.

Pushing the process further, a national workshop in Delhi was convened to bring together the field experience of the activists, professional thinking, and issues raised at state-level meetings. What emerged from this workshop was a program that included (a) mobilization of affected people, members of Parliament, and members of the Legislative Assembly; (b) involvement of NGOs and other support groups; (c) a press campaign; (d) work on amendments to the draft policy and dialogue with ministers; and (e) suggestion of alternatives to projects.

Fernandes (1995, 291) notes that the role of NGOs has evolved over the years. As NGOs involve themselves more in the policy process, they should reevaluate their situation and foster alliances that can produce a broader impact.

The rights of women are another area where alliances among NGOs have made their voice more powerful. The National Commission of Women and the Centre for Women's Development Studies (CWDS) have stated their support of NGOs as umbrella organizations that can provide a forum for influencing public policy as regards women's issues. In her introduction to the CWDS *Annual Report* (1996–1997), the director of the center emphasizes that CWDS "is committed to creating integral links between women's studies and the women's movement and has continued to blend research, action and advocacy in its work while confronting the process of marginalization of women. . . . It does not view a positive value-based social intervention as being detrimental to social science research."

In the past few years, support given in turn by various umbrella organizations to activist groups has enlarged the scope of the public debate on policy. Awareness has been raised considerably. While the government has not been impervious to new kinds of policy input, it has not been entirely receptive either. In 1999, the Voluntary Health Association of India (VHAI) submitted to the central government the voluminous report of the Independent Commission on Health in India. Based on extensive discussion and the experiences of NGOs working in the field, the report made over 350 recommendations. The government response was not, to say the least, encouraging. In a letter to the VHAI, the Joint Secretary of Health in the Ministry of Health and Family Welfare made reference to the tremendous government effort already in progress and then went on to defend government policy. The letter, absolving the government of its shortcomings, suggested that "a responsive and a conscious user will be able to revitalize the sector and make it more accountable than structural changes might be able to achieve" (Government of India letter, 18 January 1999, 3).

POLITICAL AND ADMINISTRATIVE CONSTRAINTS TO ALTERNATIVE POLICY ADVICE

While the last fifty years has seen the government opening up to alternative policy advice, the general perception continues to be that of a closed system. The political leadership within the government has neither the inclination nor institutional support to do otherwise. Crises of one kind or the other have dominated the political scene from 1970 onwards: India went to war over the creation of Bangladesh in 1971, and then in 1976, Emergency was declared. The return of democracy in 1978 was marked by a less than stable coalition, and another election was called in 1980. In 1984, a prime minister was assassinated, and another assassination took place a couple of years later.

The post-1970 period also saw the disintegration of the Congress Party, which had until then dominated the national and state governments. The major task of the leadership was to hold the party together. Thus, even though the Congress Party came back to power in 1990 upon the collapse of a coalition government, it was a minority administration, voted to power by smaller parties in Parliament. Since 1996, several coalition governments have come and gone in quick succession. With such apparent instability, politics and short-term issues have dominated the national agenda. Fire fighting has been the characteristic mode of the government, and little concern for long-term policy has been expressed. Politicians have not been able to think beyond the next election.

With the political leadership lacking research support or professional staff, as noted above, basic policy choices are left to committees or commissions appointed within specific sectors or for special purposes. In recent years, the government has relied on this mechanism for internal debate as well. Increasingly now, NGOs and representatives of influential groups have been invited to serve on these committees. Since the economic liberalization in 1991, for example, the government has turned to business organizations for advice, and the finance minister meets frequently with the Federation of Chambers of Commerce and Industry and the Confederation of Indian Industry.

To this extent, the government has opened up. Yet, the structure of the government is such that an all-powerful civil service vets all new advice. The civil service's preferred method for seeking advice is the appointment of a committee. The committee encourages wide public participation and, when necessary, authorizes a special study on specific areas of policy. Persons connected to the government in some way dominate these committees. Time has gradually seen the nomination of experts and NGO leaders to these committees, but there is less likelihood of the inclusion of persons holding opinions in opposition to the government's. This was more true during the planning era of Nehru and the liberal era of various governments after liberalization in 1991.

Usually, then, the next step in the process is that the committee makes recommendations that have been based on consensus, although dissenting notes are appended as well. The task, however, of sifting through the recommendations and deciding what will be kept and what will not, is solely that of the civil service. There will be no consultation with—or explanation to—the committee or responsible individuals.

This makes the role of the civil service quite critical. A civil servant may be named secretary or adjunct to the committee to help determine the feasibility of suggestions. But in this administrative and political capacity, the civil servant is not a neutral figure. Often he will guide the committee in a particular direction. It is unclear what takes places at this stage, but the general sentiment among committee members is that the government does not have an open mind. As noted earlier, the director of an institute was constrained to remark that politicians were more open to alternative policy advice than were civil servants.

Transfers from one position to another make the processing of recommendations/suggestions even more problematic. As a member of an NGO remarked, "Just as we were hoping that some of our suggestions will get a positive response from the government, the concerned civil servant was transferred and we had to begin the process of advocacy again."

In the political circumstances India finds itself, strong, alternative policy advice struggles to be heard. The political system grapples with the challenges of democracy, the civil service system is firmly entrenched in its own interests, and the structure of the government bears vestiges of a colonial past. As research institutions or NGOs produce policy ideas, they have the effect of lending support to the opposition groups and threatening current orthodoxy. In reaction, a precarious coalition in power responds by closing up the process rather than opening it up. As Diane Stone argues in her paper analyzing a comparable situation in Britain: "By elaborating on policy options, increasing the number of alternatives and outlining possible problems, [these] policy research bodies potentially overload the collective decision making processes, disrupt established programmes, undermine consensus and question the legitimacy of a government's chosen policy. . . . Identifying flaws in policies or promoting superior policy design does not endear these organizations to politicians and bureaucrats" (2000).

PROSPECTS AND CHALLENGES

In today's India, with changes occurring on many levels, it will be most difficult to respond adequately to the increasingly complex issues of society unless there are far-reaching changes in India's political institutions. The issue of technology offers a clear case in point. While the state of knowledge in government demands the input of experts and specialists in the field, policymakers have been loath to call upon them. The shibboleths that policy should be left to generalists and that civil servants should be coordinative and not creative have continued to prevail, and the result has been a contraction in policy ideas. Institutions are bent on keeping alternative policy advice out of the final decision-making process. While some advice does manage to enter the deliberative process, usually it is because the ideas have been filtered through concerns of political and administrative feasibility (Mathur and Bjorkman 1994, 76).

Ministers need to create new channels through which alternative advice can be solicited and advanced. Unless this is done, the powerful bureaucracy will dominate as always and choke off needed fresh policy ideas. During the last several decades, ministers have been able to install secretaries of their choosing, but these choices have been determined more by patronage than by policy. There are exceptions to the rule, but in the current climate of coalition governments and regional parties, patronage has had the upper hand.

The time-tested practice of secrecy in the operations of government has not helped. There is no way to learn the nature or the source of policy advice. The files are closed to the public, and the bureaucracy itself upholds this principle even when a government minister may wish otherwise. In a recent case, an order by the urban development minister, who is an eminent lawyer, to release such information to the public was squashed by the Cabinet secretary on grounds of public interest. NGOs have now taken up the struggle for the right to information, with proposed legislation still pending as of May 2001. It is hoped that enactment of law will create a situation of greater accountability for advice givers and takers and will expand the market for alternative policy advice.

In a system of government inherited from the British, civil servants were the protectors and promoters of public interest. This was followed by a centrally planned economy in which the planners, bureaucrats, and technocrats again knew best. The point is that, under these terms, the tradition of civil society in India has been weak. Among people there is a syndrome of dependence.

This is changing with the emergence of NGOs. Their role is still limited, however, and it is only in the last decade that NGOs have achieved such prominence that the alternative policy advice they offer has been taken seriously. Yet, the rationalist, technocratic view has not been easy to displace, its intransigence aided by well-publicized irregularities in some NGOs. The credibility of policymakers and the confidence of people must be earned continuously—an uphill task for NGOs as well as the government's own commissions.

BIBLIOGRAPHY

Bardhan, P. K. 1984. *Political Economy of Development in India*. Oxford: Oxford University Press.

Centre for Women's Development Studies. 1996–1997. *Annual Report*. New Delhi: Center for Women Development Studies.

Fernandes, Walter. 1995. "An Activist Process around the Draft National Rehabilitation Policy." *Social Action* 45(July–September): 277–298.

Indian Council of Social Science Research. 1999. *Annual Report 1997–98*. New Delhi: Indian Council of Social Science Research.

Jain, R. B. 1985. "Electronics Policy and Indian Parliament." *Indian Journal of Public Administration* 31(2): 239–274.

Jayal, Niraja Gopal. 1999. *Consolidating Democracy: Governance and Civil Society in India*. New Delhi: Centre for Political Studies, Jawaharlal Nehru University. Mimeo.

Joseph, K. P. 2000. "Budget Deficits Are Forever." *Economic and Political Weekly* 35(34): 2998–3001.

Kashyap, Subhash. 2000. "Institutions of Governance: The Parliament, the Government and the Judiciary." In V. A. Pai Panandiker, ed. *Problems of Governance in South Asia*. New Delhi: Centre for Policy Research and Konark Publishers.

Khan, Azeez Mehdi. 1997. *Shaping Policy: Do NGOs Matter? Lessons from India*. New Delhi: Society for Participatory Research in Asia.

Khilnani, Sunil. 1997. *The Idea of India*. London: Hamish Hamilton.

Mathur, Kuldeep, ed. 1996. *Development Policy and Administration*. New Delhi: Sage Publications.

Mathur, Kuldeep, and J. W. Bjorkman. 1994. *Top Policy Makers in India: Cabinet Ministers and Civil Service Advisors*. Delhi: Concept Publishers.

Mathur, Kuldeep, and Niraja Jayal. 1992. *Drought Policy and Politics: The Need for a Long Term Perspective*. New Delhi: Sage Publications.

Naik, J. P. 1982. *The Education Commission and After*. New Delhi: Allied Publishers.

National Commission for Scheduled Castes and Scheduled Tribes. 1997. *A Handbook*. New Delhi: Government of India.

Potter, David C. 1986. *India's Political Administrators 1919–1983*. Oxford: Clarendon Press.

Prakash, A. Surya. 1995. *What Ails Indian Parliament: An Exhaustive Diagnosis*. New Delhi: HarperCollins.

Robinson, Mark. 1998. "Democracy, Participation, and Public Policy: The Politics of Institutional Design." In Mark Robinson and Gordon White, eds. *The Democratic Developmental State Political and Institutional Design*. Oxford: Oxford University Press.

Rubinoff, Arthur G. 1996. "India's New Subject-Based Parliamentary Committees." *Asian Survey* 36(July): 723–738.

Rudolph, L. I., and S. H. Rudolph. 1987. *In Pursuit of Lakshmi: The Political Economy of the Indian State*. Hyderabad: Orient Longman.

Shastri, Sandeep. 1998. "Department-Related Standing Committees in the Indian Parliament: An Assessment." *The Indian Journal of Public Administration* 44(2): 184–200.

Shah, Ghanshyam. 1991. *Non-Governmental Organizations in India*. Centre for Social Studies, Surat, and Centre for Asian Studies, Amsterdam. Mimeo.

Stone, Diane. 2000. "Guidance for Governance in Great Britain." Paper presented at the Global ThinkNet Conference. Sponsored by the Japan Center for International Exchange, Tokyo, May 28–30.

Surya, Prakash A. 1995. *What Ails India's Parliament: An Exhaustive Diagnosis*. New Delhi: Indus, HarperCollins Publishers India.

Weiner, Myron. 1982. "Social Science Research and Public Policy in India." In Laurence D. Stifel et al., eds. *Social Sciences and Public Policy in the Developing World*. Lexington, Mass.: Lexington Books.

Yadav, Yogendra. 1999. "Electoral Politics in the Time of Change: India's Third Electoral System 1989–99." *Economic and Political Weekly* 34(34 and 35): 2393–2399.

8 Poland

Robert Sobiech

If one were to assess the present state of policy advice in Poland—based on existing research, bibliographies, university curricula, seminars, conventions, and the array of organizations and experts—a very pessimistic conclusion could be drawn. The concept of policy advice—or policy analysis or public policy—almost never appears in the vocabulary of decision makers and social scientists. Studies of theory and methodology are difficult to find, and in university curricula, courses in public policy are rare as well.

On the other hand, there are numerous examples of institutions and experts playing a significant role in the country's decision-making process. Almost every ministry or agency in the central administration has either its own studies and analysis department or advisory teams working on a permanent or ad hoc basis. Similarly, there are research centers affiliated to both chambers of the Sejm (Polish Parliament). Outside of government, private entities, many of them new, and respected academic centers offer a range of social-science applications. Systematic research is conducted on all spheres of Polish society, including the economy, providing detailed analysis of existing and emerging phenomena.

Why, then, is it so difficult to find rigorous assessment of the sources of policy advice? To answer this question, one must look first to the relationship between decision makers and experts that was cultivated decades ago and that seems still to influence the present situation.

ALTERNATIVE ADVICE
FROM AN ALTERNATIVE SOCIETY

Throughout the fifty years that the Communist Party was at the helm in Poland, an important distinction between the state and society became deeply rooted in public consciousness. While a majority of citizens viewed the regime as illegitimate, they could exercise no control over the government's institutions. Decision makers selected specific phenomena to be defined as problems important enough for their attention. Policy formation and policy advice were subject to ideological ends, and thus policy came to reside within the domain of party officials and the circle of officially recognized experts.

> In the political reality of socialist Poland the political activity was that performed by the government and the Communist party. The party task was to provide "political guidance in science." . . . Scientists were . . . helpless against the party line and could not change policies. Institutions such as the Polish Academy of Sciences could only execute the party's order: they could issue memorials, write reports, and forecast, etc., but they could hardly influence the government scientific policy. . . . The government . . . ordered . . . reports . . . and established teams of experts who were to prepare them. Such teams would often produce excellent analysis, which however could not have been transformed into current policy. . . . (Szczepański 1992, 308–311)

In the social science world, where the situation devolved into a clear division between a small group of government experts and everyone else, the prevailing attitude was one of passivity. Our knowledge of the government experts of that time is not extensive, but from the few recorded memoirs and written analyses it appears that even they often acted as a screen for politicians whose decisions were made with little regard to principles of effective policy. For purposes of understanding the present state of policy advice, however, the attitudes and work of those social scientists who were not in the government's sphere would seem to be more critical.

The split between the government's activities and the social scientists' fields of interest led sociologists, economists, and psychologists, who had been ready to apply their theoretical knowledge to practical ends, to focus on more basic research. For many, this served as a kind of camouflage, which facilitated research on a range of latent social problems and produced diagnoses of Polish society. As it happened, the findings of such research were available only to a very closed circle of scientific associations or university seminars. Sporadically, however, usually in times of political crises, authorities agreed to widen the dissemination of analyses that were critical of the government. These were presented to the public as an example of cooperation between the authorities and the scholarly community as well as a manifestation of basic support by social scientists for the political agenda (Kurczewski 1982, 21–32).

Among these social scientists, those who persisted with their interest in government policies found themselves becoming partisan, taking the side of citizens on the receiving end of social problems (Becker 1967, 239–247). Cloaked in their professional authority, they explained in technical terms the divergence between officially declared policy objectives and actual—and potential—socioeconomic consequences.

Academic centers enjoyed a relative autonomy, affording social scientists the chance to study such issues as alcoholism, poverty, and drug addiction, as well as to evaluate the living conditions of workers, education, and prisons (Podgórecki 1974). The research depended both on state grants allocated and on the rigor of censorship at the time.

While authorities regularly sought to restrict freedom of thought, the limits for research were not always clear—except in certain areas, where trespassing was considered a threat to the status quo. One such area was public policy. Any kind of independent research or analysis in this field was prohibited, and this stance has never officially been changed, despite changes in the political environment. The 1970s offered a situation where liberalization resulted in development of trade relations with Western Europe, the importation of technology, and the loosening of political and social control. It also raised the hopes of social scientists wishing to provide alternative advice. There were some who opened up a dialogue with decision makers and shared their studies of government programs. The belief that improvement of the system could be achieved by "enlightening" the governing elite inspired individual scholars to come up with ideas for influencing policy. Some succeeded in establishing Polska 2000, a research committee at the Polish Academy of Sciences (PAN, Polska Akademia Nauk), where they provided long-term social and economic forecasts. Theories of managing social change, known as social engineering or sociotechnics, were introduced to university curricula and disseminated in publications, seminars, and conferences (Podgórecki, Alexander, and Shields 1996; Podgórecki 1970). Many other attempts failed, including the idea of establishing a center affiliated with the Sejm, where the consequences of legislative decisions could be analyzed. At the end of the 1970s, however, most of these activities were officially ignored or viewed with suspicion.

When this quasi-official mechanism proved to be less than satisfactory, a growing number of social scientists turned to the political opposition. Some formed expert teams that worked underground, producing studies critical of the political system, the competence of authorities, and the state of human rights. Above-ground, others prepared analyses that focused on the most neglected aspects of Polish social and economic life, including poverty, access to information, and foreign debt; many of these studies uncovered social problems hidden from the public eye. Research, however, was constrained by the lack of trustworthy data and, more importantly, the lack of information on public policy that was being promoted and implemented. In the peaceful revolution that culminated in the Solidarity movement of the early 1980s, these underground attempts to influence public policy became an important tool.

One of the first acts by the strikers in the shipyards of Gdansk and Szczecin was to set up advisory teams of independent experts. This resulted in the creation of Solidarity think tanks (national and local centers for social research), which provided a wide range of knowledge for the new union and which subsequently figured large in the union's negotiations with the government. Any hope that alternative policy advice might be institutionalized (or that civil society might be created), however, was dashed by the imposition of martial law in 1981, which effectively shut down the union's think tanks.

As political conflict grew more intense in the early 1980s, so did divisions in the research community. On the one hand, there was an isolated group of experts who cooperated with the government and supported—or wanted to modify rather than overturn—the existing system. On the other hand, there was a growing group of social scientists who called for radical change. As martial law put an end to public participation, these divisions were significant in determining the role of the policy expert as well as the attitude of social scientists toward the authorities. In the period 1982–1988, almost all policy advice provided for the government was generally perceived as symbolic support for the repressive regime.

For many social scientists at that time, moral commitment was a natural component of their professional activity, and this guided their work. The traditional role of the social scientist was supplemented by the desire to assist in the development of civil society or by the expectation of being a public spokesperson. Studies that were conducted underground often took the form of critical diagnoses of various spheres of Polish life. Analyses uncovered shocking social conditions and revealed the gap between the government declarations of policy and the disparate results. Of course they were perceived as a protest against the political order, and it is no wonder that the authorities treated these researchers accordingly.

The dispute persisted through the 1980s and to a large degree explains the dearth of—and apparent disdain for—social scientific research on policy in Poland.

The need for alternative policy advice reappeared at the end of the 1980s. Despite imposition of martial law and the declaration of the union's illegality, Solidarity continued its mission of advocating civil disobedience. In 1988, after almost seven years of underground activity, strikes by trade unions and economic crises, marked by rising inflation and market shortages, finally brought the communist government to the negotiating table. Negotiations with Solidarity, which included representation by its independent experts, covered areas such as free trade, economic reform, democratization, political reform, and social policy. The final agreement was signed in April 1989, triggering a process of democratization. One element agreed upon by the parties was a compromise on elections, which would be partly free. In June 1989, Solidarity candidates won a sweeping victory, securing almost all of the limited number of seats in the Parliament. The election paved the way for the appointment of Taduesz Mazowiecki as the first noncommunist prime minister of Poland (Perdue 1995).

With this historical moment came restoration of the value of competent, independent experts in various fields. This understanding dovetailed with contemporaneous Polish attempts in the 1980s to build a civil society, which shared the conviction that independent, objective advice had a necessary place in the public policy process. A secondary dimension of this development was the reliance on the expertise of individuals rather than on outputs of an institution. Both factors were to influence the terms of policy advice in the next decade.

With the advent of a Solidarity government in 1989, the relationship between experts and decision makers changed rapidly. Suffering from a deficit of qualified policy analysis as well as professional public administration, the new government turned to the social science community. Experts who had worked for the opposition and scholars from universities were suddenly employed as senior civil servants or advisors in the central administration. Their expertise as well as their vision of society was to play a wide role in planning and implementing the political, economic, and social reforms that were initiated during the transition period.

As the new government took over, it was confronted with the dire effects of the economic and social policies of the previous five decades. In many cases, the pressing need for remedy was closely linked with the need for large-scale reform. The pace of reform adopted by the first noncommunist government, however, left very little room for profound, detailed diagnosis and research. One of the most urgent issues was provision of relevant policy advice. Collective as well as individual expertise, however, could meet the demand only to a limited extent. During the next ten years, the gap was gradually filled by newly established organizations and by development of professional experts in the field.

CURRENT STATUS OF
ALTERNATIVE SOURCES OF POLICY ADVICE

Universities, Academies, and Research Institutes

Traditionally, the first source of policy advice in Poland has been a system of scientific institutions. Research and development (R&D) has been carried out by institutions of higher education (universities, polytechnic schools, medical academies, etc.), institutes or departments of PAN, and branch units subordinated to different ministries (research institutes, central laboratories, R&D centers, science support units). Development units in, for example, enterprises, technology centers, and experimental agriculture centers have also engaged in R&D along with their main activities. These institutions all report to ministries and agencies in the central administration, and are financed by the state budget.

In 1989, there were 97 institutions of higher education, 78 PAN institutes, and 310 R&D branch units. Together they employed about 66,000 scientific staff. Of the total number of scientists, 76 percent worked at institutions of higher education, 7 percent in PAN institutes, and 16 percent in R&D branch units (Chojnicki and Czyż 1992). Data included in table 1 show that this basic system of research remained unchanged during the 1990s.

Employment statistics in table 2 show more than 80,000 persons employed on a full-time basis in R&D in the period 1995–1998. In 1998, researchers constituted 66 percent of all employed. Of the total 87,297 scientific staff, more than 34,000 worked in technical sciences, 17,822 in natural sciences, and 14,089 in social sciences. Gross domestic expenditure for R&D for that year amounted to PLZ4 billion (around US$1 billion). Of this sum, 59 percent came from the state, almost 30 percent from economic entities, 8.3 percent from the Polish Academy of Science, and 1.5 percent from international organizations and foreign institutions. PLZ3.2 billion was provided for current expenditures on research and development, PLZ0.78 billion for capital. More than half of current expenditures—PLZ1.8 billion (US$450 million)—was allocated to scientific and R&D institutions, including PLZ371.6 million for institutes of the Academy of Sciences and PLZ1.42 billion for branch R&D institutes. Development units received PLZ566.1 million, and institutions of higher education PLZ852.1 million (*Statistical Yearbook of the Republic of Poland* 1999, 322–323).

In comparison with other countries, Poland has one of the lowest rates of expenditure on research. In 1998, its gross expenditures on R&D did not exceed

Table 1. Groups in Research and Development

	1990	1995	1996	1997	1998
Scientific institutes of the Polish Academy of Science	79	80	81	81	82
Branch R&D units	260	253	255	256	246
Research institutes	111	128	130	135	137
Institutes of higher education	80	104	104	104	114
Other (development units, support units, etc.)*		300	354	379	463
Total		737	794	820	905

Source: Statistical Yearbook of the Republic of Poland 1998 (1998); Statistical Yearbook of the Republic of Poland 1999 (1999).
* Number of development units in 1990 not available in *Statistical Yearbook of the Republic of Poland.*
R&D: research and development.

Table 2. Employment in Research and Development

	1995 All Staff	1996 All Staff	1997 All Staff	1998 All Staff	1998 Researchers Alone
Scientific institutes of the Polish Academy of Science	8,089	7,705	7,262	7,600	4,745
Branch R&D units	30,900	27,836	26,158	25,160	13,107
Research institutes	24,244	21,725	21,174	20,813	11,069
Institutions of higher education	35,621	39,046	40,977	45,265	36,472
Other (development units, support units, etc.)	8,980	8,761	9,407	9,272	3,718
Total	83,590	83,348	83,804	87,297	58,042

Source: Statistical Yearbook of the Republic of Poland 1999 (1999).
R&D: research and development.

1 percent of gross domestic product—similar to Spain, Portugal, Russia, and Hungary. In Japan, the Netherlands, Germany, and the United States, the figure was about 3 percent of GDP; in Sweden it was about 4 percent of GDP. Moreover, Poland has one of the highest levels of state subsidies. Almost 60 percent of Poland's R&D funds comes from the state, while in Japan it is less than 20 percent, and in the United States and the United Kingdom, it is about 30 percent. Only Portugal and Russia have a higher share of state support (Government of Poland 2001).

Before 1989, all main decisions concerning science policy were made in a special agency of the Communist Party, with the Ministry of Science and Higher Education principally responsible for implementation of the party agenda. Since 1991, national science policy has been coordinated by the State Committee for Scientific Research (KBN, Komitet Badań Naukowych), whose chairman sits on the Council of Ministers. KBN's main tasks are to create guidelines for national science policy, prepare the budget for science research and development, and distribute funds among institutions and research teams.

KBN finances three types of research projects:

- individual research projects—by small research teams or individual researchers to be presented for peer review;
- goal-oriented projects—support for development of new technologies;
- KBN-commissioned research projects to serve regional or sectoral scientific policy—chosen on the basis of proposals submitted by central or local administrations.

The data on KBN expenditures on research projects (see table 3) show that the bulk of the funds has been allocated to individual research projects. At the end of the 1990s, there was a steady increase in both number and cost of such projects. In the case of state-commissioned projects, both number and cost have decreased.

Alternative Advice within the Government

Two institutions—the Supreme Chamber of Control and the Government Center for Strategic Studies—are at the center of the government's policy advisory system. The Supreme Chamber of Control (NIK, Najwyższa Izba Kontroli), an independent agency, serves as the highest state auditing authority, overseeing the public administration and other bodies that use public resources. Its main criteria are legality (compliance with the law), economic prudence (effective use of resources), efficacy (achievement of goals), and diligence (thoroughness, care, honesty, reliability) (Supreme Chamber of Control 2001).

The NIK undertakes audits upon order of the Sejm. It is also authorized to carry out audits on its own initiative, which in 1998 constituted about 3 percent of all the agency's efforts. The main focuses of its evaluations include the implementation of the state budget, administration of central government and local governments, financial policy, privatization, assistance funds from the European Union, environmental protection, social policy, transport and communication, defense, and the health care system. In 1999, NIK conducted 4,611 audits.

The Government Center for Strategic Studies, established in 1996, is responsible for analyzing the national economy. The center advises the prime minister and Council of Ministries on economic and social development, producing forecasts of social development and urban and rural planning. In addition to conducting evaluation research, it develops national strategies and long-term

Table 3. Research Projects Financed by the State Committee for Scientific Research

	1991	1995	1997	1998
Individual Projects				
Number	2,598	6,415	6,963	7,407
Cost (in million PLZ)	41.9	183	261.2	286.2
Goal-oriented Projects				
Number	57	732	756	777
Cost (in million PLZ)	7.1	104	196.9	181.6
State-commissioned Projects				
Number	104	105	95	
Value (in million PLZ)	38.6	31.9	28.9	

Source: *Statistical Yearbook of the Republic of Poland 1999* (1999).

forecasts, and provides policy recommendations on the economy, international affairs, and various segments of society.

In practice, the NIK focuses on legal and financial audits, with evaluation of government programs being a relatively small part of its activities. The activities of the Center for Strategic Studies concentrate on supplying analysis of the current situation and short- and medium-term forecasts with particular emphasis on the economy. Similar assessments are conducted by government departments, research institutes (especially in the area of financial policy), and independent think tanks, the result of which frequently is heated debate on the substance of forecasts and the reliability of data and methodology.

In the legislative branch, one organization plays a pivotal role in providing policy advice. In 1991, the Bureau of Research was established by the Sejm as its own agency, charged with supplying legislators with impartial information and analysis on legal issues, opinions on the consequences of submitted bills, and economic analysis of the state budget. The bureau provides deputies (that is, members of Parliament), usually on their request, with analysis on "interpretation, contents and implementation of legal acts—mainly in the fields of constitutional, administrative, civil, economic, labor, and criminal law; economic policy, agriculture, food industry, environmental protection, international economic cooperation, regional . . . cooperation; political systems of particular states, legal regulations and institutional solutions binding in these states, European integration, international relations, Poland's foreign and defense policies; work of ministries and other state institutions as well as nongovernmental organizations; taxation issues, functioning of certain financial institutions or financial mechanisms that exist in other countries; foreign general and substantial solutions regarding education, health care, social security, housing policy, youth problems, gender issues, [and] social pathology . . ." (Sejm 2001).

The bureau conducts its own research or commissions analysis by freelance experts, coordinating all external consulting for the Sejm. It also organizes seminars and conferences for deputies, government officials, and independent experts. Bureau experts often participate in committee meetings, consulting on draft bills. It bears noting, however, that all deputies are allowed to invite their own experts to committees and subcommittees, which in many cases results in lobbying hidden behind a smokescreen of policy advice.

In the executive branch as well, there are a number of alternative channels for policy advice. At the cabinet level, five committees—the Economy Committee, Social Affairs Committee, European Integration Committee, Committee on Defense, and Committee on Regional Development and Sustainable Development—are responsible for developing policy and for providing recommendations to the Council of Ministries. Usually chaired by one of the vice prime ministers, each committee consists of government representatives and invited experts. There are also advisory bodies, such as the Council on Civil Service, established by the prime minister so as to facilitate the flow of communication from external experts and political parties to the government.

A similar structure can be seen at the ministerial level. Advisory councils and temporary commissions, established in almost all ministries, are the most common forums to give independent ideas a hearing. Generally, these councils and commissions focus on monitoring government programs and supplying recommendations for policy revision.

Taken together, the range of these channels for policy advice suggests an openness on the part of decision makers to the recommendations they receive from alternative sources. This, however, contrasts with relatively underdeveloped policy units within governmental departments. The deficit of professional policy analysts corresponds to the constant change of relevant roles and responsibilities. Therefore, the formal structure of policy advice and policy implementation is always in a state of flux. Each change of government results in the emergence of new ideas and new organizational structures. Usually, the weakness of policy formation is compensated for by the establishment of a new advisory body. For example, at the prime minister's chancellery, a team of senior policy advisors reports directly to the prime minister, providing analysis and recommendations on selected domestic and international affairs. Almost every ministry or central administration office has its own analysis department dealing with relevant issues. Finally, there is a network of branch research institutes (more or less linked with line ministries) offering ongoing advice and analysis for their supervising bodies. A comparison of numerous channels of policy advice having very few separate policy units, as is the case in government departments, reveals that current concern is not about an insufficient supply of policy advice but about the very modest demand for it.

Policy Advice, Foreign Technical Assistance, and Private Consulting Companies

It is an open question whether and to what extent the various expertise gathered by social scientific institutions before 1989 can be utilized in coping with existing challenges. There are areas, like media and human rights, where the knowledge and skills of Polish experts have been adequate to the task of designing and implementing far-reaching reforms. However, in numerous cases, policy transformations have been the direct result of the policy advice offered by foreign consultants.

It is not easy to find an example of a policy or program that has not utilized foreign technical assistance. Policies regarding privatization, public management, the environment, agriculture, and many other sectors were fostered by recommendations and solutions offered to Poland through aid programs. Such support has been provided by numerous international organizations such as the United Nations, the Organization for Economic Cooperation and Development (OECD), and the World Bank, as well as individual governments and foundations. There are also examples of consulting firms—including PricewaterhouseCoopers, Arthur Andersen, and KPMG Consulting Inc.—which were contracted for policy advice for state and local authorities. Contributions of foreign expertise are generally observable in such areas as privatization, reform of public administration, and reform of pension or health systems, where solutions are directly attributable to a foreign country or inspired by the philosophy of an international organization. Due to a lack of comprehensive studies, however, the impact of such foreign expertise on the larger policy process is not easy to assess, as policy outcomes are determined by a number of factors. As the end of the 1990s brought greater economic development and political stabilization to Poland, foreign governments and international organizations began gradually to withdraw, moving on to less developed countries. Yet, there continue to be many of these foreign organizations, both public and private, that play an important role in advocating policy approaches and triggering public debate (World Bank 2000).

The transition from communist to non-communist government also saw the emergence in the country of the private consulting company. Many of these firms were founded in the first phase of the transition, prior to 1992. Having no experience or resources, they were forced to start from scratch, but after ten years, one can find numerous examples of consulting firms that got their start in such sectors as privatization and public opinion research at that juncture of history. Today, these firms enjoy a high level of public visibility and command credibility with the media and the government.

POLICY ADVICE AND NONGOVERNMENTAL ORGANIZATIONS

In addition to the two pillars of the transition process begun in 1989—that is to say, economic reform and political reform—the development of a civil society in Poland stands the third pillar. It has had significant influence on the provision of policy advice by social scientific institutions.

Lack of available research and data on nongovernmental policy advisory organizations is problematic when describing the role nongovernmental organizations have played in the country. Available information, which can be used only for secondary analysis purposes, is fragmentary. For example, the *Directory of Polish Science* for 1997–1998 lists 48 general and regional societies, 233 professional scientific societies, and 69 foundations conducting scientific activities.

However, the description of activities reveals that only five of the 69 foundations are engaged in providing any form of policy advice (*Informator Nauki Polskiej* 1999).

As regards think tanks, the 1999 directory, *Think Tanks in Central and Eastern Europe*, is quite comprehensive and useful for study. It was published by Freedom House, a U.S. nonprofit, nonpartisan organization whose mission is the promotion of democracy through research, advocacy, education, and training. The first edition of the directory was issued in 1997. In fall 1998, Freedom House, with offices in Budapest, embarked on a project to assess the work of nongovernmental research institutions in Central and Eastern Europe. From December 1998 through April 1999, two hundred fifty organizations in sixteen countries were sent standard questionnaires concerning their activities. Organizations that agreed to participate in the survey were included in the final analysis.

Freedom House used the following basic criteria:

- concentration on activities such as research, advocacy, or conferences;
- primary research interest in such fields as democratization, economic development, environment, legal reform, social safety, and security;
- independence or autonomous status within larger organizations.

The bulk of the groups surveyed were registered as nonprofit, nongovernmental organizations, although there were several examples of university centers or foundations associated with government bodies.

Of the think tanks selected for this directory, there were eleven organizations from Poland. For purposes of comparison, this chapter will concentrate on the secondary analysis of data gathered from these eleven think tanks in Poland as well as the eleven from Hungary and the six from the Czech Republic included in the Freedom House directory. It is difficult to know the extent to which these think tanks represent an accurate picture of organizations that provide alternative advice in the three countries, but the approach adopted by Freedom House offers a reliable starting point.

Almost all eleven Polish think tanks were founded in the first phase of the country's transition from communism. Only three Polish think tanks were set up after 1993. (The oldest, the Adam Smith Research Center, was founded in 1989; the newest, the Policy Education Center on Assistance to Transition, in 1996.) In Hungary and the Czech Republic, all but two thinks tanks were established before 1993. That the founding dates are weighted toward the early transition period would seem to reflect the demand for independent advice and expertise at that critical time. This observation is evidenced by the mission statements of the organizations, which place emphasis on their role in developing a free-market economy, democratic system, and virtuous society; supporting economic, social, and political transformation; developing a civil society; and providing assistance to countries in Central and Eastern Europe undergoing a similar transition.

In comparison with the Polish think tanks, five of the seventeen Hungarian and Czech think tanks were founded before 1989, when the collapse of communist regimes in Central Europe occurred. Thus, the mean year of the establishment of think tanks in Hungary is 1987, in the Czech Republic 1985, and in Poland 1992. These data seem to reflect both the history of organizational development as well as the countries' paths of transition to a democratic society.

In terms of activities, the dominant profile of think tanks in Poland is one of research, which accounted for 37 percent of their work. Conferences, seminars, and workshops were second at 23 percent, followed by publications (13 percent), advocacy (9 percent), consulting (7 percent), education (6 percent), and public outreach (5 percent).

For more than half of Poland's eleven think tanks, research constituted an important part (indicated as 35 percent–60 percent) of their overall effort. Only four of the eleven organizations declared that research takes up less than 25 percent of their time.

Besides conducting research, all Polish think tanks organized conferences, workshops, and seminars, even as this activity was a relatively minor part of their work. For only two groups did this activity constitute 40 percent of their time. Ten organizations edited their own publications. For four organizations, editing books or preparing reports constituted a considerable part (20–25 percent) of their work.

While advocacy was mentioned by eight of the eleven Polish organizations, only for two did it constitute more than 20 percent of the group's activities. Eight organizations conducted training and educational courses, but only one claimed that it required more than 20 percent of their effort. Nine think tanks mentioned different forms of public outreach, but none spent more than 10 percent of their time on it. Only five think tanks provided consulting services. However, in the case of two groups, consulting was a considerable part of their work (25 percent and 38 percent of all activities).

In terms of comparison, Hungarian and Polish think tanks engaged in similar kinds of activities. Both are research-oriented, and both focus on organizing conferences and seminars. A striking characteristic of Hungarian groups is their relative emphasis on consulting services (20 percent of overall activities). Czech groups, on the other hand, concentrate on editing publications (38 percent) and on public outreach (24 percent). It is worth noting that in the think tanks of all three countries, advocacy is not high on the list of activities.

As regards staff, the Freedom House directory reveals Polish think tanks to be relatively small organizations. The average number of permanent staff, including administrative staff, is 13.2 persons. The largest think tank, the Gdansk Institute for Market Economics, has a staff of fifty-five. Seven of the eleven Polish groups employ between three and nine people. The total number of staff in the other four organizations varies from twelve to nineteen persons. Full-time professional staff makes up almost 70 percent of all permanent employees.

A striking characteristic of Polish think tanks is the high number of professionals employed on a part-time basis. Two organizations, the Center for Economic Research and the Institute of Public Affairs, have around 200 associates. There are 52–78 part-time professionals employed in three other think tanks. Except in the case of the Institute for Market Economics, the number of part-time professionals in Polish think tanks exceeds the total number of permanent staff. In fact, in seven groups, the number of permanent staff constitutes less that 20 percent of all contracted experts. This seems to be the only major difference between Polish think tanks and their counterparts in Hungary and the Czech Republic.

Because available sources shed little light on the matter, it is difficult to determine how staff was recruited or what their career paths prior to recruitment might have been. It is likely, however, that there are no rigid boundaries among universities, research institutes, and nongovernmental think tanks. Directories of scientific establishments give many examples of experts employed on a part-time basis at different institutions. Nor are there many boundaries between scientific and government circles. There are numerous cases of former politicians, senior civil servants, and government advisors who currently occupy positions as program directors or board members of these think tanks.

Ordinarily, organizational cooperation, whether intra-nationally or internationally, is a well-developed aspect of think tank activities. In the case of Poland's think tanks, however, Freedom House data on organizational relations show very few intra-national contacts. Nine of the eleven think tanks indicated no more than three partners in the country. It is noteworthy as well that almost all groups had no relationship with other Polish think tanks in the Freedom House directory. Given the similarity of their missions, this strikes one as odd. Whether this is a reflection of intense competition among the groups or of problems related to securing financial and program autonomy encountered in the initial stages of organizational development, it is unclear. But what this may suggest is that the policy advice provided by nongovernmental organizations in Poland should be understood in terms of the individual response of relatively small groups of experts rather than as a unified system of organizational response to public policy needs.

This is reflected in the preference of Polish experts and policy analysts to establish international organizational relationships rather than create intra-national networks. On average, Polish think tanks maintain fewer contacts with their Polish counterparts than with think tanks in Central and Eastern European (CEE) countries. Six of Poland's eleven organizations maintained such international cooperation, with a mean of around three partners. Only three Polish organizations have no contact with CEE counterparts. It may be that the similarity of problems CEE countries faced during their transition process has spurred this regional cooperation.

The data on think tanks in Hungary and the Czech Republic reveal interesting differences in number of partners and their origin. For Hungary, whose think tanks tend to cultivate relationships with other Hungarian organizations, the average number of intra-national partners is three times greater than is the case for Poland or the Czech Republic. Hungarian organizations also maintained more contacts with Western think tanks, while Polish organizations cooperated more frequently with CEE organizations.

Among the eleven Polish think tanks in the Freedom House directory, financial support varies widely. Three small organizations have operating annual budgets of US$25,000–US$75,000. In the middle range are five organizations with budgets of US$127,000–US$280,000. Finally, three large think tanks have budgets of US$730,000–US$965,000.

In terms of comparison, the average annual budget of a Polish think tank is US$337,224, which is similar to that of a Hungarian organization, at US$329,035. Both, however, are significantly smaller than the average annual budget of a Czech think tank, which is US$452,299.

In terms of revenue sources for think tanks, foundations—both domestic and foreign—play the largest role in all three countries, but especially in the case of Poland (see figure 1). Polish think tanks also derive a large part of their revenue from intergovernmental organizations such as the United Nations, the World Bank, the European Commission's Phare, and the UN Development Programme. In Hungary and the Czech Republic, organizations also rely heavily upon government subsidies or fees for their services to the government.

Differences in revenue sources among Polish think tanks seem to reflect variation in both organizational

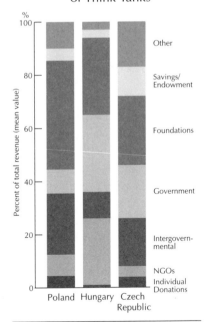

Figure 1. Revenue Sources of Think Tanks

Percent of total revenue (mean value)

Other

Savings/Endowment

Foundations

Government

Intergovernmental

NGOs
Individual Donations

Poland Hungary Czech Republic

Source: Author survey.
NGOs: nongovernmental organizations.

capacity and public recognition. For example, organizations established in the first transition period, prior to 1992, have significantly larger budgets than think tanks founded a few years later. Data presented in the following section suggest that this relationship also applies to public visibility.

IMPACT OF ALTERNATIVE POLICY ADVISORY ORGANIZATIONS

Due to the lack of systematic studies and available data, assessing the impact of alternative policy advisory organizations (APAOs) in Poland is not an easy task. Fragmentary analyses and information regarding the impact of APAOs allow only very tentative conclusions to be drawn about their role in shaping public policy.

It would seem that the widest influence exerted by alternative policy advice takes place in agenda setting. Throughout the transition period in Poland, independent think tanks, research institutes, and central executive review agencies played a large role in setting priorities for public activities, developing concepts for social and economic reforms, and influencing reforms initiated by successive governments. As public policy may occur outside the government's immediate interest, the work of APAOs helps to define new issues, initiate public debate, and encourage government agencies to respond to social problems. Accordingly, the final framework of government policies has been to a large extent developed outside the walls of ministries and central offices.

A necessary condition for exerting effective influence on public policy is the visibility of the work of APAOs. In the 1990s, most of the issues that aroused public interest were driven by the media, and in this context, the relationship between APAOs and the media has grown in importance. Elements of policy research and the resulting policy recommendations may attract media attention, offering a forum for issues at hand. Similarly, conferences organized by think tanks that are reported in the media can stimulate public discussion.

The data on the eleven Polish think tanks in the Freedom House directory (see table 4) shed some light on the impact they may have on government agenda setting through their media visibility, parliamentary visibility, and operating budgets of a wide variety of the existing organizations.

While it is clear that there are differences among these nongovernmental think tanks, the appearance of an organization in the media is not necessarily an indication of its prestige or influence. Often, visibility in the media occurs when an organization is under strong criticism or when it faces a crisis; an organization's testimony before parliament does not insure its visibility. Therefore, the real influence of an organization can be observed when both visibility in the media and regular participation in parliamentary sessions are taken into account.

Table 4. Visibility in the Media and Parliament

	Gazeta Wyborcza, (1992-2000): No. of Citations	No. of Citations/ Budget (US$ million)	Parliament (1993–2000): No. of Testimonies	Testimony/ Budget (US$ million)
Adam Smith Research Center	15	53.57	2	7.14
Center for Political Thought	0	0	0	0
Center for Social and Economic Research	217	224.87	1	1.04
Cracow Real Estate Institute	17	68.00	1	4.00
Institute for Private Enterprise and Democracy	28	220.47	1	7.87
Gdansk Institute for Market Economics	524	724.09	28	38.69
Institute of Public Affairs	166	210.45	7	8.87
Institute for Studies on the Foundation of Democracy	5	200.00	0	0
Institute for Sustainable Development	18	72.00	10	40.00
International Center for Development of Democracy	90	486.49	1	5.41
Policy Education Center on Assistance to Transition	0	0	0	0

Source: Citations are drawn from the Internet archives of Gazeta Wyborcza, the largest circulation newspaper in Poland, spanning 1,075,378 articles that appeared between 1992 and May 11, 2000. Budget information comes from Think Tanks in Central and Eastern Europe (1999). Data on parliamentary testimonies comes from Sejm electronic records of 6,492 parliamentary committee meetings in the period 1993–2000.

Given that caveat, the data in table 4 reveal the influence that the eleven organizations exercise in the country. Undoubtedly, the Gdansk Institute for Market Economics, which ranks very highly in terms of both media and parliament exposure, is the most influential. The Gdansk Institute is an example of an APAO that was established at the beginning of the 1990s, in the first phase of the transition, and successfully maintained its position.

On the other hand, the Center for Social and Economic Research and the Institute of Public Affairs are often referred to in newspaper columns but rarely participate in the legislative process. Then there are several smaller, yet effective organizations—the International Center for Development of Democracy being one example—that shape the public agenda, if their effectiveness is to be measured by their visibility in the media relative to their budgets. Finally, the list includes organizations that to date have had a more minor role in shaping the public agenda; they can be expected to lose all visibility to the general public.

Data on the participation of APAOs in parliamentary sessions also show their potential impact on policy formation and policy adoption. It should be remembered, however, that the legislative process includes many stakeholders who try to have their say. A striking feature of Polish politics is that there are no clear rules defining the extent of influence on the policymaking process, and it is difficult to distinguish between professional expertise and a recommendation of a pressure group. In fact, in many situations, the role of experts is played by lobbyists, making the policy-formation mechanism even less transparent.

The active role that APAOs play in the area of policy revision can be seen in the numerous institutionalized relationships between the above think tanks and government line departments. Apart from advisory committees at the executive level, there are advisory councils affiliated with the chancellery of the president, which were especially popular in the early 1990s, when the president's power was not limited by the 1997 constitution. Reforms recently introduced by the government—regarding public administration, the health-care system, education, and the pension system—are thus monitored not only within line ministries, but by independent organizations as well. Some organizations, the Institute of Public Affairs, for example, have introduced special units into their organizational structure, whose purpose is to analyze implementation of important reforms.

The four reforms above provide a good illustration of the opportunity for independent organizations to supply alternative policy advice that converges with official political priorities. Conferences and seminars organized by APAOs, sometimes in cooperation with government departments, on particular government policy provide a forum for discussion and exchange of views between independent experts and policymakers. However, the bulk of reform activities by these organizations is related to overall monitoring and policy revision. Except for a few cases, it is difficult to find studies that systematically evaluate the reforms themselves.

Policy or program evaluation seems to be the weakest form of alternative policy advice, a situation caused by the lack of visible demand from decision makers and by the lack of supply from APAOs. The central audit office, NIK, has traditionally focused on legal and financial audits, and its infrequent evaluation studies take the form of rather general studies. It appears that nongovernmental organizations conduct more evaluation of their own performance than of government agencies (Sobiech and Zamecka 2000). A similar lack of interest, and skill, in evaluation can be observed among APAOs.

This scarcity of evaluation may have its roots in the historical separation of social scientists from political and administrative decisions as well as the historical tendency of the social sciences to focus on critical analysis and basic research. Such analysis and research, it was discovered in the mid-1990s, had not been transformed into theories and methodologies that might be utilized in solving the acute social and economic problems of Polish society.

The other factor contributing to the negligence of policy evaluation has been the urgency of large-scale reform. The necessity of designing and implementing policy in such a compressed time period has relegated the task of monitoring and evaluation to decision makers themselves.

CONSTRAINTS AND PROSPECTS

Alternative policy advisory organizations in Poland are at an early stage of institutional development. Further progress will depend on a number of factors. Some can be defined as constraints, while others can create new possibilities.

One undeniable constraint is the scarcity of well-qualified staff. Currently, only a relatively small group of recognized experts provides policy advice in their area, and at very few universities can there be found public policy studies. It is clear that the lack of research and educational programs affects the quality of policy recommendations in significant ways. Policy units and the policies themselves, especially as regards social issues, are left wanting. Recent initiatives to rectify this situation at universities, so as to meet European Union standards, raise hopes for far-reaching changes in the near future.

A second constraint comes from the temporary structure of funding sources. Almost half the total revenue of Polish think tanks comes from grants from foundations, most of which are foreign. As these funding sources gradually withdraw this assistance, one can expect a considerable reduction of APAO activities. Recent decreases in state subsidies for commissioned projects by the State Committee for Scientific Research pose a similar threat to academic institutes and university departments.

A third constraint is the lack of transparent rules for providing alternative policy advice for decision makers. In the process by which government advisory bodies are established, the selection of members usually is done by individual nomination or invitation based on expertise. Similarly, in the legislative process, the bulk of analysis and opinion is provided by individual experts. However, with commissioned projects, which are contracted by state ministries and offices, all that can be seen is the total budget provided by the Committee for Scientific Research. The same is the case with parliamentary committees. There is no list of experts and consultants who have been invited by members of parliament or by interest groups to participate in parliamentary sessions, nor an inventory of reports and studies developed for study in the legislative process.

This lack of transparency also results in very limited access to information, especially regarding government policies. Debate on the open access to public sources began in the early 1990s. As of 2001, there are two drafts of the Freedom of Information Act, which are still being discussed in the parliamentary committee.

Scarcity of research concerning mechanisms of policy design and implementation does not allow for strong conclusions or recommendations about the prospects for alternative policy advice. On the basis of the fragmented data and analyses available, one can, however, formulate two future scenarios.

The first assumes that further development of alternative policy advisory organizations will continue to face the constraints of the existing system. The way that social scientific institutions and the government have interacted as regards policy advice has remained largely unchanged since the transition period. While the universities and institutes of the Polish Academy of Sciences are no longer under political control, they are still almost completely dependent on government funding. A similar situation exists with the branch research institutes. This has created intense competition among policy advice organizations, including private firms, for the limited resources. Those that secure access to external or internal funding sources will dominate the market for ideas in the long run.

In the second scenario, prospects for APAOs will be closely linked with the further development of civil society. Emergence of an informed and active public, which make claims and put pressure on local and state government alongside interest groups, societies, and corporations, will create a natural environment and demand for policy improvement.

Thus, the real prospects for alternative policy advice seem to depend not only on removing existing constraints, but also on the emergence of a market, which is external to the government, for such services. In other words, the future of Polish APAOs will be no less shaped by politicians' faith in the benefits of policy advice from social scientists. The greater the grass-roots pressure for a way of life that is "better for less," the larger will be the demand of decision makers for alternative advice.

BIBLIOGRAPHY

Becker, Howard S. 1967. "Whose Side We Are On?" *Social Problems* 14(Winter): 239–247.

Chojnicki, Zbyszko, and Teresa Czyż. 1992. "The Character and Role of Scientific Centers in Poland." In Antoni Kukliński, ed. *Science and Government Series.* Vol. 2. Society—Science—Government. Warsaw: State Committee for Scientific Research.

Gouldner, Alvin. W. 1968. "The Sociologist as Partisan: Sociology and the Welfare State." *American Sociologist* 3(May): 103–116.

Government of Poland. 2001. <http://www.stat.gov.pl/servis/polska/rocznik12/nakla.htm> (3 May 2001).

Informator Nauki Polskiej 1997/98, Społeczny Ruch Naukowy (Directory of Polish science 1997/98, Social movement of science). 1999. Vol. 3. Warszawa: Ośrodek Przetwarzania Informacji.

Kurczewski, Jacek. 1982 "The Old System and the Revolution. Crises and Conflict. The Case of Poland 1980–81." *Sisyphus Sociological Studies* 3: 21–32. Warsawa: Państwowe Wydawnictwo Naukowe.

Perdue, William D. 1995. *Paradox of Change: The Rise and Fall of Solidarity in the New Poland.* Westport, Conn.: Praeger Publishers.

Podgórecki, Adam. 1970. *Socjotechnika: Jak oddziaływać skutecznie.* Warszawa: Państwowe Wydawnictwo Naukowe (Polish Scientific Publishers).

———. 1974. *Diagnostyczny obraz niektórych trudnych problemów społeczeństwa polskiego oraz zalecenia socjotechniczne* (Analysis of selected acute problems of Polish society and sociotechnical recommendations). Warszawa: Instytut Profilaktyki Społecznej i Resocjalizacji UW.

Podgórecki, Adam, Jon Alexander, and Rob Shields, eds. 1996. *Social Engineering.* Ottawa: Carleton University Press, Ottawa.

Sejm. 20001. <http://www.biurose.sejm.gov.pl/eng/index.htm> at <http://www.sejm.gov.pl> (May).

Sobiech, R., and J. Zamecka. 2000. "Organizational Response to the Drug Problem in Poland." Draft. Vienna: European Center for Social Welfare Policy Research.

Statistical Yearbook of the Republic of Poland 1998. 1998. Warszawa: Główny Urząd.

Statistical Yearbook of the Republic of Poland 1999. 1999. Warszawa: Główny Urząd Statystyczny.

Supreme Chamber of Control. 2001. <http://www.nik.gov.pl/english/background.htm> (May).

Szczepański, Jan. 1992. "Society, Science and Government in Poland." In Antoni Kukliński, ed. *Science and Government Series.* Vol. 2. Society—Science—Government. Warsaw: State Committee for Scientific Research.

Think Tanks in Central and Eastern Europe. A Comprehensive Directory. 1999. 2nd ed. Budapest: Freedom House.

World Bank. 2000. "Korupcja w Polsce" (Corruption in Poland). Warszawa: World Bank, Warszawa Bureau.

9 Republic of Korea

Mo Jongryn

Governance is currently a fashionable topic. Not only is the political establishment debating the issue, but such unlikely participants as corporate boards and development banks have also been drawn into the debate. What, however, is the meaning of governance and how do we attain it? Some stress that good governance should be measured by the ability of a political system to produce good policies. Good policies, in turn, are those that (1) are generally oriented toward desirable social goals, such as economic growth; (2) are consistent and coherent; and (3) reflect broad national interests rather than excessive interest group influence. Others place more emphasis on procedural conditions than on substantive aspects of policies, focusing on the transparency of the policy-making process, the accountability of government officials, and broad participation by stakeholders. Defining what constitutes good governance appears straightforward, but in reality it is difficult to form a consensus on priorities. How to actually determine the quality of governance is also controversial and technical, as shown by recent attempts to measure the production of laws by different legislatures (Mayhew 1991).

Consequently, there is no agreement on how to attain good governance, which is surprising since the ultimate goal of political science is to identify necessary and sufficient conditions for good governance. Scholars have long searched for institutional arrangements conducive to good policy choices. Yet, while at the system level democracy supposedly produces better governance than authoritarianism, institutional arrangements also vary widely across countries with the same type of regime, whether it be democratic or authoritarian. Democratic governments, for example, have chosen either a presidential or a parliamentary system, and this choice is an important variable affecting their performance.

Furthermore, it would be a mistake to focus only on institutions without examining the broader social environments in which they are embedded. Broad social conditions are important because they affect the choice of institutions as well as their subsequent effectiveness. For example, in order for democracy to work smoothly, the existence of certain values and attitudes, such as tolerance and accommodation, is necessary.

One area of unexplored territory in the study of governance is the role of policy advice in improving the quality of governance. The concept that best captures the effect of policy advice on policy outcomes is "ideas." Along with interests and institutions, ideas are the main determinants of policy choice, affecting policy outcomes in at least three ways. First, policymakers look to act with meaning and purpose, and ideas define what is right and meaningful. Second, the choice of a policy measure is based on some understanding of cause and effect, and ideas explain the causal relationships among the phenomena affected by a given policy. Finally, ideas act as focal points. Once ideas are accepted, they influence outcomes primarily as points of reference or anchors around which actors' expectations converge. This explains why certain ideas remain influential even after their original normative and positive appeal has weakened considerably.

Discourse on policy advice has a long tradition in East Asia. Confucian philosophy was founded on the idea of good governance based on good advice. The role of the scholar-bureaucrat is essentially to give policy advice—i.e., to advise the king to follow the ideal practices of the "old kingdoms" and the teachings from classical Confucian texts. Alternative sources of policy advice are also familiar to Confucian tradition. During the Chosun period (1392–1910), government officials were not the only source of policy advice in Korea; the *sarim*, Confucian scholars out of office who were either preparing to enter the bureaucracy or were educating students in local schools, played a leading role in shaping public opinion on major policy issues. Policymakers of the Chosun dynasty firmly believed in the "politics of *sarim*," looking to those scholars who were not part of the officialdom to serve as voices of dissent and criticism. In deciding public policy, they took into account public opinion as expressed by the *sarim* and, to the extent possible, tried to form a social consensus. The democratic characteristics of Confucian governance, however, go beyond a belief in policy advice and public opinion. As I have previously argued, the ideas of transparency and accountability are classic Confucian values and political leaders of the Chosun dynasty implemented them with an elaborate and surprisingly "modern" system of agencies of horizontal accountability, called the Censorate (Mo 2000).

The quality of policy advice also explains more recent East Asian successes. In explaining the post–World War II economic performance of East Asia, scholars have explored the nature of institutional arrangements that enabled political leaders to choose and implement efficient public policies. Since Chalmers

Johnson first gave the name "developmental state" to the collection of those institutions, many have sought to understand its origins and mechanics (Amsden 1989; Wade 1990; Moon and Prasard 1994). In discussing the East Asian developmental state, three distinctive features may be observed: business-government cooperation, bureaucratic autonomy and capacity, and authoritarian rule. One popular view of East Asian economic development is that political leaders were privileged with quality policy advice from their bureaucrats. Some scholars argue that the role of bureaucrats was not limited to policy advice and that they, rather than political leaders, dominated policymaking. Indeed, this image of bureaucratic dominance still persists in East Asia, and many feel that the Korean state has become stronger, not weaker, in the aftermath of the economic crisis of 1997 (Mo and Moon 1999).

At the same time, however, growing challenges to governance have shifted attention to alternative or nongovernmental sources of policy advice. Generally, the increasing demand for such alternative sources of advice is perceived to be rooted in the rising complexity of issues, the growing demands of civil society, and the changing nature of representative government. In Korea, there are two additional reasons why interest in nongovernmental expertise has grown. First, the government has come under attack for causing and mismanaging the economic crisis. Moon Chung-in, Stephen Haggard, and I argue that government failure occurred in at least three different ways. The first concerns the government's role in the investment boom of 1994–1996, which preceded the crisis and resulted in a dramatic increase in corporate indebtedness and the banking sector's portfolio deterioration. The second centers on the government's response to impending signs of corporate and financial difficulty and to emerging problems with the external account once they became apparent. The third cut at the problem looks at the Korean political system's failure to reform the economic system, which was the fundamental source of vulnerability (Mo and Moon 1999 and 2000; Haggard and Mo 2000).

Second, there is an awareness that the settlement of policy disputes in a new democracy like Korea could be facilitated by the existence of impartial and objective mediators, including alternative sources of policy advice. The process of democratic consolidation is one of adapting to the new environment created by the democratic opening; whether or not a stable set of rules emerges depends on how principal actors coordinate their expectations and reach a procedural agreement (Mo 1996). This issue is significant because with the emergence of democracy in Korea, the bureaucracy has become less legitimate because of its ties to authoritarianism. As a result, policy advice from bureaucrats now has a weaker impact on the resolution of policy conflicts than in the past. This has in turn resulted in a greater demand for alternative sources of advice.

The purpose of this chapter is to review the current status of alternative policy advice organizations (APAOs) in Korea. I will show that APAOs are far from ful-filling their potential at the moment. I will then explain why there are so many lim-itations and constraints on APAOs, treating alternative policy advice as a product of the market for ideas. Economic logic will also be used to generate recom-mendations for policymakers interested in promoting a more vigorous APAO sector. Given the range of policy issues that APAOs engage in, it is difficult to pro-vide a comprehensive survey in one study. This chapter thus focuses on economic issues and policies.

RECENT HISTORY
OF POLICY ADVICE IN KOREA
Ministerial
Think Tanks (1971–)

Although the bureaucracy has been the main source of policy advice, its role has been transformed through several stages. During the 1960s, bureaucrats domi-nated domestic policy advice. Their only competitors were external aid agencies. In the early 1970s, however, industrialization accelerated. Korea was moving into heavy and chemical industries after successfully developing light manufacturing industries throughout the previous decade. Reflecting the changing industrial structure, there was also a change in the nature of the policy advice demanded. Thus, it is not a coincidence that in 1971 the government established its first think tank, the Korea Development Institute (KDI). A semiofficial think tank under the authority of the Economic Planning Board, KDI was instrumental in guiding the high-growth economy of the 1970s and became a model for enhanc-ing institutional capacity in developing countries.

At first, KDI was the government's only economic policy think tank. Over time, however, the scope of KDI's research decreased as other government agen-cies created their own think tanks, taking relevant research departments away from KDI. The process of dividing KDI into multiple independent think tanks began in 1976, when the Ministry of Trade and Industry created the Korea Institute for International Economics (which later became the Korea Institute for Industrial Economics and Trade), followed by the creation of the Korea Rural Economic Institute by the Ministry of Agriculture and the establishment of the Korea Research Institute for Human Settlements by the Ministry of Construction in 1978.

The number of ministerial think tanks continued to increase in the 1980s and 1990s. Their proliferation, however, has been subject to public criticism. First, there are jurisdictional overlaps. Although overlaps can in theory be a means to increase the supply of alternative policy ideas, in Korea they tend to reflect the bureaucratic desire to expand jurisdiction and secure resources rather than to offer new policy ideas. Second, they are used to support government intervention in the economy. Third, ministerial think tanks are criticized for being inefficient. In response, the government has tried several times—but failed—to consolidate and reduce the number of think tanks.

Private Sector
Think Tanks (1981–)

The year 1979 marked a watershed in Korean history. President Park Chung-hee (1963–1979) was assassinated in October of that year. It was also the year that the government began to stabilize the economy after realizing the costs of the Heavy and Chemical Industry Drive.[1] The new Chun Doo-hwan government (1980–1988) embraced this change in policy and made economic stabilization and liberalization its top priority. As the government began to rethink its role in the economy, the private sector saw an opportunity to insert its own policy advice. In 1981, the Federation of Korean Industries, one of the main lobbying groups for business, created the Korea Economic Research Institute (KERI) as an alternative source of policy advice to promote business interests and perspectives. Individual *chaebol* (conglomerate) groups followed suit by setting up their own in-house economic think tanks—Daewoo in 1984, and Samsung and LG in 1986.

Although not fully private in nature because of their vulnerability to government influence, think tanks affiliated with industry associations—especially in the financial sector—also arose around this time. Organizations such as the Korea Federation of Banks, which established the Korea Institute of Finance in 1991, thus became active in the market for policy ideas.

Social Movements and
Civil Society Organizations (1985—)

Trends in civil society since the mid-1980s are another factor for consideration. In the mid-1980s, Korea had a strong pro-democracy movement led by unions, churches, students, and dissidents. After Korea made the transition to democracy in 1987, a large number of these pro-democracy groups and activists turned their attention to civil society issues such as the environment, corruption, political reform, and economic justice. The Citizens' Coalition for Economic Justice and the People's Solidarity for Participatory Democracy have been the most successful in pushing reform agendas to the fore.

Although bureaucrats and their think tanks continue to dominate policy advice, there are now serious challenges from nongovernmental organizations (NGOs) and private-sector APAOs. With Korea currently in a transition period where the rules of the game for APAOs are being negotiated, it is important to examine the current status of alternative advice sources.

THE CURRENT STATUS OF APAOS

This section reviews the current conditions of APAOs in Korea (see table 1 for a summary). Since neither permanent independent advisory bodies nor central executive review agencies exist in Korea, this survey is limited to advisory commissions, legislative support organizations, think tanks, and advocacy tanks and NGOs.

Advisory Commissions

As of October 1998, a total of 299 advisory commissions were in operation, established either by legislation or presidential decree. Among government agencies, the Office of the Prime Minister and the Ministry of Construction and Transportation retained the greatest number of advisory committees (see table 2).

As economic issues have become more technical, sophisticated, and contentious, the government has employed advisory commissions as a mechanism to mediate conflicting interests and build social consensus. For example, the Kim Young-sam government (1993–1998) convened presidential commissions to launch its ambitious plans to reform the labor and financial sectors in the mid-1990s.

However, most advisory commissions appear to be inactive or ineffectual. Out of 347 advisory commissions active in 1994–1995, only 48 met more than ten times, 99 met only twice during the year, and 88 never met at all. Furthermore, few commission recommendations have been adopted. The credibility of advisory commissions is often questioned because members are drawn from networks of leading figures in society—"celebrities" who often lack expertise and professionalism. Line bureaucrats, not permanent staff, provide the administrative and research support for advisory commissions, thus limiting the independence of commission members. Advisory commissions have also been criticized for wasteful spending; many wonder whether the Presidential Commission on Policy Planning deserves an annual budget of 440 million won (roughly equivalent to US$440,000).

Some argue that certain commissions are ineffective and should not have been created in the first place. Government agencies set up commissions to shift the blame or shield themselves from public criticism, create patronage jobs for their retiring officials, and/or to find places to house "excess" officials. There is no system for holding commissions accountable for their decisions. Moreover, because their role is advisory, commission members do not have much authority and thus have a weak incentive to perform. Responding to this type of growing criticism, in November 1998 the Kim Dae-jung government (1998—) abolished 117 commissions, merged 27 with others, and began subjecting commissions to review every two years.

On the other hand, although permanent commissions tend to carry out routine tasks away from media attention and scrutiny, some temporary commissions

Table 1. Korean APAOs at a Glance (as of 1999)

Type of APAO	Number	Areas of Activity	Staffing	Funding	Impact
Advisory commissions (permanent)	299 (in 1998)	Attached to ministries	Outside experts; bureaucrats as administrators	Public funds	Mostly ineffectual and inactive
Legislative support organizations	5	Reference materials and other administrative support	Career bureaucrats and temporary researchers	Public funds	Insignificant
Think tanks*					
Government	14	All areas of policy	20–66 Ph.D.'s	W4–13 billion	Dominant
Private sector	3	Economic and industry	80 Ph.D.'s	W5 billion	Moderate
Party-affiliated	1	All areas	5 Ph.D.'s	less than W1 billion	Marginal
NGOs	3,649	All areas of policy, especially economic justice and the environment	20–60 for three most prominent NGOs	Around W1 billion for three most prominent ones; project-based public support	Increasingly influential

Source: Author survey.

*This data includes only major economic policy think tanks.

NGOs: nongovernmental organizations

Table 2. Governmental Advisory Commissions Active (as of 1998)

	Number of Advisory Commissions
Office of the President	7
Office of the Prime Minister	30
Ministry of Finance and Economy	15
Ministry of Unification	5
Ministry of Foreign Affairs and Trade	0
Ministry of Justice	9
Ministry of National Defense	14
Ministry of Government Administration and Home Affairs	24
Ministry of Education	10
Ministry of Science and Technology	8
Ministry of Culture and Tourism	12
Ministry of Agriculture and Forestry	11
Ministry of Commerce, Industry and Energy	17
Ministry of Information and Communication	6
Ministry of Health and Welfare	23
Ministry of Environment	6
Ministry of Labor	9
Ministry of Construction and Transportation	34
Ministry of Maritime Affairs and Fisheries	11
Ministry of Planning and Budget	6
Customs Service	5
Korea Intellectual Property Office	5
Others	32

Source: Ministry of Government Administration and Home Affairs.

have played a catalytic role in advancing important economic reform agendas, such as the Presidential Commission on Labor Relations and the Presidential Commission on Financial Reform during the Kim Young-sam administration.[2] Recognizing the limitations of the existing mechanisms of policymaking in representing the interests of all major stakeholders, the Kim Dae-jung government employed blue-ribbon commissions as a way of forging a consensus on divisive economic reform issues early in his administration. These commissions were effective for several reasons. First, they enjoyed the full support of the president. Second, the government invited policy experts and specialists as "expert commission members," as distinguished from regular, voting members. Third, the commissions allowed some of the groups excluded from the formal policymaking process, such as certain labor organizations, to participate.

Legislative Committee Staffs
and Legislative Support Organizations

National Assembly members can rely on four types of legislative support organizations. First, the Legislative Counseling Office and the Budgetary Policy Bureau (formerly a single office but now two separate entities) in the Secretariat, with more than thirty professional staff members each, offer services related to general legislative drafting and budget policies. Second, the Legislative Information and Digital Library Management Office in the National Assembly Library provides reference materials and basic legislative research to National Assembly members; this office has about 42 professional staff members, of whom 23 have Ph.D.'s. The professional staff members of standing committees are the third source of policy expertise. The number of staff members for each committee ranges from 5 to 11, with the Legislation and Judiciary Committee claiming the largest staff. Finally, assembly members can also turn to their personal staff for legislative support. Each member is allowed a five-person staff.

In discussing the effectiveness of legislative support organizations in Korea, it is important to remember that they have to be evaluated relative to those in the executive branch. In terms of size, there is no comparison between the legislative support organizations in the two branches; one ministerial think tank like KDI employs more Ph.D.'s than the entire Legislative Information and Digital Library Management Office. Given their size, legislative support organizations cannot possibly compete with the executive branch in supporting legislative activities and are not yet a credible source of alternative policy advice. Thus, it is not surprising that the legislative branch is subordinate to the executive branch in lawmaking itself. During the 14th National Assembly (1992–1996), for example, the executive branch introduced 55 percent of the bills; 72 percent of those were adopted, as opposed to just 38 percent of member-introduced bills.

Think Tanks

Three types of think tanks exist in Korea: government, private sector, and university-based research centers. In terms of policy research, government think tanks are more established, and more influential than those of the private sector, and each ministry maintains at least one research institute (see table 3).

Among ministerial think tanks, KDI remains the premier think tank. The main strength of KDI is macroeconomic analysis and forecasting, even though it retains expertise in other areas such as financial policy, fair trade and other industry-related policies, and the North Korean economy. Recently, it was KDI that provided a theoretical foundation and developed an action plan for President Kim Dae-jung's economic philosophy, dubbed "DJnomics." The basic idea behind DJnomics is the simultaneous pursuit of democracy and a market economy (in contrast to the policies of previous governments, which are alleged to have overlooked democracy in pursuit of economic growth).

Some have expressed concerns that KDI has compromised the integrity of its research agenda by committing itself to the philosophy of a particular

Table 3. Government Think Tanks, 1999

	Year Established	Home Ministry	Staff (Ph.D.'s)	1999 Budget (million won)
Korea Development Institute	1971	Ministry of Finance and Economy	204 (66)	12,993
Korea Institute of Public Finance	1992	Ministry of Finance and Economy	83 (25)	3,908
Korea Institute for International Economic Policy	1989	Ministry of Finance and Economy	107 (29)	6,747
Korea Institute for Industrial Economics and Trade	1976	Ministry of Commerce, Industry and Energy	153 (63)	8,887
Korea Energy Economics Institute	1986	Ministry of Commerce, Industry and Energy	89 (25)	5,876
Korea Information Society Development Institute	1988	Ministry of Information and Communication	116 (45)	7,677
Korea Institute for Health and Social Affairs	1971	Ministry of Health and Welfare	134 (38)	4,483
Korea Labor Institute	1988	Ministry of Labor	50 (20)	4,263
Korea Maritime Institute	1997	Ministry of Maritime Affairs and Fisheries	97 (38)	5,003
Korea Transport Institute	1986	Ministry of Construction and Transportation	130 (29)	5,482
Korea Research Institute for Human Settlements	1978	Ministry of Construction and Transportation	192 (59)	8,318
Korea Environment Institute	1992	Ministry of Environment	62 (40)	3,789
Korea Rural Economic Institute	1978	Ministry of Agriculture and Forestry	135 (56)	6,328
Science and Technology Policy Institute	1987	Ministry of Science and Technology	68 (31)	4,716

Source: Author survey.

administration. This close relationship with the Kim Dae-jung government has caused some internal discontent as well. In one incident, a senior KDI researcher reportedly left the institute after having been disciplined for publicly criticizing the government's *chaebol* policy.

The ministerial think tanks in Korea have their own staff of professional economists. Staff economists hold the status of "semipublic official," which allows them to draw private sector–level salaries. Typically, a professional economist in academia or a think tank is recruited to head a ministerial think tank, rather than a retired or seconded civil servant. Prior to 1999, ministers had the authority to appoint the president of a think tank under their jurisdiction. But after that year, that authority was transferred to special committees the government set up in the Office of the Prime Minister. The Korea Council of Economic and Social Research Institutes, for example, now has the authority to supervise the activities of all ministerial think tanks in economic and social policy areas, including the power to appoint think tank heads. Since the government holds only four seats in the fifteen-member Council, it has not been able to have much influence on the selection process.

Certainly, it is too early to conclude from this that ministerial think tanks have become independent of their parent ministries. Under the new system, ministries do not have to allocate their research projects exclusively to their own think tanks. As a result, the share of ministry think tanks' projects that are funded by the ministries as opposed to other funding sources has been declining in the past several years. Although this development can lead to more independent ministerial think tanks in the long run, as it forces them to establish their own revenue base and a reputation for independence, it can actually work to strengthen the power of the purse held by the ministries in the short run because the ministerial think tanks have yet to develop the institutional capabilities to win nongovernmental projects on a sustainable basis. Ministries can also influence their think tanks by controlling the amount of information that they release to the latter; it is difficult to carry out policy research in Korea without the cooperation of the relevant bureaus and agencies. Nevertheless, the current trend is clearly in the direction of greater deregulation and autonomy of ministerial think tanks.

Career patterns of staff economists are also changing. With the exception of a few prestigious organizations like KDI, think tank economists used to look for academic jobs. Now, the situation is more fluid. More and more ministerial think tanks are seeing their own economists rise to the post of president. Opportunities in the private sector have also expanded as many consulting companies and investment banks look for talent in ministerial think tanks. As the market for policy research is becoming more competitive, the ministerial think tanks can become more autonomous if they develop the capacity to take advantage of the market change;

otherwise, their role is bound to diminish with dwindling government support.

Private think tanks, which are few in number, specialize in economic and industry research because they are for the most part supported by *chaebol* or business associations. As noted previously, the main industrial peak association in Korea, the Federation of Korean Industries, supports a policy-oriented think tank, KERI, which has an organizational structure similar to that of KDI. Like KDI, KERI conducts policy research in a wide range of areas with its own internal staff of professional economists. In creating KERI, the *chaebol* wanted to have their own source of information and expertise, as well as the ability to present their views on the economy.

Individual *chaebol* have also founded their own think tanks. Samsung Economic Research Institute, LG Economic Research Institute, and Hyundai Research Institute are prime examples. They began as policy think tanks, but over time they have evolved into market research and consulting firms for their parent companies. Most of their revenue is now generated by contracted research projects from their parent companies, which tend to focus on management and financial market issues. Like ministerial think tanks, *chaebol*-affiliated think tanks are under pressure to reduce their dependence on the financial subsidies of the member companies of their group. As a result, they have to conduct more business-oriented projects to generate income, and public policy thus plays a steadily declining role in their activities. Moreover, the capacity of *chaebol*-owned think tanks to play a role in the public policy field is limited since the media and the public are skeptical about whether they are autonomous enough to represent the public interest rather than corporate interests.

In the wake of the financial crisis, think tanks affiliated with financial sector associations, such as the Korea Institute of Finance and the Korea Securities Research Institute, have gained influence. However, it is not clear whether they are free from government influence because the government still has the ability to influence the financial institutions whose interests they are supposed to serve.

The only think tank in Korea that is affiliated with a political party is the Yoido Institute of the Grand National Party (GNP). It was founded in 1995 with an initial endowment of 10 billion won. Since the GNP lost power in 1997, however, it has been unable to support the institute. The ruling party in Korea tends to have a monopoly on political contributions, so once the GNP became an opposition party in 1998, it could not even pay its own operating costs, making it difficult to protect the funds set aside as the institute's endowment. In short, the instability of party finances account for the weakness of party-affiliated think tanks in Korea.

The final category of think tanks that should be mentioned, namely those that are based at universities, are weak in Korea because they are funded mostly by soft money with little university support. University research centers tend to be active in science and engineering because the government runs very large research grant programs in those areas. Although the government also supports research in the social sciences, projects in this field are too small for universities to justify the fixed costs associated with independent research units.

Advocacy Tanks and Nongovernmental Organizations

Historically, NGOs in Korea have grown out of pro-democracy and opposition groups that were fighting against the authoritarian regime. Because of this tradition, NGOs have been confrontational, violent, and class-oriented in nature, and have focused on mobilizing mass demonstrations. Although roughly 68 percent of the NGOs operating in 1999 were established after 1987 (see table 4), their leaders often have ties to "old" social movements (Kim 1997). Therefore, it is not surprising that Korean NGOs have concentrated on such political and economic issues as reform of the chaebol, corporate governance, corruption, and taxation.

This is not to deny that many NGOs have sprung up to satisfy increasing citizen demands for improved quality of life and self-expression. NGOs advocating postmodern issues such as women's rights, the environment, and health care have grown in number and influence. In a way, we can say that Korean NGOs have assumed the role that advocacy tanks play elsewhere.

NGOs in Korea have been successful because they have been entrepreneurial

Table 4. Distribution of Korean NGOs by Area of Concern, 1999 (%)

	Established before 1987	Established since 1987	Total
Civil society	21.6	26.5	24.9
Local autonomy	0.9	7.4	5.3
Social services	20.4	18.1	18.8
Environment	1.8	9.6	7.1
Culture	17.4	14.5	15.5
Education/scholarship	4.9	6.1	5.7
Religion	4.4	1.8	2.7
Labor/farmers and fishermen	6.2	5.0	5.4
Economy	19.6	9.9	13.0
International	2.2	0.6	1.2
Others	0.6	0.4	0.5
Total	100.0 (1,176)	100.0 (2,467)	100.0 (3,649)

Source: NGO News (2000).
NGOs: Nongovernmental organizations.

in mixing different forms and conduits of advice. Industry associations and other established groups with existing channels to government agencies prefer informal meetings and consultations. Although they do produce reports and recommendations, these tend to be of fairly low quality. In contrast, newer groups with social movement backgrounds turn directly to politicians because they do not have ties to the bureaucracy. They tend to prefer high-profile news conferences and demonstrations. Their research output, however, is also weak, reflecting their limited resources and their strategy to take an activist rather than research-oriented approach.

Despite the recent ascendancy of NGOs, they do not have a great degree of organizational strength. Tables 5 and 6 show that most NGOs work with fewer than five full-time employees and an annual budget of roughly 100 million won. Even the three biggest civil society NGOs are financially so weak that they cannot maintain a large number of professional staff, and instead rely on dedicated volunteers and low-paid political activists (see table 7).

NGOs must overcome additional obstacles in order to establish themselves as "true" APAOs. First, it is imperative that they become independent from the government and media. NGOs have to confront the fact that they are perceived as an ally of the Kim Dae-jung government, which has promoted NGOs as a counterweight to business groups and quasi-governmental grass-roots organizations. The Kim Dae-jung government increased government subsidies to NGOs and protected a coalition of NGOs called Citizens' Alliance for the 2000 General Elections from accusations that it conducted illegitimate activities during its campaign to blacklist certain politicians.[3]

Table 5. Distribution of Korean NGOs by Number of Full-time Employees (as a percentage of all NGOs)

Number of Employees	1997	2000
1	15.4	14.1
2–5	53.8	54.9
6–10	13.7	15.6
11–20	8.6	8.1
21–50	5.2	4.5
51–100	2.0	0.8
Over 100	1.4	0.4

Source: NGO News (1997 and 2000).
NGOs: Nongovernmental organizations.

One reason the government's financial support for NGOs has risen in recent years is the economic crisis. Lacking administrative infrastructure, the government asked NGOs to undertake many public works programs that it introduced to combat rising unemployment. The YWCA, for example, was asked to manage a recycling project. More controversial has been the government's involvement with NGO-organized public campaigns. The campaigns themselves are worthwhile, since they address a wide range of important social issues such as women's

Table 6. Distribution of Korean NGOs by Annual Budget Size (as a percentage of all NGOs)

Annual budget (in million won)	1997	2000
Less than 10	9.5	20.1
10–100	43.5	29.7
100–1,000	33.0	40.0
Above 1,000	14.0	10.1

Source: NGO News (1997 and 2000).
NGOs: Nongovernmental organizations.

rights, welfare, civic education, and the environment. Government funding, however, has invited charges that the government is using the campaigns to promote its own political agenda (*Newsmaker* 14 October 1999).

The long-term impact of the increased public funding on NGOs is unclear. On the positive side, it is true that government funds have helped many NGOs to continue their programs and gain experience. But there are negative effects as well. The reputation of Korean NGOs as being politically neutral has been damaged. Moreover, most of the government-sponsored projects are action oriented, not policy based, indicating that they probably did little to increase the NGOs' capacity for policy analysis.

The main conduit for NGO activities—the media—poses a far more difficult problem. It is difficult to imagine how NGOs could have attained their current level of influence without the help of the media. Yet this cozy relationship with the media has to change because it tends to make the NGOs look away from the problems of the media. The Korean media have long been criticized for unfair business practices as well as sensationalism and inaccurate reporting.

To remain credible, NGO leaders have to refrain from entering politics or participating in government committees and commissions. NGOs also have to specialize. At the moment, they appear overextended, involving themselves in a

Table 7. Profiles of the Three Most Prominent NGOs in Korea

	Year Established	Areas of Activity	Comments
Citizens' Coalition for Economic Justice	1989	Economic justice, economic reform, political reform	50 full-time staff; 35,000 members
The Korea Federation for Environmental Movement	1982	Environment	60 full-time staff; 58,000 members
People's Solidarity for Participatory Democracy	1994	Small shareholder rights, corporate governance, economic reform, political reform, corruption	20 full-time staff; 3,599 members

Source: Kim (1999).
NGOs: Nongovernmental organizations.

large number of unrelated issues. Some quip that they are expanding their reach like an octopus-similar to the way the *chaebol* have expanded their businesses. The internal governance of some NGOs is also open to doubt. Although NGOs have attacked the *chaebol* for their lack of transparency and accountability, it is not clear whether they subject themselves to the same degree of internal or external discipline. Korea's NGO leaders could also benefit from more civility, tolerance, and moderation in their public statements and discourse. Most of all, the long-term survival of NGOs depends on the expansion of their grass-root membership base. There are limits to what they can accomplish with political activists only. Moreover, the number of political activists willing to work for NGOs will shrink as future generations will most likely not be as ideologically driven as those in the past. The orientation of the organizations will also shift to less political and more quality-of-life issues, attracting a different type of activism than that of the pro-democracy activists.

Foreign Sources of Policy Advice— Private Consulting Services and International Organizations

During the economic crisis, public trust in the government, corporations, and banks was so badly damaged that it is no exaggeration to say that foreign consulting firms and international organizations became the only trusted sources of policy advice. Korean firms and government agencies scrambled to hire foreign consulting firms to develop restructuring plans that could be "sold to the public."

Since the Korean government asked the International Monetary Fund (IMF) for emergency bailout funds, it is not surprising that the IMF has subsequently played a significant role in developing adjustment and restructuring policy measures for Korea. In its "bailout" agreements with the Korean government on December 5 and 24, 1997, for example, the IMF asked for two corporate restructuring-related provisions: greater transparency in corporate governance (e.g., the implementation of international accounting standards for Korean *chaebol*), and the reduction of mutual payment guarantees between affiliates within a single business group. The International Bank for Reconstruction and Development (IBRD) followed with more refined recommendations on corporate governance and competition policy when it signed structural adjustment agreements with Korea in February and October 1998. The February agreement, for example, focused on ways to enhance accounting transparency and financial disclosure and to improve corporate governance through better monitoring.

Thus, it appears that the IMF and IBRD played an important role in putting on the agenda two corporate restructuring issues—corporate governance and mutual payment guarantees. However, it is debatable whether these ideas originated from the two international organizations themselves. It has been widely speculated that Korean negotiators wanted to incorporate those reform measures into the agreement, implying that IMF and IBRD did not insist on them (Mathews 1998). I find this "Korean instigation" hypothesis plausible because the improvement of accounting standards and the reduction of mutual debt payments had been the main policy tools employed by the government in its attempts to reform the *chaebol* before the economic crisis.

The role of foreign consulting firms as APAOs has also increased since the economic crisis. Although the vast majority of their work is still done on behalf of the private sector, foreign consulting firms have been able to make inroads into the market for policy advice in Korea. There are three types of policy-related projects that consulting firms conduct. First, there are projects that government agencies commission for improving their own operations. For example, the Financial Supervisory Commission in 1998 asked McKinsey and Company to help them consolidate three separate financial regulatory bodies into a single, unified organization. Second, the government has also hired consultants to deal with new problems that emerged during the economic crisis. Foreign consulting firms have helped the government to sell insolvent Korean firms in international auctions and develop secondary markets for nonperforming loans. Third, private companies and banks have used foreign consulting firms as a way of enhancing their credibility with the public and government. Those firms and banks that were subject to government-led restructuring had to find some way to make their restructuring plans credible, and as a result, they often chose to hire foreign consulting services (*Sisa Journal* 13 August 1998).

As long as public trust in traditional sources of policy advice remains low, foreign consulting services will continue to be in high demand. But the long-term prospects for the role of foreign consulting firms as APAOs depend more on their substantive policy contributions than on their ethical reputation, and the evidence so far is mixed on that point. No one can deny that foreign consulting firms have introduced many policy ideas for restructuring the corporate and financial sectors. But many complain that foreign consulting firms either borrow foreign ideas ill-suited to local conditions or repackage local ones. Some go so far as to suggest that they are taking advantage of the "trust" gap afflicting other sources of policy advice without developing genuine policy innovations.

From this survey, it is clear that bureaucracies and their think tanks still dominate policy research and advice. Legislative support staffs and organizations and university and private sector think tanks are marginal in terms of resources and quality of policy research. Although private consulting firms have become an important member of the policymaking community—especially since the economic crisis of 1997—they do not regard policy research as their mission and will not invest the time and resources necessary to become an important source of alternative policy advice. NGOs have gained influence, but not based on policy research. In short, APAOs are still undersupplied in every aspect—number, resources, and diversity.

The problem is not only the amount of alternative policy advice that these organizations provide, but also their credibility. Existing APAOs are not "credible." Private sector and government think tanks represent the interests of the *chaebol* and the government respectively. Most NGOs originate from democracy movement groups and are often viewed as being overly ideological and confrontational. University organizations are too financially dependent on private business and government to be credible. This lack of independent and impartial policy research impedes the development of genuine policy debate.

The confluence of multiple factors such as tradition, political culture, and the pattern of economic and political development accounts for this unique pattern of APAO activity in Korea. Confucian tradition and the recent success of a government-led economic development strategy have created a powerful bureaucratic system where the bureaucrats dominate the policymaking process. As long as the bureaucrats maintain their power, they are unlikely to support the rise of APAOs outside of their control.

Another impediment to APAO activity is the low level of public trust in the institutions that are possible APAOs, such as big business and academia. Despite their contributions to economic development, since the transition to democracy began in the late 1980s, all of them have been discredited as having been supporters of authoritarianism. Unfortunately, critics of those institutions—i.e., pro-democracy groups—have not been able to pick up the slack as they suffer from outdated ideologies and "movement" tactics.

IMPACT OF APAOS

Government think tanks have had the greatest impact on public policy in Korea. As recently as 1992, a survey indicated that the most important sources of policy-related information for Korean policymakers were their own agencies and think tanks (see table 8). This survey also showed that media and private think tanks did not provide much information to policymakers.

Has anything changed? Table 9 indicates that private think tanks are now enjoying public prominence; their reports and activities are frequently reported in major newspapers. Nevertheless, the data shows that ministerial think tanks remain prominent, with three of them ranked among the top five think tanks in terms of visibility. It is difficult to assess the quality of research output produced by different APAOs with objective data. The consensus, however, seems to be that government think tanks, with their advantages in information and stable sources of revenue, still tend to produce the most influential studies.

Recently, NGOs have been the most prominent source of alternative policy advice. In several high-profile cases such as the movement for small shareholder rights and the fight to block the Yongwol Dam project on the Tong River, NGOs have been able to force the government to change its policy. In the first case, for example, People's Solidarity for Participatory Democracy (PSPD) spearheaded the small shareholder rights movement, using lawsuits as the main instrument of political action; they filed a series of lawsuits against corporate managers for misconduct and malfeasance. Although PSPD issues regular press releases, organizes conferences, and publishes occasional white papers on its activities, it has not published any major policy studies. In general, solid policy research does not appear to be a priority area even for major NGOs.

Table 8. Sources of Policy-Related Information for Korean Bureaucrats, 1992

	Reliance Index
Within own agency	126
Think tanks	52
Media	−4
Other agencies	−6
Agency-registered associations	−37
Academic community	−39
Private and corporate research centers	−68

Source: Yoem and Kim (1992).
Note: This chart is based on a 1992 survey of 180 senior bureaucrats in six ministries. The reliance index is calculated by subtracting the respondents who said they did not use the particular source much from the number who used it extensively.

Among the determinants of NGO success, two factors deserve further investigation. First, NGO success appears too dependent on media support. Without grass-roots support and without a strong financial base, the media is the only outlet through which NGOs can reach the public. Second, NGOs tend to succeed when they are aligned with the government—namely, when the government needs outside support for its policies. Despite the examples noted above, it is still rare for NGOs to successfully force the government to change its policy against its will. Therefore, if Korean NGOs desire to establish themselves firmly as a significant source of policy advice, they will have to find ways to reduce their dependency on the media and the government.

LIMITATIONS AND CONSTRAINTS

The picture of APAOs emerging from the previous sections is that they have a long way to go to challenge the primacy of the government bureaucracy and its think tanks. To phrase this in economic jargon, the good of APAOs is undersupplied by

Table 9. Number of Newspaper Citations of Economic Think Tanks in the Three Major Korean Dailies, 1999

Think Tanks	Workshops*	Reports†	Comments‡	Total Citations
LG Economic Research Institute	1	24	22	47
Korea Development Institute	6	15	23	44
Korea Institute of Finance	3	12	26	41
Samsung Economic Research Institute	0	12	23	35
Korea Institute for Industrial Economics and Trade	7	10	15	32
Hyundai Research Institute	3	11	13	27
Korea Institute for International Economic Policy	5	5	16	26
Korea Economic Research Institute	8	7	10	25
Daewoo Economic Research Institute	2	10	10	22
Korea Institute for Health and Social Affairs	1	11	4	16
Korea Research Institute for Human Settlements	1	7	4	12
Daishin Economic Research Institute	0	0	9	9
Korea Institute of Public Finance	1	5	3	9
Korea Energy Economics Institute	1	3	3	7
Korea Labor Institute	1	3	3	7
Institute for Global Economics	4	0	2	6
Sejong Institute	3	2	0	5
Korea Information Society Development Institute	0	0	5	5
Korea Rural Economic Institute	1	1	3	5

Source: Author survey (1999).
Notes: Using the KINDS search engine, a search was conducted for citations in the three major Korean-language newspapers, Chosun Ilbo, Donga Ilbo, and Joongang Ilbo. Only institutes with at least five citations are listed. The search was focused on economic policies, including land, finance, economic prospects, and health issues. Opinion columns were excluded.
* Workshops includes seminars, roundtable discussions, debates, and polls.
† Reports refers to official publications by think tanks.
‡ Comments are those made by think tank researchers, including their opinion on specific economic issues and remarks made at seminars organized by other institutes.

the market for policy advice. Causes of the undersupply lie both in the demand and supply sides.

On the demand side, the main problem is that policy is not very important in Korean politics. The end-users of policy advice are the politicians who use it to make policy decisions. If policy decisions are not important to politicians' interests, it is obvious that they will not demand policy advice. To politicians, winning elections is the most important goal; if policy does not determine electoral outcomes, there is little demand for policy advice. Unfortunately, this is precisely the situation in Korea. Although there are some signs that political parties have begun to define and promote their own policy positions, Korean elections are still decided by regional and other nonpolicy variables. Another problem on the demand side is that political power—i.e., the authority to make policies—is so concentrated among a few political leaders that the number of people who need policy advice is bound to be small.

APAOs are the producers of policy advice, and the amount of policy advice they produce is also affected by supply factors—i.e., the cost of inputs as well as the efficiency with which they are used by APAOs. To begin with, inputs are scarce and expensive. Because of weak traditions of philanthropy and volunteerism, it is difficult for APAOs to raise funds and mobilize volunteers. Unlike the United States, the Korean government gives little tax incentive for charity and donations. Rigid labor markets also make it difficult to recruit qualified personnel into APAOs. There is little job mobility after a certain age in the Korean labor market, so once workers start working for an APAO, they cannot expect to move to other jobs later. This discourages prospective workers from taking employment at APAOs.

Another constraint on APAOs in supplying policy advice has been access to information. As pointed out previously, one reason ministerial think tanks are still influential is their access to the information held by bureaucrats. Government agencies do not accord the same level of access to society-based APAOs. One positive development in this regard was the enactment in 1996 of the Act on Disclosure of Information by Public Agencies, which took effect in early 1998 and allows individual citizens and NGOs to request data and information from government agencies (Kim 1999). Even though bureaucratic resistance has undermined the full application of the law, a few NGOs have been able to use it to force reluctant government bureaucrats to release the requested data.

Demand and supply factors account for the undersupply of alternative advice given a reasonably well-functioning market for policy advice. Yet there are reasons to believe that sources of alternative advice also suffer from market failures and other market-retarding factors. First, there may exist certain economies of scale for policy advice production which make small markets like Korea incapable of supporting a large number of APAOs on top of the government bureaucracy.

Second, policy advice may be a public, not a private good. That is, once policy advice is produced, there is no way of preventing others—consumers or producers—from gaining access to it. Thus, APAOs have little incentive to produce at the socially optimal level because they cannot capture all the subsequent social benefits. In Korea, the weak tradition of intellectual property thus works to discourage development of new ideas because inventors are not properly credited or compensated.

Third, transaction costs may be too high. If APAOs organized themselves and engaged in collective action, they could solve problems such as externalities. Indeed, a group of 500 NGOs formed the Citizens' Alliance for the 2000 General Elections in February 2000 to push for political reform in time for the April elections. In general, however, transaction costs involved in such collective activities are too high for APAOs, which consist of a large number of small organizations with diverse interests.

Finally, the low level of public trust makes it difficult for any APAO to attain a sufficient level of legitimacy. As noted above, few APAOs in Korea are considered impartial and objective. Both APAOs and the media are responsible for this situation. While it is true that APAOs themselves should work harder to develop a reputation for objectivity, it is the responsibility of the media to objectively review the claims of APAOs and make the public aware of which ones can withstand scrutiny and which ones fail. At this point, it is fair to say that most Korean media organizations simply pass along various APAO claims to their audience unfiltered.

RECOMMENDATIONS FOR THE FUTURE

Despite limitations and constraints, Korean APAOs will continue to grow because the forces of globalization and democratization demand small government and decentralization of power. The government can help by taking measures to facilitate this process, especially on the supply side. Further deregulation is clearly needed to remove entry barriers to new APAOs and to relax restrictions on APAO activities; an important part of this reform will be more tax incentives for financial contributions to APAOs (Park 1999). The government should also be more open-minded about releasing information in response to requests made by NGOs and private citizens. New ways of providing financial support to NGOs can also be explored. For example, NGOs themselves prefer that the government set up an independent foundation to allocate subsidies instead of managing them directly.

But as is true with all forms of government intervention, the government should take caution in promoting APAO activity. The key is to adhere to certain principles that may otherwise be easily overlooked: First, there is a socially optimal level of APAOs; more APAOs is not always better. What is important for good governance is, rather, the overall quality of policy advice, including advice from the bureaucracy. Thus, policymakers should seek to improve the quality of policy advice from all sources. In doing so, they may encounter trade-offs between bureaucratic and APAO capacities. Whenever possible, APAOs should be promoted in ways that do not undermine bureaucratic capacity. Otherwise, bureaucrats will resist APAOs. One way to minimize bureaucratic resistance is to avoid totally rejecting the past and instead acknowledge the positive contributions made by the bureaucracy to date. Furthermore, bureaucrats should be given a stake in the promotion of APAOs. They should be persuaded that it is in their long-term interest to promote APAOs.

Second, although policymakers should certainly encourage more APAOs, they should also emphasize responsible participation by new APAOs. There are concerns that unaccountable APAOs may be no better than unaccountable bureaucrats.

Third, the government should pay more attention to the cultural context of policy advice. As discussed earlier, barriers to the development of APAOs are not only legal and institutional but also cultural in nature. Although a culture of philanthropy and volunteerism is difficult to establish through government policy, the government can still help by giving tax and other incentives for contributions and volunteer activities and by emphasizing them in public education and campaigns.

Finally, the benefits of APAOs can only be perceived by evaluating government performance. Thus, it is important to build objective criteria for performance evaluations. Even though global standards are used with increasing frequency, they should be complemented by domestic standards. In developing domestic criteria for government performance, the role of the media is particularly important.

While the government can certainly help, the ultimate responsibility for the success of APAOs lies with the organizations themselves. In the years ahead, APAOs in Korea will have to address many problems. APAOs should work to establish credibility with the public, the media, and the government. Only then can they secure access to the information needed to perform credible research and reach policymakers with their ideas. The best way to establish credibility is to engage in long-term, in-depth research. APAOs may maximize media attention in the short run by pursuing issues that are popular and trendy, but their long-term credibility depends on policy expertise gained through solid research, not on media attention.

APAOs must also work diligently to develop stable and sustainable bases of funding. One possible area of funding that Korean APAOs should explore is foreign donors. Fortunately, the Korean public has become increasingly tolerant toward the influence of foreign aid organizations and multinational companies in the aftermath of the economic crisis, so APAOs seeking foreign funding are less likely to face nationalistic criticism than before. APAOs should maintain independence and autonomy from government ministries.

Finally, the rapid growth of APAOs may create certain unintended side effects, such as the degradation of policy advice quality and the decreased influence of certain APAOs. To prevent these problems, the government may want to increase its oversight of APAOs in ways that do not jeopardize their independence by taking advantage of existing regulations regarding the governance structure of officially registered nonprofit organizations. If possible, self-regulation by APAOs—e.g., a code of ethics and conduct enforced by an association of APAOs—would be desirable rather than stronger government regulations. For example, an association of APAOs can formulate and recommend a code of conduct and an internal governance model for its members. Ultimately, however, the responsibility for monitoring and disciplining APAOs lies with the consumers of policy advice. It is up to all of us to be more active and alert in overseeing and disciplining badly performing APAOs.

NOTES

1. The Heavy and Chemical Industry Drive was a government effort from the mid-1970s to early 1980s to promote Korean production of steel, nonferrous metals, petrochemicals, machinery, automobiles, ships, and electronics.

2. The Presidential Commission on Reform of Labor-Management Relations was formed in May 1996, and its recommendations became the basis of the March 1997 revisions of labor laws which introduced more permissive rules on lay-offs and relaxed or eliminated provisions restricting workers' labor rights. After making progress on labor reform, the Kim Young-sam administration launched the Presidential Advisory Council on Financial Reform in January 1997 to deregulate and liberalize financial markets. Many council recommendations were passed into law in December 1997 after the financial crisis broke out.

3. Before the official campaigning period began, a group of 500 NGOs drew up a list of politicians who they opposed and wanted defeated in the April 2000 general elections. This was controversial because it violated two campaign laws, restrictions on campaigning by private groups in favor of or against particular candidates and the limitation of campaigning to the official campaign period.

BIBLIOGRAPHY

Amsden, Alice H. 1989. *Asia's Next Giant: South Korea and Late Industrialization*. New York: Oxford University Press.

Cho Hee-yeon. 2000. "A Short History of the Korean NGO Movement." Paper presented at the Briefing Session for Korean NGOs' General Information Network 2000, at the Olympic Park Hotel, Seoul, Korea, October 13, 1999.

Hahm Chaebong, Hahm Chaihark, and David Hall. 2000. *Confucian Democracy, Why and How?* Seoul: Tradition and Modernity.

Haggard, Stephen, and Mo Jongryn. 2000. "The Political Economy of the Korean Financial Crisis." *Review of International Political Economy* 7(2): 197–218.

Kim Hyuk-Rae. 1999. "NGOs in Pursuit of Public Goods in South Korea." Paper presented at the Conference on Shaping Common Futures, in Perth, Australia, October 7–9.

Kim Sunhyuk. 1997. "State and Society in South Korea's Democratic Consolidation: Is the Battle Really Over?" *Asian Survey* 37: 1135–1144.

Mathews, John A. 1998. "Fashioning a New Korean Model Out of the Crisis." *JPRI Working Paper* 46, Japan Policy Research Institute.

Mayhew, David. 1991. *Divided We Govern: Party Control, Lawmaking and Investigations, 1946–1990*. New Haven, Conn.: Yale University Press.

Mo Jongryn. 1996. "Political Learning and Democratic Consolidation." *Comparative Political Studies* 29(3): 290–311.

——— . 2000. "Democratic Implications of the Censorate." Paper presented at Yonsei

University's International Conference on Confucian Democracy, in Andong, Korea, in March.

———. 2001. "Political Culture and Legislative Gridlock: Politics of Economic Reform in Precrisis Korea." *Comparative Political Studies* 34(5): 467–492.

Mo Jongryn and Moon Chung-in. 1999. "Korea after the Crash." *Journal of Democracy* 10(3): 150–164.

———. 2000. *Economic Crisis and Structural Reforms in South Korea: Assessments and Implications*. Washington, D.C.: Economic Strategy Institute.

Moon Chung-in and Rashemi Prasard. 1994. "Beyond the Developmental State: Networks, Politics, and Institutions." *Governance* 7(4): 360–386.

NGO News. 1997. 1997 *Directory of Nongovernmental Organizations*. Seoul: NGO News.

———. 2000. *2000 Directory of Nongovernmental Organizations*. Seoul: NGO News.

Park Jong-Heup. 1998. *Legislative Administration* (in Korean). Seoul: Bupmoon sa.

Park Tae-Gyu. 1999. "Laws and Regulations on Non-Profit Organizations" (in Korean). Manuscript, Department of Economics, Yonsei University.

Wade, Robert. 1990. *Governing the Market: Economic Theory and the Role of Government in East Asian Industrialization*. Princeton, N.J.: Princeton University Press.

Yoem Jae-ho and Kim Ho-seop. 1992. "Utilization of Public Policy Research." *Korea Journal of Public Policy* 1: 85–95.

About the Contributors

R. KENT WEAVER has been a Senior Fellow in the Governmental Studies Program at the Brookings Institution since 1987. He is also an adjunct professor at the Paul H. Nitze School of Advanced International Studies of Johns Hopkins University. His major fields of interest and expertise are American and comparative social policy, comparative political institutions, Canadian politics, and the politics of expertise. Dr. Weaver is the author of *Ending Welfare As We Know It* (2000), *Automatic Government: The Politics of Indexation* (1988), and *The Politics of Industrial Change* (1985). He is the co-author and editor of *The Collapse of Canada?* (1992) and co-author and co-editor of *Looking Before We Leap: Social Science and Welfare Reform* (1995), *Do Institutions Matter? Government Capabilities in the U.S. and Abroad* (1993), and *Think Tanks and Civil Societies* (2000). Dr. Weaver graduated from Haverford College and received his M.A. and Ph.D. in political science from Harvard University.

PAUL B. STARES is Associate Director of the Center for International Security and Cooperation at Stanford University and Senior Research Associate of the Japan Center for International Exchange (JCIE), where he was previously Director of Studies. He is also a nonresident Senior Fellow of the Brookings Institution in Washington, D.C. Dr. Stares is a specialist on international security issues, currently focusing on Asia Pacific affairs. He has authored and edited seven books, including *Rethinking Energy Security in East Asia* (2000); *The New Security Agenda: A Global Survey* (1998); *Global Habit: The Drug Problem in a Borderless World* (1996); and *The New Germany and the New Europe* (1992). In addition, he has written numerous book chapters and articles on aspects of international security. From 1982 to 1996, Dr. Stares held various positions in the Foreign Policy Studies Program at Brookings, eventually becoming Senior Research Fellow. He has also been a Senior Research Fellow at the Japan Institute of International Affairs, a NATO Fellow, a Scholar-in-Residence at the MacArthur Foundation Moscow Office, a Rockfeller International Relations Fellow, and an Adjunct Professor at Georgetown University in Washington, D.C., as well as holding academic posts at the University of Sussex and the University of Landaster in the United Kingdom. Dr. Stares was born and educated in the United Kingdom, where he received B.A. (First Class), M.A., and Ph.D. degrees in international relations and politics.

KULDEEP MATHUR has been Professor of the Centre for Political Studies, Jawaharlal Nehru University, since 1986. His previous positions include Director of the National Institute of Educational Planning and Administration (1994–1997), Rector of Jawaharlal Nehru University (1993–1994), Director of the Academic Staff College, Jawaharlal Nehru University (1989–1993), Professor of the Indian Institute of Public Administration (1973–1986), and ILO Expert in Management Research of the UNDP-ILO Project (1977–1978). He is a specialist in public policy, including public policy processes, plans and implementation, bureaucracy, administration, decentralization, and state-society relations. Dr. Mathur's publications include *Top Policy Makers in India: Cabinet Ministers and Their Civil Service Advisors* (1994, co-author) and *Drought, Policy and Politics: The Need for a Long-Term Perspective* (1993, co-author). He has also edited *Development, Policy and Administration* (1996) and authored many articles. Dr. Mathur received his M.A. from the University of Rajasthan and Ph.D. from the University of Hawaii.

MO JONGRYN is Associate Professor and Director of the Center for International Studies, Graduate School of International Studies at Yonsei University; he has been a Research Fellow at Stanford University's Hoover Institution since 1991. Dr. Mo's previous positions include National Fellow at the Hoover Institution (1995–1996), Assistant Professor of Government at the University of Texas, Austin (1991–1996), and Visiting Assistant Professor at the Graduate School of International Relations and Pacific Studies at UCSD (1996). Dr. Mo received his B.A. from Cornell University, his M.S. from the California Institute of Technology, and his Ph.D. in business from Stanford University.

ANDREW RICH is an Assistant Professor of political science at Wake Forest University. He joined the faculty at Wake Forest in 1999, after completing his Ph.D. at Yale University. His major areas of interest are U.S. politics and policymaking, with an emphasis on how expertise and ideas shape policy development and decision making. Dr. Rich has published several articles on the role of think tanks in the United States and is currently completing a book manuscript entitled "Think Tanks, Public Policy, and the Politics of Expertise," which examines the proliferation of think tanks in the United States since the 1960s and their role and influence in U.S. policymaking. He spent a year as a research fellow at the Brookings Institution in 1998–1999.

ROBERT SOBIECH has been Assistant Professor of the Department of Social Policy, Institute of Applied Social Sciences, Warsaw University, since 1990 and has been Head of International Relations at the National School of Public Administration since 1993. He is also a member of the Advisory Board of the Department of Social Analysis and Forecasts at the Chancellery of the Polish Prime Minister. Dr. Sobiech has served as a member of several governmental and nongovernmental organizations. His research areas include mass communication, public policy, social problems, and social policy. Dr. Sobeich has authored three books and more than forty articles in various publications. He received his M.A. and Ph.D. degrees from Warsaw University.

AMAURY DE SOUZA is Senior Research Fellow of the Instituto de Estudos Econômicos, Sociais e Políticos de São Paulo (IDESP). He is also a business consultant and senior partner of Techne, a consulting firm in Rio de Janeiro. Dr. de Souza was a Professor of Political Science at the Instituto Universitário de Pesquisas do Rio de Janeiro (1965–1987) and the Department of Economics of Pontifical Catholic University of Rio de Janeiro (1988). He has also been a Visiting Professor at many U.S. universities. He was also a fellow of the Woodrow Wilson International Center for Scholars, Smithsonian Institution, and a member of the board of the Roper Center for Public Opinion Research of the University of Connecticut. Dr. de Souza's publications include *The Politics of Population in Brazil: Elite Ambivalence and Public Demand* (co-author, 1981); "Redressing Inequalities: Brazil's Social Agenda at the Turn of the Century," in *Brazil Under Cardoso* (1997); "Cardoso and the Struggle for Reform in Brazil," in *Journal of Democracy* (1999); and "Collor's Impeachment and Institutional Reform in Brazil," in *Corruption and Political Reform in Brazil: The Impact of Collor's Impeachment* (1999). Dr. de Souza holds a Ph. D. in political science from the Massachusetts Institute of Technology. He also holds degrees in sociology and public administration from the Federal University of Minas Gerais, Brazil.

DIANE STONE has been based in the Department of Politics and International Studies, University of Warwick, since 1996. She teaches in the area of comparative public policy and politics. She has also taught at the Australian National University (where she gained her M.A. and Ph.D. degrees), Murdoch University in Western Australia, and Manchester Metropolitan University. Additionally, she has worked in the World Bank Institute in Washington, D.C. Dr. Stone's current research interests are focused on think tanks and policy advice. Her publications include *Capturing the Political Imagination: Think Tanks and the Policy Process* (1996) and *Think Tanks Across Nations: A Comparative Approach* (1998). She is working on a third book which addresses the transnationalization of think tanks, especially their interactions with international organizations.

MARTIN W. THUNERT is Assistant Professor of political science at the University of Mannheim, Germany, and will be Visiting Associate Professor of political science at the University of Michigan, Ann Arbor, the United States, as of January 1, 2002. Dr. Thunert received his M.A. from Goethe-University, Frankfurt, and his Dr. Phil from the University of Augsburg, both in Germany. He has held appointments at the Free University of Berlin and the University of Hamburg. A former visiting fellow at Harvard University and McGill University, Montreal, his areas of teaching and research are comparative politics and political theory. His work has focused on American and Canadian politics, international student exchange, Anglo-American relations, English and Scottish political philosophy, and theories of human rights. Most recently, he has completed a comparative study on the role of think tanks in modern societies focusing on recent developments in the United States, Canada, the United Kingdom, and Germany and other European countries. His most recent publication in English is "Players beyond Borders? German Think Tanks as Catalysts of Internationalisation," in *Global Society* (April 2000).

YAMAMOTO TADASHI is President of the Japan Center for International Exchange (JCIE), which he founded in 1970. Mr. Yamamoto is currently a member as well as the Japanese director of the Trilateral Commission, the UK-Japan 2000 Group, the Japanese-German Dialogue Forum, and the Korea-Japan Forum, and a member of the Korea-Japan Joint Committee for Promoting History Studies. He also serves as a member of the boards of the Asian Community Trust and the Japan NPO Center. Mr. Yamamoto is editor/author of books on civil society and the nonprofit sector, including *Emerging Civil Society in the Asia Pacific Community* (1995), *The Nonprofit Sector in Japan* (1998), *Deciding the Public Good: Governance and Civil Society in Japan* (1999), *Corporate-NGO Partnership in Asia Pacific* (1999), and *Governance and Civil Society in a Global Age* (2001).

Index

academic think tanks, 15, 21–22, 137, 142, 166, 177, 179–181, 187, 190. *See also under specific countries*

advocacy think tanks, 16, 21, 25, 48–49, 53, 55, 60–61, 127, 138–141, 182, 190. *See also under specific countries*

alternative sources of policy advice, 2–3. *See also under specific countries*

alternative policy advisory organizations (APAOs)
access to decision makers, 8
activity of, 17, 19
autonomy from government, 6
as career path for experts, 8
and civil society, 17
credibility with policymakers, 8
credibility with public, 8
and cultural environment, 22
definition of, 3–6
development of, 19–22
durability of, 22
and financial environment, 19–20, 26–27
influence of, 23–25
and information/expertise environment, 22
institutional capacity for follow-through, 8
and labor market environment, 21
and legal environment, 19, 26
and political institutions, 20, 27
provision of independent advice, 8
responsiveness to government agenda, 8

transnational, 27
types of
academic think tanks, 15, 21–22, 137, 142, 166, 177, 179–181, 187, 189, 202
advocacy think tanks, 16, 21, 25, 48–49, 53, 55, 60–61, 127, 138–141, 182, 190
central policy review and advisory organizations, 8, 10
contract research, 6, 14, 17
independent audit agencies, 10
legislative committee staffs, 11, 20–21, 26, 259
legislative support organizations (LSOs), 10, 26
ministerial think tanks, 14, 17
permanent advisory bodies, 12, 22, 103, 186
political party think tanks, 15, 17, 25
research-oriented NGOs, 16–17, 23, 25, 125, 133, 138–140
temporary blue-ribbon commissions, 6, 12, 17, 21–22, 46, 176, 178, 189, 217
windows of opportunity for, 20, 26–27, 143, 197

blue-ribbon commissions, 6, 12, 17, 21–22, 46, 176, 178, 189, 217. *See also under specific countries*

Brazil, 11, 20
alternative policy advisory organizations, 124–125, 135, 141–142, 144, 146–147

history of, 125–130
civil society, 130
executive-based alternative
    policy advice, 131, 151
    permanent advisory councils, 132–133
    blue-ribbon commissions, 134
governance, 124–125, 130, 144–148
legislative-based alternative
    policy advice, 134, 151
    congressional commissions, 135
    congressional staff, 134, 143
    federal audits, 135, 151
nongovernmental organizations, 130, 138,
    146–147
policy expertise, 140, 142, 145, 148
quangos, 125, 147
technocrats, 126, 128
think tanks, 135, 144
    academic think tanks, 129, 134, 137, 139,
        141–142, 147, 153
    advocacy think tanks, 129, 138, 143, 147, 154
    contract research, 133–134, 136–137, 139,
        141, 143, 147, 151
    outside of government, 138, 148, 154
    political party think tanks, 140, 156
transnational networks, 140

Canada, 13
central policy review and advisory organiza-
    tions, 8, 10. See also under specific
    countries
civil society
    and APAOs, 17, 19
    and governance, 3
    See also under specific countries
contract research and ministerial think tanks,
    14, 17. See also under specific countries
Czech Republic, 242–245

democracy, 3, 8, 207, 252. See also under spe-
    cific countries

Germany, 15, 17, 21–22
    alternative policy advisory organizations,
        157, 186, 188, 192, 195, 197, 201
    history of, 159, 161
    blue-ribbon commissions, 176, 178, 189

civil society, 165, 168
cultural environment, 159, 199
executive-based policy advice, 161–162, 167,
    189
federal-state councils, 176
independent advisory bodies, 174
legislative-based policy advice, 168, 171, 189,
    198
    Office of Technology Assessment, 169–170
    legislative study commissions, 170, 173,
        189, 192, 198, 200, 203n. 8
    reference and research services, 172
policy expertise, 157, 159, 172, 187–188,
    191–192, 196, 199
political environment, 158, 191, 194
think tanks, 159–160, 165–167, 182, 192,
    194–198, 200–202
    academic, 166, 177, 179–181, 187, 189–190,
        194–196, 202, 203nn. 10, 11
    advocacy, 182, 190
    political party–affiliated, 184, 190, 203n. 12
globalization
    and governance, 3, 119. See also under
        specific countries
governance
    definition of, 1, 28, 252–253. See also under
        specific countries

Hungary, 242–245

independent audit agencies, 10
India
    alternative policy advice, 208, 213, 217,
        226–228
    blue-ribbon commissions, 217–219
    bureaucracy, 209, 211–212, 216, 227–228
    democracy in, 207–208, 226
    economic policy of, 209–210, 212
    Education Commission, 218
    globalization and, 211
    and governance, 208, 211, 227
    Indian Civil Service (ICS), 210
    Indian Council of Social Science Research
        (ICSSR), 214, 216–217
    National Commission for Scheduled Castes
        and Scheduled Tribes, 219–220
    National Human Rights Commission, 220

nongovernmental organizations, 208, 211, 221, 223–229
parliamentary committees, 221
policy concerns, 208–209
policy experts, 213, 222–223
public policy processes, 208, 212–213, 216–217, 219–221, 228
research institutions, 213–214, 225
and the state, 209, 212
statutory commissions, 219–220
voluntary agencies, 223
women's rights, 225
International Bank for Reconstruction and Development (IBRD), 267–268
International Monetary Fund (IMF), 27, 211, 265, 267

Japan, 19, 27
alternative sources of policy advice in, 76, 82, 84, 86
bureaucracy of, 74, 76–77, 79, 84, 87
and civil society, 71, 86
globalization and, 71
governance, 72, 84
legal environment in, 74
legislative process in, 72–73, 76, 85
nongovernmental organizations, 73, 80, 86
nonprofit organizations, 73, 78, 80, 85–86
The NPO Law, 73
policy expertise in, 77–79, 84–86
The Prime Minister's Commission on Japan's Goals in the 21st Century, 72, 84
private advisory councils, 82, 83
research councils of political parties, 78, 85
think tanks, 78–80, 85

Korea, 19–20, 27
advisory commissions, 23, 257
advocacy tanks, 257, 264
alternative policy advisory organizations, 257, 265, 269–270, 273
alternative sources of policy advice, 254, 270, 272
bureaucracy, 254–255, 268, 270, 273
civil society organizations, 256
democracy, 254, 264
foreign sources of policy advice, 267

globalization and, 273
governance, 253, 273
legislative support organizations, 259, 268
nongovernmental organizations, 264, 269–270
nongovernmental policy expertise, 254, 256
policy advice in, 253–254, 271–272
recent history of, 255
social movements, 256
think tanks, 255–257, 260, 262–263, 267–269, 272
careers in, 262
chaebol-affiliated, 263
ministerial, 255, 260, 262, 268–269
political party-affiliated, 263
private sector, 256, 263, 268–269
university-based, 263, 268

legislative branch, and policy making, 3. *See also under specific countries*
legislative committee staffs, 11, 20–21, 26, 259. *See also under specific countries*
legislative support organizations (LSOs), 10, 26. *See also under specific countries*
"line" departments or agencies, 2, 3. *See also under specific countries*

Netherlands, 15

Organization for Economic Cooperation and Development (OECD), 241

permanent advisory bodies, 12, 22, 103, 186. *See also under specific countries*

Poland, 19
alternative policy advice, 233–235, 240
alternative policy advisory organizations, 246, 249
academic, 235–238
civil society, 234–235, 241
democratization, 235
foreign technical assistance, 240
government-based advice, 238
executive-based, 239
legislative-based, 239
ministerial, 240
nongovernmental organizations, 241, 244

political opposition, 233–234
policy advice, 231, 240–241, 244, 248
policy expertise, 234–235, 240
public policy, 233
social scientists, 231–234
think tanks, 242–245
political party think tanks, 15, 17, 21–22, 92,
140, 156. *See also under specific countries*
policy expertise
and APAOs, 6, 52
and Asia, 253
role of, 1, 52, 60
policymaking, 3
and alternative sources of policy advice, 4

research-oriented NGOs, 16–17, 23, 25, 125,
133, 138–140, 152. *See also under specific countries*

United Kingdom, 17, 21
academic research centers, 96, 105, 109, 112,
116
AIDS policy, 93
alternative policy advisory organizations, 91,
102, 105, 110, 113, 116, 118–120, 141–142
careers in policy, 105, 141
Central Policy Review Staff (CPRS),
100–102, 110
civil service, 89, 102–103, 106, 114, 117–118
civil society organizations, 90–91
commercial policy advice, 95, 114
commissions of inquiry, 90, 97–98, 107,
110–111, 116
and European Union, 104, 117, 119
and globalization, 103, 119
governance, 95, 117, 119–120
government-based alternative advice, 97,
100, 114
interest groups, 93–94, 111, 114
international networks, 94
new public management (NPM), 110, 114,
116–117
nondepartmental public bodies (NDPBs),
90, 99, 106–107, 116
nongovernmental organizations, 93, 105, 114
parliamentary committees, 90, 97–98, 103,

109, 111–112, 115–116
policy advice, 89, 111, 115, 119
professional associations, 94, 106, 111, 114
quangos (see also nondepartmental public
bodies), 96, 99, 117–118, 120*n. 1*
think tanks, 90–93, 95–97, 99–100, 102–103,
105, 108–116, 119–121
United Nations, 109, 130, 136, 241, 245
United States, 11, 17, 20, 21, 28
alternative policy advisory organizations, 31,
44, 59–60
history of, 35
civil society–based APAOs, 34, 47, 53, 59–60
academic institutes, 49, 59
consulting firms, 13, 31, 33, 48, 50, 53,
59–60
interest groups, 50, 53
nongovernmental organizations, 46, 50, 53
think tanks, 31, 33, 47–49, 53, 55, 59–62*n. 2*
executive-based APAOs, 36
advisory committees, 33, 39–40, 59
Council of Economic Advisers, 37, 59
National Economic Council, 37, 59
National Security Council, 37–38
Office of Management and Budget
(OMB), 36, 53, 55, 58
Office of Policy Development, 38, 55, 59
intermediate APAOs, 53, 59
task forces, 45–46, 59
health-care reform, 45
government reorganization, 45
research-and-development centers, 46, 53,
59
contract research, 5–6, 15, 47–48, 53, 55,
59
legislative-based APAOs, 40
Congressional Budget Office, 20, 31, 42,
52, 58, 60
congressional committee staff, 43
Congressional Research Service, 22, 40,
58, 62
General Accounting Office, 11, 41, 53, 55, 58
Office of Technology Assessment, 23, 42
policy experts, 31, 34–35, 51–53, 58, 60
political parties, 33

World Bank, 27–28, 109, 140, 211, 241, 245

The Japan Center for International Exchange

Founded in 1970, the Japan Center for International Exchange (JCIE) is an independent, nonprofit, and nonpartisan organization dedicated to strengthening Japan's role in international affairs. JCIE believes that Japan faces a major challenge in augmenting its positive contributions to the international community, in keeping with its position as one of the world's largest industrial democracies. Operating in a country where policymaking has traditionally been dominated by the government bureaucracy, JCIE has played an important role in broadening debate on Japan's international responsibilities by conducting international and cross-sectional programs of exchange, research, and discussion.

JCIE creates opportunities for informed policy discussions; it does not take policy positions. JCIE programs are carried out with the collaboration and cosponsorship of many organizations. The contacts developed through these working relationships are crucial to JCIE's efforts to increase the number of Japanese from the private sector engaged in meaningful policy research and dialogue with overseas counterparts.

JCIE receives no government subsidies; rather, funding comes from private foundation grants, corporate contributions, and contracts.

Other JCIE Books
on Governance and Civil Society

Governance and Civil Society in a Global Age, edited by Yamamoto Tadashi and Kim Gould Ashizawa

The Third Force: The Rise of Transnational Civil Society, edited by Ann M. Florini (Copublished with the Carnegie Endowment for International Peace)

Deciding the Public Good: Governance and Civil Society in Japan, edited by Yamamoto Tadashi

Corporate-NGO Partnership in Asia Pacific, edited by Tadashi Yamamoto and Kim Gould Ashizawa

Changing Values in Asia: Their Impact on Governance and Development, edited by Han Sung-Joo